# Before Columbus
## Exploration and Colonisation from the Mediterranean to the Atlantic 1229–1492

University of Pennsylvania Press
MIDDLE AGES SERIES
Edited by
*Edward Peters*
Henry Charles Lea Professor
of Medieval History
University of Pennsylvania

A listing of the available books
in the series appears at the
back of this volume

# Before Columbus

Exploration and Colonisation from the
Mediterranean to the Atlantic 1229–1492

FELIPE FERNÁNDEZ-ARMESTO

University of Pennsylvania Press
Philadelphia

Copyright © 1987 by Felipe Fernández-Armesto
All rights reserved

First published 1987 by Macmillan Education Ltd

First published in the United States 1987 by the
University of Pennsylvania Press.
Third paperback printing 1994
Printed in the United States of America

Library of Congress Cataloging-in-Publication Data

Fernández-Armesto, Felipe.
    Before Columbus.
    (University of Pennsylvania Middle Ages series)
    Bibliography: p.
    Includes index.
    1. Mediterranean Region—History.   2. Atlantic Coast
(Europe)—History.   3. Atlantic Coast (Africa)—History.
I. Title.
DE94.F47   1987      909'.09822      87-10764

ISBN 0-8122-1412-9

# Contents

# PART TWO: ... TO THE ATLANTIC

# Preface

Nowadays there are international conferences on Mediterranean history, and in the University of Oxford, in very recent years, seminars have been dedicated to it. 'Atlantic studies' have spawned books and articles with increasing frequency for nearly 40 years and, since 1955, a distinguished Spanish periodical has been devoted to them. This book is an attempt to explore some of the more promising possible connections between the two subjects. Part One gives an account of late medieval theatres of expansion in the western Mediterranean. Part Two sketches the beginnings of exploration and colonisation in the Atlantic. Throughout, the main quest is for elements of continuity or discontinuity between the Mediterranean and Atlantic worlds and for approaches to an answer to Horace's question:

> . . . quid terras alio calentis
> sole mutamus?

– which I would paraphrase, 'Why do some of us bother with alien climes?' At the cost of some cross-references and summary repetitions, I have tried to make each chapter independent of the others, as many readers find this convenient. A few pages of introduction are devoted to a conspectus of the problems which afflict students and absorb historians. Conclusions, which are intended to address these problems, are advanced chapter by chapter, as I go along. If I try to suggest new arguments wherever they occur to me, this is not out of contrariness or 'revisionism' but simply because, in an adult life largely given to teaching, I have come to value books which seek to be stimulating at the risk of being wrong. In any case, I like the subject too much to see it fossilised in rocks of orthodoxy.

Much of the material, including the whole of Chapter 9, was accumulated with the aid of a Leverhulme Research Fellowship: I take pleasure and pride in acknowledging the kindness of the Trustees. A travel grant from the Trustees of the Arnold Historical Essay Fund allowed me to do some research in the Canary Islands. Chapter 5 is based on lectures given in the Modern History Faculty of the University of Oxford in 1984 and Chapter 6 on a lecture to the External Studies Department of the University of Manchester in the same year. I am grateful for these opportunities and sources of stimulation. The book in its present form was the work of the vacations of 1985 and the spring and early summer of 1986. The unerring eye of Mr Christopher Butcher saved me from many infelicities of style, the careful scrutiny of Dr Maurice Keen from errors of fact and judgement. To the wise talk and scholarly examples of Professors Edmund Fryde and Peter Russell the book owes more, I fear, than they may care to acknowledge. Defects of my own devising remain. I owe a further debt to the Warden and Fellows of St Antony's College, Oxford, who have let me pursue a subject only marginally relevant to the collective interests of the College, and who, with the other members and staff, make it an ideal place for learning and teaching.

F.F.-A.
Oxford, 7 July 1986

# A Note on Names

For personal names transliterated from Arabic, I followed standard practice, but place names follow the guidelines of the U.S. Board on Geographic Names: this results in some inconsistencies, but enables readers to check the places named in a widely available and comprehensive gazetteer. Where other forms are current in books in English, I give them in brackets at the first mention of the place concerned.

Other names are given in English wherever there is a well-established form, but otherwise in the national language. I make an exception in the case of the Infante Dom Henrique of Portugal for reasons explained on p.185. The names of monarchs of the House of Barcelona are given in Aragonese (and here I prefer the form, 'Jaime' to the archaising 'Jayme') if they were kings of Aragon, or in Catalan if only kings of Majorca, or in Italian if only kings of Sicily. This has the merit, for instance, of distinguishing Jaime II of Aragon from Jaume II of Majorca. Catalan place names are given in Castilian, where well-established equivalents exist (e.g. Lérida, Gerona) in the absence of established English forms, because this is the practice of most atlases which readers are likely to consult.

# List of Maps

# Introduction

## Problems and Approaches

A few years ago, an advertising campaign of the Greek national tourist authority strewed the pages of glossy magazines with pictures of nubile tourists cavorting amid Doric ruins over the slogan, 'You were born in Greece'. Taken literally, the words would have been obscure. Yet no reader can have had any difficulty in interpreting them as an allusion to the doctrine that 'western society' derives, by unbroken tradition, from Graeco-Roman origins. The doctrine may not be true; the terms in which it is commonly expressed may be misleading. Yet its influence is such that it forms part of the self-perception of almost every educated person in Europe and the Americas and much of the rest of the world today. Studies of periods of crisis in the transmission of the supposed legacy – in late antiquity or the early middle ages, when rival cultural traditions were received, or in the 'age of expansion' when western society is thought to have broken out of its heartlands – have concentrated, like Theseus in the labyrinth, on following as if it were a lifeline this single, tenuous thread.

One of the most conspicuous differences between what might be called 'western society' or 'western civilisation' and its presumed Hellenic origins lies in its geographical configurations. The Mediterranean 'frog-pond' of Socrates has been replaced by the Atlantic 'lake' across which we traffic in goods and ideas and around which we huddle for our defence. Rather as the Romans had colonies in northern Europe, which extended their world beyond the Mediterranean basin, so we have our outposts elsewhere: Pacific and Indian Ocean colonies and a worldwide spread of cultural influences, which are sometimes thought to justify talk of a 'global civilisation'. But our essential axis is the Atlantic, whereas the Romans' was the *Mare Nostrum*. The questions therefore arise: when, how and why, if at all, did this remarkable displacement from the Mediterranean to the Atlantic take place, and how – and to what extent – did it happen without loss of continuity with the Mediterranean original?

Historians who think along these lines have tended to seek 'the

1

origins of Atlantic civilisation' – the phrase belongs to the great Belgian scholar, Professor Charles Verlinden – in the late middle ages and early modern period. That may be the wrong place. After the discoveries of the fifteenth and sixteenth centuries, the New World tended to drift away again from the Old, developing internal economic systems, 'creole' identities and finally independent states. Only with the improved communications and mass migrations of the late nineteenth century, perhaps only with the transatlantic partnerships of the world wars in the twentieth, did it become possible for scholars to formulate questions about Atlantic civilisation. On the other hand, a genuine achievement of the late middle ages was the creation of awareness of Atlantic 'space', which was there to be exploited for what it was worth, and into which features of Mediterranean life may be seen, with hindsight, to have been funnelled or squeezed.

This book makes no pretensions to charting the fate of civilisations, but it does attempt to describe the contribution made by explorers and colonists to that growth of awareness. By separating some of the ingredients of 'civilisation' – personnel, ways of life, institutions, forms of government, economic techniques, habits of thought and belief and behaviour – and by tracing their movement from the Mediterranean to the Atlantic, it may be possible to cast some light on changes which, whatever their implications for the 'course of history', command attention because they involved or affected a large number of late medieval people.

At another level from that of 'civilisations' – and one better calculated to appeal to English-speaking readers – the problem can be seen as one of 'economies'. Naturally and historically, western Europe has two economies – a 'Mediterranean' and a 'northern' – separated by a narrow strait, with widely differing sailing conditions along the two seaboards, and a chain of breakwaters which determines the flow of rivers and therefore the directions of exchange. For much of Europe's history, communication between these two zones was not easy. Limited access through the Toulouse gap, the Rhone corridor and the Alpine passes kept restricted forms of commerce alive, even in periods when commercial navigation from sea to sea was abandoned. When Mediterranean craft resumed large-scale seaborne commerce in the late middle ages, they faced enormous problems of adaptation and acclimatisation. Heavy seas threatened ships low in the gunwales; Finisterre was their 'Cabo de Não', beyond which lay a long excursion out to sea around or across the Bay of Biscay. Galleys, which carried much of the trade, depended on huge inputs of victuals and water from on shore. All in all, the journey called for great sang-froid and was, in its way, when it started in the late thirteenth century, almost as bold a venture as the Portuguese swoop out into the south Atlantic, 200 years later, in search of the westerly trade winds. The gradual integration of the northern and southern economies depended on the navigation and exploration of the Atlantic and became increasingly tied up, from the fifteenth century onwards, with the development of an Atlantic economy which embraced both zones. In this context, it seems proper to look to the subject and period of this book for help with the problem of how the gap between the two halves of the modern European economy came to be bridged, and what contribution was made during the late middle ages.

These questions beg a deeper one. The experience of Europe's age of expansion is unique in the history of the world. Other imperial societies have expanded into areas contiguous with their homelands. Some have migrated over great distances in search of the means of life. Examples of both phenomena occurred in Europe before the start of our period. Yet only in Europe (except perhaps in the copy-cat case of Japan), and only since the late middle ages, have imperial and commercial ends been pursued across the world without restraint. Europe's idiosyncracy seems even more acute when compared with the experience of the Chinese – a people better fitted for a worldwide imperial role, because of their density of population, unity of command and superiority in technology. In the mid-fifteenth century, however, when the Indian Ocean had been explored and the foundations of an overseas empire laid in Java, the Chinese pulled back, perhaps because the decision-making élite there was not as dependent on or committed to long-range trade as was that of much of Latin Christendom.

This singularity of European history and its evident effects on the rest of the world have inspired historians to seek explanations, often by examining the individual motives of participants in the process of expansion – whether pious or greedy, crusading or chivalric or commercial, whether sprung from a syndrome of self-confidence or from the psychology of escape. Sometimes the examination of motives has overspilled into a search for collective mentalities or else yielded, among historians who see overseas expansion as a mass movement, to a quest for the grinding 'structures' of economic determinism, such as relentless demographic pressure, cyclical commodity shortages or social systems productive of desperate or ambitious outcasts; others stress economic 'conjunctures' – mysteriously generated demands for gold or spices.

There is also a tendency among historians of this subject to distinguish motives from means, as in popular detective fiction, and treat both as preconditions of European expansion. While the motives were of long standing – indeed, it is hard to discern any 'new' motives in the critical period – the means were of late medieval contrivance, and lay in the development of techniques of shipbuilding, navigation and cartography. There is something in this analysis. Atlantic commerce and exploration were facilitated by the cogs and carracks of the high middle ages and the caravels of the fifteenth century. Long-range navigation in the northern hemisphere required no new instruments or techniques, but beyond the line, out of sight of the pole star, the demands of an unfamiliar heaven were different. Yet all the technical developments of the period were achieved in the course and as a result of experiments in navigation which were being made anyway. It seems that the search for 'causes' or 'origins' of Europe's overseas expansion can be rewarded only by taking a very long-term view, acknowledging that, like appetite, exploring or empire-building 'vient en mangeant', and that the process grows, cumulatively but slowly, from modest beginnings.

If from some perspectives Latin Christendom seems an unlikely candidate for expansion, the leading role of improbable communities within it – particularly from Portugal and Castile – is one of the most beguiling aspects of the problem. In a sense, it is to be expected that poor and peripheral peoples should espouse initiatives that convey a promise of wealth. In exploring neighbouring seas, late medieval Castilians and Portuguese were like certain 'emergent nations' today, desperately drilling for offshore resources with foreign capital and foreign technicians. In recent years, the search for an explanation of Iberian fortunes has concentrated on the partly covert role of the foreigners – especially Italians and chiefly Genoese, who brought the resources of a more developed economy and the experience of long colonial and commercial traditions to bear on the difficulties of exploring and exploiting the Atlantic. The question of the extent of the foreign stake in the Iberian empires is sometimes thought to be related to that of how far 'modern' colonisation is continuous with 'medieval', as if the depth of Italian involvement were a measure of the profundity of the Iberian empires' medieval roots. In part, this may be a result of the myth that Iberians were 'shy traffickers' or that their own medieval experience was irrelevant to the erection of commercially orientated seaborne empires. In order to make progress with the investigation of the problem, it will be useful to dispense with such assumptions and look afresh at all three of these late medieval 'empires' – Portuguese, Castilian and Genoese – to identify the 'roots' of each and the relationship between them.

The conspicuous failure, among the peoples who took part in the overseas expansion of the late middle ages, is that of the Catalans. The 'lost tribe' of the age of expansion, virtually ignored in most books on the subject, they tend to be regarded either, like the Venetians, as a people with no Atlantic vocation, or else dismissed as gripped by an inexplicable 'decline'. Yet for the first generation of Atlantic exploration, Catalan-speakers, especially from Majorca, contributed by far the most. Their traditional trading links with north Africa made them well placed and well disposed to break into the Atlantic; their colonial experience was almost as extensive as and in some ways more varied than that of the Genoese, and, because it included the establishment of sovereign island-colonies, seems peculiarly relevant to the Atlantic. No explanation of the 'rise' of Portugal or of Castile can be complete without a thorough retrospect on the frustrations of the Catalans. In the same context, the failure of France – in many ways, the kingdom best placed to dominate the early Atlantic world – also needs to be considered. In the past, the debate about the relative contributions of various 'national' or proto-national groups to European expansion was pursued jingoistically and concentrated on rival claims to priority in major discoveries. It is still worth pursuing today, but for other reasons: if we could tell why the French and Catalans held back, we should better understand why the Portuguese, Genoese and Castilians sallied forth, and so come closer to identifying some of the dynamic features of the late medieval Latin Christendom.

In all cases of the expansion of particular peoples, whatever their relative importance, the immediate results embraced a common feature: the establishment of colonial societies – settler communities in new and sometimes uncongenial environments, often in close proximity to indigenous cultures. In defining the natures and describing the behaviour of those societies, it seems wise to bear some basic questions in mind. First, what difference did environmental change make? However tenacious, for instance, the traditions which early Atlantic settlers brought from the Mediterranean, Atlantic islands were different from Mediterranean ones and Atlantic archipelagoes differed widely from one another. Were these 'frontier' societies, moulded and changed by new challenges and opportunities, or were they 'transplantations' of metropolitan society, which they resolutely aped or unconsciously mirrored? Or, rather, as these descriptions are not mutually exclusive, what was the balance, in each case, between creation and innovation? Secondly, what did it feel like to live in one of these societies? What self-perception, and what perception of the community to which they belonged, did settlers at various levels of society and in different occupations have? The sources only allow sporadic insights, but it is helpful to try to make the most of them if we are not to be distracted, by problems of historians' invention, from seeing what participants saw. Finally, where there was an indigenous society – and sometimes, as in Madeira and the Azores, colonists were the only inhabitants – what mental image did the colonists form of the host culture? It is rarely possible to say anything about what the natives thought of their 'guests', but only through a consideration of the problem of what they thought about each other, can the problem of how they behaved towards each other be approached: colonial societies, economies and institutions sprang from mental attitudes which were products of mixed traditions and experience.

The question of 'cultural contacts' and particularly of the mental images to which they gave rise, suggests more general problems about the intellectual impact of the discoveries – both geographical and anthropological – on the metropolitan societies, as well as the colonial ones. The implications of the discoveries for cosmography and the 'rise of science' have been much discussed in the past. Historians have tended to see explorers as empiricists and exploration almost as a form of scientific experiment, which exploded the reputations of written authorities. The delight which Columbus took in disproving Ptolemy, or Ramusio in compiling explorer's revelations, suggests that this analysis is not altogether silly, but the enormous amount of recent research on late medieval and early modern science has identified so many other influences that explorers are left with little room for a role. A more promising field of enquiry is the possible impact of the encounters with newly found and previously unsuspected societies of pagan 'primitives' on the development of a science of anthropology and on ways of understanding the nature of man. The debates provoked by the American Indians in the sixteenth century have become well known and some scholars have begun work on the medieval origins of the terms of those debates. In the period covered by this book, the potential significance of two major new encounters has to be considered. Black people had always been known in Latin Christendom, but late in the first half of the fifteenth century, Europeans began to come into contact with Blacks in their own 'habitat' – Black societies, which had previously been subjects of speculation only. Even earlier, in the 1340s, the aboriginal Canary Islanders (a neolithic and probably pre-Berber north African people) had begun to baffle and intrigue scholars. Most of what was said about American Indians was precisely foreshadowed in literature about the Canarians.

Part of the purpose of this book is to provide material with which to contemplate or approach these problems, and even to confront them directly. First, however, a confession must be made, which may console some readers and exasperate others: my interest in most of the problems has gradually diminished, except as an aid to writing questions for examinations. I no longer share historians' common anxiety to explain change and prefer, on the whole, merely to describe it. The question I most want to ask myself about the past is, 'What did it feel like to live in it?' Not even, 'What *was* it like?', because we have so few means of answering or, indeed, exploring that question. A book addressed to a variety of readers cannot, however, be written self-indulgently, and I shall try to mix attempts to evoke, from the sources, experiences of people who took part in exploration and colonisation with discussion of the questions which readers are likely to ask or be asked.

My method will be to look in turn at the 'arenas' of colonial life in the western Mediterranean and Atlantic in our period, trying to suggest what each was like and classifying them tentatively, in terms of similarities and dissimilarities, as I go along, before returning at the end of the book to consider some implications, for

Latin Christendom, of the discovery of Atlantic 'space'. In the first five chapers I examine the great theatres of western Mediterranean expansion: the island-conquests of the House of Barcelona; the 'first Atlantic empire' created in the south-west of the Iberian peninsula, chiefly from Castile; the 'Mediterranean land empire', as I call it, in Levantine Spain, which, because of its differences of character must be separately treated; the Genoese colonial outposts which spanned the Mediterranean from west to east but which, though scattered, constituted a distinctive 'world' of their own; and the north African coast, with its Atlantic aspect, where Catalans, Provençals and Italians contended for commercial mastery. The subjects of the last four chapters of the book will be the course and characteristics of early European penetration of the Atlantic.

Two limitations must be stressed: the enquiry closes in 1492 on the assumption that the beginning of the story is less well known than the middle and end; a further and more tentative assumption is that the western Mediterranean in the late middle ages is a proper area of enquiry. It might be objected that the colonisation of the eastern Mediterranean by Latin peoples from the late eleventh century, or the medieval commerce and navigation of northern European peoples, is an equally good subject to start with if an understanding of the ultimate nature and direction of the expansion of western Christendom is the aim. The only principle on which I might try to justify my approach is that of 'first things first'. Apart from a relatively small number of Flemings, relatively late in the story, and one 'French' episode which will be discussed (pp.175–84 below), it was western Mediterranean peoples alone – Iberian and Italian and, of the latter, chiefly Genoese – who explored and settled in the Atlantic in our period.

One problem of the historiographical tradition I am happy to ignore, even though it can be detected, remotely underlying historians' treatment of all the others. The question of the usefulness of distinguishing medieval from modern times and of when, if ever, distinctive or essential features of the modern world can be detected, is a hoary old historiographical chestnut which I am content to leave, blackening amid neglected embers, until it finally explodes with a shattering pop.

# PART I

# From the Mediterranean . . .

Map 1
THE BALEARICS, SARDINIA, CORSICA AND THE
CATALO-PROVENÇAL AND NORTH-WEST ITALIAN
COASTS
places named in the text

# 1. The Island Conquests of the House of Barcelona

THE Portuguese poet, Gil Vicente (*c.* 1470–1536) was able, without incongruity, to liken a lovely woman to a ship and a warhorse. The comparisons were intended to flatter. The ship must be pictured starlit and with sinuous sail, the horse girthed and caparisoned for knightly combat.

> Digas tú, el marinero . . .
> Si la nave o la vela o la estrella
> Es tan bella.
> Digas tú, el caballero . . .
> Si el caballo o las armas o la guerra
> Es tan bella.[1]

> Sailor, declare
> If ship or sail or star
> Can be as fair.
> Rider, declare
> If horse or arms or war
> Can be as fair.

Poets can winkle images of pulchritude from unlikely places and it would be easy to dismiss Gil Vicente's lines as an outrageous conceit. Yet at the time they were written, they would not have sounded strange. The associative bond between seafaring and chivalry, and the beauty of both, were so widely remarked in late medieval Europe, especially in and around the western Mediterranean world, as almost to be commonplaces. It was as if romance could be sensed amid the rats and hard-tack of shipboard life, or the waves ridden like jennets. There is no reason to doubt that the sentiments were sincerely felt and could be genuinely inspiring: they are voiced by men of action – navigators and conquistadores – as well as men of letters. They infuse and animate the story of the overseas expansion of Latin Christendom, especially in the period which forms the subject of this book. Gil Vicente was writing at the end of the period dealt with in this book, but one of the most splendid evocations of seaborne chivalry dates from its beginning.

King Jaime I of Aragon (r. 1213–76) has left us that rare thing – the autobiography of a medieval king, reasonably authentic, reflecting royal inspiration and probably, in large part, royal composition. At the very least, it captures the self-image which the king wished to project and resounds with the chivalry which was, it seems, Jaime's only source of abiding and deeply espoused values. When he described his conquest of Majorca, the arguments which moved him to undertake it and the experience of crossing the sea to carry it out, the king revealed that he saw maritime war as a means of chivalric adventure *par excellence*. There was 'more honour' in conquering a single kingdom 'in the midst of the sea, where God has been pleased to put it' than three on dry land. The voyage was lingeringly and lovingly described: the numbers of ships, the sailing order of the fleet, the location of the guiding lanterns, the waiting for a wind, the cries of the watches exchanged when the ships made contact, the changes of breeze, the shortenings of sail, the heaving of the sea in a storm and the resolution and faith in God it called forth. No moment matched the moment of making sail. 'And it made a fine sight for those who stayed on shore, and for us, for all the sea seemed white with sails, so great a fleet it was.'

Jaime's enthusiasm for seafaring was already shared by many of his Catalan subjects. Now it infected the warriors of his realm and helped to inspire a series of seaborne conquests. 'The best thing man has done for a hundred years past,' the king later wrote, 'God willed that I should do when I took Majorca.' Jaime probably meant that it was the 'best' by the standards of chivalry, the deed of most daring and renown. It was an achievement of great importance, too, for the political future of the House of Barcelona, which began to create a network of island dominions, first in the western and central Mediterranean, later – with less success – in the Atlantic. By the end of the thirteenth century, the chronicler, Bernat Desclot, could claim with pardonable exaggeration that no fish could go swimming without the King of Aragon's leave.[2]

The colonisation of Majorca is thus an important episode, which demands scrutiny. The sources only permit a patchy reconstruction, but at least the questions to be asked – and addressed in turn – are clear: who took part in the conquest and why? How was the Catalan colonisation organised? What became of the indigenous people? What was the role of other non-Catalan minorities, such as Genoese, Jews and imported slaves? What sort of economy and society resulted? How was the island governed and what was its relationship to the Aragonese world? The subjugation and colonisation of Ibiza, close in time but different in character, and of the later island conquests further east, can be reserved until after these problems have been broached.

## Majorca, 'The Kingdom in the Sea'

Despite the sea's appeal for King Jaime and, increasingly, for members of the Aragonese nobility, landlubbers could not engage in seaborne exploits unaided. The merchants and masters of Catalonia and Provence were called on to provide shipping and expertise. Pere Martell, citizen of Barcelona, played the same sort of role, organising logistic support for the conquest of Majorca, as Ramon Bonifaz of Burgos was later to play in the Castilian conquest of Seville (see p.53). It is, however, clear that more than commercial motives were involved. In the circle of the king, where the idea of the expedition seems to have arisen, other impulses – chivalric, dynastic and political – were stronger. The House of Barcelona had an acute sense of dynasty. Atavistic appeals to common ancestry were often capable of ending clannish conflicts; if a particular policy could be represented in council as ancestral, that was always a useful, and sometimes a compelling argument for its espousal. Majorca was a longstanding focus of the cupidity of Jaime's predecessors. Count Ramon Berenguer III had attempted the conquest in 1114–15, in alliance with Pisa, at a time when Catalan commercial interest in the island was still underdeveloped. The memory of the exploits had been kept vivid by an 'epic' poem in Latin and vernacular versions, the *Liber Maiolichinus*, just as the memory of the conquest of Valencia was to be sustained and revived by the diffusion and versification of the story of the Cid. At intervals throughout the twelfth century, further attempts to organise a conquest were made: first, new efforts in alliance with Genoa and Pisa by Ramon Berenguer III and Ramon Berenguer IV, later with Sicily by Alfonso II. In 1204, the pope authorised the creation of a see in Majorca when its conquest should have been accomplished.

King Jaime, susceptible as he was to the nostalgia of 'lineage', also had more urgent political reasons to take his magnates abroad. The minority with which his reign began aroused rivalries for the regency and invited aristocratic usurpations of authority. Only in 1227, after ten years of almost continuous civil war, did Jaime make good his claims to have attained his majority. He was nineteen years old, heir to a depleted patrimony, legatee of troubled times. The cause behind which he might most easily have united his realm was the conquest of Valencia, a Muslim land abutting Catalonia to the south. But, even if successful – and Jaime, who had tested Valencia's defences, had reason to think it would fail – such an enterprise could only fatten aristocratic domains of already indecent corpulence. Jaime's cause was better served by peace with Valencia, secured by the payment of tributes directly to himself. He preserved the peace with – or at least deferred the war against – Valencia, even at the risk of another magnate uprising.

To judge from the versions of debates in council preserved in Jaime's chronicle, Majorca proved an acceptable alternative partly because of its traditional appeal and partly because the king was lavish with promises of rewards. The relationship of the king to his Aragonese nobles was never one of control. At its best, it was an entente. The debates unfolded with successive renewals of the pledge of feudal loyalty, by erstwhile rebels, under strict conditions. Entirely representative was the declaration of En Nunyo Sanç, Lord of Roussillon and Cerdagne, who would make the biggest contribution to the conquest and would claim the largest reward: he reminded the king of the equivalence of their lineage, which they both owed equally to God; he acknowledged himself to be the king's vassal and to hold his lands by grant of the king's father, but he implied that part of his patrimony was attributable to divine election, rather than royal investiture. The Count of Ampurias, who spoke after him in council, made this point explicitly on his own behalf and that of his kinsman, Guillem de Montcada: God had 'made them' and they held lands not only of the king but also 'of their own allod'; indeed, all the dominions accumulated by the House of Barcelona were and would be circumscribed by a fudged line between sovereignty and suzerainty. Nunyo Sanç went on to confirm his peace with the king and the terms of his tenure of his lordships; he conceded to the king, as of his own free will, the right to levy the pasture tax, the *bovatge*, in his dominions; he promised to aid the conquest with horse, foot and ships, including a hundred of his household knights. Next came the explicit condition: 'And you will give them part of the land and the movable wealth,' before the affirmation, 'And I have to serve you in that land since God gives it to us to conquer.' Jaime's response was embodied in a charter issued at the representative assembly or *Corts* of Barcelona in 1228, before the expedition sailed, addressed to all the nobility: 'We shall give just portions to you and yours, according to the numbers of knights and men-at-arms whom you take with you.' The decision to attempt the conquest of Majorca was a good example of how contractual kingship worked.[3]

As well as the work of contingents from this 'feudal' world of aristocratic give-and-take, the conquest was the work of militias, mercenaries and ships from the 'commercial' world of the cities of Catalonia and Provence. These worlds were more thoroughly interpenetrated than is commonly supposed. Trade and land were distinct sources of wealth, but substantial amounts of both were often in the same hands and there was no 'class antagonism', but rather common interest, between them. King Jaime's *Book of Deeds* gives the impression that the idea of the conquest originated in commercial circles. He describes the great banquet at Tarragona in November or December, 1228, when Pere Martell entertained the king 'and the greater part of the nobles of Catalonia'; the question of Majorca is represented as arising by accident, but Martell was well prepared for it, explaining to the magnates the whereabouts of the Balearics as if with an early map spread before him.

In fact, the decision had been made by then. The preparation of a fleet against Majorca is mentioned in the king's 'contract of concubinage' with Countess Aurembiaix of Urgel of October, 1228 – a document vital to the king's interests, in which he secured the reversion to the crown of the biggest territorial principality in his realms. This is not to say either that the Tarragona banquet was a fiction or that the conquest of Majorca was without commercial allure. Jaime regularly liked to discuss business after dinner: it was a typical social ritual of the Catalonia of his day. The account books of the city of Majorca after its conquest show that banquets to honour great events or stimulate appetites for civic transactions were a major source of expense, like the 'business lunch' today. It was characteristic, too, that a nautical technician and merchant like Pere Martell could act as host to the king and sit down with 'the greater nobles' without social embarrassment. Some nobles, like Nunyo Sanç, had coastal jurisdictions and ships of their own. Many merchants, especially from Barcelona, possessed investments in land. Unlike Venice and Genoa, Barcelona had always maintained intimate links with its hinterland. The city's eschewal of a republican constitution helps to demonstrate this, but more vivid examples can be found in individual merchants' careers. The very origins of Barcelona as a great commercial centre can be sensed in the records of the activities of Ricart Guillem, who in the course of 50 years in the late eleventh and early twelfth centuries built up a fortune not only from selling wine but actually producing it on a growing domain of his own, which extended ever farther into the hinterland. Doubling as a moneylender, he ended as a castellan as well as a citizen, a vassal of the Montcada and Cabrera families, acquiring castles and seigneurial rights by purchase or holding them from his lords. This was still *le style barcelonais* in the time of Pere Martell.[4]

Barcelona, alone or even in combination with the other great Catalan port of Tarragona, could not launch enough ships to conquer Majorca. The shortfall was made up by aristocratic shipowners and by the King of Aragon's subject-ports and allies, beyond the Pyrenees, at Collioure, Perpignan, Narbonne, Montpellier and Marseilles. The Marseillais contribution – though the city was not beholden to the Crown of Aragon – may have been equal to or greater than that of Barcelona. The shipping for Jaime's expedition was in a sense a joint effort of the Catalan and Provençal worlds. It is tempting to see the cities of this region playing collectively in the conquest of Majorca the same role as the Venetians in the Fourth Crusade, transporting respectively Aragonese warlords and 'Frankish pilgrims' for a share in the spoils. But none of them was a city-state in quite the same sense as Venice, and no 'empire' was created for them in the Balearics. The territorial rewards were modest plots for individual participants, as was promised by Jaime I to the men of Barcelona and Tarragona: 'May you have lands allotted to you, held from us and our successors and in fealty to us according to the customs of Barcelona [meaning, perhaps, without intervention of intermediate lordship, or else with the guarantee of heritability in the female line] . . . and the portions which you will have there you will be able to sell and alienate, saving our fealty and lordship.'[5]

The strictly commercial rewards which therefore justified such widespread adhesion to the king's enterprise must have been considerable. Nothing is known of Majorca's trade before the conquest, except that the island was a notorious hotbed of piracy. Though a rather rough-and-ready form of exchange, piracy should probably not be too sharply distinguished from trade in this period. Most seafarers and most ships slipped in and out of both vocations without specialisation. King Jaime made the depredations of the corsairs the *casus belli*, but it is reasonable to suppose that the merchants in his fleet aimed not only to suppress the pirates because they were pirates but also to supplant them in their more legitimate lines of business. Though many new products seem to have been introduced to Majorca by the conquerors, the island's role as an entrepôt or staging post of the western Mediterranean seems to have been well established for generations, perhaps for centuries, before Jaime's conquest. The entrenched position of Moorish traders, and of their privileged partners from Genoa and Pisa in the early thirteenth century, adequately explains the jealous anxiety of the Catalans and Provençals to break into the cartel, by force if necessary, on equal or preferential terms.

Crusading rhetoric justified the expedition and papal indulgences helped to launch it. Can religious motives be distinguished in the background of the conquest? The distinctively spiritual motives of Hold Land crusaders who were spurred by the redemptive virtues of pilgrimage are not explicitly attested by any source for the conquest of Majorca. It remains possible that in a more general sense the conquest was seen as salutary because divinely ordained, even perhaps sanctified by the unbelief of the enemy. Pious avowals, beyond conventional invocations of Providence or assurances of godliness of purpose, are rare in King Jaime's *Book of Deeds*. Usually it is interlocutors – bishops, for the most part – who are made to convey the more profound or more eloquent appeals to religion, which may be the work of a clerical interpolator or amanuensis. The conquest of Majorca, however, did inspire passages of exceptional fervour in the king's own mouth. When adverse winds made some of his company desire to abandon the voyage, Jaime answered them, by his own account, 'We are going on this voyage out of faith in God, and against those who do not believe in Him, and we are going against them for two purposes, either to convert or destroy them, and so that they may return that kingdom to the faith of Our Lord, and since we are going in His name, we confide in Him to guide us.'[6] Votive effusions in time of peril are a long tradition of Mediterranean sailors, and it may be that this passage in the chronicle faithfully records a moment of uncharacteristic spiritual transport on Jaime's part. Seastorms, which recall Christ's stilling of the waters and the shipwreck of St Paul, easily induce moods of exaltation. More than merely just, Jaime represented the conflict almost as hallowed by the promise of Moorish blood or baptismal water. Yet even here the accent was on the legitimation rather than the sanctification of the conquest: Jaime went on to justify his war in terms of traditional just war theory, as waged for the recovery of usurped lands. This is the usual context of pious allusions in western Mediterranean texts; the numinous east, where Christ trod and relics seemed to pullulate, was more productive of purely spiritual motives.

So the conquest was determined and the subsequent colonisation shaped by cupidity for commerce and land. Majorca was genuinely a crucible of colonial experiment, in which the problems of adjusting the balance of indigenous and incoming populations, native and new elements of the economy, were tried. Initial solutions were modified by experience. A pattern was established which remained influential throughout the history of the expansion of the Crown of Aragon – indeed, in some respects, throughout the history of western Mediterranean expansion generally. The problems were not considered in advance. The king's obligation to distribute the soil of Majorca among his magnates and city men imposed the necessity of dispossessing, perhaps of expelling or exterminating the Moors. Until practical problems supervened, the conquistadores probably envisaged a Majorca created from scratch, and thickly planted with new settlers and their crops. The scale of the division of the city, house by house, and of the soil – plot by plot, where detailed records survive – suggests a conscious attempt at comprehensive colonisation, a genuine repeopling of the island. Sixty thousand hectares are unaccounted for in the surviving sources; this may correspond to a portion for the natives or may be a trick of the uneven survival of evidence. The rest was divided up, according to the promises the king had made to the *Corts* of Barcelona, by one of the most efficient and pernickety royal bureaucracies in Christendom. Most of the large grants are known only in outline. Nunyo Sanç and his followers got the biggest single domain: Valldemossa, Bunyola, Manacor and 89 houses in the city. The see of Barcelona was rewarded with half the city and the coast as far as Bunyalbufar. The Count of Ampurias and Bishop of Gerona received Muro, with two-thirds of Sóller and half of Albufera. The remainder of Sóller and Cala Rotja went to the Viscount of Béarn and the archdeacon of Barcelona. The subdivision or alienation of these big fiefs is usually hard to trace. The pattern discernible in the case of the Viscount of Béarn, who distributed fees from his portion among his household, was repeated in some instances; in others, the estates might be rapidly transferred *en bloc*, like those of the Bishop of Gerona, who sold most of his share to Guillem de Toroella (helping to make the latter one of the period's biggest gainers in patrimony, by conquest and purchase in the Balearics and inheritance on the mainland). The magnates' portions in the city probably evolved in a way similar to those distributed directly to individual townsmen by the king. Nunyo Sanç's share, for instance, between 1232 and 1235, was settled by 27 Catalans (from Ampurias, Barcelona, Cambrills, Collioure, Gerona, Lérida, Montcada, Montblanch, Ripoll, Sabadell, Tarragona, Tortosa, Vich and Vilafranca), 20 from southern France outside the dominions of the House of Barcelona, 14 Italians, 7 Aragonese, 5 Navarrese and 20 Jews.[7]

The most detailed evidence of land distributions survives, however, from outside the magnates' portions, in the so-called royal 'moiety', the *medietas regis*. At the first comprehensive division in 1232, this comprised 57 000 hectares (in Inca, Pollensa, Sineu, Petro, Artà, Montuiri, Albufera and the mountains, of which almost half was granted away, in a total of 300 separate properties (not counting those of the city), to the Templars, the towns and various nobles just below the dignity of the 'big three' who had received, with the Church, a moiety between themselves. Guillem de Montcada, Ramon Alemany and Guillem de Claramunt are examples of those who benefited from this distribution of royal land. This left the king with direct control of more than twice the land granted to the biggest magnate proprietor (the approximately 13 500 hectares of Nunyo Sanç). There would be further depletions as time went on, but it was a huge bonanza for the impoverished crown. The king's half of the city went in rewards to the soldiers of his urban militias, the sailors of his fleet and the merchants who backed his invasion: 307 houses to Tarragona, 298 to Marseilles,

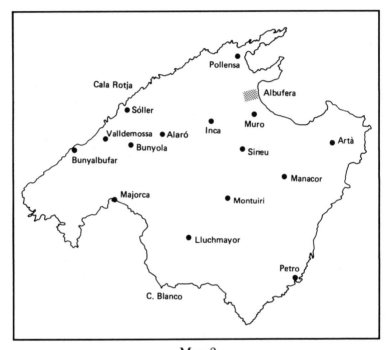

Map 2
MAJORCA
places named the the text

226 each to Barcelona and Lérida, 100 to Montpellier and small portions to Cladells, Cervera, Gerona, Huesca, Manresa, Montblanch, Tarrega, Tortosa and Vilafranca.[8]

This *repartiment* or *partitio* of the island suggests a programme of intensive colonisation at every social level. The same intention is betrayed by the exhortations distributed around the western Mediterranean basin by Pope Gregory IX. He encouraged all potential settlers (with the exception of Cathar heretics) 'who wish to inhabit lands newly won or to be won' with indulgences equivalent to those of pilgrims to the Holy Land.[9] Enough colonists responded to make the island Catalan-speaking, with marked influence from the dialects of Ampurias and Roussillon, and to saturate the toponymy of the lowland areas in Catalan forms. But the extent to which this colonial population displaced the Moors and, among the surviving Moors, the problem of the degree of enslavement, are much debated topics of Majorcan history. The myth that the Moors were all enslaved or expelled seems to have arisen from a misreading of the chronicles, fortified by a false analogy with what happened later in the island of Minorca. It is true that of the major chronicles of the next century, one says that the island was 'altogether settled by Catalans' but in a context where Jewish and 'Saracen' elements have just been mentioned, while the claim of the other that 'it was all peopled with Catalans' clearly relates, from the context, to the city of Majorca, not the island at large.

Evidence of Moorish survival, in both free and servile status, is overwhelming. First, there were Moors whose resistance in the mountains was not ended by the conquest. The largest contingent, submitting conditionally in June, 1232, and specifically exempted from enslavement, can be reckoned, by implication, from the king's own chronicle, to have numbered 16 000 – but such estimates are notoriously unreliable. Then there is considerable evidence that in the interests of keeping the island well populated, the king and other proprietors rapidly came to value their Moorish subjects and tenants, whatever their initial posture of hostility. The Templars soon brought free 'Saracens' into the island from their peninsular properties in order to stimulate exploitation of the soil; the king encouraged Moorish immigrants, especially from Minorca, and promised them the same rights as Moors had already established in various localities in the island. Pope Gregory IX favoured this policy, hoping that it would lead to conversions among incoming Moors. Finally, the large number of documents from within the island, from the thirteenth and fourteenth centuries, attest the continued presence of Moors on a considerable scale, especially as artisans in the towns – smiths, goldsmiths and other metalworkers, leather and textile workers, shopkeepers and even a painter.

Many of these documents are records of slavery, but they do not show a population that was enslaved wholesale. On the contrary, it is apparent that many Moors purchased indemnity from enslavement or expulsion at the time of the conquest, even if they did not of right enjoy the specific exemptions conceded to some communities by the king. It was common for those who had paid this impost 'pro stando in terra ista (for remaining in the land)' to slip into and out of slavery for debt, to the annoyance of royal officials who tended to insist that during spells of slavery their freemen's poll tax should continue to be paid by their masters. Contracts in which slaves, who were given land to work for the purchase of their freedom, stayed on as serfs or tenants allow us a glimpse of the means by which many seigneurs must have exploited their land-grants. Finally, the toponymical evidence is probably as good a guide as any to the relative distribution of natives and settlers. Place names in the poorer uplands and central mountain region remained Arabic. Though we shall probably never know the scale either of indigenous survival or settler penetration, it seems evident that both happened. The thoroughly Catalan appearance of Majorca in the next century was a result of Catalan predominance in the main centres of population and of commerce.[10]

Alongside the Catalan predominance, Majorca retained and developed, in the commercial ports, a cosmopolitan feeling, because of growing numbers of resident foreign merchants and a lively trade in slaves of diverse nationalities. The Genoese were one of the most important foreign communities tolerated – or, during the period of Majorcan independence, actually encouraged – even in times of war between Genoa and the Crown of Aragon. During the hostilities of the next century, the Genoese, with the Pisans, were accused of having encouraged Moorish resistance to Jaime I's invasion, but the conquest did not disturb the Genoese in the enjoyment of their trading privileges. On the contrary, Andrea Caffaro negotiated the confirmation of their status; in 1233 the king granted them a trading precinct in the street that led to the Templars' castle and ordered the local authorities to protect them. Their presence is documented in the *Capbrevació* of Nunyo Sanç's portion of the city of 1232. Fourteen Italians, including eight Genoese, are mentioned, with Otgerio de Mazanello as their consul. They were a valuable property, more profitable to persecute fiscally than by embargo or expulsion. Between 1320 and 1344, for instance, they paid an import tax ten times as big as that charged to the Pisans: the high level was justified on the grounds that it provided indemnities for Majorcan goods against Genoese piracy.[11]

The Jews were even more numerous and at least as important to the economic life of the island. At the time of the conquest, the prosperous Jewish community already established in Majorca seems to have acted as a magnet for poor co-religionists from all over the western Mediterranean. Ships' masters had to be deterred by royal decree, issued on the request of Majorcan Jews, from embarking Jewish immigrants on credit in the expectation that their unwilling potential hosts would meet the bill. Poor Jews – or, at least, those who pleaded inability to pay their taxes – remained a problem for the community throughout its history. Such was its constitution – with a measure of self-government by a council of 30, assisted, and increasingly directed, by 4 elected 'secretaries' – that its considerable burden of taxation was incurred collectively and discharged by an often painful process of mutual agreement, negotiated by the secretaries, among its members.

Pleas of poverty, however, leave intact an overall impression of comfortable wealth. The Jews were regarded as a 'treasure house . . . from whom the trades and traders of this kingdom in peacetime derive great abundance [*haurament*]'. Most Jewish wealth was accumulated in crafts or professions. In the fourteenth century, for instance, Jews were active as silversmiths, silk merchants, veterinarians, peddlers, freelance postmen, armourers, cobblers, tailors, drapers, dyers, kosher butchers, carpenters, physicians, illuminators, bookbinders, soap makers, mapmakers, wet-nurses, wine merchants and millers. They were disadvantaged in long-range trade by fiscal victimisation, by discriminatory terms sometimes imposed on them in payment for certain staple products, and by exclusion from some ports. The only routes on which they played a major role in the fourteenth century were to the Maghrib (see p.135), where they were too deeply entrenched to be extruded. They had a peculiar relationship with the crown, which, as in much of the rest of Christendom, generally worked to their advantage. They were 'the king's coffers of money', generously endowed by Jaime I with privileges – of which the most valuable was that no Jew could be convicted by Christian or Moorish testimony. Though their secular leaders were chosen by a mixture of seniority and ballot, the office of rabbi was a royal gift or, at least, subject to royal confirmation. Their privileges were gradually modified and, especially under King Sancho (r. 1311–24), fiscal exploitation of the Jews became more abrasive; but almost throughout the fourteenth century Jews maintained, in some respects, a favoured and protected status. Despite occasional token prohibitions from 1285 onwards, they continued to hold public offices up to the level of members of the royal council.

Growing popular resentment in the second half of the fourteenth century was their undoing. Their public delinquencies afford scant clues to their fate. Two characteristically Jewish crimes were false coining and – in the reign of Jaume II, when it was an offence, – 'dwelling in Saracen lands'. The first reflects their prominence in the handling of precious metals, the second their leading position in the Barbary trade. But what most seem to have vexed their Christian neighbours were, first, their discharge of detested functions as moneylenders and tax farmers and, secondly, the conspicuous distinctions which set their society apart. They lived apart, in their own ghettos or *calls*, where they were numerous enough to do so, as at Inca or in the city. With few exemptions, granted, as in the case of the renowned cartographer, Cresques Abraham, for exceptional services, they wore the dress prescribed by the Lateran Council, or a modified form of it. They remarried on divorce, by royal leave, and, as is shown by the case of Moses Obeyt, whose plea of 1258 was made on grounds of childlessness, were allowed lawfully to contract bigamous marriages. All their Hebrew marriage contracts were valid without registration by a public notary. They flouted the Christian sabbath and incurred odium in the marketplace by their pre-emptive habit of early rising. As their legal privileges were greater than those of Christians, so were their punishments more severe. A Jew guilty of a hanging offence was suspended upside down – 'mouth downwards' – to protract the death and aggravate the agony.

The natural resentment of a community apart, which ensued from these invidious distinctions, was exacerbated by accusations of usury. Isaac Addenden behaved like a stage Jew, when, in March 1338, he foreclosed on his mortgage of Salvador Gisbert's tavern in Castellitx; the king's lieutenant upheld the Jew's rights on appeal and set a date for the auction. When Isaac Solomon went to collect debts in Porreres in 1356, he sought the *batle*'s protection. These were representative incidents. The Jews were anyway under an ancestral cloud. Their taxes fell due at Easter. Holy Week yielded an annual crop of violent outrages. Hard times or febrile preachers could stir popular hatred with astonishing ease. In 1374, the king had to quell demands for the Jews' expulsion at a time of famine by recalling that they had paid for royal relief ships. In 1370, the preaching licence of the rabid, footloose mendicant, Fray Bonanato, was withdrawn because of his anti-Semitic excesses. The pogroms and forcible conversions of the next generation – the near extinction of the *call* after the blood-letting of 1391 – were being prepared.[12]

Most other aliens were slaves. Majorca's large servile population seems to have come more from *razzie*, piracy and trade than from any supposed mass enslavement of native Moors. Its provenance was wide, reflecting the range of the Mediterranean slave trade. Sards were numerous during the Sardinian wars of the House of Barcelona. So were Greeks, whose status as schismatics made them vulnerable. Most of the slaves who worked the quarries for the builder, sculptor and architect, Pero Mates, in the mid-fourteenth century were Greeks. Majorca – indeed, the Balearics as a whole – was probably more of an emporium than a market for slaves in its own right.

The island was a centre of re-export for the entire Arago-Catalan world for these and all manner of other goods. The iron of Bayonne and Castile – the latter usually shipped from Seville – figs of Murcia and Alcudia, Ibizan salt, Sevillian oil and 'Greek wine' – perhaps Calabrian rather than strictly Greek – were, with slaves, the commodities brought in the largest quantities to Majorca, en route for elsewhere. The Aragonese dominions and north Africa predominate among the destinations represented in surviving shipping contracts. Between 1321 and 1340, for instance, 48–59 per cent of sailings for ports outside the kingdom of Majorca were bound for Catalonia and 20–28 per cent for Valencia. North Africa came a good third, with over 2800 sailing licences surviving from the fourteenth century.[13]

Majorca was dependent on trade, but that is not to say that she was incapable of fostering new industries after the conquest. Commerce bred shipbuilding, especially after Sancho I turned one of the Jewish cemeteries into a shipyard; an appeal to the crown over conditions of employment of carpenters employed on the building of six cogs in 1340 shows the scale of activity attained at a single moment. Some of the materials and skills of the shipwrights may also have been deployed in the remarkable armaments industry: in and around the 1380s, for instance, Pere de Vilalonga shipped literally thousands of crossbows to Flanders and England. The greatest industrial success of post-conquest Majorca was textiles, the most important product of the medieval industrial revolution, which fostered commerce wherever it was produced. Majorcan cloth was probably already coveted in the late thirteenth century; its production is documented from 1303. Its origins are obscure. Italian influence has been postulated to account for it, and Italians were generally the technicians and financiers of new colonial enterprise in late medieval Mediterranean islands; but the first evidence of Italian involvement in the Majorcan cloth industry is of Florentine operatives at work in the late fourteenth century. The industry may well have come, in the first place, with the majority of colonists, from Catalonia.[14]

The range of new commercial and industrial activity, the prodigious economic growth of the century after the conquest, made Majorca a land of medieval *Wirtschaftswunder*, comparable with Madeira in the next century with its new products and 'nodal' trade. The chronicle of Jaime I eloquently expressed the potential of Majorca: it was the finest land, with the most beautiful city in the world; it was the king's favourite conquest, 'of more esteem than the kingdom of León'. In the eyes of Ramon Muntaner, writing in about 1325, the king's confidence seemed to be fulfilled. Muntaner was, of all the Catalan chroniclers, the most indiscriminate in his praise and the most ready with superlatives; but his encomium of Majorca rings true. It was a 'goodly isle, and an honoured one'. The king had 'made great grants to all his men, and great graces. And he peopled the said city and isle by means of more exemptions and privileges than any other city in the world; wherefore it has become one of the good cities of the world, noble and of greater wealth than any, and all peopled with Catalans, all of honoured provenance and good worth, whence have descended heirs who have become the most businesslike and best endowed people (la pus convinent gent e mills nodrida) of any city there may be in the world.' The concentration on the 'city of Majorca', in despite of the rest of the island, is revealing. When outsiders thought of Majorca, they thought only of its entrepôt just as today they think only of the tourist complex, on the same coast, centred on the same city. Muntaner also accurately perceived the conditions that enabled Majorca's economy to thrive: the economic freedom and low taxation that accompanied a sustained effort to draw settlers to the island.[15] The pattern became normal in the subsequent history of colonisation in the western Mediterranean and Atlantic. That history is often represented – quite rightly – as slow and painful, riven with 'checks' and reversals; yet the successes are in some ways more surprising than the slips and they could not have been procured without lavish concessions to settlers.

In the generation after Muntaner's encomium, Majorca's economic miracle seems to have run out of steam. Between 1329 and 1343 the population of the city of Majorca, for instance, fell dramatically, from 5256 hearths to 4124. The loss of feudal 'independence' in 1343, and the reabsorption of the island under the direct lordship of the king of Aragon, may have helped to bring the pioneering period to an end, to remove a source of incentives and to make Majorca a less stimulating place to live in and operate from. Yet if expansion was halted, prosperity continued, and if dynamism subsided, complacency prevailed. The *Manual de reebudes e de dades* – the municipal accounts of 1349 – captures the epicene contentment of the city fathers in the very year of plague. Theirs was a world of status linked to consumption, measured in costly feasts and ostentatious displays of loyalty to the mainland dynasty. At least 76 craftsmen and decorators were employed – some Moors, some Greeks, a few specifically slaves – to adorn the city chambers for the banquets. Two 'painters of altarpieces and battle flags' decorated hangings to celebrate the obsequies of the mainland queen. And the large sums spent on defence against the pretensions of the extruded island dynasty included the pay of eleven surgeon-barbers to serve the fleet. A society so abundantly supplied with quacks and craftsmen must have wallowed in surplus wealth.[16]

The government of this society presented problems which the Aragonese kings found hard to resolve and historians have found hard to classify. Like the mainland dominions of the house of

Barcelona, it combined devolution of power in the localities to municipal communities and lords, mediated through a bureaucratic layer of royal or seigneurial representatives called *batles*, with sophisticated representative institutions at the centre to advise the king and regulate taxation. Under the king or, in periods of rule from the peninsula, his lieutenant, the *jurats* performed the function of a council, and the *Consell* that of a representative institution. Because so much of the great nobility was based in the peninsula, and represented in the island by administrators trained in the law, both institutions had a deceptively bourgeois air. The *jurats* were royal nominees, the *Consell* an elective body, partly nominated by the *jurats*, partly elected by syndics in the localities. The representatives of the *part forana* – distinguished from those of the city – were chosen by bodies of rural syndics, appointed in turn by a combination of election and lottery; the growth of their numbers – from 3 after the conquest to 10 in the reign of Sancho I and 63 by the end of the century – reflects the growth of population and of the importance of the hinterland. Each rural town was to have between four and eight representatives; the relatively large settlements – Inca, Pollensa, Sineu, Sóller, Manacor, Lluchmayor – predominated.

The *Consell* met infrequently, for the enactment of ritual, the approval of taxation or the codification of privileges. The day-to-day business of government, as in all medieval states, lay not in legislation but the administration of justice. This was nicely divided between frequently absentee kings and lords. As early as July, 1231, the king and the principal beneficiaries of the *repartiment* agreed that seigneurial jurisdiction would be limited to the appointment of *batles* in seigneurial lands and the hearing of civil and minor criminal cases, though criminal jurisdiction at any level could be, and often was, granted away by the king. The profits of justice seem to have been shared variously, according to no fixed rule but rather to the power of the baron concerned. In his own lands, for instance, Nunyo Sanç scooped the pool, though the crown was able to secure varying shares, from time to time, elsewhere. When law-making was required, the process reflected this effective division of power among the absentee élite: the *jurats*, among whom representatives of the magnates predominated, were the decision-makers.

Of greater interest to historians than the details of the island's institutions has been the question of the relationship of the

Kingdom of Majorca as a whole to the Crown of Aragon and the other dominions of the House of Barcelona. The controversies over whether the Aragonese dominions can properly be called an 'empire' and over the nature of the models of government inherited by 'modern' colonisation from the 'medieval' past have deflected enquiry into some arid byways. Certainly Majorca was typical of the Aragonese dominions in the vagueness with which its place in the monarchy was defined. Like most other areas of Arago-Catalan overseas expansion, it was often hived off to local rulers – at first called 'lord' and later 'king' of Majorca – whose loyalty, secured only by oaths of vassalage and participation in the general *Corts* or representative assembly of the Crown of Aragon, was generally unreliable.

The first lord was that extraordinary condottiere-cum-gigolo, the Infante Dom Pedro of Portugal. Exiled to León in 1211 at the age of 24, and unable thereafter ever to make a wholly successful intervention in Portuguese affairs, this freelance prince served first with Alfonso IX of León against Portuguese and Moors, then in Morocco as commander of a foreign legion (see p.126). He seems to have entered Aragonese service in 1228, but not to have taken part in the conquest of Majorca. Instead, the king employed him to be husband of the discarded royal concubine, Countess Aurembiaix of Urgel. The countess saw the prince as a means of vengeance on her lover, settling the county of Urgel on him in the event of her death, defying the terms of her 'contract of concubinage', which guaranteed the reversion of that desirable principality to the crown. But, in a secret deal, Pedro agreed to respect the king's rights. His reward, together with a few minor lordships of his wife's, was the seigneury of Majorca. At about the time – perhaps on the very day – of his wife's death at Michaelmas, 1231, he was invested with the lordship of Majorca and Minorca; the latter was a nominal dignity, save for the prospect of future tribute, since the island was still in Moorish hands. He also received the right of conquest, to be shared with Nunyo Sanç, of Ibiza. He was granted possession of the strongest castles on Majorca – the Almudaina, Alaró and Pollensa, – a life-interest in a relatively extensive domain and the right to pass a third of it on to his heirs.

Pedro's lands seem to have been intended as a fund of patronage, from which he could reward his own entourage, rather than as a fisc with which to pay for government. He had 103 divers and widely separated properties, of which 52, amounting to well over half the domain, were given to members of his household, generally in the form of grants from the king. The total at Pedro's disposal – 6100 hectares – took about a ninth of the royal moiety and was not large by the standards of the magnate beneficiaries of the *repartiment*: Nunyo Sanç, for instance, had well over twice as much. Pedro's rights were ill-defined. He made grants within the royal moiety, but so did the king. He nominated and dismissed royal *batles* and justices, including those of the city. He received acts of homage from new settlers; he sat with the *jurats* to make laws and frame decrees, as for instance when water for irrigation was redistributed in 1239 after the loss of records of the system which had prevailed under the Moors. From the pope he received a special right or duty to extirpate 'perverse usages and wicked customs or unlawful practice (*ritum illicitum*)' perhaps because Majorca was being used as a refuge by Cathar heretics. But none of these functions implied any form of long-term autonomy for Majorca. Indeed, for the greater part of the time, Pedro was probably absent, like most of the feudatories of the island. In 1235 he was away conquering Ibiza and in 1238 Valencia. In 1239 he appointed a lieutenant who was not relieved. Throughout the first period of his tenure of the lordship, his presence is only attested by documents briefly in 1239 and again in the summers of 1241 and 1242. Thereafter, he probably did not return until 1254, and in the meantime he had surrendered his lordship in exchange for a substantial fief in the newly conquered Kingdom of Valencia.[17]

Still, he did resume the lordship in 1254 for the last two years of his life. Thus, when the firstborn of the House of Barcelona died in 1260 and the patrimony was prospectively divided between the king's other heirs, there was a recent precedent for Majorcan autonomy, which from Jaime's death in 1276 would be precariously sustained, with attenuations and interruptions, until 1343. Majorca became the treasury and granary of a kingdom of enclaves and islands – the Balearics, Roussillon, Cerdagne and Montpellier – on the fringes of the Arago-Catalan world. At times, its kings, like other, lesser vassals of the kings of Aragon, could break their oaths of fealty and defy the senior line; until 1279, it was even possible for Jaume II of Majorca to claim that he owed no loyalty to the Crown of Aragon, as his father's testament had not specifically obliged him to take an oath. But Majorca was never genuinely viable as a wholly independent state. Its inhabitants were Catalans, who retained habits of loyalty to the historic dynasty; it was dependent on its peninsular trade; its magnates were for the most part peninsula-based. Jaume II was powerless to resist Pedro III's demand for homage in 1279 or to oppose the Aragonese invasion of 1285. His restoration in 1299 was made in the interests of the dynasty as a whole by the decision of Jaime II of Aragon. When the ambiguities of the relationship were finally swept away by the definitive Aragonese conquest of 1343, the operation took a week. The invaders were welcomed almost everywhere and there was little or no local support for Jaume III's later attempts at revanche: only the heavy-handed government of Pedro IV in 1347 gave the exile a hope of success, which ended with his death in a hapless invasion two years later.

## Ibiza and Formentera

Ibiza and Formentera constituted a better example of an island principality within the Aragonese dominions. Like Majorca, they were conquered by 'crusaders', but, unlike Majorca, by private enterprise. The crown played no part, save as a source of legitimation. Because Pedro of Portugal and Nunyo Sanç failed to take up their right of conquest, it was reallocated, with their agreement, between December, 1234, and April, 1235, to Guillem de Montgrí, sacristan of Gerona cathedral. The king reserved the possession of fortified places, the right to make war or peace and the exclusive right to the homage (save any owed to ecclesiastical superiors) of the participants in the conquest, but all costs and risks were borne by the would-be conquerors.

In conquering Ibiza, Montgrí was acting on behalf of the archbishopric of Tarragona, which had got little out of the conquest of Majorca. For a while, however, he was to rule Ibiza as an unchallenged paladin. Dom Pedro and En Nunyo were to hold their portions of the principal port in fee from him and perform homage. The town and castle were to be divided equally among the three of them, and the rest of the island in proportion to the number of combatants each brought to the conquest. Like the Genoese conquest of Chios in the next century or the Castilian conquests of the western Canaries in the fifteenth, this was a private speculation for gain. Despite the exalted language in which the pope exhorted the conquerors 'to snatch the island from impious hands', the conquerors' bargain was quite explicit: their investment would be recouped from the spoils of conquest.

When castle and town were taken by storm in August, 1235, it seemed as if the partners would have a free hand to exploit what they had acquired. Jaime I did not enforce his rights over the fortified places. Montgrí, who had provided the biggest contingent, appointed himself governor of the principal castle, and took half the land outside the town and half the yield of salt – the island's main source of wealth. Dom Pedro and En Nunyo divided the rest equally. Gradually, however, the crown's superior lordship and right to the strong places was reasserted. Pedro's fief passed, via the *infant* Jaume, to the crown, Nunyo's to the see of Tarragona. After about a generation, the island thus became a royal-ecclesiastical condominium.

The society of post-conquest Ibiza seems to have resembled Majorca in miniature, save that subenfeoffment was rare. The big exception was the island of Formentera, granted by Guillem de Montgrí in fee perpetual to Berenguer Renart, with exemption only of Pedro's share and a few sites intended for a hospice and hermitages. The lord was to receive a quarter of the profits of justice and a tenth of wheat and meat 'according to the custom of Ibiza' in addition to the dues owed to the church: in colonised areas, the seigneurial economy evidently relied on ecclesiastical dues. That, perhaps, was why Nunyo Sanç sold out to the church. Renart could appoint a *batle*, who, however, was obliged to swear fealty to the lord, as were all new settlers. The office of notary was to remain in the lord's gift; so was jurisdiction in the surrounding sea. Fishing rights were for Renart and the free use of salt deposits for the settlers.

Throughout Ibiza, settlers were at first difficult to attract. In 1237, Pope Gregory IX authorised the see of Tarragona to readmit to communion arsonists, profaners of sacred persons and suppliers of illicit arms to Saracens on condition that they settled Ibiza in person or by proxy. Like Majorca, Ibiza relied on the survival or reintroduction of Moors. Those who surrendered at the conquest could redeem themselves from captivity for seven-and-a-half ducats, but in numerous cases the payment was probably waived or worked off. Many were sold in Minorca, Majorca and Barcelona – the authorised markets – and others illegally in Valencia and Orihuela. The fact that they or others soon found their way back to the island as freemen infuriated the pope, who felt 'that they should live alongside Christians in such a way that, deferring to the same, they should recognise that they are placed beneath the yoke of slavery'. Pedro of Portugal, before he renounced his portion of the island, was instrumental in its resettlement with Moors, doubtless bringing some of them from his Valencian estates.

Nothing better illustrates the difficulty of attracting settlers and the narrow economic base of the island than the failure of the lords to increase revenues from salt, dividing them between the needs of public works and the demands of their own pockets. Their efforts lasted for eight years before they yielded to the necessity of exercising liberality in allowing settlers use-rights in the salt. It was, apart from slave-trading, the only economic resource of the island, and the only 'perk' that would attract settlers.

And yet, despite the early preponderance of Moors, the fragile economy and the hesitant colonisation, Ibiza was remarkably successful – reflecting, perhaps, the glow of the tail-light of Majorca's 'take-off'. By the late fourteenth century there was an island council of 250 members, divided into 5 groups of 50, each group holding office by turn. This was a large élite for a small island. Of the five *jurats*, introduced in 1299, one represented the 'greater estate' (*mà major*) 'of the best and richest men' and one the 'middle estate'; a third, chosen by the lords, came from the *mà forània*, the hinterland, outside the port, reflecting a division comparable to Majorca's, which transcended the old concept of estates. These three between them elected two more. These institutions seem to belong to a solidly established society, with deeply rooted settlements. Yet in about the same period – in the mid to late fourteenth century – the insecurity of life on small islands in corsair-infested seas was thrown into relief by the abandonment of Formentera. By 1403, there was nobody left there.[18]

## 'Proceeding Eastwards': Minorca and Sardinia

Majorca and Ibiza were the first in a series of islands, of the western and central Mediterranean, conquered by the House of

Barcelona at long intervals over a period of about a hundred years. The next burst of activity came in the 1280s and 1290s, some two generations after the first conquests, when Minorca and Sicily, with Malta and Gozo, were conquered, and a title to Sardinia and Corsica acquired. At about the same time, Majorca's client status was asserted from the mainland by force of arms. No serious military effort was ever mounted against Corsica; Malta and Gozo were not long retained; but in the 1320s an aggressive imperial policy reduced Sardinia to precarious obedience. Meanwhile, vassals of members of the House of Barcelona made conquests even further east, in Jarbāh (Djerba, Gerba) and Qarqannāh (Kerkennah) and Greece (see pp.131–32). The impression of a growing island empire, reaching out towards the east – perhaps to the Holy Land, perhaps the spice trade, perhaps both – was reinforced by Aragonese propaganda. King Jaime II, writing to the pope in 1311, justified the growth of Aragonese *Hausmacht* in terms calculated to appeal to the crusading fervour of the Council of Vienna. Aragonese conquests, he claimed, were made so that

> the Christian army, in proceeding towards the east by way of the sea, might always have islands of Christians to cling to: that is, Majorca, Sardinia and Sicily, from where they might always be able to draw victuals and refreshments and men to re-inforce the said army and settle new homelands and by acquiring a base might be able, with God's help, to reach the Holy Land.[19]

Perhaps this was not altogether disingenuous: the House of Barcelona did toy from time to time with grand crusading schemes, and Catalan trade reached Alexandria and Constantinople. But as a guide to the nature and motives of Arago-Catalan expansion, the king's words are unreliable. The easterly vassal-states were only, at best, nominally 'Catalan' in character and tenuously linked juridically with the other dominions of the House of Barcelona. The Grecian dominions, for instance, were conquered by a macedoine of mercenaries of various provenances, whose lingua franca was Catalan, who called themselves the 'university' or company of Catalans, and who included a strong, genuinely Catalan contingent. But other nationalities predominated and the company's allegiance to the House of Barcelona was weak. Their acknowledgement, for most of the period of their survival, of the suzerainty of the heirs of the Sicilian throne, was calculated to maximise their effective independence. After 1380, the territorial principalities they founded, the duchies of Athens and Neopatria, depended directly on the overlordship of the king of mainland Aragon: but that was a desperate throw, at a time of irresistible Turkish strength. Kings of Spain preserved the picturesque titles of 'Dukes of Athens and Neopatria'; memories of the company's exploits were preserved by the popularity of the chronicle of Ramon Muntaner, who devoted an enormous amount of space to an episode in which he had been a participant and which he believed illustrated Catalan prowess. Subsequent generations of Catalan nationalist historians were happy to follow Muntaner's lead. In the light of current knowledge, however, it seems best to leave the achievements of the Catalan Company out of any account of the Mediterranean career of the Aragonese royal house.

The same applies, in lesser degree, to the principality of Jarbāh and Qarqannāh – which was conquered by the private enterprise of a *condottiere* and ruled as a fief variously of Sicily or the pope (see p.131) – and even to the kingdom of Sicily itself. Except for its kings and a few élite families, introduced into fiefs carved from the royal demesne or wrested from earlier generations of foreigners, Sicily remained an island *sui generis*, untouched by personnel or institutions from Spain. Even the intruded Aragonese aristocrats rapidly became 'Sicilianised' and intermarried with native families. Catalan merchants were favoured in Sicily from the moment of the conquest, but their permanent settlements were concentrated in Syracuse, Agosta and Catania; they, too, married locally, as is known from Martin I's and Ferdinand I's regulations for their communities. If there was such a thing as an 'empire' of the House of Barcelona, it remaind confined to the western Mediterranean and can be explained, as we shall see, by Mediterranean motives.[20]

The most trenchant Aragonese imperialism was practised in Minorca and Sardinia, and in both islands, in different ways, the policy failed. At the time of the conquests of Majorca and Sardinia, Minorca was left undisturbed, save for nominal client-status and token tribute, as a Moorish vassal-state: this was a common solution within the Iberian peninsula for Moorish states which could not be practically or profitably absorbed by Christian kingdoms. In the 1280s, however, Minorca assumed a new importance on the way to Sardinia and Sicily. It was an island of invitation to potential commercial rivals, Pisan and Genoese, as well as an embarrassment to the Aragonese kings' crusading propaganda. It offered, moreover, an opportunity for the young king, Alfonso III, to demonstrate his mettle. Its conquest in 1287 was the most brutal in the history of the Aragonese monarchy. Departing from the practice evolved in Majorca and Valencia, Alfonso aimed at a radical extirpation of the native population and its replacement by settlers from the mainland. He was barely able at the time to restrain noble factionalism at home from breaking out in civil war, and he may have hoped to buy support from magnates and churchmen by a lavish display of patronage at Muslim expense. Over 100 'Saracens' of Minorca were allowed to remain 'pro causa populandi' and perhaps there were others of whom the record has not survived. But the great bulk of the population was rounded up and sold into slavery, temporarily glutting the markets of Ibiza, Valencia and Barcelona. Minorca was not an attractive island to settlers: without the mineral resources of Ibiza, it was too small to support any life that was not laborious, precarious and poor; the dispersal of the native labour force and the break in the continuity of agricultural exploitation made the prospects even bleaker. The demographic holocaust could not be made good. A century after the conquest, the wreckage remained. In 1370, houses abandoned by the Moors and never reoccupied were in a state of collapse. Shortage of the means of life was chronic: every cornbearing ship that stopped at Minorca was obliged to offer its cargo for sale. Nor were the means of civilisation in greater abundance. In 1358, a lieutenant-governor of the island was killed by a blow on the head from a candlestick in a brawl at the high altar of the island's main church. Such was the tenor of life in this showpiece-conquest of Aragonese imperialism.[21]

Alfonso 'the Benign' repeated his namesake's mistakes in Sardinia in the 1320s. Aragonese kings long coveted Sardinia and, to understand why, it is not necessary to invoke their supposed concern with crusaders' lines of communication to the east. A constant anxiety of members of the House of Barcelona was their own conviction of the paucity of their patrimony. Pedro III complained that neither he nor any of his ancestors possessed treasure. Catalan poverty and avarice were mocked by Dante and were proverbially notorious.[22] From the political consequences of poverty – the overweening truculence of noble leagues or 'unions' in Aragon and Catalonia, the threat indeed of oligarchy – kings sought to escape, whenever their strength permitted, either by conquering lands with which to boost their resources of patronage or by stimulating commerce in order to generate alternative sources of wealth. All their conquests must be understood against this background, and none more so than Sardinia, which was an exceptionally large island – the world's largest, according to the mistaken authority of Herodotus – and which was endowed with peculiar commercial attractions. Not only did it produce in commercial quantities two vital products – silver and salt, about which Aragonese official sources are strangely silent in the period leading up to the conquest – but it lay athwart important trade routes and was fringed with communities of Genoese and Pisan merchants, staging-posts on the way to the Maghrib. Pope Clement VI thought Genoese commerce could not survive without access to Sardinia.[23] Increasingly in the second half of the thirteenth century, the Aragonese crown was becoming involved in commerce. With members of his merchant-entourage, for instance, Pedro III seems to have sought a large interest – perhaps control – in the western Mediterranean grain trade; his conquest of Sicily in 1282 was, in part, an attempt to reinforce Barcelona's pretensions to being a sort of 'staple' for grain – that is, a monopolistic centre of distribution – by seizing the main granary and centre of production; the great grain merchants, intimates of the king, like Guillem de Perelada and the House of Fiveller, helped to finance the expedition.[24] After the subjugation of the emporium of Majorca, and the granary of Sicily, the acquisition of the staging-posts of Sardinia could almost be seen as a logical next step in the evolving proto-mercantilism of the Crown of Aragon. The western Mediterranean might even have become – had the policy succeeded – a Catalan gulf in the same way as the Adriatic had become 'the gulf of the Venetians'. Basic commodities of the western Mediterranean might have become subject to Catalan domination, if not control, as those of the eastern Mediterranean almost passed under the control of Venice. At the very least, it would be appropriate to see the military and naval strength of the kings of Aragon reinforcing the claims of 'excluded' merchant-communities of the Tyrrhenian Sea, and especially that of Barcelona, to break into an area of established

Genoese and Pisan preponderance: hence, the main contributions to the conquering host came from trading cities – Barcelona, Valencia, Tortosa, Tarragona.

Alfonso IV's vision of Sardinia, however, encompassed more than merely commercial exploitation. The displacement of Pisa's entrenched merchant-quarters and the substitution of Catalans around the coast might have been practicable within the limited resources of Alfonso's monarchy. To challenge the Genoese as well, and thereby drive them into alliance with Pisa, was foolhardy. To attempt a wholesale takeover of Sardinia's wild and intractable hinterland and turn it, like Majorca, into an overseas extension of Catalonia was a wild fantasy, induced by the land-hunger of a traditionally impoverished dynasty. Beyond the luxurious, bourgeois toeholds of the foreign merchants, Sardinia was a savage land. There were only two sources of authority in the interior: the predatory sway of a few great families, of foreign (generally Genoese) origins or affiliations, who exploited large tracts of land and exacted tribute or imposed jurisdiction in villages on or around their domains; and the intense, local loyalties of a society that was still tribal in its configurations. Indeed, the Aragonese regarded the Sards as semi-bestial barbarians, whom they had no compunction in enslaving and whose Christianity they declined to acknowledge. The only formal institutions which spanned the whole island were the four 'Judiciates', divided between the Pisans and the island notables. It was the prospect of expelling the Pisans and monopolising power that made the island élite, and especially the most powerful of them, the House of the Judges or Arborea, at first cooperate with Aragon. But the realisation that they had exchanged a present nuisance for a putative master, soon induced a series of rebellions, not quelled for 100 years, which bled Aragonese energies. Sardinia was the 'Spanish ulcer' of the House of Barcelona or, even more appositely, Aragon's Ireland.

The militant hand of Aragonese imperialism was revealed early. Sassari (Sásser), for instance, was one of Alfonso IV's first attempts at creating a comprehensively Aragonese colony. The native Sards were peremptorily and informally dispossessed by Catalan conquerors in 1329. The king immediately set about the rationalisation and formalisation of this takeover by means of a 'compartment', essentially resembling the 'repartiments' of the lands of Majorca or Valencia. Between 1330 and 1333, 166 fees, comprising proprietorship of land, rights of jurisdiction and the obligation of knight-service, were distributed, at least on paper, with 1393 smaller plots of which only the use-right was granted away. Of the beneficiaries whose provenance is recorded, almost half were Catalans, nearly a third Valencians, over ten per cent Roussillonais and nearly five per cent Majorcans. Though the terms of the distribution, with the accent on knights' fees, were feudal, the breakdown of the settlers by designation reflects the commercial priorities of the conquest. Of those specified, 163 were merchants and their grants on average were worth double the mean. A large number of valuable grants made in 1330 went to members of a consortium who proposed to establish a silver foundry. The only other substantial categories were artisans (155), peasants (34), members of the liberal professions (30) and public officials, chiefly notaries (29).[25]

The policy of 'Catalanisation' was pursued and extended with extraordinary tenacity. To some extent, like the Norman conquest of England, it was conceived as a sort of tenurial revolution, to be achieved by introducing the language of feudalism into a society that in the past had barely known it. Fees were granted *iuxta morem Italiae*: the recipient had to reside in his fief (so that the beneficiaries were aristocratic cadets rather than great mainland lords), render a portion of its produce to the king in war, maintain fortifications and provide knight-service. Fiefs were heritable in the male line but not alienable without royal leave; the lord's rights of jurisdiction were generally limited to civil cases. To kings of Aragon, accustomed to remote overlordship of great fiefs that were virtual territorial principalities, in which royal rights were ill defined and reluctantly admitted, this system must have represented – had it worked in practice – a vast accession of power. By 1335, 38 great fiefs had been created for Iberian nobles, and the native chiefs and *judices* had been turned into feudatories. But the latter were not easy to buy off. The Doria, in the north, were in almost continuous rebellion. The Arborea, driven by the insistent imperialism of Alfonso's successor, the splenetic and combative Pedro IV, rebelled in the early 1350s and never returned to wholehearted allegiance. At Pedro's court, elaborate plans were drawn up for the dispossession of the native aristocracy and the wholesale deportation of the commonalty as slaves. Sardinia would become a feudal Utopia, paying for itself. The holding of the first intended victim, the Donoratico family, would yield enough revenue for 50 knights; two years later, the Pisans could be eliminated, then the Doria and the Arborea.[26] These plans were never implemented but Sards were shipped off, enslaved, in thousands, especially between about 1370 and the end of the last revolt in 1442. Abused for the replenishment of depopulated Minorca, they made that island ungovernable. Most had to be repatriated as the price of peace.[27] The only lasting colonial achievement to emerge from this febrile royal programme was the settlement by Pedro IV of the port of Alghero – Alguer in Catalan – which remained defiantly Catalan-speaking until the present day. Even this success was procured with difficulty; many beneficiaries renounced their grants rather than take them up; absentees had to be punished; widows and bachelors were compelled to marry.[28] For a while, in the late middle ages, Alghero, Sassari and Cagliari (the last gradually and bitterly extracted from Pisan grasp) were a sort of Catalan pale, beleaguered enclaves surrounded by a frequently hostile and largely indomitable world.

Experts are divided over whether the Aragonese kings wished to exclude foreign merchants from Sardinia altogether; on balance, it seems more likely that they would have been satisfied with restricting or eliminating rival merchant-quarters and encumbering foreign trade with prejudicial tariffs. But they never got the chance. Every rebellion forced concessions to Pisa or Genoa. The Aragonese paid heavily for what was in effect a commercial and political condominium.[29]

Much of the crippling cost seems to have been borne by merchants of Barcelona, who, for the sake of commercial footholds on the coast, were prepared to finance a continuing war for an inland empire in which they had little interest. Their enthusiasm, unrestrained at first, lasted at least until the mid-century. After another half-century of war, the disillusionment of Barcelona was complete and in the *Corts* of 1408–9 the merchants called for withdrawal from the Sardinian imbroglio.[30] The modified victory – at least, the lasting peace – won in the next generation came too late. The Sardinian adventure contributed to the exhaustion of Catalonia-Aragon's powers of expansion and to the diminished commercial prominence of Barcelona in the fifteenth century. In 1972, amid much rhetorical Catalan nostalgia, Alghero was officially twinned with Tarragona; the return ceremony on the Spanish mainland had to wait until after the death of General Franco, so that the Catalan language could be freely used and Catalan nationalism freely indulged. It was the last feeble echo of a great imperial effort of the middle ages.

## Aragon's Dynastic 'Empire'

Whether one cares to call it an empire or not, the loose dynastic agglomeration that constituted the Arago-Catalan world of the thirteenth and fourteenth centuries was meant to function cohesively, as a kind of fraternal alliance, a tenuous confederacy bound more by atavistic appeals to loyalty and the force of oaths than by common institutions. That the system failed makes it no less of a system. The civil wars of Caesars and Augusti make the Roman Empire no less of an empire. It is a fallacy of modern historians to confuse centralisation with strength, institutional complexity with common purpose and 'despotism' with statehood. No state, until quite recent times, could command obedience, especially in outlying lands, by force, without consent. Institutional minimalism, like that of the Crown of Aragon, could be as effective as more purposeful or more creative statecraft.

The nature of the ties that bound the Aragonese dominions were defined in a letter patent of Alfonso III to the men of Majorca, written in 1285 to justify war against the king of Majorca. The two crowns, he claimed, were obliged to help each other against any and every foe 'with their castles, lands and men'. The subjects and vassals of each were always to aid the others. The disloyalty of Majorca's ruler was 'an abominable thing . . . an atrocity against God, men, oaths and natural duty'. Alfonso adjured the Majorcans to uphold 'that loyalty in which you were brought up, from your mothers' breasts'. On the whole, they responded to his call. Like the Roman Empire, whatever its institutional deficiencies and practical shortcomings, the kinship of the dominions of the House of Barcelona was something in which its subjects seem to have believed: at least, its Aragonese and Catalan subjects, and none more so than Ramon Muntaner, whose entire chronicle was inspired by his king's vision of an end to fraternal dissension and something approaching a coalescence, if not a unification, of the Arago-Catalan world:

And so, lords of Aragon and Majorca and Sicily, who are descended from that saintly lord, King Jaime, be of good heart, be of one mind and will; and do not let evil tongues sunder you for any reason, for to part company would be against what God has sealed; and hold yourselves well recompensed with that which God has given and will give you.[31]

Early European Atlantic expansion, when it began in the fifteenth century, 'hopped', like that of the House of Barcelona, between island stepping stones; as we shall see, Majorcans and Catalans were in the vanguard of early Atlantic exploration. On the other hand, the subjects of the Crown of Aragon were not the only people to form a network of maritime outposts in the western Mediterranean in the late middle ages; and within the Iberian peninsula itself, two distinctive types of 'land empire' took shape, which also deserve to be considered as scources of influence on later Atlantic expansion. The problem of how much Arago-Catalan island empire-building contributed must be postponed until the other possible influences and the other spheres of Aragonese 'imperial' activity have been examined.

# 2. The First 'Atlantic' Empire: Andalusia and its Environs

An Atlantic empire of sorts existed already in the thirteenth century. Of the parts of the Iberian peninsula which were conquered from the Moors in one of the most active and sustained periods of the so-called 'Reconquest', between the 1220s and the 1260s, the kingdoms of Valencia and Murcia constituted a substantial 'Mediterranean front', subjugated largely by Aragonese and Catalan forces. The conquests of Castile and Portugal, however, in the south-west of the peninsula, in lower and upper Andalusia, Extremadura, the Alentejo and the Algarve, belong to a different, Atlantic world. Their coasts were washed by the Atlantic; into the Atlantic their rivers drained. They were or became, for the most part, colonial *tierras vagas*: lands empty or emptied of indigenous population or, at least, where the natives were depleted or displaced. They were the seedplot of a colonial people and, in some respects, a nursery of colonial experience. They resembled the future terrains of Atlantic colonisation, but were radically unlike those of most of the Mediterranean, where native labour forces and indigenous economic systems were essential to colonial life. The difference would be appreciated by any film-goer or aficionado of historical romance: the Mediterranean conquests were a sort of Raj, the Atlantic a sort of wild west. The political boundaries, unfortunately, failed to mark these typological distinctions because Murcia, though conquered and colonised chiefly by subjects of the Crown of Aragon fell, by enforcement of ancient treaties, to the lot of Castile. Towards the end of the fifteenth century, Castile acquired another, similar province – Mediterranean-facing and peopled with Moors – in Granada, also conquered with foreign help. Until then, Granada survived, independent, between two distinctive types of medieval land empire. We shall consider them in order of creation, looking first at the Atlantic type, in this chapter, and returning to the Mediterranean in the next.

43

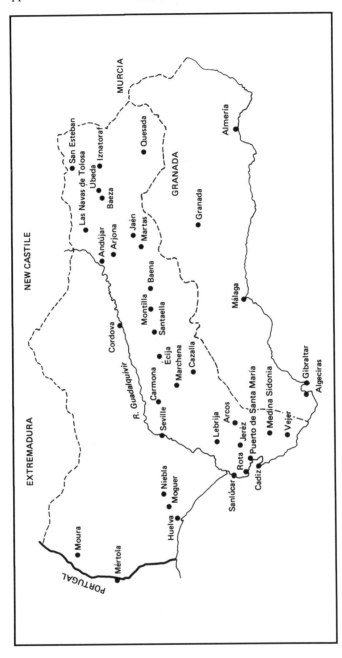

Map 3
ANDALUSIA
places named in the text

## The Conquest of Upper Andalusia

The search for medieval precedents for modern European expansion leads naturally back, through the history of the conquistadores and navigators, to the Portuguese and Castilian Atlantic imperial experience of the thirteenth century. Yet the relevance of this background to the story which follows has rarely, if ever, been properly understood. Traditional Iberian historiography has represented the Reconquest as a continuous process, begun almost at the moment of the Moorish invasion of 711 and sustained, with checks and interruptions, of course, but without essential mutation or substitution of 'spirit', until the fall of Granada in 1492. Spain and Portugal are represented as nations forged in the white heat of a long crusade. In fact, the creation of these states was a fitful process which rarely and briefly depended for its progress on awareness of confessional distinctions. It would be no more convincing to portray Spain as the product of conflict between Christians and Moors than, for instance, to see Britain as the result of the struggle between Saxons and Celts, or Germany of that between Teutons and Slavs. In this respect, the processes which brought Castile or Portugal into being are no different from those which produced other major European states, all of which have had their frontiers drawn and redrawn many times and all of which are in some sense the results of phenomena of expansion.

What is distinctive about the Iberian states is not their supposed conflictive or confessional origins, but their colonial ones. The making of Castile and Portugal was less in the reconquest of lands peopled by Moors than in the repeopling of lands which the Moors devastated or deserted: a repeopling with scarce resources, which demanded the attraction of foreign capital and personnel and which required lavish inducements to immigrants and settlers. Of other European peoples, only the Germans had a similar medieval experience, for like the Castilians they thrust great peasant settlements deep into the Ostmark, while, like the Catalans, scattering merchant-quarters way beyond their frontiers. The German expansion, however, was launched from a large and populous heartland, such as the Spanish kingdoms never possessed.

It is therefore not surprising that the conquests and colonisations were fitful. They were the work of widely interspersed bouts of phrenesis in the tenth, eleventh, thirteenth and fifteenth centuries.

The thirteenth-century conquests were decisive in the making of 'Spain', because the Andalusian provinces, the conventional Spain of foreigners' perceptions, where Carmen would sing and Figaro snip, were then added to the dominions of the crown of Castile.

Before we consider how, and by whom, the conquest was launched, a conspectus of the character of the kingdom of Castile at the start of the enterprise can be gained from a look at its three greatest surviving monuments, the cathedrals of Burgos, León and Toledo; together with the wars against the Moors, they were the products of the big collective efforts, the major 'public spending projects' of the period. That of Burgos recalls the wealth of a great landlocked 'port', linked to the sea by daily mule trains in the season, swelling beyond its walls and soaring within them, building extramural parish churches and thrusting a fashionable cathedral heavenwards, all on the profits of the export of wool. That of León bears witness to another sort of civic and diocesan pride. Where Burgos was booming, León was declining, and its pride was in its past; a former 'capital' and royal pantheon, it was degraded to a provincial town when it lost its status as an independent courtly centre. In 1230, the last phase of León's technical independence was ended by the definitive union of the Castilian and Leonese crowns. These circumstances, in the cases of Burgos and León, account both for why new cathedrals should have been erected in the thirteenth century and why, for motives of prestige, they should have copied the latest fashion, prescribed by French models.

The cathedral of Toledo, by contrast, owes its genesis, and, perhaps, the distinctive features of its style, directly to the progress of the 'Reconquest'. For, in the first place, unlike its sisters of Burgos and León, it was not a 'replacement' cathedral, but newly created on the site of the great mosque. Extraordinary as it seems, although Toledo was the primatial see and the second richest in Christendom – the ancient seat of councils and the pride of Spanish Christians since its reconquest in 1085 – still, despite the ample time which had been available to embark on such a natural labour of piety and prestige, it possessed no purpose-built cathedral. Twelfth-century struggles to establish and maintain their pre-eminence had inspired the primates to do no more than think about the erection of a suitably dignified church; and the ostentatious corporation to which they belonged continued its curiously crabbed and eremitical habitation of the old mosque's abandoned shell. For, to a surprising degree, during a century and a half after it was repossessed, Toledo remained the metropolis – or, rather, the garrison – of a frontier zone. From here, during St Ferdinand's campaigns in the south, his queens and princesses rode to meet him or encounter his news. Until Andalusia was conquered. Extremadura and La Mancha were no man's lands, heavily fortified but sparsely settled. The adaptation of Toledo's mosque to be a cathedral was a consciously temporary arrangement, but, like all such arrangements, it lasted in unsettled conditions for a surprisingly long time.

The building of the new cathedral and the southward thrust of the frontier happened at about the same time, under the influence of a single genius. The design of Toledo's cathedral was the product of its patron's imagination, as much as that of the St Denis of Abbot Suger. Like Burgos and León, it was indebted to France and reflected the period of study which Archbishop Rodrigo Ximénez de Rada (died 1247) spent in Paris. At the same time, the odd upper levels of its choir and its curious, spiky profile proclaim an aggressively distinctive character. An elaborate fancy would see it as the embodiment of the 'Reconquest' idea, which Rodrigo professed and even championed. Certainly, without the context of renewed and successful war against the Moors, Toledo cathedral would have been impossible.

Don Rodrigo, who became archbishop in 1208, was a model alike of episcopal vice and virtues. He was a state-churchman whose pastoral vocation was felt and exercised mainly in defence of the privileges of his see; a 'civil servant' with an almost erastian understanding of kingly rights and duties; a great patron of architecture and a great architect of policy. He was also a prolific historian, whose writings helped to determine the historical self-perception of Castilian kings.[1] In partial consequence, the acquisition of an Andalusian land empire was actually seen in Castile as an 'imperial' venture. The concept of 'empire' seems to have been variously, perhaps confusedly, understood in medieval Spain, but it always carried connotations of rule over a variety of lands, communities or crowns. A so-called emperor might be a 'king of kings' (lord, that is, of other vassal-kings), or 'king of two religions' (ruler of Christian and Muslim communities) or an aspirant to rule over the entire peninsula. Don Rodrigo developed or revived the myth of an imperial legacy of the Castilian crown, which he traced back to the Visigothic successors of the Romans.

The imperial title affected by earlier Spanish monarchs was renewed within two generations and, soon after Rodrigo's death, Alfonso X made a bid for the most numinous phantom of a genuinely imperial past, the *sacrum imperium* itself, the name of Holy Roman Emperor. When in his writings Rodrigo conferred the purple on Castile, he had an eye on the pallium of his own see. Toledo, the metropolis of Roman and (for much of the time) of Visigothic Hispania, had a special claim on the supposed heritage. It may not be too fanciful to see the last tatters of Rodrigo's standard in the street bunting and car stickers which today proclaim Toledo 'ciudad imperial'. In his own day, the imperial theme was widely echoed and the mood of exaltation, the thrill of expansion, widely shared. For Vincentius Hispanus, for instance, combative canonist of the Portuguese royal service, Spain was a 'Blessed Lady *(domina)*', whose dominion Spaniards were creating or extending and whose 'empire' had been won by merit.[2]

In part, Rodrigo's commitment to the idea of a 'Reconquest' grew out of experience, in part it was precipitated by events. He was entrusted by Alfonso VIII of Castile with the organisation of a coalition of Hispanic kingdoms against the Almohads (see p.124 below) and took an active part in the subsequent campaign of Las Navas de Tolosa in 1212. Conventionally, this is regarded as a 'turning-point' of Spanish history; certainly, Almohad power never recovered. He engaged in unsuccessful warfare on his own account in Moorish Extremadura. And in 1217, he performed, for Castile, a vital task by deflecting some of the crusading zeal of the Lateran Council from the Holy Land to the war against the Moors. When, in the middle of the next decade, circumstances were propitious, he influenced the inception and assisted the progress of the royal campaign of conquest in Andalusia.

For, despite tension and discord in other fields, Rodrigo's partner and protégé in this enterprise was the young king, Ferdinand III, whom later generations would worship and formally canonise in imitation of St Louis. In fact, the king's piety was unremarkable, but he was a conventional monarch who accepted the ideal of kingship as service and the object of his obligations as God. The service of God and the enlargement of his kingdoms were the aims to which he most frequently alluded, and he missed no chance to seem to combine them – while, in practice, readily allying with infidels when it suited him, – waging war on the Moors and stressing the identity of his political and confessional foes. Even before his death – and it was not for another generation, after the life and death of St Louis, that sensitive noses began to detect the odour of sanctity in the vicinity of his tomb – Castilian propagandists cast him in the role of *miles Christi*, knight of Christ.

He came to the throne in 1217, at the age of sixteen, the beneficiary of a coup engineered by his doughty mother at a time when indefeasible hereditary right had not yet been established as the rule of succession. It was 'a time of silence' – that is, of truce with the Moors, a normal time by medieval Spanish standards. Ferdinand's path to the cross is unclear, but his position was precarious and his personality was impressionable: the imperial course advocated by Archbishop Rodrigo would quell aristocratic unrest by employing the warrior class beyond the frontier and increasing the crown's resources of patronage; Don Rodrigo's Lateran diplomacy gave the king the tools with which to finish the job. Ferdinand, however, did not even make a start until 1224, when the apparent disintegration of the Almohad state seemed to render the prospects sure.[3]

His opportunism was almost his undoing. Strategically, it would have made the best sense to roll up Andalusia's oriental carpet from its corners: Extremadura in the west, where Don Rodrigo had focused his campaigns, and Jaén, the 'high ground' which blocked Castilian expansion to the east. These two provinces were the east and west gates, so to speak, of the heartland and treasury of Andalusia, the Guadalquivir valley. But Ferdinand found progress on these fronts uneven and slow. He twice laid seige to Jaén, in 1225 and 1230, with no lasting result. His invasion of the lands beyond, with a brief investiture of Granada, was a frustrated parade, more a grandiose raid than an attempted conquest; with unsecured communications, Ferdinand was bound to withdraw before long. The need to seize the Leonese succession, which fell to him in 1230, interrupted his southern campaigns, but in 1232 he returned to the Extremaduran front, where most of the gains of 1232–35 were registered by expeditions of the knightly orders.

Christendom was spreading slowly south, as if by a process of titration rather than flood. In 1235, however, a chance arose, albeit at considerable risk, for King Ferdinand to ease the flow. Cordova, in the heart of the Guadalquivir valley, was probably not envisaged as an immediate objective; it commanded the main axis of communications between Upper and Lower Andalusia; it possessed the faded prestige of a former metropolis and it was a useful base from which an invader could practise 'the strategy of the central position'. But it was too exposed to counterattack from Moorish strongholds on its flanks to constitute a prime target. In attempting its capture, Ferdinand was launching a sort of battle of the bulge.

It was the complacency of his enemies that allowed him to seize it and their dissensions which permitted him to hold it. The decline – now accelerating to collapse – of the central power of the Almohad dynasty left Andalusia riven by faction. Kinglets ruled or would rule defiant in Niebla, Jaén and Arjona. From Almería, Ibn Hūd plotted an indigenous Andalusian revanche which was aimed at expelling the Almohads while preserving unity. The restlessness of Seville broke out in successive, open, self-seeking revolts against each possible contender for Andalusian allegiance: the Almohad dynasty, its local rivals and the safely distant emir of Tunis. In retrospect, it seemed to the great Muslim historian, Ibn Khaldūn (1332–1406), that 'every qa'id and man of influence who could command a score of followers or possessed a castle to retire to in case of need, styled himself sultan and assumed the insignia of royalty'.[4]

This emulous environment, which characterised the whole of the Andalusian and Maghribi worlds, was mirrored in miniature in most Andalusian strongholds and cities. Mutual rivalries were intense, the prevailing sense of insecurity strong: so much so, that one Cordovan faction denied the fortified suburb of Ajarquía to its Muslim foes by confiding it to a party of mercenary Christian knights. Ferdinand recognised these symptoms of internecine conflict at once, it seems, and rushed to the scene with a following of only a hundred knights. He exaggerated his opportunity and underestimated his risks. It took him five months to reduce the city to his control, and then at the cost of the evacuation of its inhabitants. The king was saved again by Muslim disunity: because Ibn Hūd took it upon himself to try to redeem Cordova to the potential credit of his own programme of self-exaltation, Ferdinand was able to invoke the alliance of the ruler of Jaén, first to prevent the city's recapture and then to perpetuate its occupation.[5]

In the nearly four years which Ferdinand now spent away from the front, there was no serious attempted counterattack, while disarray increased and deficiencies multiplied among his enemies.

The fact that Ferdinand was opposed by no comprehensive Muslim coalition seems to show that the conquest was not the fruit of a religious conflict. Precisely because coexistence was the norm, because shifts of alliance were habitual, because two great confessional communities had lived side by side for so long with litle mutual hostility and – for much of the time and in many cases – with little awareness of their mutual exclusiveness, the idea of an unremitting war along religious lines rarely occurred and almost never commended itself either to Christians or Moors. Muslim poets lamented the loss of each 'city of my heart', each 'garden of Islam', but with little apparent sense that life would not continue, in a larger sphere, along the same lines as before. Moorish rulers had no 'domino theory' at their disposal to explain their plight: the dethronement of a coreligionist might imply as much for their future security as their future peril. Ferdinand would probably not have retained Cordova without Moorish acquiescence nor would he have been able to seize Seville without Moorish help. It is doubtful whether even Ferdinand himself shared historians' common notion of the Reconquest. The political testament he left for his heir shows that he saw his work in the peninsula as accomplished, despite the great tracts still ruled and inhabited by Moors. He had, he said, reduced to submission or tribute 'all the land this side of the sea, which the Moors took from King Roderic'. That was enough for him. If his son retained the same degree of supremacy, he would be as good a king as he; if he extended the system – by which the father meant, to Africa – he would be a better one.[6]

## The Conquest of Seville

When at last he returned to Andalusia, it was to prosecute the conquest on two fronts from his base at Cordova. The amity of Jaén had outlived its usefulness. The third and final siege was prepared by the reduction over two years of its outlying strongholds and maintained, to final victory, for nearly nine months. Meanwhile, Ferdinand's son, Alfonso, won his spurs in Murcia, where it was vital to stake out the territory claimed for Castile in the face of Aragonese advances from the north-east. The cooperativeness of the Aragonese, in the event, was almost equalled by that of the Moors themselves, who in Murcia were generally prompt with at least token submissions. Only Cartagena, Lorca and Mula required the force of arms at this stage. But, as Alfonso later found out, a people readily yielding to his suzerainty proved dangerously intractable to his control. By the middle of 1245, there was nowhere in Castile's sphere of influence that was not Ferdinand's client or conquest, except in Lower Andalusia. In that region, however, lay the greatest prize of all: Seville, the biggest and richest city of Atlantic Spain. The physical extent of the city was enormous for its day: 187 hectares were enclosed within its curtilage, without counting the extension of the built-up area to the south of the river. This suggests a population which must have approached, and perhaps exceeded, 70 000,[7] a figure so large by the standards of the time – twice the size of Barcelona – as to beggar belief. Seville was also a prize of great psychological importance. If Cordova was enhanced by the memory of its days as the home of the caliphs' court, Seville was actively regarded as the actual metropolis of Andalusia. As an independent kingdom, it had housed the dynasty of the Banū-'Abbād, who had ruled most of Andalusia in their day; and it had been the normal courtly and administrative centre ever since.

Seville, like Cordova, fell victim to the jealousies of internal factions; like Cordova it was a sudden and opportunistic conquest for Ferdinand: if the desirability of taking it, as a prize or a client, was felt continuously, the actual occasion was unforeseen. In the twenty years after 1228, the Sevillans changed their nominal lords many times, but their self-interest never wavered. All their revolutions were conservative. The object always was to maintain the autonomy of the city government, sometimes despotic, sometimes patrician, and of the power it exercised in the region of the lower Guadalquivir. At the eclipse of the Almohads, Seville wavered between Ibn Hūd and Tunis; after Ibn Hūd's death, between Tunis and the Almohads. These mutations of allegiance were, of course, the results of both calculation and conflict: calculation of where Seville's best hope of protection and patronage lay, conflict between factions within the city. By 1245, only two options remained untried: internal sovereignty and the overlordship of Ferdinand of Castile. Two revolutions of 1245 and 1246 may have represented attempts to try these options. The first putsch was by an ambitious administrator, the second by discontented generals. The administrator was Ibn al-Jādd, who deposed his superior and sent him in chains to Tunis. Without repudiating his Tunisian master, he moved Seville towards Ferdinand's camp and may have aimed at overt clientage. But his schemes were given no time to unfold, for in the following year he was assassinated and replaced by a junta of frontier generals, for whom a rapprochement with Castile and a policy of peace were an unprofessional and unpalatable prospect.

Ferdinand was caught by surprise. He had no fleet capable of closing the siege of Seville. That he had not planned such a campaign in advance is shown by the fact that he only extemporised the means it demanded in the first months of 1247. His instrument was a burgher of Burgos, Ramón Bonifaz, made equally for conquest and colonisation. Bonifaz was himself a colonist or son of colonists, one of the *francos* with whom the population of medieval Castile was swollen by the design of the kings; a merchant-oligarch, who, despite his residence in an inland mercantile centre, could evidently command ships in large numbers; a pugnacious and talented seafarer, to whom Ferdinand owed the success of his Sevillan campaign. The merchants of Burgos shipped their wool, transferred by mule train, from the Cantabrian ports, and it was presumably from this stock of shipping that Bonifaz supplied, under his own command, a squadron of thirteen vessels in response to the king's command 'to prepare the biggest and best fleet possible and hasten with it to Seville'. This alliance of king and merchant, capitalism and chivalry recalls the conquest of Majorca and suggests that Andalusia, or, at least, Seville, was an object of mercantile cupidity as well as of royal zeal. Bonifaz's contribution was decisive in two respects: it broke the boom by which the Sevillans maintained contact with their codefenders on the southern bank of the river; and it deflected the seaborne blow struck by the Almohads in an attempt to raise the siege. Yet even with amphibious forces at his command, Ferdinand could never take Seville by storm. Only the defeat of their relief and the failure of their supply convinced the inhabitants, by the summer of 1248, of the necessity of submission. Even thereafter, the siege was prolonged by the defenders' quest for favourable terms and Ferdinand's customary reluctance to make concessions to a stubborn foe.

These irreconcilable postures could be met only by the evacuation of the city, which was agreed on 23 November 1248, and largely completed by the time of Ferdinand's ceremonial entry a month later. Victor and vanquished alike recognised the fall of Seville as the culmination of Ferdinand's conquests and the virtual consummation of the history of al-Andalūs. The best of the Arabic threnodies, by Abū'l-Baqā' al-Rūndi, although well known, is worth quoting extensively, because its conventional imagery suggests a mood of resignation rather than despair:

> This is a disaster to leave men inconsolable.
> Uḥud has collapsed because of it and Thahlān has tumbled.
> The evil eye has gazed on Islam, which has sunk down, leaving whole countries void.
> Ask Valencia what has become of Murcia, and where is Játiva and where Jaén?
> Where is Cordova, the dwelling of all learning, and all the sages whom she made so great?
> Where is Seville, elegant as she was, with that delicious river, brimming like mother's milk?
> These great cities were the pillars of the land. It cannot stand without them.

After bemoaning the displacement of believers by infidels, the poet continues:

> Oh, you who live at ease, indifferent to the call of Destiny, though you were asleep, Fate will awaken you.
> What can you do with the leisure of your homeland? Can any man lie idling in his land when Seville is lost?
> This stroke of fate has blotted every previous disaster from memory. And it will never be forgotten, as long as time endures.[8]

From one point of view, the poet's prediction was too gloomy: Moorish rule survived in a large fragment of al-Andalūs for two and a half centuries; in the Mediterranean provinces, sizable Moorish populations and tenacious ways of life survived thereafter for over a century more. The 'pillars' of Islam were not as fragile as they seemed. They sustained a tent, which, at a pinch, could always be folded and stolen away. It was true, however, that Andalusia was totally and definitively transformed. The hegemony of Castile, the confinement of Islam were fixed as never before. Ferdinand died dreaming of extending his conquests to Africa, in 1252, leaving only comparatively minor adjustments of the frontier to be accomplished by his son. Relative security for the colonisation of Seville was obtained by the liquidation of the enclave of Niebla, the reduction of the stronghold of Jeréz de la Frontera and the devastation of the frontier-in-depth between Jeréz and Gibraltar. Murcia, formerly cajoled but not yet cowed, had to be conquered in earnest with forces loaned by King Jaime of Aragon, who wished to set an example to his own Moorish subjects in neighbouring Valencia. All these achievements, as well as Alfonso's barren tinkerings with an African crusade against Salā, were concentrated in the early 1260s, provoked by the disobedience of Moorish clients and subjects and the hostility of Moorish neighbours. After the most active period of its history, the 'Reconquest' had subsided.

## The Fate of the Moors

The completion of the conquest of Andalusia implied the commencement of the labour of settlement. For, like the frontiers of earlier phases of Castilian expansion, the newly acquired Andalusian provinces were seriously underpopulated, dotted with deserts and wastes and 'ghost' towns. The conquest and its aftermath drove refugees away, especially from strategic centres. A new, colonial society had to be constructed among the ruins and inside the discarded shells of Islamic Andalusia. Suddenly (in the scale of history), within two generations, the land ceased to be Moorish and became 'Spanish'. The problems of who the Moors were, where they settled and what became of them after the conquest have to be tackled. For an understanding of the importance and intractability of these problems, an historiographical excursion is necessary first.

The Moorishness of Spain generally has been much exaggerated, especially by foreigners, who think that Africa begins at the Pyrenees and that the vices of the oriental character are responsible for the ills of Spain, as the virtues of oriental craftsmanship are credited with her beauties. The insistence on the importance of this supposed oriental legacy is part of a greater myth: that Spain, in the old tourist-office slogan, 'is different', and has an extra-

European character, derived from a non-European experience. The myth is as vital to Spain's *europeizadores*, who lament it, as to the *hispanizadores*, who are proud of it. Generally, modern Spanish writers adopt one of two postures on the contribution of the Moors to the supposed strangeness of Spain, following either of two equally great and, in this case, equally deluded historians. To the partisans of Claudio Sánchez-Albornoz, the Moor is what he has become in popular stereotype: the alien foe who participated, so to speak, in the making of Spain only by his exclusion. Concentrating Spaniards' hostile energies, uniting them – or most of them – in a common cause, inspiring in them an alleged catholic self-consciousness, the Moors, despite themselves, made Spaniards what they are. Demographically, according to this school of thought, the Moorish contribution has been negligible to a 'nation' or even 'race' fixed in what might be called its genetic pool, before the invasion of 711. The opposite school is that of Américo Castro, an historian whose credentials are as liberal as those of Sánchez-Albornoz but whose theories are more generous. His followers see Spanish culture as the product of a symbiosis between Christian and Moorish and, incidentally, Jewish as well. Spaniards accustomed to revile the Moors as necessary enemies are reminded of the long periods of peaceful coexistence, of cooperation and even of alleged cultural cross-fertilisation. The three strands are given comparable prominence in the fabric of Spanish history; and the probable paucity of the numbers of two of the three communities is dismissed in consideration of their cultural abundance. But the Moor is no less important for the *anti-castristas*, in their way, than for the *castristas*. As other or brother, he is essential to both versions of Spanish history.[9]

There is some merit in both theories. The Moor is the traditional bogey-figure of Spaniards' collective psychology. Goya illustrates the fact for us when he paints French invaders as Mamelukes, in mustachios, turbans and pantaloons; 'Moor' and 'infidel' were terms of abuse exchanged by the sides in the Spanish Civil War. In Spanish proverbial usage there are still 'Moors on the coast'. Yet the adversarial relationship implied by these images was by no means continuous in the middle ages. On the contrary, the *castristas* are right to stress the normal coexistence. The Moor was elevated or degraded to the status of bogey only when he had vanished from Spain. On the other hand, his cultural legacy was neither ample nor original. Sánchez-Albornoz was right to argue that medieval Castile was a colonial world from which the Moor was largely absent or, if present, in retreat. Al-Andalūs had its splendid centres, but most of them were short-lived; Madina al-Zahrā and Madina al-Zahira were ruins two centuries before the conquest of St Ferdinand; at its height, under the late amirate and caliphate, Moorish art was at once the beneficiary and victim of values of conspicuous consumption, which yielded lavish objects and chance survivals. Before that period, the Moors were cultural parasites; after it, their splendours, like the Alhambra itself, were decadent by comparison. Great tracts of al-Andalūs were unexploited except for the erection of fortresses, unpeopled and untilled. Save in the rich vocabulary of most of the language of the Iberian peninsula, Moorish cultural influence is conspicuous by its paucity.

The problem which no attempt to estimate the importance of the Moors has yet surmounted is a basic one of quantification. No one knows how many Moors there were. Strictly understood, the term applies to Arabs and Berbers, but is justly, if loosely, applied to relatively larger numbers of 'acculturated' indigenes and imported Slavs, Moorish in guise or affectation. In the noontime and twilight of Spanish Islam, the numbers of inhabitants of al-Andalūs who stood outside the majority community seem to have been negligible. No native Christian population is mentioned in any source in the lands of Ferdinand III's conquests. But the population of al-Andalūs, and the Moorish population of Spain, was also very unevenly distributed. The extent and ease of the Arab conquests of the seventh and eighth centuries have beguiled historians into thinking that Arabia and north Africa were inexhaustible breeding grounds and that Islam was infinitely elastic, stoppable only by Christian resistance. Gibbon's joke that but for the battle of Poitiers the divines of Oxford might expound from their pulpits the 'truth and sanctity' of the Qurān has, in one respect, been taken seriously. The confidence with which historical cartographers draw political boundaries on maps of medieval Europe induces unwary scrutineers to think of Spain as thickly carpeted with Moors to the Duero or even the Cantabrians, like the pile of an oriental rug.

Most of the rug, however, was threadbare and the pile patchy. Moorish settlement was determined by three constraints. It was confined to areas which could be exploited by the traditional means of the Arab and Berber economies: that is, the eastern and southern river valleys and some pastoral uplands. It was limited by a general insufficiency of numbers: the economy of al-Andalus demanded intensive settlement in key areas where market gardening was practised or rice produced, and soaked up huge populations in sponge-like cities which were among the biggest in the western world. And it was governed, in its overall modalities, by problems of communication across a wide and mountainous peninsula, behind a long and exposed frontier, along roads laid in Roman times for quite different strategic purposes. The great concentrations of Moorish population were in the valleys of the Ebro in the north and the Guadalquivir in the south and the coastal areas between them. The main axis of communication, the old Roman road from Cordova to Saragossa, lay well outside the area of settlement, though it passed through an important outpost of al-Andalūs at Toledo. To the defence of this exposed flank, the extension of Moorish political power across the northern Castilian plateau was directed; a deep frontier from the Tagus to the Duero was established; and a policy was devised and sustained of launching raids even beyond that frontier into the abandoned, unwanted north. Like the Roman empire, Moorish al-Andalūs was doomed by its unwieldy frontier, easily breached by any ruler of the north who persevered in pretensions to conquest or who was genuinely animated by a 'spirit of crusade'.

The overall numbers of the Moors are impossible to estimate. The first comprehensive census occurred at the final expulsion of the Moriscos in the early seventeenth century. But the computation was entrusted to those responsible for the expulsion. The figures were calculated, with suspicious precision, by interested parties. Even if the global figure yielded by these accounts – some 275 000 – were reliable, it could not provide a starting-point for back projection. Too many events had disturbed the fluctuations of the Moorish population. The Moriscos' alarming growth in the late sixteenth century had been preceded by a long period of decline, of successive expulsions and enforced migrations, of a continuous if unspectacular trickle of exiles. It is likely that by the time of St Ferdinand's conquests, the decline had already begun, or was beginning, as the export of Moorish captives to foreign slave markets rose, refugees departed in increasing numbers to Africa, the conquest deterred new arrivals and the cultural shock, which accompanies defeat, registered its usual effects.

Nevertheless, the conquest of Andalusia brought Castilian invaders for the first time – if we except Toledo – into the heartlands of Moorish settlement, where, after the original configurations of al-Andalūs were broken, the Moors were penned like sheep. The crown of Aragon had already absorbed two big Moorish communities in the Ebro valley and, recently, the kingdom of Valencia. But previous Castilian experience had been largely confined to reclaimed wastelands and sparsely populated uplands. The pattern of Castilian colonial habits – settlement at all social levels, including peasants who would work the soil themselves – had been established. Now for the first time Castilian expansion met a large indigenous subject population. The Castilian reaction, faced with this problem was, on the whole, to sweep it aside. In strategically sensitive places, where the natives resisted the conquest, they were expelled by the terms of surrender. Among the conquests of St Ferdinand's reign, for instance, the cities of Baeza, Andújar, Martos, Úbeda, Iznatoraf, San Esteban, Quesada, Cordova, Seville and Cartagena were surrendered as empty husks and in Jaén and Mula only selected residents were allowed to remain. Alfonso X intensified this policy. In 1262–63 he drove out the inhabitants of Écija; as he spread his conquests to the south-east of Seville he expelled the Moors from Jeréz, Arcos, Lebrija and Puerto Santa María to secure the safety of his frontier. Alfonso was a curiously Fuastian figure with a passion for knowledge as well as power; but like Frederick II, whom he admired, he was ruthless under his civilised crust. Happily his poetic talent enabled him to discharge the obligations of conscience a king incurs by writing delightful 'canticles' in praise of Our Lady. When the Moors replied to his rough treatment with recalcitrance – in the uprising of 1264 – he took even sterner measures. The Guadalquivir valley began to empty of Moors, forced or pressed into exile. *Morerías* began to diminish, like those of Carmona and Jeréz, which dwindle in the documents and are last mentioned in 1294. In some surviving grants of houses in the towns, the names of former Moorish occupants are specified. The Seville address of Ibn Khaldūn's ancestor could be consulted in the records when he visited in the 1360s. While it was from the cities that most recorded expulsions took place, it must not be assumed that the countryside was spared. The descriptions of rural devastation in Castilian chronicles tend to be stereotyped. 'Everything' is destroyed – 'gardens and vines and cereals'. But these formulae reflect royal policy: Alfonso X reduced the frontier from Jeréz to Gibraltar to a wasteland. The most telling evidence for the displacement of the Moorish population derives from place names. It is not only modern dictators who try to expunge the past by changing the names and the wholesale substitution of Christian for Moorish names was usually by royal command. It was not always successful: Alfonso X, for instance, could never get the same 'Estrella' to stick; people called it 'Medina Sidonia'. In other places the new name struck popular roots: Alcanatif, for instance, became Santa María del Puerto (or Puerto de Santa María) by a popular acclamation which Alfonso attributed to a miracle of the Virgin.[10] To a remarkable extent, and especially outside the big towns, the new names were established by the early fourteenth century.

Canonists seem to have been scandalised by the severity of Castilian policy. Even writers who were harshest on the subject of the rights of infidels, and who were willing to deny true sovereignty to the Moors, objected to expropriation and despoliation as 'openly contrary to the precepts of charity'.[11] To Oldradus de Ponte, whose words these were, Spanish kings seemed to victimise the Moors on religious grounds; the expulsions appeared, from Rome, dangerously like a device to procure conversions by force. But this was to misunderstand the mental world of the Spanish conquests, where, though crusading rhetoric was exploited, the conflict was not conceived in confessional terms. Like other Spanish kings, Alfonso, who was only carrying a common policy to new extremes, expelled enemies from their property not because they were infidels, but because they were recalcitrant. His actions were justified, not under the laws governing the rule of confessional minorities, but those of war.

## The Nature of Settlement

The scale of this displacement of population imposed on the conquerors a labour of resettlement which stretched manpower resources to the limit. It was not only Andalusia that had to be colonised: indeed, its fertility made the south easier to repopulate than the former frontier lands south of the Tagus. Hence the chronicler's admiration for St Ferdinand, 'who peopled not only what he conquered from the Moors, which had been inhabited before, but also what was previously uninhabited'.[12] Perhaps, however, this praise was too lavish. The resettlement was remarkable because in the circumstances every achievement was registered against the odds; but it was a halting, frustrating and long unfulfilled labour. No systematic body of materials exists to study it, but an idea of its character can be gleaned from the six known surviving landbooks – *libros de repartimiento* – which present digests of the division and allocation of property in particular towns and, in most cases, their environs. The book of Jeréz is limited to the town, and that of Cádiz is fragmentary, but those of Seville, Écija, Carmona, and Vejer, are more complete. The grants they record are of two classes, designated by different names: *donadíos*, large landholdings given to royal personages, aristocrats and military or religious orders for purposes of patronage or of defence of the frontier; and *heredamientos*, small units intended for the direct exploitation of their owners and for the encouragement of settlement. The extent of seigneurial lands is a measure of the colonisation's limited success. If *donadíos* were settled at all, it was only very gradually, because the inducements available to intermediate lords were few and the profitability of tenancies doubtful. In the seigneurial lands pastoral exploitation predominated – the ranching which would become the classic model of a frontier economy. More often than not, it was cattle-ranching: the grasses of Andalusia were lusher than the sheeplands of New Castile. The lands in lordly hands tended to increase – gradually by royal grant, rapidly by the acquisition of the lands of failed settlers. At a conservative estimate, by the last decade of the thirteenth century, in the reign of Sancho IV, about a quarter of Andalusia was in seigneurial hands; the biggest shares went to the knightly orders, especially that of Santiago, which owned perhaps half of the lands in question, and to the archbishopric of Toledo. At that stage, the distribution of seigneurial land reflected an obvious element in royal policy. The *donadíos* stretched along the frontier in a deep and almost continuous band, broken only for two short stretches to the south of Jaén and the south-east of Seville. They were a product of two inescapable imperatives: shortage of settlers and want of soldiers. The ecclesiastical lordship of Quesada included 37 fortified places, some of them substantial castles; their defence demanded 400 men. The early grants reveal the kings' struggle to colonise. The first flush of royal favour was shown to footsoldiers and sergeants and undubbed cavaliers. They got the better part of the first division of Seville in 1249–53.[13] In Carmona, conquered in 1247, there were, at the best estimate, 244 settlers who received allocations recorded in the landbook; 198 were footsoldiers, who received modest portions of a house and land enough to yield 180 bushels of wheat. Their land accounted for six-sevenths of the total distributed. Over 80 per cent of recipients in the first division of Jeréz were footsoldiers, without counting the separately classified archers. Allocations to nobles, of which there were 31 in Carmona, were distinguished more by quality than size; they included land designated as 'gardens', well watered and suitable for the specialised fruits, nuts, vegetables and condiments which were Andalusia's more prized products. The queen's portion was fifteen times the size of a footsoldier's (and that of the prince, Don Fernando, ten times), while the five knightly orders between them got about twice as much as the queen. The *repartimiento* of Carmona was thus a smallholders' – one might almost say a 'yeomen's' charter. The attempt to encourage women to settle marks it as a colonial endeavour in the fullest sense. The number of married settlers is unknown, but twenty women received allotments in their own right, most of them widows 'with their sons', who might have equipped the little colony with a ready-made second generation. At Jeréz, the 1828 first settlers were accompanied by 1277 women.[14]

In general, however, the first *repartimientos* seem to have been failures. That of Seville was completed only in 1253. Even then, in what was acknowledged to be the most attractive city for colonists, the population was little more than a quarter of what it had been before the expulsion of the Moors. By 1255, the king was complaining that settlers were actually moving away; the emptiness of the city made him hesitate to carry the conquest further. Many grants after that time reapportioned lands abandoned or neglected by their original grantees. New distributions of abandoned lands took place in 1255–57 and 1263. When Écija was divided up in 1263, 'at the time when it was emptied of Moors', as the landbook says, the grants were much bigger than formerly. Most were *donadíos*; precious few were as small as a footsoldier's share at Carmona.[15] And the task got harder as the conquest wore on. Royal desperation is most evident – but not unrepresentative – in the records of the colonisation of Vejer. At the first attempt, by Sancho IV in 1288, nearly 35 per cent of the settlers were footsoldiers and nearly 30 per cent bowmen and sergeants; but many of them failed to take up their grants or transferred them to comrades or superiors. Of 176 who exercised their rights, 37 had departed by 1293, when a second division reallocated their abandoned lots and added some big holdings of aristocratic proportions. The drift away continued. Sancho attempted further distributions of land in 1294 and 1295, but in 1304 it was still necessary for Ferdinand IV to order sharing of 'what could be acquired abandoned' among the remaining settlers.[16]

The kings' frantic efforts to transfuse new lifeblood into the stricken corpse of Andalusia are apparent in the landbooks. But the 'official' record, revealing as it is, may of course conceal something more. The *repartimientos* were highly formal acts, and the fact that they had to be recast so often shows that they were at best imperfectly reflected in reality. In freshly conquered cities, emptied of their inhabitants and full of licentious and cupidinous soldiery, the natural course of events is unlikely to have been suspended while the bureaucrats responsible for the division of the spoils received their commissions from the king, made their stately entrance, set up their court, conducted their investigations and tendered their recommendations over a period of time rarely amounting, even in small towns, to less than two years. The *repartimientos* were often conducted in an atmosphere of ritual designed to satisfy the two most marked mental features of Castile's small intellectual élite: legalism and ritualism. At Écija, for instance, the town was divided into four quarters in memory of the cross – a ritual reminiscent of Jaime I's practice, on the fall of a Moorish city, of facing east and kissing the ground, to the unresolved satisfaction of Muslims and Christians alike. Unless such acts were merely 'propaganda exercises', it was as if the repeopling of erstwhile Moorish homes and the reploughing of erstwhile Moorish tillage were perceived by the devisers of such rituals, like the reconsecration of an erstwhile Moorish mosque, as acts of purgation and sanctification after profanation and bloodshed. As the appropriation of Moorish goods was of dubious legal validity, there were delicate consciences which are peculiar to élites, to appease. It is possible that while *repartimiento* had a strong appeal for intellectuals and bureaucrats, the concepts of usurpation and loot, which it sought to occlude or euphemise, were more readily grasped by the soldiers, impatient for reward and ignorant of law or religion, who were the first settlers.

At another level, the *repartimiento*, perhaps like the Domesday survey of England or the *encomienda* in the New World, was an attempt to regularise a less formal division of the spoils which must have happened anyway. The idea that immovable property could be distributed by those in authority under the crown had figured occasionally in earlier Iberian conquests. But the division of Andalusia was novel in its comprehensive scale. Traditionally, one established title to a *res nullius* simply by occupying it, and even while the apportionment of the lands of Andalusia was in progress, this principle was embodied in the *Siete Partidas*, the royal attempt to codify the laws of Castile. In the first years of the conquest of Andalusia, while there were still landless *écorcheurs* scouring the frontier for easy pickings, many Castilian soldiers seem to have put the precept into practice. Cordova, for instance, was filled to bursting at its fall by eager landhunters who seized Moorish farms in the hinterland and drove off the inhabitants. Not until after the Moorish unrest a generation later was the area formally allocated for Christian settlement and the usurpers' position confirmed.[17] But to judge from the difficulty with which settlers were induced to go further south, this land hunger was rapidly assuaged and the supply of frontiersmen soon attenuated.

The same was true of the Algarve. Although the character of the area would change markedly towards the end of the middle ages, and diverge from the patterns established in Andalusia and the Alentejo, the Portuguese conquests of the thirteenth century generally seem to have resembled those of Castile. Their threshold was the wasteland of Ribatejo and the northern Alentejo, like the La Mancha and Extremadura of Castile. To the south lay vast stretches of underpopulated and underexploited countryside sprinkled with towns on a much smaller scale than those of Andalusia, with populations normally of between one and five thousand. Until the Almohad debacle, permanent Portuguese conquests from the Moors had been sideshows of the crusades; on the way to each of the great Levantine crusades, northerners had stopped off en route to wrest a town or castle. Lisbon was even more of a frontier garrison than Toledo; seized in the second crusade it had remained an enclave ever since, with only Moors to landward. This pattern of reliance on crusader help continued as late as 1217, when Alcácer was captured with the aid of pilgrims bound for the camp at Damietta. Sancho II (r. 1223–48), however, was a king determined to exploit the disunity of al-Andalūs, and the dislocation caused by Castilian and Aragonese invasions further east, to make territorial gains in Portugal's sphere of conquest. He was also willing and able to make vast alienations in favour of the knightly orders, especially those of Santiago, Calatrava and the Hospital, to raise the necessary force. The Alentejo and eastern Algarve, except for some strongholds, were absorbed between 1226 and 1238; Silves, Faro and the western Algarve had to be left to be mopped up by Alfonso III after the fall of Seville. Little work has been done, and few documents published, on the colonisation of these conquests, but enough has emerged for some of the features typical of Andalusia to be glimpsed in southern Portugal too: the prominence of the knightly orders, the lavish terms of alienation, the sporadic evidence of efforts to introduce settlers. In 1235–36, for instance, Sancho gave two reconquered castles to the Order of Santiago, and another three in May and June, 1236. This open-handedness provoked riots, which drew in turn papal and episcopal censure. The order was not quick to exploit the lands, though some, near one of the castles, at Mértola, were alienated in 1269 in circumstances which might suggest an attempt to induce settlement.[18]

Where did the settlers come from? It has often been pointed out that the biggest single category in the Andalusian landbooks came from Old Castile. But that is not surprising, for it was where most Castilians lived – over 42 per cent of them in the sixteenth century, when reliable demographic sources begin, therefore assuredly a higher proportion in the thirteenth century, before the settlement of so much future territory. What is remarkable is the number of colonists from elsewhere. First, one can detect a large number who resettled from within Andalusia – that is, migrants who moved south with the frontier, a core population with a genuinely frontier vocation – 25 per cent, for instance, of those of specified provenance in Carmona, 31 per cent of those of Vejer. At Jeréz, over 28 per cent of settlers came from former frontier zones, including those of

New Castile and Extremadura. This footloose manpower was the stuff of dynamism. Without it, there could have been no Spanish empire, in the old world or the new.

Secondly, the colonisation of Andalusia evidently depended on non-Castilian settlers. Castile had too many open spaces and too few people for a policy of *farà de se* or self-help. Even in the sixteenth-century New World, theoretically the exclusive perquisite of Castilians, the rejection of foreigners was a slogan rather than a policy, honoured in the breach. In the medieval Castilian 'empire' foreign participation was acknowledged as invaluable. At first glance, the most surprising alien community to be welcomed among the settlers was that drawn from among the Moors themselves. The expulsions were far-reaching and thorough, but the subsequent readmission of Moors was by no means negligible. Even while Moorish quarters disappeared from Andalusian towns in the late thirteenth and early fourteenth centuries, others appeared elsewhere, although of course, on a much smaller scale. Cordova got its *aljama* back in 1254 and Seville not long after. But the quarters were tiny, accommodating perhaps two or three hundred people, and these were the biggest concentrations of Moors in areas from which they had been expelled.[19]

An almost equally remarkable, and perhaps even smaller, minority was formed by Jews. The Jews of Andalusia later became such an affront to the Christian community that they were the first victims of the pogroms of 1391 and eventually had to be expelled, in the 1480s, ahead of the Jews of the rest of Spain. Yet most of them had been brought by Christian conquerers in the first place. To eke out the meagre settlement, they were eagerly welcomed and lavishly privileged; indeed, in some respects, those very privileges which accompanied their settlement later excited their unpopularity and so led to their massacre or ejection. But in the late thirteenth and early fourteenth centuries, when expulsion, because they were unwanted, was forced on them in much of the rest of western Europe, they were welcomed, because they were needed, in Spain. The most conspicuous example is that of Seville. Though Jews had flourished there in the eleventh century, no Jewish community seems to have existed in the period immediately before the conquest. Implanted by St Ferdinand and Alfonso X, it grew to become the second largest in Spain, numbering perhaps some 450 heads of households by 1391, when it reached its peak. Its introduction was a sudden and deliberate step. A spacious quarter of sixteen hectares was assigned to the Jews in what is now called the Barrio de Santa Cruz, north of the Alcázar, by St Ferdinand, and three synagogues were granted to them, as early as 1252, by his son. This ample accommodation was too optimistically delineated: it seems never to have been filled. But some Jews resided outside its limits and Seville's preponderance among Jewish centres in Andalusia is shown by the relative tax returns yielded by Jewish communities. In 1294, Seville's Jews paid over 115 000 *maravedíes*; only Cordova yielded a remotely comparable figure – a mere 38 333 *maravedíes*. From Jaén, Úbeda and Baeza together, 25 000 *maravedíes* were collected, but no other single town paid more than 7000. Most of these taxes were the fruit of post-conquest settlement. Even where Jewish inhabitants were documented under the Almohads, they seem to have increased in the wake of the conquest, as at Cordova, where, in 1250, they annoyed the cathedral chapter by building a lavish new synagogue.[20]

So far, what we have said of the settlement of Andalusia may seem to carry little hint of the region's future importance in the colonisation of the Atlantic, or, in particular, of the role of Seville, with neighbouring ports, as the great emporium of Atlantic trade in the sixteenth century. One must remember that the region's prominence in Atlantic navigation was still a long way off – emerging, as we shall see (p.155), for the first time nearly a century after the conquest. On the other hand, the ports of Andalusia did prove attractive from the first to settlers with an established maritime vocation: some from outside the realm, others from the seaboard lands of the Castilian crown. Cadiz, for instance, was devilishly hard to colonise: Alfonso X put his best efforts into it because he fancied the most remote of his conquests for his mausoleum; yet it took eleven years for settlement to strike roots. Eventually the city was colonised, among others, by Cantabrians and Basques.[21] Cadiz was one of the stepping stones of late medieval Basque penetration of the Mediterranean. In various Andalusian ports, a small but significant number of Catalans received grants in the *repartimientos*, despite the claims on their attention of their own Mediterranean and African colonies, and in Seville Catalan merchants had their own quarter and warehouse from 1281. But the most significant maritime community to be introduced in the aftermath of the conquest was the Genoese. By a

Latin privilege of St Ferdinand's, known in a confirmation of
Alfonso X's of May, 1251, they were given a quarter in Seville,
looking for all the world like an African *funduk* (see below, p.137),
with its bath, bakery and quay, its chapel and its peculiar legal and
commercial privileges.[22] Their initial interest was in olive oil, but
Seville would grow into the main entrepôt of Genoa's African trade
in the fifteenth century. The settlement of small maritime
communities in conquered Andalusia was the springboard of the
region's future long-range seaborne trade – something on which the
Moors, more shy traffickers than the dark Iberians, had never
ventured.

The tenor of life in these first Atlantic 'empires' of south-west
Spain is hard to capture. For the Arab eulogists of the high middle
ages, Andalusia had been a paradise, a garden of earthly delights,
because its climate and fertility suited their way of life. If, leaving
aside the well-known poets, we turn for example to Ibn al-Awwām,
the twelfth-century agronomist, we seem transported into a world
of epicene contentment, in which he mingles aromatic vinegars,
concocts foie gras and happily devises recipes for compost to please
his sybaritic king.[23] 'Il faut cultiver notre jardin', is his message.
Though the climate continues to be praised, Christian Andalusia
never speaks to us with that sort of lush, rich voice. Its material
advantages, its fertility, the good economic performance of its
crops, were well known and appreciated; otherwise, even the
modified success of the colonisation would have been impossible.
In some respects Andalusia was a land of opportunity, where the
great bulk of the urban citizenry enjoyed the status of direct vassals
of the king and where wages were high and land prices were low –
about two-thirds those of Old Castile, it seems, on average, in the
years before the Black Death. But the opportunities were hard to
exploit and the conditions of life variable. It was difficult to make
the most of Andalusia's rich soil, with the hazards of the frontier,
shortage of labour and the relentless progress of aristocratic tenure
imposing pastoralism on much of the country. Olive oil, the liquid
gold of Moorish Andalusia, though prized by Genoese merchants,
was little esteemed by Castilians, who had scant tradition of olive-
growing and tended to rely, for their source of edible fat, on lard.

As under the Moors, it remained an urban world, with big towns
lapped, like oases, by sparsely populated hinterlands, making on
the productivity of the countryside large demands which led to

frequent breakdowns of supply. Remote communities strove, with the self-consciousness of an urban culture, to preserve the amenities of civilised life. Among the settlers of Vejer there were two priests, a miller, two gardeners, a tiler, a blacksmith, a shoemaker, a butcher and no fewer than three surgeon-barbers – though presumably they must have plied some other trade as well. Almost within bowshot of the Moors, one could go, shriven and shod, to the hairdresser's. Yet the fate of most post-conquest smallholdings was to be absorbed, over the next two centuries, into the growing and economically inefficient latifundia of the Church, the orders and the aristocrats; their owners' successors would become wage-labourers eking a poor subsistence from seasonal work; and the free towns, whose status as direct dependants of the crown, without intervention of intermediate lordship, the kings so jealously conserved, would slip under the control of hereditary councillors who were the kin or clients of the great territorial nobility. By the late fifteenth century, the thirteenth-century reconquests had become lands of poverty and day labour, which would provide the cannon fodder of remoter conquests and new, oceanic colonies.

# 3.   A Mediterranean Land Empire: Sharq al-Andalūs

'In all Biscay you will not find an orange,' wrote Bishop Palafox in an attempt to explain to himself the diversity of Spain, 'and in all Valencia not a chestnut.'[1] No contrast so thoroughly undermines the myth that Spain is one country than that between Mediterranean and Atlantic Spain. The differences, which remain apparent today, were of course more marked in the middle ages, before the political unification and cultural assimilation of these two unequal moieties. It was easier to make a pilgrimage from Barcelona to Rome than to Compostela. Jaime I, who claimed with some exaggeration 'to rule from the Rhone to the Ebro', was typical of his fellow countrymen in sensing the kinship of the lands of the western Mediterranean basin. Conventionally, the territorial ambitions of the House of Barcelona in what is now southern France are held to have been decisively reversed by the battle of Muret in 1213. Yet even at the end of his reign, Jaime was prepared to risk conquests from the Moors in favour of a trans-Pyrenean adventure.[2] The Catalan and Aragonese route to Africa lay through western Mediterranean islands; within the Iberian peninsula the eastern seaboard conquests of both Aragon and Castile have a distinctively 'Mediterranean' flavour which marks them out from areas further west. A certain common sentiment united the communities of Hispania, but practical economic and geographic realities gave them divergent characters and divergent interests. Mariners from Atlantic Spain penetrated Mediterranean commerce in the late middle ages, while those from the Mediterranean explored the Atlantic, but their predominant courses remained distinct. Spain, in short, was a Janus. The head, however, was not set rigidly upon the shoulders, but capable of swivels and nods in different directions as it faced both ways.

The changes of the thirteenth century both confirmed and modified this character. For the first time, the kingdom of Castile acquired a Mediterranean seaboard. The partition of the peninsula, envisaged as early as the Treaty of Tudilen of 1151, and ratified by Alfonso VIII of Castile and Alfonso II of Aragon in 1179, was at last fulfilled. Still, it was less by the force of a long-sustained

Map 4
VALENCIA AND NORTHERN MURCIA
places named in the text

design, rather by a compromise cobbled together to avoid a fratricidal war between Aragon and Castile, that Murcia became a kingdom of the crown of Castile, while Granada was confirmed by political geography, as it had formerly been assigned by treaty, to Castilian conquest. Castile's 'real presence' on the eastern seaboard remained slight. Murcia was conquered largely by Aragonese and Catalan arms, by virtual courtesy of Jaime I. Its Christian community, settled after the conquest, was predominantly Catalan-speaking. Its abiding Muslim population gave it a 'Mediterranean' flavour. It behaved, as it were, more like an Arago-Catalan than a Castilian colony, following the model of Valencia, with its large native population and general economic continuity, rather than the denuded ranchlands of Andalusia.

### Valencia and Northern Murcia: Conquest and Division

The predominantly Moorish character of conquered Valencia is relatively easy to exemplify and explain. It was a result of the nature of the country, the circumstances of the conquest and the limited manpower resources of the crown of Aragon. Famed for its infinite variety, within a relatively small compass, Valencia really comprised two countries: mountainous, pastoral extremities in the north and on the southern border, where sheep and goats outnumbered people and the opportunities for settlers were greatest because the numbers required were least; and rich lowlands with a well watered plain in the centre, where most of the population had lived and worked from time immemorial and where the cultivation of cash crops, surviving the conquest and imposing labour-intensive demands, made the natives irreplaceable. Expulsions were infrequent, by comparison with Castilian reconquests, readmissions extensive and settlement of newcomers sparse. Towards the end of his reign, Jaime I complained that only 30 000 settlers had come to his new kingdom, whereas 100 000 were needed to guarantee its security.[3] The king was notoriously given to numerical exaggeration, but the message of his claim is clear. The immovable spoils of the kingdom of Valencia were undersubscribed.

The course of the conquest, so different in crucial respects from that of Andalusia, helps to account for this. Everywhere, Christian Spanish conquerors exploited the divisions among the thirteenth-century Moors, but in Valencia, more than anywhere else, the conquest had the character of a Moorish civil war, into which Jaime I profitably intruded. Though called by Christian observers a 'kingdom', Valencia was technically an Almohad governorate, whose ruler, Abū Zayd, derived from his Almohad masters authority without power. As the Almohad empire crumbled, Abū Zayd maintained the semblance of continuity in Valencia where it lasted for longer than anywhere else in Spain. But his position was ambiguous. He found himself obliged to defend Almohad legitimacy with his own resources and at his own risk against a medley of factions similar to those of the rest of al-Andalūs. He confronted ambitious castellans, like the Banū-'Īsā at Játiva; charismatic captains of banditti such as the redoubtable al-Azraq, who would prove the wiliest and most intractable of Jaime's enemies; partisans of the Hafsids; friends of Ibn Hūd, and, most formidable of all, the usurper Zayyān, who threatened to become an Ibn Hūd of Valencia. Though his real origins were questionable, Zayyān claimed, with apparent verisimilitude, descent from the pre-Almohad rulers. While the north remained loyal to Abū Zayd, and the castellans of the south flirted with Ibn Hūd, he was able to create a state which stretched to the Júcar, including the city of Valencia, in the strategic and economic trunk of the country. Zayyān's sultanate wanted the two great requisites of head and tail. Events would prove that it also lacked heart, since most of the countryside put up little resistance to the Aragonese invasion of the next decade. But it looked formidable enough on the map, and for Abū Zayd represented a threat which could not be faced alone.

In these circumstances, Abū Zayd resorted to a traditional expedient of Andalūsi politicians: alliance with the infidel. He took his first step in the direction of Jaime's camp in 1226, when he agreed to pay tribute to Aragon. Ostensibly, this was for the castle of Peñíscola, which Jaime besieged in 1225 in the course of a tentative incursion into Valencian territory, a youthful cavalcade, a premature adventure. But Jaime's attack was ill prepared and it was probably not necessary for Abū Zayd to buy him off; rather than payola to a predator, this was a retainer to a potential mercenary. Its immediate effect, however, was to render the mercenary unavailable, for it provoked a revolt by most of the nobility of Aragon, who would have preferred a war, which might have enriched them, to an accommodation which benefited the king. Only after winning the subsequent power struggle in his own kingdom and uniting his fractious aristocracy in the successful war against Majorca, was Jaime free to come to Abū Zayd's help. By then his tributary was in desperate straits. In 1229 Abū Zayd offered a condominium in conquered lands and a quarter of the revenues of the realm, in 1232 the entire city and jurisdiction of Valencia itself. With most of the governorate cowed or controlled by Zayyān, the old pro-Almohad élite could survive only as collaborators with a foreign conqueror. Yet an air of legitimacy still clung to the side on which Jaime intervened, at least until Abū Zayd enfeoffed himself, soul as well as body, to his ally and became a Christian. Thus many communities within Valencia submitted to and sided with the conqueror. This fifth column could count on a privileged and secure place in post-conquest society.

Even beyond the relatively narrow compass of Abū Zayd's allegiance, much of the kingdom submitted without a fight. The war was launched in 1232, and the last fortress to hold out, at Biar, did not surrender until 1245. Fighting continued or recurred for a generation after that. This long struggle makes Valencia seem a model of indomitable resistance; yet had it really been so, it might never have been conquered at all, for in manpower and resources the kingdom was a match for Jaime. The fierce but patchy resistance was the work of Zayyān and of a few more or less independent chieftains: it was the impregnability of their positions, and the invader's domestic distractions, which made for a long war. On a few occasions, Jaime declined to accept a proffered surrender, because he needed a victory; in others – Burriana and Valencia itself – the offers came too late and Jaime found it expedient to make an example. In 1237, a litany of strongholds fell bloodlessly: Nules, Castro, Vall d'Uxó, all on the same day. During the great siege of Valencia in 1238 Jaime was able to secure by accommodation the surrender of most of the remaining castles of the central zone. Silla showed exceptional spirit in holding out for a week.[4] In many ways the conquest was a royal progress, faltering at times as much from Jaime's own hesitancy as from the strain of fierce confrontation.

For Jaime entered the war reluctantly and pursued it tentatively. It was never a particular cause of his own, as his 'favourite' conquest of Majorca was. On the contrary, it was the pet cause of the nobles who fought him in the civil war of 1226–28. He pulled back from it in 1226 and had to be persuaded into it even in 1232, when his alliance with Abū Zayd gave him an ideal pretext. He professed himself astonished at the nobility's enthusiasm for Valencia. The war was only precipitated by the private initiative of the nobles who supported it, led by En Blasco d'Alagó, who had been one of Jaime's most voluble critics and, after his two years of exile in Valencia, the spokesman in council for the Valencian adventure. Some of them occupied Morella, one of the northern strongholds which eluded Abū Zayd. Forces of the knightly orders followed. Only after that did Jaime rally a few hundred men and join the war in person.

This opportunistic reaction was typical of the man and provides the key to his conduct in the conquest of Valencia. In his autobiography, Jaime dignified the process by invoking providence and his own, pretended, longstanding ambition, or by claiming to have adumbrated in advance the entire conquest strategy: 'And now I shall tell you how we shall take Valencia and all the other land'.[5] In reality, however, the conquest was improvised at every turn. En Blasco's success at Morella convinced the king that it was expedient to invade. Abū Zayd's compliance made it worthwhile to proceed with an attempt on Valencia itself. And once Valencia had fallen, the king was unable, by his own explicit admission, to resist the opportunity to make a dependency of Játiva and levy tribute from the south. Until 1236, he intended to keep Abū Zayd as a puppet king, but in that year he unceremoniously arrogated the title of King of Valencia to himself: this may have been the fulfilment of a long-term strategy, but more closely resembles another extemporisation. Jaime's only consistent quest was for chivalric glory, for the 'bon preu et tan gran nom' that great conquests promised. His reason for prizing Majorca above Valencia was that a conquest by sea, because more difficult, brought more honour. The barons who sought to interest him in Valencia tried every argument: his ancestors had coveted it; it was the 'best and most beautiful' kingdom in the world and 'the most delectable'; 'and if God will that you conquer it – and so He shall – you will have the conquest of the best thing there may be in the world, of pleasances and strong castles'; compared with Valencia, Majorca was as nothing. But in Jaime's account, the final argument seems to have been decisive: 'If you take it, well may you say that you are the best king in the world, and he who has wrought most deeds.'[6]

It was, as usual, an indiscriminate love of 'deeds', not any specifically Christian or 'crusading' fervour, certainly no animus against Islam, that inspired Jaime. He later became Catalonia's candidate for canonisation in imitation of those other warriors against Islam, St Louis and St Ferdinand.[7] Deservedly unsuccessful, he was the least likely saint, even in potentia, of the three. He was an 'hom de femnes', a ladies' man, with respect neither for a chaste sex nor a celibate order. He brutalised the Archbishop of Saragossa and cut out the tongue of the Bishop of Gerona. His models were not Christ and the apostles but Alexander and the Cid. Often impatient with his coreligionists, he could be indulgent towards the Moors, especially when he found that they spoke the same chivalric language as he. Of all his Moorish vassals, he said, only al-Azraq disappointed him on a point of honour. The representative of Játiva, for instance, who came to negotiate terms of surrender with the king, seemed the 'wisest of men of Játiva and one of the best men there,' who 'expounded his argument well'. The Muslim sage's argument is worth quoting:

Well do you know of what kind is the castle of Játiva and that there is none better in all al-Andalūs, and that if you were to have the castle at so little cost, Moors and Christians would consider it ill. And though the governor and the Moors do not observe your way of life [literally, 'law'] they would receive dishonour from you if they did what you demand. And they ask you not to desire them to do so.

The tone of this exchange is typical of Jaime's dealings with Moors. He 'knew their customs' and showed it by offering them fresh meats and live gifts and traditional greetings. Jaime was of course capable of expressing satisfaction, when addressing clerical interlocutors, that the 'name of Christ and His Holy Mother' could be invoked where formerly only that of Muhammad was heard. But as long as the 'enemies of God' were good and loyal subjects of the king he wished neither to destroy nor displace them, nor even – as far as his wider obligations permitted – unnecessarily to disturb them.

In a famous passage of the Book of Deeds, he described an audience he had of two leading citizens of Murcia, whom Alfonso X had knighted, but who had complaints of the treatment they received at Christian hands. When he heard they were coming, he had his tent draped in Saracen fashion, and seating spread. He ordered live chickens and sheep and goats and had them slaughtered in the Moors' own manner and made the dignitaries feast with him. After they had knelt and kissed his knees he dismissed all save his Jewish interpreter and addressed them confidentially:

> And we told them that we had sent for them for this reason, that they might well know that there were many Saracens in our own lands, and that from times past our dynasty had kept them in Aragon and in Catalonia and ourselves in the Kingdom of Majorca and that of Valencia, and all keep their own way of life, as well as if they were in a land of the Saracens, and they had come before our mercy and had submitted to us. And those who would not submit we had to take by force and people their land with Christians.[8]

This was an accurate statement of royal policy and a helpful source of explanation of why Valencia under Jaime's rule remained a predominantly, indeed overwhelmingly, Moorish kingdom. The bloodless surrender of most of the realm, the king's preference for the criteria of loyalty over those of faith in the narrow sense, and historical memories all combined to guarantee the Moors' survival. The example Jaime mentioned, and which he had experienced himself, of the recent history of Majorca was evidently influential. In Majorca, the initial attempt to extirpate the native Muslims, inspired as much by cupidity as by crusading zeal, had proved impracticable. But a remoter example was equally germane: that of the Valencia of the Cid, who had demonstrated the viability of a largely Moorish state under Christian governance and the coexistence – normal in medieval Spain but dramatically instanced in Valencia – of Christian and Muslim communities with their peculiar privileges and laws.

There were, of course, exceptions: places in Valencia where settlers were introduced and where Moors were, at least, dispossessed and, at worst, expelled. Over twenty landbooks yield a detailed picture of the distribution of conquered territory in Valencia. The greater efficiency of the royal bureaucracy has bequeathed a more exact and comprehensive account than is possible for Andalusia. The Valencian records are 'domesday books' – often accounts of *ex post facto* rationalisations of land distributions on the basis of territorial units which predated the conquest; many date from the 1270s, when the frustrations felt by the native population at unauthorised expropriations helped to provoke a major rebellion, to which the king's command for surveys of distributed lands was part of the royal response. In other cases, like that of Valencia, the *repartiment* was recorded as it happened. In terms of the treatment of the conquered lands and of the nature of settlement, four regions can be distinguished and demand separate review: the north as far as the limits of the province of Castellón; the zone from Segorbe south to the *horta* of Valencia, with a separate but similar area south of the capital to the Júcar; Valencia proper, city and plain; and the south, beyond the Júcar, with northern Murcia, which, for present purposes, can be treated jointly with southern Valencia. In every case it is important to remember the shortcomings of this type of evidence. Royal wishes, even when formulated by an efficient bureaucracy, are not always translated into action; a tenurial revolution does not necessarily imply any serious mutation in the population on the ground.

Settlement was scarcely attempted in the north. Its few economic attractions made it unpromising terrain. Its pastoral economy doomed it to become the 'Extremadura' of Valencia, a land of vast, underpopulated estates, chiefly in the hands of the knightly orders and often settled, if at all, with Moors brought in from elsewhere, as was particularly a Hospitaller practice. There were some unusually active proprietors, such as the monastic community of Poblet, which succeeded in settling its lands at Benifasar, in the extreme north, in the second half of the century. Blasco d'Alagó pursued a vigorous settlement policy in the fief he held around Morella until 1249: this was in the traditions of the great aristocratic 'populators' of the 'reconquered' lands of Aragon and Catalonia in the twelfth century.[9] But such individual fiefs were exceptional in the kingdom of Valencia. The king did reserve some lands to the crown, perhaps with the intention of attempting a policy of settlement at some future date: in Castellón, for instance, fourteen per cent of the territory, but much of this was subsequently alienated without having been colonised. Except possibly at Morella and certainly at Burriana, there is, on the other hand, no evidence of any loss of Moorish population, either through expulsion or voluntary emigration.

Burriana is the great exception. This was, as En Blasco hastened to tell the king, 'a flat place', attractive to colonists and adaptable to the plough. Here, moreoever, an outright victory – 'in despite of the devil', as King Jaime averred – rather than the usual bloodless capitulation was essential for morale. Expulsion from the city were the most benign terms Jaime was prepared to permit the population. Jaime calculated, with suspect precision, that 7032 men, women and children departed the city, while the *repartiment* of 1233 introduced about a thousand families. Yet even here, it is not clear how far the expelled Moors were removed – perhaps only, as at Valencia and, later, Murcia, to a suburb of their own. Outside Burriana, Moorish survival can be assumed in this region, even if it is not actually documented as at Chivert and Borriol. The apparently generous terms of Chivert's surrender, in which Islamic tenure, law and worship are guaranteed, are probably typical.[10]

Southwards from Segorbe, which was originally intended as a milksop-fief for Abū Zayd, the Cerberus who had left the gates of the kingdom unguarded, and which remained virtually untouched by Christian settlement for most of the rest of the century, lay a zone unpenetrated by the system of *repartiment*. The only large-scale expropriations were of the lands of the mosques, which here, as everywhere, went to the Church. This was the Church's share of the conquerors' booty. Most of the castles of this region opened their gates to Jaime without more than token defence and here the rights of the natives were entrenched by generous terms of surrender. Moreover, it was an area from which the king evidently wished to limit intermediate lordship, whether of knightly orders, nobles or the church. The seigneurial 'sector' was limited to small individual grants not much larger than those of commoners. Where the king hastily projected the creation of a fief, as at Segorbe or Sagunto, he soon thought better of it. Repossession was followed by the confirmation of preconquest tenures, as at Segorbe, or by a programme of colonisation, as at Sagunto, where, exceptionally, the natives disappeared and the lands were assigned to contingents from Barcelona and Montblanch. There were a few places, like the strongholds of Moncada, Torres Torres and Puig (at the most sensitive spot in Valencia's defensive rim), which had qualified for allocation to settlers by virtue of their resistance; at Moncada, indeed, Jaime described with some pride his massacre of the population – men, women and children – in the cramped confines of the keep. But even in these locations the post-conquest pattern shows little change. Torres Torres remained so thoroughly Moorish that it had to be reconquered in every rebellion of the next three decades.

The area which formed the southern flank of the Valencian *horta*, between the Turia and the Júcar, was in practice treated in a similar way, although Jaime had considerably more freedom of action: Zayyān's terms of surrender put all the inhabitants and lands as far as the Júcar, except at Cullera, at Jaime's disposal. Some acts of dispossession took place and some small seigneuries were created. At Chiva, for instance, a lay lord was introduced and, exceptionally, given the lands of the mosque; yet the population of Chiva descended from its Moorish inhabitants until the expulsion of the Moriscos in the early seventeenth century. There may have been some loss of population from Silla, since the Hospitallers resettled a group from there on underexploited land just over the Aragonese frontier. Alcira, however, was more representative, remaining overwhelmingly Moorish and successfully claiming from Jaime I in 1245 the return of lands seized without good title by Christian soldiers in the heat of the conquest.[11] This contrasts with Castilian policy in the *campiña* of Cordova, where usurpations were generally confirmed.

In the city and *horta* of Valencia, however, an influx of colonists was inevitable. Here was the most sought-after real estate in the kingdom, reputed in Islam to be 'the dwelling of all beauty', in Christendom 'the finest place in the world'. It was a large oasis of incomparable fertility, stretching from Albufera to Puzol and inland from the coast as far as Manises and Paterna. Here the inexorable detail of the *repartiment* seems to show Catalans and Aragonese swarming into the vacant smallholdings of which the plain was composed like bees into the cells of a honeycomb, though Moors also received lands, not necessarily those they had formerly occupied, on the fringes of the area. There was continuity of a sort here – of the modalities of the division of the soil, of the boundaries of plots and of methods of exploitation in this intensively cultivated, cooperatively irrigated market garden – but not of land ownership. How far was this a genuine expulsion as well as an expropriation? Abundant evidence of Muslims continuing to live and work in the *horta* for the next quarter of a millenium, as slaves, labourers, sharecroppers, tenants and artisans, shows that the *repartiment* gives only a fragment of the whole picture.

The case of the city of Valencia provides perhaps the best example of the insufficiency of the evidence of the *repartiment*, even when supported by the chronicles. Here the evidence of expulsion of the indigenous population could hardly be stronger. The exodus is explicitly, unequivocally enjoined in the city's terms of surrender. It is described vividly in many contemporary accounts; in the king's own description the very groans and lamentations of an alleged 50 000 refugees resound. Only 34 Moorish families received grants of houses within the city. In reality, however, there was little more than a token removal. The walls of Valencia only enclosed enough space for a population of some 15 000. It was a metro-city, a conurbation, its walls surrounded by a dark penumbra of suburbs, villages and densely-populated countryside. In practice, the expulsion of the Moorish citizens meant their removal to an extramural suburb or *aljama*. Expulsion carried none of the same connotations in Valencia as it possessed in Andalusia. And it is important to remember that expulsions even of this modified character demonstrably took place in Valencia, in the immediate aftermath of the conquest, in only two cities: Valencia and Burriana. In all other documented cases, except arguably that of Morella, evacuations applied only to small quarters within the city which thenceforth constituted, as it were, Christian *aljamas* in predominantly Moorish towns.

Just as Jaime I used the pastoral lands of the north as a fund of patronage with which to reward one of the most significant components of his armies – the military orders – so he exploited the arable lands of the centre for the satisfaction of the towns, whose militias supplied his bowmen and footsoldiers. Instead, however, of granting fiefs to the municipalities, he allocated areas to the citizenry and plots to individuals from particular towns. Thus 900 citizens of Teruel and its vicinity received a block of some 5000 hectares between them and there were shares of the *horta*, allocated even before the fall of the city of Valencia, for Jaca, Montpellier, Tortosa, Lérida, Saragossa, Daroca, Tarazona and Tarragona. The greatest grant went to Barcelona: a fifth of the houses inside the city and a sixth of the lands of the *horta*, though the latter was later compounded for ten hamlets and lands in Sagunto. Additionally, particular groups of men who actually fought in the conquest might receive rewards independently of those of the communities from which they came. 73 sailors of Tortosa were settled at Castelo and 64 'Catalan sailors' got a block of city dwellings and lands in Ruzafa. Plots in the *horta* were small, not only because of the scale of rewards the king was seeking to confer, and the social structure he was seeking to contrive, but also because yields were high from the excellent soil. Even the occasional aristocratic beneficiary normally received an allotment little bigger than a yeoman's. The average size was about that of a footsoldier's in the Andalusian *repartimientos* – but this implied a much higher value and could support a more intensively settled population, frequently including slaves, tenants and sharecroppers who in most cases were probably Moors.

The *repartiment* within the city seems comprehensive at first: it is not possible to trace the destiny of every individual building, but of some 2600 available, at least 2500 seem to have been distributed to incoming colonists, if one can set any store by the asseveration that Barcelona's share of 503 buildings constituted a fifth: on the other hand, only 393 expropriated Moorish householders are named in the *repartiment* of Barcelona's quarter. The division of the city looked well on paper, a formal plan designed to balance the interests of different groups in the conquering army and among potential settlers. As a guide to such actual settlement as took place it may be of little or no value. Of the fifteen unequal wards into which the city was traditionally split, seven were assigned to Catalan and seven to Aragonese towns, apparently in rough proportion to the size of their military contribution, with one large quarter reserved for the men of Montpellier. Within and around these wards, suburbs, neighbourhoods, courts, blocks, streets and alleys were awarded to other sectional interests. The Jews and Moorish allies got quarters of their own; if all the grants to Jewish families were taken up, Valencia must have become the home of one of the largest Jewish communities in the mainland dominions of the Crown of Aragon, but what really happened is not clear: the 'terminus Judaeorum' of 95 households, mentioned in the *repartiment*, probably predated the conquest; there are Jewish names among grantees – at least 134 of them – and dispossessed alike. On balance, the conquest seems to have increased the Jewish community's size, which continued to grow under successive kings:

among the beneficiaries of Alfonso III's grants to Jews in the city was Joseph Ravaya's widow (see below, p.136).[12] It was no disgrace to be assigned a suburb, along with such Christian allies as the Navarrerese and Béarnais and even Roussillonais, who were subjects of the crown. Catalan and Aragonese towns whose contributions were too large to be rewarded within the walls also received suburbs: Vich, Huesca. There were particular trades which demanded rewards or encouragement, as the streets assigned to shoemakers and drapers show, and the knightly orders received blocks in prominent corner positions, like banks during a depression: the Templars' block of 50 buildings within the walls may have been larger and more valuable than those assigned to most towns. By the completion of the *repartiment* in 1244, 3191 settler families, not counting the Moors and Jews, had received grants. Christian households may have been smaller than Muslim ones, on average. But this still suggests a respectably populous city, albeit with plenty of space to spare – interstices of the higgledy-piggledy street plan of the old *madina* – in which Moorish artisans and small shopkeepers, to judge from the air of normalcy with which they appear in documents of the next generation, could acquire premises and, presumably, live.[13]

South of the Júcar, the mixture was different again. Here were two types of magnet for colonisation. First, the zone was studded with attractive spots, especially in Denia and Gandía, where colonists had an incentive to settle. In the extreme south, however, and in the parts of northern Murcia which were annexed to the Crown of Aragon between 1244 and 1304, frontier conditions prevailed, which gave the monarchs good cause to settle reliable soldiery: throughout the late middle ages, the great manpower problem of the kingdom of Valencia was that its large Moorish population could not be effectively mobilised in time of war, in part because the Moors' privileges limited their military obligation, in most cases, to the vicinity of their homes, in part because their loyalty (though often reliable when actually tried) was doubtful. Even so, settlement of these areas was thin – a few dots on the map. Montesa was repeatedly threatened with clearance, but when population was really lost after the revolt of 1276–77, the king relented and pleaded for the Moors' return. At Játiva, that great stronghold, 500 grants were made in *repartiment* but it is doubtful how many were taken up. Under the chroniclers' bluster, it is easy to see that Jaime I never really conquered the area at all: he merely benefited from one of those temporary shifts in nominal allegiance at which the Moors of thirteenth-century al-Andalūs were adept. His son had to conquer it anew and in earnest. In the far south, where *repartiments* were densest, the number of grants was always tiny. Only the Guadalest valley, with 125 grants, represents a potentially sizable intrusion; other communities of settlers, to judge from the grants, varied from about 15 to 40 families. Here, more even than in any other part of the kingdom, they were truly 'Christian atolls in a sea of Moors'.[14]

## Colonial Society in Valencia

In a famous passage of his chronicle, the forthright swashbuckler, Ramon Muntaner, delivered an impressive eulogy of the Catalans, the main point of which was to stress the populousness of Catalonia:

And let no one think that Catalonia is a poor province, but I would rather all men knew that in Catalonia there is found, in general, a nobler people than any that I know or have seen in any province, although most of the other people of the world make them seem penurious by comparison. It is to be seen that in Catalonia there are none of those great treasures of money esteemed by certain men, such as there are in other lands; but the common people is the best endowed of all that inhabit the earth and they live better and in better conditions in their dwellings with their wives and children than any people there may be in the world. And, on another point, let me tell you a thing which shall astonish you, albeit if you look into it closely, you shall find it to be true: that of those with a single common language, there is no people so numerous as the Catalans.

And he goes on to compare their numbers favourably with those of the Castilians, English, French, Germans, Italians, Greeks and even Tatars, ending with further excessive protestations of the veracity of his claims.[15] The passage makes a fascinating study of a mentality defiantly confronting and traducing fact. It was not, of course, the numbers of the Catalans that explained their extraordinary dispersion in the Mediterranean world of the late middle ages, much less their prosperity, but precisely the confidence and aggression which Muntaner expresses so well. In reality, the total population of Aragon and Catalonia combined was probably about a quarter of that of Castile; by the time of the colonisation of Valencia, the Catalans were already committed to a demanding programme of settlement in Majorca and to a long process of intensification of settlement on the northern march. The formidable Catalan diaspora of the next century, in the Byzantine empire, Sicily, Sardinia, northern Africa and the Atlantic islands, would be the work of a strategic smattering of purposeful individuals and desperate warbands, not a mass migration. The heartlands of the Crown of Aragon did not provide a sufficient demographic base for the creation of a colonial frontier world in the same sense as that of Castile, not, at least, after the exhausting expansion into 'Catalunya Nova', the Ebro valley, Tortosa and Lérida, in the twelfth century. Behind the Moorish character of the kingdom of Valencia, beyond the royal policy of conservation of the Moorish population, lay inescapable and constricting demographic realities.

There was scope for a perceptible, but not fundamental, adjustment of the balance of population in Valencia in favour of the settler community, at the expense of the natives, in the course of the late thirteenth and early fourteenth centuries. The energy of colonists quickened, the repression of the Moors hardened, with the rhythm of revolt. The rebellion of al-Azraq of 1247–48 was not the unique event it has sometimes been taken for. Unrest was endemic. A long period of revolt always simmering, often overboiling, can be discerned at least until the ruthless general pacification – the 'second reconquest', as Muntaner called it – of Pedro III in the 1270s but al-Azraq's defeat does seem to have been a turning point for many communities. Even in the north, outside the area of al-Azraq's operations, the Moors were expelled from Peñíscola, though there were no colonists with which to replace them. At Sagunto, a new *repartiment* seems to indicate the removal of the last Moors. There were expulsions from Játiva, Alcira and allegedly, Montesa, though chroniclers were prone to exaggerate their scale. In general, terms of surrender grew harsher with each revolt and this may have encouraged Moorish emigration, after 1248 and again after 1276. From 1264 onwards, strenuous efforts were made to attract settlers to the fragile Aragonese conquests in northern Murcia, in Elche, Alicante and Orihuela. Jaime's and Pedro III's new *repartiments* – some 5000 after 1264, a further instalment in Elche in 1272, 1000 in Orihuela early in the next century – must have had some effect. The endeavour was painful, the results unrewarding. At Alfandech, for instance, the community was singled out for despoliation following its part in the revolt of 1248; Jaime allocated it to 250 Christian families including 40 bowmen from Tortosa and 40 men of Montpellier. Yet there was little sign of the fulfilment of this plan until after the war of 1276, when a church was at last built in the valley. In 1297, the original surrender privileges of the Moors were confirmed. At Eslida, Jaime made a virtue of necessity and renewed the local privileges after the uprising; the town had no priest for a generation after the conquests; the only occupation for a Christian was selling wine.

On the other hand, there was, over the same period, a largely undocumented Moorish immigration, especially from the Balearic islands, and possibly a positive balance of trade in Moorish slaves. Ironically, for instance, to attract Moors to settle or resettle, Jaime I was lavish with fiscal concessions, especially in the third quarter of the century, perhaps in partial reaction to the excessive zeal with which expulsions had been carried out in the wake of al-Azraq's revolt.[16] There was no great or sudden growth in the availability of manpower for colonisation: on the contrary, the commitments of the Crown of Aragon grew in the fourteenth century with the attempted colonisation of Sardinia, while the population fell. Throughout the period, the kingdom of Valencia remained a Raj contiguous with the mother country, an imperial province bearing a relationship to the Crown of Aragon comparable, perhaps, in its combination of contiguity and cultural disjunction, with that of Bosnia to Yugoslavia or Turkmenia to the Soviet Union today. Jaime I called himself 'King of Valencia' but to most of his subjects he was probably 'sultan'.[17]

The society of this colonial world was strictly unprecedented, save in Majorca: the realms of Frankish Syria, which most resembled it, adopted quite different institutions, where the native population was subject to a feudal nobility, with tributary relationships and forms of tenure introduced by the conquerors, whereas in Valencia seigneuries were, at least in the thirteenth century, relatively few and small and the Moorish majority was shot through with thin veins of colonists. Yet Valencian society, though distinctive, probably did not feel strange to those who lived in it. The interpenetration of confessional and ethnic groups, and the political subordination of some to others, was a typical form of Mediterranean life, albeit not formerly on this scale, and its usual features – a degree of attempted physical separation, rigid endogamy, the coexistence of separate law codes, religious establishments, languages, diets and dress – prevailed in Valencia and were presided over, as usual, by dual local heirarchies, only remotely overlain with a colonial administrative élite.

For the Moors it was in many ways, as Jaime boasted, like living 'in a land of the Saracens'. Most urban occupations remained open to them: in Valencia we find small shopkeepers and every kind of craftsman, even a painter, though long-range commerce does not seem to have been practised by Muslims on any significant scale. There are a few cases, like that of the Moor who bought a ship in company with Christians and Muslims of Tunis and Bejaïa (Boujie) in 1270, but even before the conquest long-range trade seems to have been a speciality of foreigners. Muslim patricians with capital to spare seem to have preferred to deal in land.[18] For the rural majority, changes in tenure made little practical difference. There were no wholesale enslavements as in the Balearics. The intrusion of 'Christian' understanding of forms of allodial tenure, serfdom and tenancy seem not to have modified the basic reality that most tillers of the soil lived after the conquest, as they had before, by some form of sharecropping. Religious liberty and Islamic law were genuinely respected. The tax burden was based on that of the Almohad period; and the records of tax returns seem to suggest that the Moorish community remained and increased in prosperity. The average expectation of life was greater than among their Christian neighbours.

And yet the atmosphere of discontent persisted; the climate of revolt seemed inescapable. King Jaime professed himself astonished. Justifying his desire for vengeance in the face of al-Azraq's revolt, he claimed to expect better of them, 'keeping them in my land and not turning them out of their homes, that they might live plenteously with us and our dynasty'.[19] The paradox which baffled the king has been explained by a modern historian. Robert I. Burns has seen the shell of continuity penetrated by cultural shock waves; the intrusion, however gradual and slow, of alien colonists and Christian symbols made the Moors 'guests in their own home . . . a remnant in psychological rather than demographic terms'.[20] The higher the social and educational level, the less consoling the continuities and the more traumatic the colonial experience. In Murcia, all the blandishments of Alfonso X could not keep the great Moorish sages from emigrating; in Valencia, too, after a couple of generations of slow extrusion there was little place left for the old élite, above the level of the village *qadi* and *imam*. Al-Azraq, chafing in exile, returned to die a hero's death in the last revolt. Two leading castellans, transformed into rulers of fiefs under the king by the cultural alchemy that made a baron of a *qa'id*, were eventually deported to Africa in a hired Genoese ship. After a long war of nerves in their fief south of the Júcar, the Banū-'Īsā of Játiva at last disappeared from the lists of the king's tenants-in-chief and their castle became the home of a knightly order. Poets, calligraphers and sufis of Valencia would also be found in exile, writing their laments in Morocco, Tunis and Granada. The case of Abū Zayd shows the alternative to flight: transformed into the convert, En Vicent, he was shunted to ever smaller fiefs and an ever more obscure role in society, ordering or suffering his tomb to be inscribed, as an ironical epitaph, with the names of the towns which, after the revolt of 1248, 'he seized from the hands of the infidel'. Yet even this *converso* crusader continued to blend with the predominantly Moorish cultural context, wearing Moorish dress, sitting in Moorish style and proclaiming, with his profession of Christian faith, his descent from companions of the caliph.[21]

The sense of insecurity was greater, the break in the continuity of life more acute, for the settler minority. In Valencia, Burriana and the *horta* they may have been numerous enough to cocoon themselves from disquietening experiences like those of the handful of Christians in Segorbe, whose taxes were collected by Moorish revenue farmers. They aped the ways of home. What bottled peas were to Anglo-India was lard to Christian Valencia. The sort of dislocation and isolation many settlers suffered can induce a sense of distinctiveness, a '*laager* mentality' and a form of aggression against the host culture.[22] Crimes of violence by Christians against Moors and riots, by Christians who must have been greatly outnumbered, against Moorish persons and property in the cities, occurred widely in 1245 and seem on the whole to have increased, despite firm treatment by royal justice, in the rest of the century. This sort of behaviour is common in politically dominant, numerically beleaguered cultures. *Convivencia* – the fabled coexistence of religious communities in medieval Spain – was capable of working, but it worked best in contexts where the intermingling was not too thorough. In Valencia, which really was 'a land of two religions' – in a way that most of Spain was not – it produced no fruitful cultural cross-fertilisation, but a sullen apartheid, sometimes relieved by violent tension, which continued, weakening as the relative size of the Moorish community shrank, until a sudden new increase in Morisco numbers led to a final expulsion, after three and a half centuries in which *convivencia* somehow never quite stuck.

## Southern Murcia

Southern Murcia, despite its distinct political destiny, belonged to the same cultural and, after the conquest, to the same colonial world as Arago-Catalan Valencia. The native Muslims acknowledged the continuity between these two Mediterranean kingdoms in the common name they assigned to them: 'eastern' Spanish Islam, Sharq al-Andalūs. Indeed, Murcia became Castilian only in a modified sense. Although Castilian kings coveted it from the mid-twelfth century, and sought to include it with the kingdom of Granada in the zone assigned, by agreement with other Spanish kings, to Castile's right of conquest, no obvious providential design earmarked it for Castile. In the early 1240s, it seemed more likely to fall to Aragon's lot: Jaime I was on the frontier, whereas St Ferdinand had not yet subdued Jaén. En Ramon Folch, one of the most restless magnates of Aragon, was making up for his absence from the conquest of Valencia by raiding Alicante. This was intended to precipitate a full-scale conquest, like En Blasco d'Alagó's earlier invasion of Valencia. It was not Aragonese respect for Castile's ancient treaty rights that stayed Jaime's hand; rather, it was a successful manoeuvre by Murcia's Banū-Hūd rulers. To forestall Aragonese conquest, they tendered nominal allegiance to Castile. Jaime I seems to have been prepared to accept this solution, though he kept an eye on the chances of smaller territorial gains on the Murcian frontier, perhaps because it provided a degree of cheap security for his southern flank and partly because he feared over-extension of his meagre resources for war.

Jaime traded his acquiescence for a frontier fixed south of Biar in March, 1243. A Castilian 'conquest' or – even less appositely –

'reconquest' of Murcia is often ascribed to the years 1243–45, but, although St Ferdinand's heir, the infante Alfonso, did enter Murcia on 1 May 1243 he did so as the representative of the overlord of the Banū-Hūd and the object of his campaign of the next two years was to quell their dissidents, chiefly at Lorca, Mula and Cartagena, who challenged the validity of Murcia's submission to Castile. He left garrisons in those cities, and the forms of Castilian municipal life. He visited Murcia again during the first six months of 1257 and may have strengthened the Castilian presence, but Murcia was in no sense yet a Castilian colony, rather an independent vassal state or tributary kingdom, as Granada then was.

The widespread repudiation of Castilian overlordship in 1264, however, convinced Alfonso of the need for more active intervention. A seaborne expedition reoccupied Cartagena by force, but by then Castile's resources were fully committed and Alfonso might have been powerless to retrieve, let alone, enhance his position had Jaime I not come to his rescue. It seems curious that the Crown of Aragon, which had so recently disputed the prize with the Castilians, should now conquer Murcia on Castile's behalf. Jaime gave three reasons for his commitment: for God, to save Spain and for the sake of chivalric honour.[23] The second of these reasons implies a political interest: Jaime had a huge and rebellious Moorish subject population to control in Valencia, for whom an independent Moorish Murcia would be an incitement and a source of aid.

Aragonese forces invaded Murcia in 1265 and continued to occupy much of it at intervals until 1304. This was genuinely an Arago-Catalan rather than Castilian conquest. Except at Lorca, Orihuela and Cartagena, Jaime's forces were everywhere instrumental in procuring submission. Surrender terms were generous, as in most of Valencia, ensuring Moorish rights and conserving the Moorish population. In the city of Murcia, the articles of surrender divided the city equally between Moors and incoming settlers. The Banū-Hūd did not go into exile but remained as the feudatories of an initially large territorial principality, like Abū Zayd or the Banū-'Īsā in Valencia, with the title of kings. Because the modalities of the conquest followed the Valencian pattern, so did the configurations of post-conquest society, with a largely undisturbed Muslim majority. The myth of Murcia's 'Castilianisation' is largely based on some ambitious and probably bootless schemes of Alfonso X's to introduce Christian settlers by means of *repartimientos* (as they were called here) similar to those of Andalusia, from 1266–2500 in Murcia, 600 in Lorca, 80 in Mula, and so on. But the success of this project was severely limited, first because of the shortage of settlers which had already been so marked in Andalusia; secondly because many grantees left the Moors as tenants on their lands, as at Cotillas and Alquerías; thirdly because many recipients were foreigners and even Moors; and finally because during the Castilian-Aragonese war and Aragonese occupation of 1298–1304, Alfonso's *repartimientos* were unscrambled and lands and settlers flung back into the crucible. After the Moors, the next largest community in the resultant *mélange* was Catalan. As the chronicle of Alfonso X admitted, 'Because he could not have people from his own land, there came to settle many Catalans from among those who had come to settle in the kingdom of Valencia'. In the city of Murcia, 45 per cent of recorded settlers came from the Crown of Aragon, against only 18 per cent from Castile. Thirty-nine per cent of settlers of the *huerta* were of Aragonese or Catalan provenance. In the fourteenth century, the Christians of Murcia were Catalan-speaking, and Catalan remains influential in the local dialect to this day.[24]

Where Christian settlement was densest, in the city and *huerta* of Murcia and Cartagena, the *repartimientos* were on the same scale as those of Valencia. Ironically, this seems to have been by virtue of the policy of Alfonso X, acting in defiance of Jaime I's advice. 'At no time,' counselled the Aragonese king,

> will Murcia be worth anything unless one thing is done, which we may explain to you thus: what you must do is see to it that there remain in the city one hundred men of worth who know how to give you the welcome which befits you when you go there, and, moreover, that these hundred should live there with ample estates, because with a hundred or two hundred *tahullas* [an average footsoldier's portion in Andalusia would be equivalent to about 52 *tahullas* of Murcia] a man of worth can hardly be said to possess an estate. Let the rest be for artisans and thus you will have a goodly city.

In other words, Jaime was recommending the intrusion of a large aristocratic garrison, maintained by large domains: very much the sort of plan Alfonso himself seems originally to have conceived for Cadiz, and consistent with the traditions of Castilian colonisation, as they had developed in practice, in Andalusia. The contrast with Jaime's own distributions of small plots to large numbers of townsmen in and around Valencia could hardly be more marked. Alfonso's fear, however, was 'that a few men of great wealth might come and buy up many inheritances and that few settlers would take root in the city.' He therefore provided in his own *repartimiento* for a solution much closer to Valencian precedents, distributing nearly six times as much land in *donadíos* as in *heredamientos* (or some five times as much in terms of value), and making grants to 285 horsemen and 1333 foot. This tenurial pattern seems to have survived the political upset caused by Aragonese occupation in 1296–1304.[25]

Outside the isolated patches of settlement, neither the land nor the available resources lent themselves to the promotion of change apart, perhaps, from a slow depopulation of the countryside and informal despoliation and emigration of Moors from the wealthiest area which had been assigned to them, the Arrixaca. Like Jaime I in Valencia, Alfonso X used lavish fiscal concessions to discourage emigration, but the drain of population from the Arrixaca seems to have been marked by the end of the century. By 1264, the commune of Murcia felt free to grant away its Moorish cemetery.[26] For most vacant Moorish land, Christian settlers were simply unavailable. When Pedro Gueralt, for instance, bought Fortuna from its Moorish owners, he risked forfeiture by failing to introduce colonists: the land was taken from him in 1307, and given to the Order of Santiago. Because this made no difference, and because of the protests of the lively municipal corporation of Murcia, the estate was restored to Gueralt before finally being abandoned altogether.

Like St Ferdinand in Extremadura and the frontiers of Andalusia, and Jaime I in northern Valencia, Alfonso alienated large tracts to the knightly orders in marginal and frontier lands; but these proved discouraging of settlement. By the early fourteenth century, it seemed that the most likely potential colonists were Moors – especially émigrés who might be attracted back by lavish privileges. Ferdinand IV wanted them back in the very city of Murcia itself and its environs. He promised them exemption from almost all taxation, regulation by officials of thier own community, under their own laws administered by their own *qādis*, citizenship of Murcia with membership of the commune, immunity from arrest for debt, their own prison, and – almost incredibly – the privilege of having cases brought against them by Christians tried in their own courts.[27] This was hardly a testimony to successful 'Castilianisation'.

As in Valencia, there was a gradual extrusion of the Moorish élite. The Banū-Hūd 'Kings of the Moors of Murcia' saw their patrimony shrink, much as Abū Zayd had done, halved in 1272, then unceremoniously abolished. Before the conquest, their court had briefly been the intellectual and artistic beacon of al-Andalūs. Alfonso X · tried to retain the services of the sages, but their dispersal was inevitable in the face of tempting offers from more congenial, Islamic courtly centres in Granada and north Africa. It was symptomatic of the torpor into which this once distinguished and populous kingdom abruptly declined. It remained a Moorish land, as the records of the expulsion of the Moriscos show, but, compared with Valencia, a benighted and increasingly barren one. When detailed statistics became available in the sixteenth century, Murcia is markedly the most underpopulated province of Spain, despite the vigour – and, indeed, the growth – of the city of Murcia itself.[28] Ferdinand IV evidently exaggerated when he declared in 1305, 'The greater part of the Moors are dead and the remainder fled, wherefore the land is much depopulated and diminished'. But his desperate tone captures the gravity of conquered Murcia's plight.

## An Imperial Formation

It is no exaggeration to call the Iberian conquests of the thirteenth century 'land empires'. The Portuguese crown increased its territory by nearly 70 per cent, that of Castile and León by over 50 per cent. In territorial terms, the Kingdom of Valencia represented a more modest gain for the House of Barcelona, but in terms of wealth and population it was the biggest bonanza of all. Its revenues were thought to exceed those of Catalonia. All the conquests were exploited by imperial masters – Valencia for its ample revenues, the Castilian and Portuguese conquests for the great store of patronage conferred on the king by the acquisition of disposable lands.

In the political management of these empires, Aragonese methods evidently differed markedly from those of Portugal and Castile. For Jaime I, Valencia was genuinely a kingdom apart from his other realms; for the Castilians and Portuguese, the sonorous titles with which they prefaced their writs – kings of Murcia, Seville, Cordova, Jaén, of the 'two Algarves' and so on – were window-dressing, flattering to royal vanity but implying no continuing institutional identity for the subdued kingdoms. Alfonso X maintained the fiction of a 'kingdom of the Moors' in Murcia, but that was only because he fancied himself as an imperial figure and liked to have vassal kings, in imitation of some of his ancestors. Culturally, there was a more profound division between the former lands of Sharq al-Andalūs – Valencia and Murcia – on the one hand and Andalusia, Extremadura and the Alentejo and Algarve on the other.

Looked at collectively, however, the Iberian empires of the thirteenth century were a threshold land between the Atlantic and Mediterranean. They constituted a laboratory of colonial experiment – with an 'Atlantic' type in the west, a 'Mediterranean' type in the east, a Raj in Valencia and Murcia, a 'frontier' in the other lands. The conquest of Andalusia, in particular, facilitated navigation between the two seas and increased the opportunities for Mediterranean communities – especially of Genoese and Catalans – to establish quarters in Atlantic ports; Seville was an invaluable staging post for the increased penetration of the Atlantic by both these peoples in the later thirteenth and fourteenth centuries.

The Iberian peninsula is often thought of as a sort of diving board on which merchants and mariners bounced from the Mediterranean pool – the shallow end, as it were, of the history of European expansion – into the deep end, the Atlantic 'lake'. It is as well to remember that the conquests of the thirteenth century stimulated traffic in the other direction, too, and launched Atlantic seaboard peoples on an increasingly intensive career of penetration of Mediterranean piracy, shipping and trade in the late middle ages. Despite the jejune colonisation of Murcia's hinterland, the acquisition of a stretch of Mediterranean coastline by Castile is, in this context, an event of great importance. Castile became a corridor between the two seas. Murcians were trading in Majorca before 1300. The Cantabrians who colonised Cadiz and the international merchant community of Seville did not lag far behind them. A few Portuguese names occur in the *repartimiento* of Murcia.

Though Portugal had no Mediterranean outlet, the southward extension of the frontier brought the Portuguese incomparably closer to the Mediterranean than ever before; Lisbon, formerly a beleaguered enclave, became, potentially, a great emporium. The route of these peoples who went, so to speak, from the Atlantic to the Mediterranean and back again is at least as important as the 'one-way' course of, say, the Majorcans and Genoese. But to do justice to the colonial formation of the Genoese, which was gained in scattered outposts all over the Mediterranean, we must assign them a chapter of their own and make an excursion as far east as Byzantium and the Black Sea.

# 4. The Genoese Mediterranean

In his mid-sixteenth-century *Cosmographia*, Sebastian Münster chose to illustrate Genoa with a Janus-figure brandishing a large key.[1] A more popular medieval legend derived the city's name from the supposed Trojan founder, Ianos, but Münster's conceit better represents the character of Genoa, as it had come to be defined in the late middle ages: a Janus facing east and west, towards the trade of the Levant, the Black Sea and the Orient, as well as towards the western Mediterranean, the Maghrib and the Iberian peninsula. From the late thirteenth century, that westward gaze was extended ever farther into the Atlantic. Though punningly thought of as the 'door' (*ianua* in Latin) to Italy along the Ligurian coast road, Genoa never controlled access by land around or across the Alps. Her growing maritime power, however, her sketchy but far-flung 'empire' of merchant colonies along the Iberian and Maghribi sea routes to the Atlantic and her hugely disproportionate stake in Mediterranean-Atlantic trade gave her a privileged position in the late medieval opening of the Atlantic. The key Janus holds in Münster's drawing should be thought of as opening the 'door', not of the *via Francigena*, the old Roman road from Gaul to Italy by the coast, but of the Pillars of Hercules.

The Genoese network of centres of production and exchange was an 'empire' only in the feeblest of senses: firstly, because it lacked central direction from the institutions of the state; secondly, because it contained few sovereign colonies; thirdly because of the ambivalence of Genoese traders, whose success owed much to their mutual solidarity but more to their adaptability and gift for distinguishing and serving private or family interests rather than those of their nation. Furthermore, Genoese policy had a 'hermit crab' character, content wherever possible to work within or alongside other states, from Byzantium and the Khanate of the Golden Horde in the east to Portugal and Castile in the west, and accept the protection of foreign princes: the result was a form of covert colonialism or surrogate empire-building, in which, for example, much of the profit from Castilian overseas expansion was drawn, by a flick of the purse strings, into Genoese hands. An examination of each of these features in turn may help to yield some useful notion of the character of Genoese expansion.

## The 'Absence' of the State

Genoa might have launched an overseas empire in much the same period as Venice or Barcelona. Visiting on a preaching tour for the Fifth Crusade in October, 1216, James of Vitry was in no doubt of the city's suitability for such a role:

> For there are powerful and rich men there, practised in arms, and warlike, who have a great store of the finest round ships (*navium*) and galleys, and they have skilled sailors who know their way by sea and have often penetrated Saracen lands in pursuit of gain.

James thought them the people best equipped to succour future crusades and sustain the Christian colonies of the Levant – better, therefore, by implication, than the Venetians, who had acquired their overseas empire by acting as crusaders' shippers and allies.[2] As much as Venice, and more than Barcelona, Genoa was 'wedded' to the sea. Mountains cut her off from any prospect of viable exploitation of her hinterland, more effectively than the lagoons which isolated Venice: Genoa never enjoyed the sort of 'land empire' beyond the Ligurian coast that Venice was later to create lower down the Po valley. Nor did the opportunity exist for the close interdependence with the countryside which, as we saw in Chapter 1, distinguished Barcelona. A maritime vocation was inescapable. 'Genuensis ergo mercator' was already a common proverb in the thirteenth century, and informal Genoese merchant colonies were at least as far-flung as those of Venetians and Catalans: consuls 'per diversas mundi partes' were receiving letters from the commune in the 1220s.

The history of Genoa down to that time, moreover, resembles the imperial prehistory of Venice in suggestive ways. Genoa developed later, after a long piratical apprenticeship, spent preying on the wealth and commerce of the western Mediterranean Muslim world of the tenth and eleventh centuries. By the time of the first crusade, however, in 1095, Genoa's position as a community of long-range traders and shippers, resembling the Venetians, was established. Genoa won similar concessions to those of Venice and Pisa in the first crusader states. The dictates of geography were comparable in Venice and Genoa, points of reception and distribution at the furthest reach of mighty gulfs, where commodities of long-range trade could be disembarked for the centres of dense population and high consumption in northern Italy, or for freighting by the traditional land routes north. Venice stood in a relationship to the mouth of the Po similar to that of Genoa to the mouth of the Rhône. Both cities were therefore committed to aggressive policies towards rival ports on the shores of their gulfs. Genoa fought Pisa, on terms of approximate equality, and outstripped Marseilles, while Venice ground down Zara and Ferrara. Genoa tyrannised her 'Riviera' while Venice struggled to control Illyria and Dalmatia. Both cities sought to establish themselves, in their respective spheres, as staples for the distribution of key products, or to monopolise carriage, resorting to force as necessary. Looking beyond these 'domestic' bases in the 'home waters' of the Adriatic and the Tyrhennian, Venetians and Genoese alike were aware, as were all Italian traders, that the biggest profits of the high middle ages could be made in the Levantine and Byzantine trades, which presented the wealthiest markets and yielded some of the most valuable goods. None baulked at fighting for the sake of these gains.

Thus Genoa looked poised for an imperial destiny. Indeed, towards the end of the twelfth century it seemed as if she might anticipate both Venice and Barcelona and found a seaborne empire. Corsica and Sardinia were the likely victims. Bonifacio, first and last of Genoa's sovereign overseas colonies, on the southern tip of Corsica, commanding the Sardinian strait, was founded in 1195–97. The context was the struggle between Genoa and Pisa – or, rather, between powerful Genoese and Pisan families – to control the production and trade of Corsica, which, exploited for foodstuffs, wine and wool, might have made up for Genoa's lack of a hinterland. More alluring still was Sardinia, which was a major producer of silver and salt. In both islands, the unsettled states of the tribal interiors and the bitterness of warfare along the coasts made exploitation difficult. Bonifacio was the key to a strategy of direct control and of exclusion of the Pisans that was potentially imperial in character. At first, the settlement consisted only of a castle, built to be impregnable, at inescapably vast cost, on a scale which must have demanded collective action rather than mere private adventurism. In the environs of the castle, an agricultural colony was envisaged, of 1200 Genoese and Ligurian settlers, with land grants which they were initially obliged to work themselves, drawn and sustained by lavish fiscal privileges on a rising scale contingent on marriage and procreation. Government was to be strictly controlled from Genoa, represented by a *podestà* in whose appointment the settlers would have no voice.[3]

It may be that, in conception, Bonifacio was never the starting point of an overseas empire at all. In a sense, the settlement was another strong point of the Genoese riviera, an outwork of the 'Genoese main'. In practice, certainly, its military and agrarian characters were alike quickly attenuated. It soon became a commercial outpost, functioning exclusively as an entrepôt; it grew, moreover, increasingly autonomous, so that, while remaining in theory a sovereign colony, it came to resemble a typical Genoese overseas merchant community, linked to the metropolis by little more than volatile sentiments. Bonifacio was called the 'seaward eye' (*oculus marinus*) of Genoa, but the eye was odd. Direct exploitation of the soil rapidly proved to be both impractical, in the narrow and ill-favoured coastal strip around Bonifacio, and unnecessary, as the Corsicans were willing to increase production. The settlers' privileges, which gave them limited immunity from taxes on trade, stimulated participation in commerce, for which the proximity of Sardinia gave them an opportunity. Control from Genoa, even of a colony so close at hand, proved impossible for that war-torn and faction-riven city. For most of the duration of the Pisan wars, which lasted intermittently until 1288, the people of Bonifacio had to be largely self-reliant for defence and were rewarded with progressively more generous statutes which, by the end of the thirteenth century, conceded virtual administrative and judicial independence. Not until the fifteenth century did Genoa have significant jurisdiction in the hinterland. A form of colonial exploitation of the native population was practised, but it was by contract and for payment. The produce of the countryside was bought in; and domestic labour was provided by hired rural serving-girls, with relatively little help from imported slaves.[4]

The history of Bonifacio illustrates the singular character of the Genoese 'empire', from which the state was 'absent' or in which it 'withered away'. Despite the comparisons made with Venice and Barcelona on the eve of their imperial careers, Genoa was different in a crucial respect. It had neither a king, like Barcelona, to adopt a 'policy' of overseas expansion and to command and control it, nor, like Venice, a cohesive élite with a common, transcendent sense of identity which could animate imperial action and make expansion an act of state. Thus the Venetian empire was created virtually at a stroke, in the aftermath of the Fourth Crusade, when Venice took a share of the dismembered Byzantine territory. The Doge of Venice became 'Lord of one quarter and a half of one quarter of the empire of Romania'; homage to any suzerain was explicitly excluded and thenceforth most Venetian acquisitions were thought of as areas of extension of Venetian sovereignty. Most conquests were made by collective effort and ruled by proconsuls from home; unless local dynasts, like the Sanudi in Knaxos, usurped authority for themselves, Venetian colonies remained part of a single, and largely uniform, administrative system. Not even the Venetian quarter of Constantinople was allowed more than once to elect its own *podestà*. By no such central purpose or common method did the Genoese spread abroad. The process was fissiparous, chaotic, variegated. It depended on the divisions within Genoa. Many colonies were found by extruded warlords – Grimaldi in Monaco, where they have endured to this day, Doria in Sardinia, Boccanegra at both ends of the Mediterranean, in Aegean islands and a Castilian port. Others were the work of emulous merchants, competing with their compatriots as much as with foreigners, or escaping from turbulent Genoese faction fighting which at times limited credit and inhibited trade. Others were the domains of rootless condottieri, like the Lesbos of Francesco Gattilusio, or, like Chios, as we shall see, products of Genoa's civil wars. Genoa, in short, was an amoeba, with an almost infinite capacity for self-anatomisation. Her colonies often, like the offspring of amoebae, closely reproduced the image of their parent. But they were only rarely or loosely controlled from home. Genoa never possessed Venice's consistent 'direction from above'. The constitution was too often in flux. The Genoese were never too fussy to submit to despots or foreign lords, whom Venetians abhorred with credal passion; yet the rule of one system – much less of one man – rarely lasted for long.

## The Sovereign Colonies

All expatriate merchant quarters in the middle ages enjoyed protected status and many had some measure of self-regulation or even privileges of extraterritoriality, but the Genoese founded only few and late colonies of a fully sovereign kind on the Venetian model. The exceptions were: the large and effectively self-governing Genoese colony of Pera, abutting Constantinople across the Golden Horn; Kaffa and its dependencies on the northern shore of the Black Sea, in what the Genoese called 'the empire of Gazzaria' – the land of the Khazars; and Chios, Genoa's mastic yielding island, commanding the Black Sea approaches and providing an offshore emporium for the trade of Asia Minor. A very short-lived fourth imperial domain was Cyprus, acquired in the late fourteenth century in approximate imitation of Chios.

All came to Genoese hands as an indirect result, and perhaps in conscious mimicry, of the eastern Mediterranean empire of Venice. Venetian hegemony damaged Genoese trade, without destroying it. When, in the mid-thirteenth century, that hegemony slackened and the Latin Empire, with whose fortunes it was bound, first tottered and then, in 1261, finally fell, Genoa's obvious interest lay in preventing any possibility of a recurrence. The means of doing so – strong, permanent colonies directly dependent on Genoa and invulnerable to the mutable whims and changing identities of local rulers – were adopted only gradually and with some reluctance. Genoa did not 'succeed' Venice in the east, and, in a sense, did not seek to. But on a smaller scale, the three main Genoese colonies did compose an 'empire' which, for all that has been said, was in some ways reminiscent of Venice's.

The first Genoese quarter in Byzantium had been founded early in the second half of the twelfth century, but not until 1202 was the commune of Genoa satisfied with its site, coherence and defensibility. The disaster of the Fourth Crusade brought the exclusion of the Genoese, to the profit of the Venetians, within two years. Thereafter, though Genoese traders continued to deal at Constantinople, there seems to have been no Genoese quarter for as long as the Venetians and their allies occupied the city. A permanent Genoese installation, located at Pera, started anew only in the late 1260s. The establishment at Kaffa dates from about the same time. Certainly, the context was the same: Byzantine revanche, overthrowing the

Latin Empire, breaking the Venetian monopoly, selectively favouring Genoa and, in this instance, admitting and encouraging the Genoese in the Black Sea. Similarly, in 1267, the alum centre of Phocaea became, by grant of the Byzantine Empire, the Zaccaria family's fief, extended to Chios in 1304.

In all these cases, however, it took a long time for the Genoese colonies to prise themselves from the authority of the locally dominant powers – Byzantium in the cases of Pera and Chios-Phocaea, the Mongols in the case of Kaffa. Pera and Kaffa were commercial 'conquests'. Once they had made themselves indispensable, the Genoese wrung or attracted concessions or else quietly usurped autonomy. The process could be painful. For example, by the time the major surviving series of notarial records begins in the 1280s, Kaffa seems to have established de facto direct dependence on Genoa; but, if its status was assured, its survival was precarious. Mongol attacks forced the abandonment of the town in 1307–8. Only in their absence did the Genoese become fully appreciated by the mainland Khans. Allowed to return, and stimulated to spread to other Black Sea ports, to the Sea of Azov and along the Central Asian trade routes, the Genoese found their perseverance rewarded. Relations with the Mongols broke down in war again in the 1340s. Thereafter, for as long as the Mongols' power lasted, they limited their hostility to periodic encouragement of Genoa's Venetian rivals.

Meanwhile, Pera underwent a similar – indeed, more spectacular – stabilisation and growth. Its commune behaved from the mid-1320s like a traditional Mediterranean city-state in its own right, loosely federated with Genoa and deferential to Byzantium, but self-consciously distinct from both. By the mid-fourteenth century, Byzantine emperors seem to have abandoned effective authority in Pera. From Chios, meanwhile, the Zaccaria were expelled in 1329, victims of their own feuds, the Chians' hatred and Byzantine reconquest. But the years of Zaccaria rule had created an indelible interest in Chios among the Genoese. Despite the distractions of civil strife and war with Aragon, intrigue at Genoa for the recovery of Chios did not cease, and at least two ill-starred expeditions were organised, until an opportunistic conquest was at last successfully mounted in 1346. Characteristically, this was not a state expedition, but the private enterprise of a company of freelance venturers. Volunteers for a sortie against the Monaco of the Grimaldi, cheated of their expectations, were diverted eastwards, in the pay of the state, for the defence of Kaffa. Apparently, they alighted by accident on Chios as an alternative outlet for their energies, perhaps chiefly to prevent it from falling into Venetian hands. Or it may be that the Monegasque expedition (or, at least, the Kaffan) was a feint to conceal the conquerors' real intentions. After a conquest of less than four months' duration, under the command of the resourceful and far-sighted Simone Vignoso, the invaders falteringly established control: only in February, 1347, did they agree on the effective division of power between themselves and the commune of Genoa, whose sovereignty they acknowledged; between 1347 and 1349, local and Byzantine forces drove them out of Phocaea; and for a time in the mid-1350s they had to pay tribute to Byzantium. But within a few years, Chios was pacified and governed as a Genoese overseas territory, similar to Venetian Crete, or the Arago-Catalan Balearics.

Institutions varied between the three great focal points of Genoa's empire. At Pera a *podestà* and at Kaffa a consul were appointed annually to represent the commune of Genoa at the head of the government. But, increasingly in the fourteenth century, real power resided with the local notables, who dominated the communal assemblies and composed the consul's or *podestà*'s councils. In Chios, disposal of a complex structure of offices was divided, equally in theory, between the Genoese state and the private transferable-share company, known as the Maona di Chio, which had effected the conquest and possessed all rights of usufruct. The *podestà* was appointed by Genoa, his vicar by the Maona, and so on. In practice, however, the Maona's power was preponderant, because Chios represented a large area by the standards of Genoese colonies and the Maona was responsible for local government and defence.[5]

In some ways, it was less their institutional superstructure than the tone of life that made these colonies Genoese in more than provenance. That tone was established by non-institutional means: the affectionate recollection of Genoa, the street plans and street names, the building styles, the family ties that bound the settlers to home, the language and the transplanted social substructures – guilds, cults, confraternities, commercial companies. The biggest contribution – in a sense, it was the defining characteristic of Genoa's sovereign colonies – was made by the supremacy of

Genoese law, which each successive *podestà* or consul swore, on taking office, to uphold. Its strength was its flexibility. It suited the cosmopolitan merchant communities which flourished alongside the Genoese in Genoese territories; it accommodated both the small western minorities – Italian and Catalan – and the big oriental ethnic groups, the Greeks, Armenians and Jews. All were comprehended within the 'tutelage' of a system of law administered locally but formulated in the metropolis of the Ligurian Sea; this was a large part of the attraction of Genoa and her colonies to foreign immigrants and hence of her success.[6]

It took even longer to populate the colonies with permanent settlers than to define their institutions. Thirteenth-century Pera and Kaffa had no permanent residents from among the great families of Genoa, and few Latin womenfolk. Not yet settled communities, the towns were disembodied *fondaci*, points of trade or transit, and their 'inhabitants' were birds of passage. Peaceful conditions in the early fourteenth century transformed Pera into a self-conscious commune, in which representatives of the Embriaco, Cattaneo, Doria and Lercari families, for instance, set up their principal homes. Not until the second half of the fourteenth century did anything of the sort happen in Kaffa or Chios. The latter was anyway a special case, because the island's Latin aristocracy was formed by the successors, by inheritance or purchase, of the conquerors: they formed the Maona, and took the distinguishing name of Giustiniani.

The basis of successful colonisation, however, was in all cases the same: commercial and cosmopolitan. In none of the three colonies was exploitable land available on a large scale: Pera was a suburb of Constantinople, Genoese 'Gazzaria' a chain of towns along a cramped coastal strand; even in Chios, most of the land was confirmed by treaty in the hands of its Greek owners, though Simone Vignoso granted some confiscated estates of vineyards and olive groves to farmer colonists. Nowhere could the experiment of Bonifacio be repeated, even had it been wished.

A more practical model was land-starved Genoa itself. Owing to the dearth of land, settlers were necessarily merchants, artisans and fighting men. A strong garrison was a priority everywhere: one of Simone Vignoso's first demands of the Greeks of Chios was for 200 houses for the billets. Once a colony began to grow, craftsmen and traders comprised most of the Genoese population. In Chios, for instance, the majority worked or dealt in cloths, hides, dyes, spices and drugs: the main trade, in mastic, was reserved to the Maona. The Latin population was overwhelmingly Ligurian and Genoese: 84 or 85 per cent in all 3 colonies by the most authoritative count. But they were infiltrated by Greeks, Armenians and Jews, following in many cases similar occupations to those of prominent Genoese, and interpenetrated – often, in the Greek case, intermarried – with the Genoese at every social level. What distinguished the Genoese from these other members of the international corps of merchants were religion, language and, above all, the possession of formal political power. As a ruling élite, they were extraordinarily secure in view of their numbers – tiny even in relation to their own domestic slaves from northern and central Asia and the Balkans. Though they tended to occupy the citadels and commercial quarters of the colonies, they were surrounded by aliens: in the fifteenth century, two-thirds of the free population of Genoese Gazzaria were Armenian; the Genoese and Lugurians numbered 2000 out of a total of some 70 000 and there were 3 official languages.[7]

Except in their paucity of numbers and their receptivity to foreigners, these sovereign Genoese colonies were atypical. Most Genoese in the eastern Mediterranean and the near east probably operated outside their confines, as individuals or in much smaller communities, accepting foreign rule. It is time to turn to the typical features of the Genoese diaspora, and to follow them westwards towards the Atlantic.

### 'Ambivalence': Typical Genoese Colonisation and Trade

What turned the Genoese dispersal around the Mediterranean into a 'network', if not an 'empire', was not the state, but a sense – sometimes a muted sense – of national solidarity, supplemented and often exceeded by family ties. In differing degrees, this was characteristic of Mediterranean trading communities generally. The outstanding example is formed by the Jews, who had no state of their own but passed with ease, from port to port or market to market, among their coreligionists, and made their investments on the recommendations of brothers or cousins (see p.136). Even in Venice, where commercial law was highly sophisticated by the thirteenth century and where people unrelated, and even unknown, to each other could form a mutual society or take part together in a share venture, most successful trading enterprises had a family basis. Genoese versatility did not exclude nostalgia for the metropolis. If the traders were successful in adapting to every economic environment and every political climate, the obverse of their ambivalence was an abiding sense of being Genoese and an enduring capacity to exploit Genoese connections. The street names of fourteenth-century Kaffa recalled those of Genoa. The poet known as the Anonymous of Genoa linked the adaptability of his fellow countrymen ('destexi', he called them – literally, dexterous, which I translate below as 'sure-footed') with their ability to replicate the feel of home:

> So many are the Genoese
> And so sure-footed everywhere,
> They go to any place they please
> And re-create their city there.[8]

This nostalgia may have been the basis of expatriates' national fellow feeling. They were capable of displaying a welcome for a fellow citizen. Columbus was the best-known beneficiary of it, first saved by Genoese in Lisbon, after his shipwreck in 1476, then 'made' by the Genoese of Seville, who deployed influence at court on his behalf and raised money for his enterprises (see p.206). But commercial considerations outweighed the obligations of common provenance: the cutthroat competition of the Centurione and Lomellini, based respectively in Castile and Portugal, for a stake in the gold trade from the 1440s, is a case in point.[9] Only links of consanguinity or affinity were thick enough to provide a reliable bond.

The same surnames crop up repeatedly all over the Genoese world, from the Black Sea in the thirteenth century to the Caribbean in the sixteenth. The Cattaneo, who were among the first great families to sprout a branch in Kaffa and the earliest meddlers in Mytilene, were also the first to open a 'branch' in Santo Domingo. Transferable share-companies, like the Maono di Chio, for all their importance, were rarer than the family firm, and even the Maona adopted for its members a common surname and some of the formal characteristics of a family. Every late medieval

Genoese business which has been studied in detail has turned out to be, in some sense, a family business.[10] Even for the most closely knit families, to operate – indeed, to survive – amid competing allegiances in widely differing milieus required adaptability, and adaptability implied ambivalence. Most of the leading members of the Rivarolo clan in the late-fifteenth century were naturalised Castilians, but they never gave up their house in Genoa. Their debtor, Columbus, never forgot that he was Genoese and charged his heirs in his will to maintain a house in Genoa for ever. Yet he was indignant when his loyalty to Castile was impugned 'as a poor foreigner'.[11] In the fourteenth century, Benedetto Zaccaria could serve successively Castile, France and Byzantium and the Malocello Portugal and France.

Such ambidextrous talents were never, perhaps, in greater demand than in Muslim lands. Two important and accessible examples are provided by Málaga and Tunis. Málaga was among the most remunerative of Genoa's colonial entrepôts in the fourteenth and early-fifteenth centuries. Of perhaps 300 Genoese trading houses with agencies in Iberia, at least 20 were represented by permanent residents in Málaga in the mid-fifteenth century, when the port's trade was already in decline. In the previous century, the size of Málaga's Genoese community may have equalled those of Seville and Cadiz and certainly exceeded those of Lisbon and Valencia. Málaga's importance was threefold: it was a harbour of unsurpassed excellence on the sea route from the Mediterranean to the Atlantic; only Cadiz could rival it, among peninsular ports, for size and depth and security of approach. But Cadiz had a relatively unproductive hinterland, and here lay Málaga's second advantage. The Kingdom of Granada, which, with her sister port of Almería, Málaga served, was an alternative spicerie or garden of exotic supplies for the Genoese, whose access to the eastern spice trade was limited or rendered costly by the Venetians.

Genoa's traders had been attracted eastwards by spices in the twelfth and thirteen centuries. In the course of the fourteenth century, however, they switched the greater part of their effort (enormously the greater part in bulk terms and perhaps a little over 50 per cent in value terms) to the local products of the northeast Mediterranean basin, bulkier of carriage but dependable of supply: above all, the mastic of Chios, the alum of Phocaea, the grain of Cyprus and of the Danube and Black Sea basins, Danubian and other northern forest products and the slaves of the Black Sea. Spices, properly understood, tended to be channelled through Beirut and Alexandria, where the Venetians were supreme. The Genoese galleys went out of commission and were replaced – almost entirely by the end of the fourteenth century – by bulk-carrying round ships. In roughly the same period, Chinese silks, which had been a valuable perquisite of the trade of Genoese Romania in the early-fourteenth century, grew rare as a result of the rupture of the 'Mongol Road' (see p.121).

As if to remedy these deficiencies, until, under Genoese auspices, Sicily and the Algarve began to yield commercial amounts of superior sugar and silk, Genoa found a silk and sugar-land near home, at the western end of the Mediterranean, in Granada. Though a Levantine rather than a fully 'oriental' spice, sugar was classified, with pepper, cinnamon, nutmeg, mace and cloves, as an exotic condiment. Saffron and dried and preserved fruits were other Granadine products in much the same category. Granada's sugar industry had its own port at Almería, where most of the Genoese of Málaga maintained agents.

Finally, as well as being, as it were, a displaced oriental land, Málaga enjoyed privileged access to the Islamic Maghrib and therefore to Saharan gold – always, as we shall see in the next chapter, the magnet and motor of European interest in Africa and the African Atlantic in the late middle ages. In the fifteenth century, Málaga normally occupied third or fourth place among the Iberian ports which made direct shipments of Maghribi gold to Genoa. Seville, Cadiz and Valencia were the other entrepôts. But these statistics may obscure Málaga's primordial importance. The gold trade, once seaborne, travelled by complex routes. The Genoese seem to have found it convenient to buy their gold in Castile and Valencia, where the silver price was relatively low. And while much of that gold, especially in Valencia, was the result of direct trade with Barbary, one of Castile's major sources was Granadine tribute, which must have passed virtually under the eyes of the Genoese of Málaga on its way to the hands of their brothers, cousins, partners and bosses in Seville.[12]

While the commercial activities of the Genoese of Málaga are well known, glimpses of their intimate lives are rare. Dramatic evidence of the insecurity of life is presented by the *Liber*

*Damnificatorum* of 1452, which itemises the losses, indemnified by
the Genoese state, incurred when the entire community was
victimised, and its property confiscated, as a reprisal for the illegal
enslavement of Muslims by a Genoese sea captain in Syria.[13] This
sort of incident seems to have been rare and might have occurred,
with a different pretext, as much in a Christian as in a Muslim
country. But opportunities for giving offence were legion in Islamic
lands, and a certain diplomatic delicacy, especially on the part of
the consul of the community, was essential for survival. This is
brought out in a precious series of notarial records from Tunis,
covering roughly the first six months of 1289. The commercial
importance of Tunis is explained in the next chapter (see p.141)
but the value of the 133 surviving documents of the notary Pietro
Batifoglio lies in their chronicle, day by day and, on some days,
hour by hour, of the life of the Genoese merchant community in
one of the major Muslim ports of the west.[14]

First, they evoke the huge scale of the Genoese operation in
Tunis. Even in this tiny, fragmentary survival, allusions are made
to the work of eighteen Genoese notaries, their *acta* distributed over
only seven years. There seem regularly to have been at least three
notaries at work among the community at a time: this must imply a
colony of several hundred persons. It was not only a large
community but, by the standards of Christian colonies in Maghribi
ports, a settled one. The sons of resident or formerly resident
fathers were often in business there. Some merchants had established
households with womenfolk of their own. Waldo di Budi's was a
temporary arrangement: his form of marriage to a former slave girl
was annulled on grounds of her previous marriage in her homeland.
But others were more permanent; a Genoese woman living in the
Marseillais quarter – presumably as a result of a marriage –
claimed burial in the Genoese cemetery; Jacobina de Savignano
stayed on after her husband's death and married again.

It was a society with established rituals and a well-defined élite.
Most business was conducted in 'the old warehouse (*fondacus*) of the
Genoese', where the first merchant quarter had been founded in
the twelfth century and which it had now far outgrown. But
particularly solemn acts might be recorded in the Genoese church
or major disputes with the local authorities in the amir's palace.
Occasionally an urgent matter connected with an arriving or
departing ship might be transacted in the open on the quayside. A

more popular venue was the wine warehouse, natural rendez-vous of Latin expatriates in a Muslim state. Everything worthy of report – whether a purchase on credit, the acknowledgement or liquidation of a debt, the formation of a company, the registration of a shipping contract, the purchase or sale of a house, the making of a will, a divorce or a deposition of paternity, a dispute or demand addressed to the Muslim authorities, the conferment of a power of attorney, the attainment of majority – all passed before the notary to be inscribed and witnessed with prolix formulae. The triad of notables, the consul, the priest and the leading merchant, were often at the notary's elbow. Tealdo, the priest, was a universal helpmeet, witness or proxy in nearly twenty per cent of recorded transactions, frequent donee of powers of attorney or commissions as agent in particular matters. Cibo da Cibo and his numerous family were the most important – in terms of the amount of business transacted – of Pietro Batifoglio's clients and therefore, presumably, of the Genoese merchants of Tunis, challenged only by the Embriaco, Santo Ambrosio, Sigenbaldo and Usodimare families: they had a share in no fewer than 50 of the 133 recorded transactions. But the acknowledged leader of the community was the consul, Balianno Embronio. The fact that he was more sought after as a witness even than the priest reflects his presiding 'godfatherly' role. His practical importance lay in his duty of representing the common interests of the community to the amir.

This was no easy job. In the brief spell covered by these records, Embronio had twice to complain about breaches of Genoese-Hafsid treaties. He resisted attempts to interfere with the established procedures for purchasing and selling wine by putting up the tax or 'rent' on the warehouse; he locked the premises and gave the key to Tealdo until the status quo should be restored. He upbraided customs officials for exceeding their powers and was obliged to denounce the amir's refusal to give him audience twice a month in accordance with agreed practice. Strained relations overspilled into violence on 3 May 1289. Two days previously, the consul had gone to the amir's palace to claim the revenue owed to Genoa on the sale of oil by some Genoese merchants: part of the tax had to be remitted to the Genoese state and it seems that the merchants concerned withheld it for that purpose. The Tunisian authorities refused to yield their right to the amount in question, except to the *podestà* of Genoa in person, and sent a force armed with stones and clubs to impound the oil against full payment of the tax. According to the notary's account, the Tunisians threatened to act 'by force and even contrary to law': presumably, he was putting these words into their mouths, but the tone of shock is genuine enough. By the hour of Vespers, the siege was over. The prudent consul had capitulated, and the merchants agreed to foot most of the bill, referring the consul 'to the court of Tunis or the purchasers of the oil' for the recovery of the disputed share of the tax.

The local authorities were not the only source of threats. Pisan outrages against Genoa could be as destructive at Tunis as at Constantinople. Claims were still outstanding, after 7 years, for compensation for a riot in 1282, in which Genoese property worth over 20 000 ducats, including ships and their entire cargoes, was destroyed by fire. Generally, however, in Batifoglio's records, Genoese relations with other Christian merchants seem relaxed. The notary substituted, on occasion, for a Catalan colleague, or recorded business involving Genoese partners in the Marseillais or Sicilian quarters. Amicable partnerships with members of these and other communities – Pisan, Florentine, Venetian, Majorcan – were common.

The colonies of Málaga and Tunis lay on the routes that led to the Atlantic: Málaga's deep-water harbour on the way north; Tunis, terminus of Barbary trades, on the route south. But for Genoa's future in Atlantic trades, the most important of her merchant settlements were those of Castile, and particularly of Andalusia. Technical and geographical reasons made Cadiz and Seville and their regions Genoese merchants' most substantial bases in Spain. The technical reasons were a matter of ships and cargoes. As early as 1216, James of Vitry had praised Genoa's big round ships, which could sail in winter and 'keep food and water fresh' – that is, exhaust shipboard supplies at a slower rate than the relatively overmanned galleys. Thus the Genoese had large sailing vessels as well as galleys available to make the Atlantic run from its earliest days in the late-thirteenth century. Commercial galleys disappeared from Genoa in the next hundred years.[15] It can probably be safely assumed that the Atlantic routes, where conditions least favoured the galley, were the first to be converted to the round ships. The use of round vessels, however, was not solely or even chiefly for the convenience of the navigators: Venetians sailed regularly to England and Flanders in galleys; when the Atlantic commerce of Florence started in the fifteenth century, it was carried exclusively by galleys which demonstrated their worthiness for the task and continued to do so until the time of the Armada. The Genoese preference for more economical shipping was a result of their reliance on relatively low-value bulk commerce. The consequence was that a short run from the mouth of the Mediterranean to the English Channel was possible and, to some extent, vital, since by exploiting the seagoing properties of round ships to reduce the number of calls at ports en route and shorten the length of the voyage, merchants could ensure an improved return. Nor was there much point in hawking small quantities of the goods the Genoese carried; they were better held over for the big markets of the north, where the holds could be restocked with wool and cloth. Finally, the Genoese ships required spacious deep-water ports, like those of Cadiz and the mouth of the Guadalquivir. It became normal for Genoese northbound ships to bypass Portugal, the Cantabrian and Atlantic France altogether.

Andalusia was thus a 'frontier' land of Genoa as well as of Castile. The colonisation which had begun before the Castilian conquest grew exponentially in the fourteenth century, once Genoa's northern commerce was established, and again in the fifteenth when opportunities in the east diminished. An idea of the scale and character of the colonies can be gained from a look at the region of Cadiz and Jeréz in the fifteenth century.[16] First, the growing pace of Genoese settlement and its changing, increasingly mercantile character are apparent. The first Genoese to settle in Jeréz, in the thirteenth century, for instance, were Benedetto Zaccaria, the naval commander, and Gasparo di Spinola, a retired ambassador. Zaccaria seems personally to have forsaken commerce during his residence in Castile and it was common for early Genoese colonists, especially in centres, like Jeréz and Cordova, in the hinterlands of the great ports, to marry into the local aristocracy and become rentiers rather than traders. In Seville and Cadiz the process was reversed and Genoese influence helped to convert the aristocracy to commerce in more than two centuries of increasing infiltration and intermarriage. By the time of the *nouvelle vague* of Genoese immigrants of the late-fifteenth century, new settlement was exclusively mercantile and artisan. By the sixteenth century, three-quarters of the nobility of Seville had Genoese surnames; and Jacopo Adorno was there to defend for them the idea of the compatibility of commerce and nobility. As the pace of immigration grew, so did the incidence of fixed settlement. Most Genoese newcomers of the fifteenth century tended to become 'citizens' (*vecinos*) rather than 'transients' (*estantes*): this presaged the relative immobility of the Genoese community of Castile in the sixteenth century, when they took part in Castilian empire building vicariously, from their fixed centres, by way of banking and investment, rather than continuing to settle new frontiers.

At the same time, these increasingly settled communities were, in the fifteenth century, points of support for further Genoese colonisation to the westward in Portugal, Africa and, above all, the Atlantic islands. Family homes established in Andalusia were ports of call for relatives from Genoa en route for or from the west. After taking up service with Portugal, for instance, in the exploration of the west coast of Africa, Antonio di Usodimare was sheltered by his brother, Francesco, in Cadiz in 1462. The Franchi di Luzzardo sent sons on to Tenerife and Barbary, the Ascanio to Gran Canaria, the Nigro or Negrone to Portugal and Madeira. Nothing better illustrates the elastic properties of the Genoese family as an instrument of colonisation than this ability to maintain mobility while cultivating roots.

Finally, the Genoese of Andalusia demonstrated a typical Janus-like versatility. They were able to camouflage themselves in local society by intermarriage, formal naturalisation, bilingualism, service to the community and the crown, and even modification of the orthography of their names; and, at the same time, to conserve, in the big centres like Seville and Cadiz, 'another Genoa' of their own. Apart from their exogamous habits, their record in office-holding is the best indicator of their success in local 'acceptance worlds'. Francesco da Rivarolo, for instance, and Francesco Pinelli were councillors of Seville and close confidantes of the crown; Francesco Adorno sat on the town council of Jeréz and Gianbatista di Ascanio and Christoforo Maruffo of Cadiz. At a humbler level, Agostino Asilio was treasurer of his parish in Puerto de Santa María. Yet these positions of confidence in Castilian society were generally won without sacrifice of Genoese identity, especially in Seville and Cadiz, where the Genoese colonies were defined by their ancient privileges and their proper consulates and quays. It was common to have a home in Genoa – Rivarolo's was cited as evidence of the invalidity of his naturalisation – perhaps as a bolt hole; even fabled

Genoese thrift served this sort of versatility: notarial records of Cadiz show them spending sparingly, outside trade, save on jewels, rugs and small, movable luxuries. By the 1480s, there was a particular Genoese confraternity in Cadiz, with its own chapel, dedicated to St Mary and St George, in the cathedral, and there may have been similar organisations elsewhere. The confraternity of the Name of Jesus in Jeréz, for instance, had been founded by Genoese tailors. In Seville, the Genoese 'nation' continued into the sixteenth century the custom of making collective addresses to the crown. The effects of ambivalence were most vividly expressed by Columbus: 'Sirs,' he wrote to the directors of the Genoese state bank of San Giorgio, 'although my body wanders here, my heart is continually in Genoa.' They may also have enhanced the sensibilities shown by the Castilian verses of one of the leading poets of fifteenth-century Seville, known as Francisco Imperial, and always described as 'native of Genoa, dweller in the very noble city of Seville'. He loved his adoptive city, 'choicest in the kingdom', praised the beauty of its women and the justice of its kings, exhorted and admonished it, in an explicitly Dantesque vision, to purge itself of heresy and vice; but he never forgot his native city, either, and was mindful to the end of Ianos of Troy.[17]

Their ambivalence protected the Genoese in times of tension, even of war, between their republic and the states in which they settled or with which they traded. One effect of Venice's state-directed history of empire building was that much of the empire was the work of war. This method had its perils. Repeatedly, from the Ferrara war of the early-fourteenth century to that of the League of Cambrai in the early-sixteenth, the entire structure of Venice's empire was threatened by the uncertain outcome of wars of aggrandisement. The Genoese, less successful warriors, on the whole, than the Venetians, could not have done it. Genoese wars were waged – it is probably fair to say – never for dominion but only for the protection or extension of Genoese trade. Genoese merchants typically had a gift for tolerating the rule and even absorbing the aggression of other states.

No case illustrates this more strikingly than the pattern of Genoese trade with the Crown of Aragon in the period covered by this book. The relations of the two states were characterised by a growing – at last proverbial – enmity and frequent war. The survival, even faltering growth, of trade was based on the favoured position in the dominions of the House of Barcelona which the Genoese had contrived in the twelfth and early-thirteenth centuries: as we shall see, this had made Genoese and Catalan commerce inextricably interpenetrated (see p.139). Divisions, moreover, among the Arago-Catalan kingdoms generally left the Genoese with freedom to operate somewhere within the Catalan world. Finally, the rapid syncopations of war and truce meant that breaks in continuity never lasted for long. But underlying all these causes of continued trade, was the adaptability of Genoese traders, whom no difficulty or discrimination could deter.

The trenchant measures of Alfonso IV, for instance, seem to have left them unscathed. From 1329, the Genoese were subject to swingeing tolls. Whereas the Provençals paid four per cent on imports and three per cent on exports, the figures for the Genoese were eight and four per cent respectively. At intervals from 1332, they were banned from Catalan ports altogether, with no visible effects. Indeed, there is every indication that trade grew in the warlike conditions of the fourteenth century, and that nominal bans were evaded or unenforced. Even in the heat of the Sardinian wars, when each state's shipping was the legitimate prey of the other's corsairs, Catalan vessels were welcomed in Bonifacio and those of Genoese merchants in Sassari and Cagliari. The frequency with which truces were proclaimed, especially from 1360, bears witness to the importance for both communities of the survival of trade. The biggest growth element was probably the wool and dyestuffs trade between Barcelona and Genoa, but raisins, rice, wax, salt, anchovies and fish generally were also important products carried by the Catalans to Genoa. Ironically, even these were exceeded by goods which, in time of war, were officially prohibited: fats used as oil sources in shipping, gluestuffs and pitch. The only effect of prohibitive regulations seems to have been the disappearance of the arms trade from the records: but even this may have continued clandestinely. For most of the fourteenth century, the balance of trade favoured the Catalans and between 1376 and 1454 the Genoese deficit grew almost continuously; but this was not necessarily to Genoa's net disadvantage. The Catalans supplied raw materials which Genoese industry turned into profitable products marketable elsewhere. Each community needed the other.[18] The same overall cooperation with Catalans marked Genoa's Majorcan and Barbary commerce (see pp.138–40).

## The Transmission of Genoese Influence

Although the biggest concentrations of Genoese merchant-settlers in the eastern Mediterranean were in the three sovereign colonies of Gazzaria, Pera and Chios, individuals, agents and 'family businesses' were scattered widely in the Aegean and in Levantine and Egyptian ports – to say nothing of the lower Danube (where the Genoese were particularly active), the island despotates, the Ottoman Empire, the shores of the Caspian, Persia (especially Tabriz) and, for as long as the China road stayed open, eastwards along the silk routes as far as Beijing. It would therefore be imprudent to suppose that Genoa's eastern Mediterranean colonial experience was essentially different from that of the Atlantic, or necessarily uninfluential further west. If we make an exception of the sovereign colonies, which were unsual even in the east, there is no distinction of type to be made between Genoese colonies in all spheres of expansion: everywhere, it was the non-sovereign merchant quarter, imbedded in indigenous society and dependent on foreign protection, which prevailed.

Moreover, there was continuity of personnel: most of the big Genoese trading families spread their business and their agents over huge segments of the Genoese world, often encompassing the whole length of the seaborne trade routes from the Black Sea to Bruges. The Zaccaria, for instance, were one of the first Genoese businesses to operate on a large scale in England. They were drawn by the alum trade, which they already dominated at its other great terminus, in the Byzantine empire and particularly at Phocaea. The fact that alum was an important primary commodity of the cloth industry, for which England was a major supplier of wool, illustrates the importance of divers sources of supply, which might often be widely separated, and the names of Zaccaria, Lomellini, Vivaldi, Pinelli, Lercari, Cattaneo, Doria, Usodimare, Malocello, Cibo – to take only the most familiar in the regions traversed by this book – are to be found in all of them.

All the industries served by Genoese trade implied geographical specialisation, which in turn implied long-range commerce. Textiles depended on concentrating wools and dyestuffs in industrial centres; 'food processing' on the meeting of fresh foodstuffs with salt. The gold industry of Genoa itself, which turned raw gold into coins, leaf and thread, relied on supplies of African gold to Italian technicians;

shipbuilding demanded a similar marriage of raw materials with technical expertise, and a matching of wood, iron, sailcloth and pitch.

Part of the stimulus, therefore, for Genoese penetration of the Atlantic derived from the commercial needs and opportunities generated by Genoa's presence in the eastern Mediterranean. And when Genoese colonial activity began in earnest in the Atlantic archipelagoes, the eastern Mediterranean supplied vital economic models and new commodities, which would transform the islands' ecologies and form the basis of the early Atlantic economies. These powerful products were sugar and the Malvasia grape. Sugar attracted Genoese attention with a new intensity in the fourteenth century in Cyprus (although Genoa exploited Cyprus chiefly for grain)[19] because of the extensive Venetian-owned sugar estates in the south of the island. Uniquely among the exotic condiments favoured by palates in Latin Christendom, sugar could be grown in the Mediterranean. It was technically possible for merchants to control the sources of supply themselves instead of playing the 'middle man' role to which they were accustomed in the oriental spice trade: this was the basis of the Venetian experiments in sugar production in the Kingdom of Jerusalem in the twelfth century and of the Venetian Corner family's vast sugar operation in Cyprus. The first Genoese-owned sugar estates on a commercially influential scale seem to have been in Sicily, from where, in the fifteenth century, the crop was taken first to the Algarve, then to the Atlantic islands, where (in Madeira, the western Canaries, the Cape Verde Isles and those of the Guinea gulf) it became the basis of the islands' economy by the end of the century.[20] The Malvasia grape followed a similar route from the Venetian-dominated islands of the Aegean, where it was indigenous, through Genoese estates in Sicily to Madeira and the Canaries. It yielded 'specialist', luxury wines, which were uniquely suited to long-distance trade, because, sweet and liquorous, they travelled well, commanded higher prices than drier, thinner local wines and appealed particularly to northern European tastes. Malmsey and Madeira are their descendants. Malvasia was already established in Madeira and the Canaries by the late-fifteenth century; within half a century it began to challenge – and soon displaced – the predominance of sugar. By the time sugar completed the Atlantic crossing and began production in the New World – the first sugar mill was of

1513, in Hispaniola – the effective model, it is usually supposed, was no longer the eastern Mediterranean but the Canaries. But it is worth remembering that Columbus, who first planted sugar in the New World, carried some Mediterranean images in his mind. He claimed, for instance, apparently wrongly, that Hispaniola produced mastic: he must have been thinking of it as another potential Chios, which he had visited in the 1470s.

The main nurseries, however, of Genoa's Atlantic experience were in the western Mediterranean; in the seas contested and the trade routes shared with the Catalans; and in the Castilian 'empire' of Andalusia, with its emporia of African gold and its deep-water harbours for Atlantic navigation. The nature of Genoese Atlantic colonisation would follow the mercantile, small-scale, family-centred, 'ambivalent' and 'stateless' tradition which typified the Genoese experience generally and monopolised that of the western Mediterranean. Just as in the fourteenth century the main theatre of Genoese commerce moved from Egypt and the Levant northwards to 'Romania' and the Black Sea, retreating from Venetian supremacy, so in the fifteenth, a gradual displacement westwards was impelled by the rise of Ottomans, who proved to be rapacious conquerors and unreliable partners in trade. By the end of the century, Chios was the only surviving Genoese sovereign possession: those of Cyprus, Pera and Gazzaria had been abandoned or overrun; and Chios had become an entrepôt for the distribution in the east of Atlantic sugar. Some adventurous spirits among the Genoese of the east had been tempted beyond the reach of the Turks into the Persian Empire, India and even Abyssinia. But there they operated without contact with their motherland. The main thrust of collectively, consciously Genoese action reverted to Genoa's 'home' waters and nearby bases and therefore to the Atlantic: Genoa stood in a similar geographical position, relative to the Atlantic, as Venice to the Orient. The Genoese, it seemed, had penetrated everywhere: there were places named after Genoese adventurers on the Sea of Azov and in the Canaries. But the Atlantic was their proper sphere.

Yet when the opportunity to exploit the ocean arose, Genoa lacked resources, especially of manpower, to make full use of it. Genoese expansion, despite its extraordinary powers of extension, was not infinitely elastic. Partly because of the drain of colonial enterprise, or simply because there was no more room to build inside the notoriously crowded city, Genoa's growth seems to have been checked. Working from the physical dimensions of the city and a reckoning of the number of buildings, Heers calculated a mid-fifteenth century population of over 100 000; his estimates of density, of heads per hearth and of hearths per house, seem, however, to have been generous. Census figures of the sixteenth century suggest a total of only about a half of Heers's value – comparable, therefore, with Valencia or Barcelona rather than Venice or Seville.[21]

It is instructive to look back to the heyday of the early fourteenth century, vividly captured by Petrarch (1304–74), who saw the city as a child of seven and thought it 'an heavenly dwelling . . . a truly regal city'. Returning in the mid-century as an adult, he was still impressed: 'The very sight of her proclaims her mistress of the sea.'[22] Those judgements would not have been inappropriate a century and a half later, but the impact of the sight of Genoa, untouched by the Renaissance, unenlarged by growth, relatively unadorned by expatriate wealth, seemed much less. In the Atlantic trade of the sixteenth century, Genoese no longer figured as pioneers or even, to any great extent, as participants. They were limited to a vicarious role, with Castilians as their main surrogates. Columbus was virtually the last such pioneer and his Genoese backers were representative of a new breed, who preferred the bloated purse to the billowing sail. These advantages and limitations – a talent for vicarious expansion, a severely constricted domestic base, a tradition of commercial 'conquest' and non-sovereign settlements – help to explain why Genoa made a vital contribution to the exploration and colonisation of the Atlantic without establishing a sovereign Atlantic empire.

The Arago-Catalan islands; Andalusia and its environs; Sharq al-Andalūs; the Genoese diaspora: all the theatres of expansion we have considered so far seem to have made some contribution towards the penetration of the Atlantic by Mediterranean civilisation. But it was the north-western rim of Africa, the last area of western Mediterranean colonial activity in the late middle ages which led, in a sense, most directly into the ocean, partly because the Maghrib had an Atlantic aspect of its own and partly – and more importantly – because the exploration of its trade routes demanded and rewarded Atlantic navigation. It was, moreover, as we shall now see, an arena of competition between all the European peoples most closely involved in the process of Atlantic discovery and settlement. Consideration of the late medieval Maghrib will complete our survey of the western Mediterranean colonial world and prepare us for our exploration of the Atlantic.

# 5. The Rim of Africa

## The Condition of the Maghrib

Petrarch was an eloquent witness of an excitement widely shared in his day: the excitement of geographical discovery. His *Senilia* are enlivened with recommendations of the pleasures of imaginary travels, seated in one's chair, with maps and books. He even boasted that he could 'lead his readers through all lands with a pen'.[1] He was reflecting a prevalent taste. Yet he could report only selective progress.

European knowledge of the remote orient, for example, actually underwent a contraction in his day. For over a century from the 1230s, the power of the Mongols had made access relatively easy across the causeway of the steppes. Even in Petrarch's maturity, in the late 1330s and early 1340s, Italian merchants and missionaries could travel to Beijing on a road 'safe by day or night',[2] sending letters home, albeit without adding to the stock of geographical and ethnographic news transmitted by thirteenth-century travellers. But in the next generation, as contact was lost and the flow of information stemmed, the revelations of Marco Polo (recorded in 1289–99) came to be regarded with incredulity; Chinese silk became a rarity again in western markets, and Petrarch was obliged to 'confess that I do not know what the Chinese or Indians are doing'. Later medieval accounts of the Orient tended to depend on thirteenth-century sources. Most were taken directly from the encyclopedic compilers of high medieval wisdom, especially from Vincent of Beauvais. From having been a great theatre of mercantile and missionary endeavour in the late thirteenth century, China became for Petrarch what it had been for his idol, Horace: an exoticist device, a name to conjure with, to evoke associations with the curious and strange.[3]

As the perspective eastward faded, Petrarch, like many of his contemporaries, fixed his gaze on new areas of expansion nearer home. The apple of his eye, the cynosure of his time, was perhaps his 'pulcherrima Africa', which he chose for the eponymous title of his unfinished masterpiece: an epic of Scipio, which, he believed, would establish his reputation for all time. The name of 'Africa'

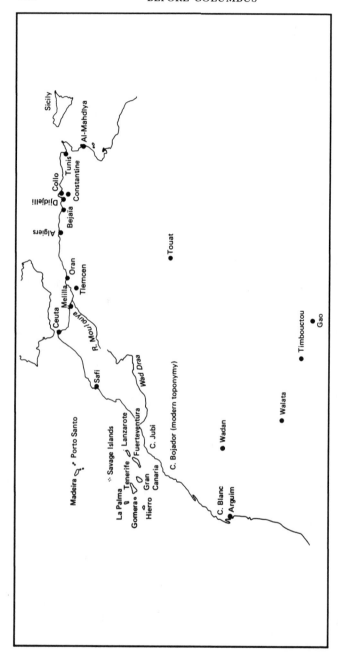

Map 5

NORTH-WEST AFRICA AND THE CANARY ISLANDS

places named in the text

usually denoted the old Roman province, the 'Ifriqīya' of the Arabs, or, more generally, the Maghrib: the segment of the continent which lay closest to the dynamic powers of western Mediterranean Europe in the late middle ages. It was, as we shall see, an economically attractive area; and it had formed part of the Roman world. Therefore it may seem surprising that Latin Christendom should appear to have neglected it for so long. Why was it only in Petrarch's day that it became the main theatre of 'the expansion of Europe'? Part of the explanation lies in the pull exerted on occidental energies by two of the great eastward movements of the high middle ages: the Mongol mission and the Holy Land crusade. As they were stymied or repulsed, Barbary assumed a new relative prominence. The crusading strategy of St Louis, 'deflected' to Tunis in 1269, is a case in point.

Like the deviation of the Fourth Crusade from Jerusalem to Constantinople in 1204, St Louis's change of direction has excited suspicions of the crusaders' motives. Some deception seems to have been practised on Genoese participants, who took out insurance for a voyage to Syria but found, on reporting to the crusaders' place of assembly in Sardinia, that a decision to go to Tunis instead had already been taken. How far St Louis himself was the author of the deceit, or how far the new destination was contrived by his brother, Charles of Anjou, who, as king of Sicily, was interested in control of the coast opposite his own realm, is a matter of debate. Charles had a stake in unrecovered debts owed in Tunis to Provençal traders. He stood to profit from the recovery of Tunisian tribute, formerly paid to Sicily but suspended since 1266. Louis may have been duped into thinking that an attack on Tunis offered easy rewards, or that the amir might be willing to embrace Christianity. He may have believed that a north African foothold would render future crusades easier or that Tunis was near Jerusalem, or that his blow would strike just as serviceably against an undifferentiated Islamic world. Even in its day, the Tunis crusade was regarded as a pallid substitute for the real thing: Louis's biographer, Joinville, refused to serve on it and declined to mention it, save to thank God he was not present.[4] But it belongs in the context of the gradual westward shift of the crusading trajectory. As the sun set on the Holy Land crusade, the crusaders followed it westward.

This is not to imply that the forces of late medieval European expansion could be stoppered and released as if by a system of valves: they more resembled the contents of Betjeman's geyser, with 'steam escaping here and there', leaking where it could. The Maghrib in the thirteenth and fourteenth centuries was a land of opportunity for adventurers. Politically divided, vulnerable to Christian intermeddling, it was Islam's soft underbelly. Impressive but short-lived unity had been imposed on the region in the eleventh and twelfth centuries by two movements of frenzied chiliastic ascetics from the desert, known respectively as the Almoravids (al-Murābitun, garrison folk, a name signifying ascetic withdrawal as well as holy warfare) and Almohads (al-Muwahhidun, followers of the oneness of God). But millenarian movements run out of steam; charismatic leaders die; and desert warriors get corrupted by the soft life of the civilisations they conquer. All political authority in western Islam had tended to be displaced in the past by one of three means: conquest from the desert, usurpation from the extremities and Putsch from within. After almost a century of dominance in north Africa, the state ruled by the Almohad caliphs succumbed, in the 1230s and 1240s, to a combination of all three. In the eastern Maghrib, power was seized by the Hafsids, the family of the local governor; in the centre, by the Banū 'Abd al-Wād, a tribe whom the caliphs had employed to keep control; in the west, by a predator tribe from the south, the Banū-Marīn. A brief look at the states they formed will illustrate the condition of the Maghrib.

An invaluable witness to the instability of north Africa in this period is the historian and *haut fonctionnaire*, Ibn Khaldūn (1332–46), who served successively in the courts of each of the three Maghribi states at Tunis, Fez and Tlemcen. His theory of history as the interplay of tension between sedentary civilisation and the 'Bedouin' savagery beyond reflected the actual political experience of his lifetime.[5] In Hafsid Tunis, for instance, the amirs were virtually powerless inland, outside the two 'oases' of urban life at Constantine and Kairouan. Pretenders and usurpers were rife, precisely because they could always recruit short-term help from nomads. Yet Tunis was at first the most redoubtable of the successor states to emerge from the Almohad debacle. Its ruler, Yahyā, could feel the attenuation of his masters' authority in Spain and the feebleness of their power generally. In 1229 he effectively repudiated their supremacy, in the characteristic Muslim fashion, by deleting specific reference to them from the Friday prayers. In

1236, he completed this assertion of independence by having the prayers proclaimed in his own name. His son, Muhammad I (known as al-Mustansir) called himself caliph from 1253 and in the early 1260s was widely recognised as the bearer of the Mahdi's mantle. This usurpation excited envy from within his own dynasty and enmity from without; nor did he have the means to enforce widespread obedience. From his death in 1277 al-Mustansir's legacy was prey to subdivision and internal war between rival pretenders, exacerbated by interventions from Aragon and from the other Maghribi states. Only under Abū Bakr (1318–46) did Tunis again represent a formidable power, claiming hegemony over virtually the whole Barbary coast. Thereafter, the re-establishment of some sort of unity had to await the reign of Abu 'l-Abbās (1370–94).

Marinid Morocco was founded in an act of nomadic aggression. The Banū-Marīn, after generations of impatience with Almohad pretensions, in which successful resistance was followed by outright aggression, passed in 1244 under the chieftaincy of a leader of genius: Abū Yahyā-abū Bakr saw that his tribe had the means not merely to maintain its independence but actually to capture the state. Marinid Morocco, however, never fulfilled its promise. Successive rulers dreamed without success of reconstructing an empire, like that of the Almohads and Almoravids, which would cover the Maghrib and al-Andalūs; but, like previous desert conquerors, they found sedentarism enervating. By the time of their final extirpation of the last Almohad strongholds in 1269 they had already absorbed the culture of their reluctant hosts: the sultan Abū Yūsuf built himself a pleasure palace outside Fez to celebrate his victory and dabbled in connoisseurship and bibliophilia. The sultans of the fourteenth century, increasingly, because of retiring habits and royal minorities, tended to withdraw into the life of the palace and the seraglio, abandoning government to their hereditary vizirs, the Banū Wattā. The rule of mayors of the palace nearly always ends in a palace coup: in the case of the Marinids, it is remarkable that this consummation was delayed until 1420.

For most of the fourteenth century, though Morocco was the most promising of the Maghribi states, Tunis was the most formidable. Neither was capable of uniting the Maghrib or resisting Latin influence for long. The third state, Abdalwadid Tlemcen, maintained a precarious existence between them, transferring or withholding allegiance as seemed best from time to time. The Abdalwadids never controlled more than Tlemcen and its environs; but it was such an important emporium that its neutrality suited all its neighbours and its tolls enriched its rulers out of proportion to the breadth of their political sway. Thus the Abdalwadids achieved, as a dynasty, remarkable longevity, surviving all comers until their obliteration by the Turks in 1554. Meanwhile, the earliest and longest-sustained attempts to exploit Maghribi disunity from outside came from Spain – a part of Christendom which had contributed relatively little to the Levantine crusades – and, originally and particularly, from the Crown of Aragon.

## The Aragonese Protectorate

Catalan and Aragonese mercenaries, missionaries, monarchs and merchants began to take an active interest in the Maghrib, all at roughly the same time, in the early thirteenth century. Mercenaries from Christian kingdoms of the Iberian peninsula had a long tradition of service among the Muslim Hispanic states, emulating the exploits of Fernando of Carrión, who was paid with the corpse of St Zoil, or of El Cid himself, who after his exile from Castile spent as much time fighting alongside Muslims as against them. It was natural that this mercenary life should spill over the straits into northern Africa. A Portuguese contingent served at Marrakesh from the 1220s. Its leader followed devout precedents and was paid with the relics of Franciscan martyrs of Ceuta. The Hafsid rulers of Tunis had their own Catalan Company from 1256, The permanent loan of Catalan soldiery to Tunis was enshrined by treaty from 1279. Missionaries were intermittently active over the same period. They came and went in frenetic and often fatal descents. Opportunities to proselytise were limited. When, for instance, the Pope asked the Moroccan ruler to tolerate the friars in 1246, he assumed that their ministry would be confined to existing Christian residents. Franciscans and Dominicans were in Tunis, on and off, from 1235 at the latest, but only the Dominican *studium*, established in 1250 to promote missionary study of Arabic, gave their presence any chance of permanence. Mercenaries served longer turns and were always at their posts in the main courtly centres of the Maghrib. But they lived in ghetto-like 'quarters' reserved for their use and rarely established their own households. They and their mendicant counterparts created colonial toeholds, not colonies.

In the course of the thirteenth century, the pace and nature of Latin involvement in the area began to be transformed by the sharpening intrusion of the political ambitions of the Aragonese kings. The Crown of Aragon was, after all, a successor state of the Almohad empire and had an interest in maintaining Valencian and Majorcan trade with the Maghrib. North Africa may, moreover, have come to be seen as a potential sphere of Aragonese expansion as a result of the apprehension excited by French interest in the area at the court of Jaime I. In 1248, at the time of the preparation of St Louis' first crusade, Jaime ordered his Genoese agent, Nicolosso Cigala, to seek assurances that the crusaders would not attack Tunis.[6] On that occasion, his fears seem to have been unfounded. But when Louis launched another attempt twenty years later, Tunis was evidently under imminent threat, and Jaime acted as the amir's protector. From then on, Aragonese rulers pursued, almost continuously, a policy of the extension or defence of their influence in the Maghrib. Tunis became an Aragonese dependency and tributary; Jaime and his successors sought to make the relationship permanent and to extend it further along the Barbary coast, or supplement it with firmer forms of political domination elsewhere in the Maghrib. Jaime's initial, over-ambitious strategy was evidently to take the Maghrib, as it were, from both ends. The claim made in his *Book of Deeds* that he had launched raids against the Moorish coast as early as the 1230s has been confirmed by archival discoveries.[7] While, in the east, he made Tunis his client, Catalan fleets attacked Ceuta in the west. In 1274 Jaime made a treaty with the ruler of Morocco which called for cooperation over Ceuta.[8] Gradually, however, Aragonese royal attention became focused on the eastern Maghrib, between Tunis and Tlemcen.

The potential scope of these ambitions is best illustrated by an episode of 1291, the very year of the Vivaldi voyage from Genoa into the African Atlantic (see p.152). That November, in one of the dramatic personal encounters favoured by medieval Spanish kings as occasions for diplomacy, rather like the 'summits' of modern leaders, Jaime II of Aragon and Sancho IV of Castile agreed to a partition of Africa, dividing spheres of influence or zones of conquest at the River Moulouya, which flows a little to the west of

Tlemcen. Little came of this shadowy pre-enactment of the Congress of Berlin, perhaps because no Christian state in the middle ages had sufficient strength to make extensive conquests or exercise more than a fragile protectorate in any part of the Maghrib: the internal strains which kept the area divided militated equally against overall control from outside. And Sancho's interest in Moroccan conquest was ephemeral, being connected with short-term political fluctuations in the Iberian peninsula, although susceptible, perhaps because of the strength of 'Reconquest' tradition, of periodic revival. Nevertheless, Jaime's agreement with Sancho was portentous. It is tempting to see it as prefiguring the Treaty of Tordesillas, in which, a little over 200 years later, Portugal and Castile defined zones of conquest in the Atlantic, just as it is tempting to see the Vivaldi as precursors of Columbus. At least the agreement of 1291 testifies, on the Aragonese side, to an abiding interest in extending the political influence of the dynasty in Africa. The lions that strutted in the Aragonese royal menagerie implied unrealised hopes of exotic dominion, like the giraffes of the court of the Ming.

The background of Aragonese ambitions in north Africa is formed by the developing island 'empire' of the thirteenth century. Majorca (conquered, it will be remembered from Chapter 1, in 1229), Ibiza (1235), Sicily (1282), Minorca (1287) and Sardinia (of which the conquest was projected in the 1290s) stretched like stepping stones across the western Mediterranean. Whether they were stepping stones towards Africa or the Levant is a matter of debate. In order to understand the relevance to Africa of the Arago-Catalan islands, it is necessary to consider the evidence for linking them to the Levant. This entails a brief excursion eastwards in the direction of much Aragonese propaganda and of some projected Aragonese conquests.

Jaime I intended to make an expedition to the Holy Land, though nothing of the sort materialised. He had been brought up in a crusading milieu and his daughter died on pilgrimage in Jerusalem. He exchanged ambassadors with the Tatars and by attending the Council of Lyon, alone among the monarchs of Christendom, in 1274, appeared to lay claim to the mantle of St Louis. The realm of Sicily, which he coveted, had long associations with the kingdoms of the eastern Mediterranean and with the crusading cause. And, in the early years of the next century, the allegiance averred for the Sicilian branch of the Aragonese dynasty by the mercenaries of the autonomous Catalan Company, who conquered Athens for their own benefit in 1311, lent some colour to Aragonese pretensions in the east. At the Council of Vienne, as we have seen (p.34), the Aragonese represented their conquests as the potential supply line of a crusade.

The possibility that this was more than bluster, and that the Aragonese kings genuinely aspired to rule in Jerusalem, is vividly suggested by the millenarian prophecies of Arnau de Vilanova (died 1311). His 'ravings'[9] deserve to be taken seriously. Court physician to Pedro III of Aragon from at least 1281, intimate adviser of the king's sons, *soi-disant* interpreter of the dreams of Jaime II of Aragon and Federico II of Sicily, Arnau was well placed to reflect and perhaps to influence the self-perceptions of his masters: he retained the confidence of Jaime until about 1308 and of Federico until his death.[10] He dabbled in every abstruse art. From physic he passed to alchemy and from astrology to scriptural divination. This last art had been perfected in Sicily, which was conquered by Arnau's first royal master in 1282. There, perhaps, Arnau conceived his interest in the seminal prophet, Joachim of Fiore, who, nearly 100 years before, had tried to chronicle in advance the last convulsions of human history: the rise of the Last World Emperor, the conquest of Jerusalem, the advent of Antichrist, the pontificate of the Angelic Pope, the cosmic struggle, the Age of the Holy Spirit. From 1289, Arnau was a professor in the University of Montpellier (then a fief of the Aragonese kingdom of Majorca), finding himself in a milieu where Joachimite prophecy was studied and where there were numerous Franciscan 'Spirituals' – followers, that is, of St Francis who evoked the founder's spirit, transmitted through his testament and the tradition of his friends, and who applied rigorously the doctrine of apostolic poverty. Though a layman, Arnau became saturated in the Franciscan spiritual tradition. Since many spirituals regarded their own movement as the embodiment or prefiguration of the Age of the Holy Spirit foretold by Joachim, these contacts probably reinforced his Joachimism.[11]

In 1292, Arnau began a series of writings which reflect these influences. His *De tempore Adventus Antichristi* of 1297 – intended as the first part of a trilogy of the Antichrist – was the first of his visionary works to prophesy an eschatological role for the Aragonese kings. In the *De Mysterio Cymbalorum*, written not later than 1301, this was refined into a programme. It has a Sicilian flavour. Arnau's programme was essentially that of the chiliastic propagandists of the Sicilian-based Emperor Frederick II (died 1250): renovation of the church, conquest of Jerusalem, extirpation of Islam, unification with Byzantium, creation of a universal Christian empire from Sicily. This suggests that the Aragonese may have 'caught' their learned millenarianism from Sicily and that the conquest of Sicily may have been the inspiration – as much as the outcome – of Aragon's Hierosolomitan orientation.[12]

It is worth stressing, however, that Arnau de Vilanova's programme also includes a distinctively Aragonese element: the conquest of Africa. For however alluringly Aragon's island conquests may have pointed the way towards Jerusalem, they also constituted a sort of system of outworks of the Maghribi coast – a defensive line drawn across the sea, guarding routes of access to north-west Africa and threatening to envelop it. Potential bases for a mainland conquest, they were also, perhaps more importantly, strategic *points d'appui* of economic 'warfare': they lay athwart the African trade routes of other trading states. Majorca was a regular staging post for Genoese trade with the Maghrib. Sardinia was the natural base of Pisan traders, and one they were willing to fight hard to control. Sicily lay on the way from Naples, Amalfi and Venice to the Barbary ports. The Aragonese, as we shall see, did not attempt systematically to curtail the use of these routes, but they may have aspired to control them. It is not necessary to assume that the pattern of Aragonese island conquests and mainland ambitions reflects a single coherent strategy. But it is possible to detect one, not so much *inspiring* the extension of Aragonese conquests beyond the 'reconquests' of the early thirteenth century, as *arising* from it.

The nature and extent of the Aragonese kings' commitment to political involvement in the Maghrib are not easy to define. Some historians have been reluctant to take their projects of conquest seriously. The most impressive armada, for instance, launched by Pedro III against Collo (Alcoll) in 1282, has generally been dismissed as a feint for the conquest of Sicily. Pedro may have been an opportunist, happy to strike at more than one target as the occasion arose. But the very intensity of his propaganda, while it may disguise the subtleties of his policy, testifies to the strength of Aragonese feeling about the Maghrib. The chronicle of 'Bernat

Desclot' was written, probably within a few years of the event, by a royal household official who helped to prepare the expedition. His account can be taken to represent the 'official' Aragonese version: the king's desire to seize Constantine and subdue all Africa was genuine, and espoused for the honour of God and the sake of all Christendom; if the pope lent him aid, he would stay in Africa, and his barons professed themselves ready to send for their wives and children. The next chronicle in the Catalan tradition is that of Ramon Muntaner, an 'artless', impassioned and chivalrous writer who fought in many of the campaigns he commemorates: with him, the facts have grown more distorted and the propaganda more shrill. Muntaner's presence in Sicily is not attested before 1300 and he seems to have played no part in the conquest. He muddles the chronology and conflates the king's achievements: Pedro is another Alexander, who excels Roland, Oliver, Tristan, Lancelot and numerous other heroes of romance; the Saracens skulk and hide from him; the entire coast is subdued. Muntaner's strength of feeling is more intense than that of the chronicle of directly royal inspiration. The lost glory of the potential conquest of Africa afflicts him deeply. His bitterness against the pope is more acute than his predecessor's. However unrealistic the ambition, and however faint of heart the kings, African conquest was a powerful image in the mental world of Catalan knights of the late thirteenth and early fourteenth centuries.[13]

Whether or not north Africa was King Pedro's main objective when he landed there in 1282, the first enduring Aragonese conquests in the area date from his reign. In 1284–86 the islands of Jarbāh (Djerba, Gerba) and Qarqannāh (Kerkennah) were added to the Aragonese dominions – loosely added, for they were ruled thenceforth as fiefs variously of Sicily or the pope. The conqueror was Ruggiero di Loria, one of Pedro's most swashbuckling warlords, who had occupied Malta and Gozo in June, 1283, and served the dynasty as admiral or pirate all over the Mediterranean. His south Italian provenance and Norman ancestry are obscured by the common Catalan rendering of his name as 'Roger de Lluria'. But he ruled Jarbāh consistently with the traditions of Norman conquest, terrorising the inhabitants, driving 2000 of them from their homes and, in 1289, building a hugh castle – al-Qastil, as it was unambiguously called – to dominate them. The islands were suitably qualified to count as Europe's first African colonial possession. Though reputedly indomitable, the Muslim Berber inhabitants were in some respects disposed to collaboration with a foreign occupier. As Kharijites, they were Islamic heretics, uneasy in their fellowship with their erstwhile rulers from the mainland. Divided among themselves between two mutually hostile tribes, they were incapable of sustaining unity in the face of attack. Their commercial relations with Latin Christendom were of long standing, and they were reviled in the Muslim world for the willingness with which they sold coreligionists into European slavery. Their islands produced vines, dates, olives and pasture. Cloth and cotton were made up for export. And they offered the chance of creating an offshore emporium for European interlopers in Maghribi trade – a role for which islands would be sought at intervals during the next century and a half.

Loria was a patron of Roman Muntaner and may have shared the chivalric mentality of a romantic conquistador: the private passion for conquest, however widespread in the knightly estate, and the spirit which animated individual conquests, like that of Jarbāh, should be distinguished from royal policy. Yet some form of protectorate, albeit not of formal mandate, in the Maghrib, does seem fairly consistently to have been sought by Aragonese monarchs. The history of the quest can be traced in a series of treaties between Aragonese kings and north African rulers, especially those of Tunis, in the century after St Louis's Tunis crusade. Sicilian merchants had been protected by agreed conventions in Al-Mahdīya since the late eleventh century. Commercial treaties had been common since the early twelfth century between the Almoravids and their successors on the one hand and the merchant city-states of western Mediterranean Europe on the other. The first such agreements may have been made by word of mouth alone, for some of the earliest examples are known only from the records of chroniclers: the Almoravid convention with Pisa of 1133, the treaty which Marseilles sought, with Genoese help, in 1138 and Genoa's treaty with the Almohads of 1153–54. The terms survive, recorded in a chronicle, of a Genoese treaty of 1160–61, which bound Genoese merchants to pay a levy of eight per cent on all their imports into the Maghrib, except at Bejaïa (Bougie) where they were committed to a toll of ten per cent by an existing treaty. From the 1180s it was common for such agreements to be written down in synallgamatic form and from the 1230s onwards survivals are numerous.[14] It is possible that the Aragonese kings, or their Catalan subjects, made such agreements in the early to mid-thirteenth century. Certainly they had customary trading and residential rights in various Barbary ports by the 1250s.

The Aragonese treaties from 1271, however, exceeded the terms of these traditional trade conventions and continued to differ sharply from subsequent agreements made by other Latin states in north Africa.[15] They all had an at least partly political character and in many cases they imposed tribute (*trahut*) or at least some unreciprocated payment to the crown of Aragon from the north African parties. This tribute went under various guises. In the treaty made between Jaime I and Tunis in 1271, for instance, it appeared as a payment for the loan of a mercenary militia. A similar line was taken in the treaties of 1274, 1309 and 1323 with Morocco and 1309 with Bejaïa. In each case, the payments were for troops or galleys or both. The Tunisian treaty of 1301 represented the tribute as compensation for a despoiled shipwreck. In some cases, after the Aragonese conquest of Sicily, the claim to tribute from Tunis appeared as a continuation or revival of the sums demanded or extorted by Sicilian rulers since Hohenstaufen times: the very tribute which had been withheld by al-Mustansir from Charles of Anjou, helping to provoke St Louis' crusade. The tribute specified by Pedro III in 1285, for instance, was called 'lo trahut de Sicilia' and fixed at 33 333⅓ besants: it continued to be paid to Alfonso III· of Aragon even after the separation of the kingdoms, when his brother ruled in Sicily.[16] In many treaties, the tribute was perceived as a return on the trade of subjects of the Aragonese monarch. The treaty with Bejaïa of 1314, for instance, agreed a payment to the king of Aragon of 5000 ducats a year from the yield of the 'robes e mercaderies que pagaren dret en la duana de Bugia'. The treaties of 1314 and 1323 with Tunis allotted to the king 4000 ducats a year out of the dues paid by his subjects. In all such cases, the amirs were bound by the treaties to pay the full tribute, even if the value of business from the crown of Aragon was insufficient to cover it.[17]

The precedents for Aragonese exactions of tribute from north Africa may be sought in various directions. it was normal for medieval Hispanic Christian states to mulct Moorish neighbours for protection money. Frequently this tributary relationship was a prelude to conquest. The rights of legitimate 'reconquest' (*reconquista*) which Hispanic Christian kings claimed from the Moors were universally assumed to extend into north Africa. The Sicilian tribute was specifically invoked by Sicily's Aragonese legatees. And there may have been longstanding commercial precedents for the trading partner state to reclaim a share of customs revenues from Barbary ports: as early as 1161, the terms agreed between the Genoese and the Almohads stipulated the return to Genoa of a quarter of the dues paid in Bejaïa. In any event, the Aragonese treaties can hardly be read as mere commercial conventions. They represent political stake-claiming, a stage towards the establishment of an Aragonese protectorate. If that protectorate was never transformed into empire, if the Crown of Aragon seemed equivocal or vacillating about the degree of control to be enforced in the Maghrib, this was not necessarily for lack of the will to conquer. Sardinia – Aragon's Ireland – bled the kings' energies. Prosecution of an active policy in Africa was possible only in the rare and brief intervals of the Sardinian conflict. It was, for example, during a temporary respite in Sardinia after 1324, that the Aragonese kings made their most intensive efforts to impose tribute on the Abdalwadids. Well might they have sympathised with Petrarch's Syphax, who wished he had forever left that evil island to the pestilent wind and sea.[18]

## The Merchant Colonists

While royal policy may have had chivalric, traditional and imperial motives, to which conquest was appropriate, the main reason for the Aragonese presence in Africa was commercial, for which a protectorate was enough. As a general rule, political involvement seems to have been tuned to commercial ends. The structure of the Aragonese dominions, so far as one existed, was 'feudal': the loosely associated states – chiefly Aragon, Valencia, Catalonia, Majorca and Sicily – were covered by a finely spun web of lordship and vassalage. But that did not mean that economic priorities were excluded. The kings may have had 'imperial' pretensions, such as the prophecies of Arnau of Vilanova suggest, but the impulse which created and conjoined the chain of dominions was mercantile. One of the early manuscripts of the chronicle of Jaime I depicts, in rich illumination, the banquet given to the king by the merchant

Pere Martell. King and host, merchant and magnates sit together, as if in knightly companionage, without the intervention of social distance – except that the king has his own table – jointly plotting the conquest of Majorca.[19] The advantage to the Crown of Aragon in maintaining ties in the Maghrib lay not in enforcing obedience but in creaming off the profits of trade. The island possessions of the western Mediterranean were 'toll bridges' on the routes of Italian-Maghribi trade as well as 'fortresses' which guarded the Catalans' Barbary commerce. Their treaties with mainland rulers enabled the kings to milk the same trade further by levying tributes from north African clients in the form of fixed shares of customs dues.

The commercial relations regulated by these treaties were well established by the mid-thirteenth century. In 1227 Jaime I granted the shippers of Barcelona the right of first refusal of any cargo bound for Ceuta; in Tarragona in 1243, a special toll applied to exports to Barbary, though 'Saracen' captives are the only commodity mentioned.[20] By the mid-century, the Catalans maintained consuls in Tunis and Bejaïa. The *funduk* – the community of Catalan merchants – operated in Tunis throughout St Louis' crusade. A list of sailings from Majorca survives for the period 25 January–18 March 1284: departures from Barbary, leaving once every other day on average, and including some vessels from Genoa or Barcelona, represent two-thirds of the total, although in most cases tonnages are small compared with those of ships making longer runs.[21] Building on these thirteenth-century origins, the Catalan traders in the fourteenth century, their position enhanced by the political activity of their monarchs, developed their commerce and entrenched their merchant-colonies throughout the Barbary coast. By the 1320s, at least 150 Catalan subjects were making roughly annual trips to Barbary.

Some of them – and probably all those who penetrated the interior – were Jews. The kings of Aragon had a relatively large number of Jewish subjects, partly because they attracted and protected them when they were persecuted elsewhere. From 1247, Jaime I encouraged them to enter his realms 'for the sake of dwelling and settling in our lands'. They remained welcome in Aragon's peninsular dominions for most of the next century and a half. They found refuge there from sufferings in outlying parts of the Aragonese world, when they were expelled from Roussillon and

Montpellier, for instance, in 1307, or vexed by Sancho I of Majorca, who held their community to ransom. They played conspicuous roles in royal service: until the confirmation of ancient liberties obliged the king to discharge them from high office in 1284, the brothers Joseph and Moses Ravaya, for example, were architects of the financial success of Pedro III, liberating him from reliance on representative institutions and raising money for the conquest of Sicily.[22]

The Jews complemented their legal privileges in Aragon with natural advantages in the Barbary trade. Jews could elude the restrictions to which Christian merchants were subject in Muslim cities. They could set up house outside the appointed quarter. They could gain access to the markets of the interior, where every European merchant wanted to trade. A pitch even a little way inland, like that enjoyed by the Genoese at Constantine, was highly coveted. Jews, travelling between communities of their coreligionists, equipped perhaps with some manual for Jewish travellers, like Benjamin of Tudela's *Itinerary*, could go far afield unchallenged, even (when not obliged to wear distinctive garb) unobserved. The cases of the Majorcan Jews, Abraham and Solomon Malachi, who had dwellings in both Majorca and Tlemcen in the 1320s and 1330s, suggest the possibilities: the fraternal basis of the Jews' 'family business' made it strong at its centre; their membership of an international community made it broad in its contacts; 'branches' could be maintained, with permanent resident 'staff', at both ends of a trade route, in mutually hostile lands. The Jews were pitiably vulnerable to discrimination and persecution in Christian countries, but they were never successfully excluded from Barbary.[23]

Apart from Jewish penetration of the interior, on an unknown but no doubt numerically modest scale, the merchant colonies were confined to the coast. Their quarters in the early fourteenth century were cramped and retiring, their houses humble and 'rather small', as Al-Tidjāni observed on his journey round Tunis, where Latin traders were relatively well ensconced, in 1306–9. Such were the beginnings of the splendid modern European sector of Tunis which Leo Africanus was to describe in the early sixteenth century. The fourteenth was the crucial century of growth: by its end, the *funduks* and the mercenary quarter together occupied nearly half the city.[24]

Even during this period of expansion, life in the *funduks* remained pecularily constrained. The numbers of permanent residents were small; the terms of most treaties assumed that merchants would come and go with their cargoes and not dwell habitually in the Muslim ports. Factors from the big trading houses were tolerated for long stretches at a time. The Peruzzi of Florence, for instance, maintained two factors in Tunis throughout the fourteenth century; their countrymen, the Acciauoli, from 1332. The customs officials of the *funduks* were normally appointed from within the resident community – among the Florentines they were known as 'bancheri'. The Aragonese-Tunisian treaty of 1341 mentions European officials in Tunisian employ. Most communities had permanent chaplains, who were safe as long as their operations were prudently confined.

The tenor of life in these outposts of the Latin world is admirably captured in the terms of some of the surviving treaties. That of Pisa with Tunis, for instance, of 13 May 1353, granted the same 'protection, honour and favour' as other Latin nations enjoyed: the Genoese were specifically mentioned. The most modest amenities of civilised life and Christian death were provided: a church, a cemetery and a bakery 'according to longstanding custom', and weekly access to a bath.[25] Most merchant colonists were prevented from putting down roots in Africa not by the narrow compass of the way of life which these conditions imply, but by the dearth of womenfolk. They usually lived in enforced celibacy. As we know from an early Marseillais regulation forbidding the practice, sexual relief was provided by casually imported prostitutes,[26] though, as we have seen (p.109), some of the Genoese of thirteenth-century Tunis had wives or concubines and settled households: such exceptions may have been more numerous, concealed only by shortage of sources.

In any case, Latin colonialism was shallow and feeble in the African mainland in the fourteenth century, compared with the extensive and full-blooded settlement of the Mediterranean island 'empires'. Only the Crown of Aragon attempted systematically to erect a structure of political influence or control in the Maghrib in this period. Except in Jarbāh and Qarqannāh which closely resembled the insular seigneuries established in other parts of the Mediterranean by Catalans, Venetians and Genoese, the colonies were exclusively mercantile; and even in the restricted merchant quarters it was unusual for settled patterns of life to be established.

Those quarters were, however, self-governing, with the privileges of extraterritoriality. The Aragonese treaty with Tunis, for instance, of 1 May 1323, made it clear that the consul of the Catalans was to administer justice in the colony, and further insights into life in a typical *funduk* are yielded by some surviving grants of offices of this sort by Aragonese kings in Tunis. In early May, 1261, for instance, Jaime I appointed a chaplain to his Tunisian *funduk* and farmed out the consulship to Ramon Arnau and Felip de Denia for two years for 5500 besants. For their money, they got the yield of the shops, bakery and tavern (terms slightly better than those specified in a similar grant of 1258), but they had to supply a suitable person to hold the office of notary. They would be reimbursed if the Moors made their task impossible. But life seems to have been less insecure than they feared; though the normal tour of duty supposed in the surviving documents of this type was from one year to five, a stay could be indefinitely protracted by royal renewals. Felip de Denia, for instance, was still at his post in 1280 with a break of no more than two years, during which he may have continued to be based in Tunis. Renewal was worthwhile, even at an increased charge. In 1272, Ramon Ricart, who had twice been the king's ambassador to Tunis and how knew the accounts of the *funduk* well, thought it worthwhile to go into partnership with him. The king's revenues from the *funduk* must have been substantial to cover the costs of his embassies: on his mission of 1272, he spent more than 23 000 *solidi* of Barcelona on the hire of a ship, horses and mules. The consulship of Bejaïa seems also to have been desirable: Berenguer de Reguer held it for most of the 1260s and 1270s, first at 750 besants annually, then at 800. Competition for these consulates was keen. At Tunis, in the 1250s and 1260s, the king alternated between the rivals; at his other 'royal' *funduk* of Bejaïa, the competitors – one from Barcelona and one from Majorca – sued one another, while the king solomonically favoured each in turn.[27]

One of the most striking features of the Latin quarters of the Barbary ports is perhaps their international character. Even in Hafsid ports, which were subject to the uneven but exacting protectorate of the Aragonese, *funduks* of all the Latin trading states flourished. According to the *Pratica della mercatura* of the mid-fourteenth century, the main trade of Tunis itself was with Italy. Merchants of Genoa, Pisa, Florence and Venice could be found in all major ports from Tunis to Safi. The Crown of Aragon never attempted to exploit its political influence to give the Catalans a monopoly. Nor did it use command of the sea lanes to exclude foreign vessels. The island curtain which the Aragonese controlled across the western Mediterranean from Majorca to Sicily was never fully drawn against rival commerce. The reason for this apparent paradox is not hard to find. Because they levied tolls on trade and tributes on customs duties, the Aragonese benefited from the volume of commerce, whoever carried it. Because they ruled the island staging posts, the nationality of the traders who used them was usually a matter of indifference. It is remarkable, for instance, that Aragonese kings took an indulgent view of Genoese trade with the Maghrib, even in times of enmity or open war, probably because the worlds of Catalan and Genoese commerce were thoroughly interpenetrated and and interdependent – rather like those of Portugal and Genoa in the western Mediterranean in the next century.

With only rare punctuations by embargoes and confiscations, the Genoese enjoyed a privileged place in the lands of the Crown of Aragon, even while the two peoples were building up their mutual perceptions as inveterate enemies. The Genoese, like the Pisans, were explicitly excluded from many general measures taken against Italian competition. Their prior rights were recognised in some Aragonese negotiations with Maghribi rulers. And individual Genoese never ceased to enjoy royal confidence, serving in diplomatic, administrative, military and espionage roles despite the potential conflicts of loyalty.[28] This remarkable cooperation illustrates a general feature of medieval warfare: outright economic war was rare in a world where war was waged for profit. Trade often incubated under the shell of hostility; and 'national' odium had to be very strong before it assumed priority over economic interest.

Notarised records of Genoese commerce are relatively scarce in Catalan archives. Of 241 surviving commercial shipping contracts from Barcelona up to 1464, only 13 mention Genoa.[29] But Genoese records supply a picture of prolific trade. Particulars of the *Drictus Catalanorum*, the levy paid by subjects of the Crown of Aragon on goods shipped through Genoa, survive for two years of the fourteenth century. They show frequent sailings – about thrice weekly in the season – which covert commerce must have doubled: for August, 1386 (at the end of a spell of warfare between Genoa and Aragon), when the *Drictus* records show 12 sailings, 28 are mentioned in the Datini correspondence.[30] Nor do the *Drictus* records do justice to the spread of Catalan-Genoese commerce:

Tunis is mentioned only once. Though Cyprus, Alexandria and 'Romania' feature, over half the entries mention no more distant port than Pisa; the western coast of Italy, the main ports of the Crown of Aragon, the Balearics and Sicily between them account for almost all mentions. This is probably because the compilers of the *Drictus* records were interested chiefly in the immediate provenance or destination of the ships rather than in remoter legs of their journeys. Fortunately, Genoese notarial records supply the deficiencies: Genoese-Catalan trade – that is, Catalan trade through Genoa, Genoese trade with the Crown of Aragon, and commerce in which traders and shippers of both peoples were associated – linked Genoa to Barcelona and Tunis and Valencia to Sicily, Chios and Pera.[31] By no means were the Genoese squeezed from the western Mediterranean by the Catalans in the fourteenth century. It would be more realistic to see the area as a de facto condominium, from which the commerce of both countries made forays into the eastern Mediterranean, sometimes in company. And on the western edge of the Mediterranean world, beyond the reach of Aragon's informal protectorate, and especially at Ceuta, the Genoese remained supreme, partly through their traditional connections and partly through their increasing presence in southern Castile and Portugal.

Among the goods shipped by Catalan-Genoese trade, wool and woollen textiles overwhelmingly predominated, with 248 mentions for wool and fine fleeces in the *Drictus* records and 240 cargoes which included various types of woollens. Otherwise, only gold in various forms (74 cargoes), iron (59), saffron (55), pitch (33), canvas (32) and leather (31) feature in more than 30 cargoes. It is worth noticing the relative importance, in value terms, of gold – most of it, doubtless, despite the scarcity of explicit references to the Maghrib, of African provenance. The dearth of oriental spices is not surprising. It was a general feature of Genoese Mediterranean trade, which concentrated on the products of the Balkans, the Caspian, Turkey and Chios.[32]

## The Lure of the Gold Trade

What drew western merchants to Barbary? What trade was so valuable that it was worth braving the cramped and comfortless conditions of a *funduk* for? And what, from the Catalan point of view, was the prize for which Pere Martell and his successors were prepared to finance the creation of an island empire for their kings across the Barbary sea lanes? In a famous essay of 1957, the great Catalan historian, Jaume Vicèns Vives, posed the question whether the Aragonese island route was a 'route of gold' or a 'route of spices'. At that time, he was prepared to answer tentatively, 'Spices'.[33] Today, we can unequivocally answer, 'Gold'. To see why, an excursion among some more of our sources is necessary: they yield a surprisingly comprehensive picture of the sort of goods the Catalans shipped out of the Maghrib.

For instance, a remarkable insight into Catalonia's Barbary trade in the fourteenth century is given by a merchant's manual (analogous to the *Pratica della mercatura* and other surviving Italian manuals) compiled in Catalan, probably in Barcelona, in 1385. Intended, like its Italian counterparts, to provide instruction in the trader's 'art', it is self-consciously a didactic work, opening with an adumbration of the perfect merchant. Almost every noble, even kingly virtue is stressed. The emphasis on the importance of good faith is so reminiscent of the self-perception presented by the *Book of Deeds* of King Jaime I, who kept faith even with Moors and was taken on trust by them, that only the chivalric touch seems wanting to make the ideal merchant a regal figure. His 'art' is not an esoteric one. After the didactic section, the work goes on to convey practical information with concision and clarity. It is an unusually rich source: 207 types of merchandise are mentioned, of which 146 are described – far more than in any of the Italian handbooks. The book's title, *Llibre de conexenses de spícies e de drogues e de avissaments de pessoas, canes e massures de diverses terres*, portends concentration on spices and on the Levant trade. Indeed, these receive their due attention. But the distribution of the material reflects unambiguously the African priorities of Catalan trade. At least seventeen Maghribi ports are mentioned – more than Italy, Flanders, Castile or the Levant. The concentration of Barbary toponyms is greater than for any other area, save Catalonia and Provence.[34]

But the most important revelation of the document for our purposes is its detailed study of the customs tariff of Tunis and of the commodities traded between Tunis and Barcelona. Two items are conspicuous by their absence. Sardinian salt was an important product for Catalan carriers who shipped it all over Mediterranean

Europe; yet (despite the importance of salt from elsewhere in the Saharan gold trade) none of it found its way to Tunis. Apart from silver, the only Sardinian commodity demanded in the Maghrib, it seems, was cheese.[35] The omission of Barbary wool is equally surprising: it was a traditional export of the region and had played an important part in the commerce of Majorca during the period of Majorcan independence between 1276 and 1343. The only reference to Barbary fleeces in the *Llibre* is slighting: 'aquestes so avols (these are contemptible)', says the compiler.[36] They figure neither in the breakdown of Tunisian customs dues nor in the list of Tunisian exports.

Grain is singled out as the most important of 'the goods which go from the said place of Tunis'. This is what one would expect from other sources: grain and fodder were exempted from customs duties in almost every treaty imposed on north African rulers by the Aragonese in the fourteenth century. Throughout the late middle ages, the Maghrib remained a net exporter of grain, though the *Llibre* also shows the Catalans carrying a staple starch to Tunis in the form of rice – chiefly, no doubt, from Valencia. Other foodstuffs exchanged were gastronomic delicacies or rare flavourings or aromas, many of them entering Tunis chiefly for re-export: every kind of saffron, liquorice, lavender, pepper, sultanas, cream of tartar, three kinds of nuts and wine. The book's evocation of the fig trade is particularly resonant: Murcian figs from Alicante, white figs of Morocco or Majorca, figs of Valencia or Denia, all imported into Tunis with no mention of re-export, are treated as separate products and subject to different tolls; more than a delicacy, they were a major foodstuff – almost a staple when grain was short. At a humbler level, Tunis imported cheese and exported oils, fats, semolina and the products of apiculture.[37]

Evidently the Catalans' biggest market in Tunis was for finished textiles. Sixteen distinct types of cloth are enumerated, as well as Alexandrian linen. Leather and cotton were purchased in Tunis. The textile trade supported lucrative exchanges of dyestuffs and other products employed in the textile industry: at least eight sources of dyes are mentioned, together with 'gleda', a gritty substance used for cleaning fleeces. Tunis also required lacquer, hemp rope and paper. Human cargoes were not negligible: the *Llibre* refers to 'testes', which perhaps means slaves, and lists 'Christian captives' among the other merchandise with no sense of incongruity. Ransomed Moors are not mentioned in exchange, although they figure in Catalan customs schedules of the thirteenth century. The only other major category comprised metals: the compiler of the *Llibre* expected his countrymen to take silver, tin, lead and copper to Tunis. In exchange, they would export the most lucrative single commodity of the Barbary trade: gold, ready coined in the form of 'Moorish ducats'. Tunis imported gold in the form of thread, but the only other finished metal product to feature among the imports is hawks' bells: these were typical of the small items of truck that might have been traded on from Tunis along the Saharan goldroad. Analysis of the commodities mentioned in Aragonese treaties with Tunis yields a similar picture, albeit less complete than that of the *Llibre*, with emphasis on grain and gold.[38]

Further confirmation can be drawn from notarised commercial shipping contracts from Barbary voyages from Barcelona: these survive from 1239 onwards. In the early years of the trade, it was necessary to take gold to Barbary to make purchases: this is also suggested by the fact that Jaime I began minting 'Arab' coins of gold for the Levantine and Maghribi trades in the 1230s. But evidence of the practice disappears from surviving contracts after the 1270s. Generally, the commodities specified in the thirteenth-century evidence are reminiscent of those of the *Llibre*: predominantly, textiles, wine, dyestuffs and figs are exchanged for wax, leather and gold.[39] There were, of course, also clandestine trades not reflected in these records: the fruits of contraband and piracy, and above all the illicit sale to Muslims of arms of Christian manufacture. It is reasonable to guess that the arms traffic contributed to the flow, from Africa to Europe, of gold.

Despite fluctuations in the precious metals market, gold could almost always be traded with advantage across the western Mediterranean, throughout the fourteenth century. The story of the Majorcan Jew who borrowed 40 gold dinars, valued at 30 silver Majorcan solidi, in Tunis and sold them for 50 solidi on arrival in Majorca may not be literally true; but it illustrates the point: the silver-price of gold was generally higher on the northern than on the southern shores of the Mediterranean.[40] In 1330, the widely employed north African unit of account, the besant, was reckoned at 1.5 grams of gold or 15 grams of silver. This ratio of 1:10 may be taken as normal. The comparable norm in Christian Europe was not as high as the tale of the Majorcan Jew might suggest, but in the markets of

Valencia, for instance, a ratio of 1:13 was average in the fourteenth century. Towards 1350, it was 1:10.5 in Naples, 1:11 in Florence. In Portugal in 1383 a ration of 1:11 prevailed. Fluctuations of supply and demand were not necessarily unfavourable to the gold trade. In Aragon, the gold-price of copper and silver fell by about 30 per cent between 1280 and 1330: this reflected the merchants' success in obtaining large quantities of Barbary gold, but it might have ruined them. In fact, however, the effect was to stabilise demand for their merchandise by inducing a general adoption of gold coinage throughtout western Mediterranean Europe. Into Sicily Pedro III introduced the 'pierrale d'oro'. The *reial d'oro* was coined in Majorca. Even Sardinia, traditional producer of silver, got the gold *alfonsino*, introduced by Pedro IV in 1339. The gold florin became the basis of the coinage of Aragon proper in 1346. The Aragonese kings thus had a seeming Midas touch. Its source was Maghribi gold.[41]

The auriferous reputation of the Maghrib was well established by the mid-thirteenth century, when the plausible legend of a Genoese expedition to Safi in 1253 suggests a search for the source of the Saharan gold-trade. The early Genoese interest is corroborated by the depiction of Sijilmassa – on the trans-Saharan camel route that brought gold to Tlemcen – in Giovanni di Carignano's map of the early years of the fourteenth century. One of the reasons for the early Latin – especially Genoese – interest in Ceuta was probably that a form of coral, highly esteemed as truck on the goldroad, was available there. Ceuta was, moreover, on the way to Sijilmassa and to the starting point of a journey by a 'cardinal's messenger' towards the land of the Negroes, reported by Ramon Llull in 1283. By then, the Genoese presence at Ceuta was at least 100 years old. In 1183, Ibn Jubair could travel from Ceuta to Alexandria in a Genoese ship.

The source of the gold was deep in the west African interior, around the middle and upper reaches of the Niger and Volta. Across the glare of the Sahara, through the darkness of the jungle, the glint of gold could be glimpsed only with difficulty in the coast-bound *funduks* of Barbary. The location of the gold source and the route by which it came north were closely guarded secrets of the black monopolists of the empire of Mali, through whose lands, between the Niger and the upper Senegal, the trade passed, and of the Saharan merchants who dealt with them. Procured, according to all accounts – written perhaps from convention rather than

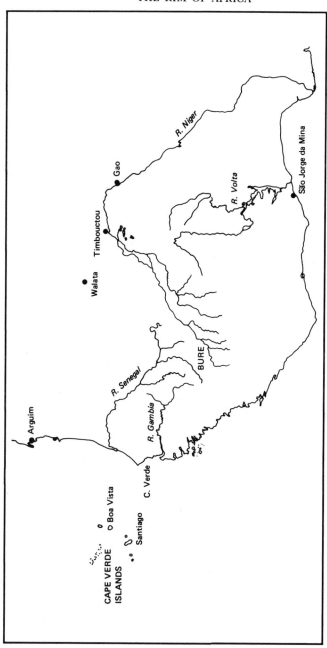

Map 6
WEST AFRICA AND CAPE VERDE
places named in the text

conviction – by 'dumb trade', in which goods were exchanged by being left exposed for collection, the gold generated bizarre theories about its origin: it grew like carrots; it was brought up by ants in the form of nuggets; it was mined by naked men who lived in holes. Its probable real provenance was in the region of Bure, around the upper reaches of the Niger and the headwaters of the Gambia and Senegal rivers. Additionally, some may have come from the Volta valley. The middlemen of Mali never succeeded in controlling the production of the gold: whenever their rulers attempted to exert direct political authority in the mining lands, the inhabitants adopted a form of 'passive resistance' or 'industrial action', ceasing to produce the gold. But Mali controlled access from the south to the emporia of Walata and Timbouctou, on the fringes of the Sahara. Its marketing, so to speak, was therefore in their hands, and they took the nuggets for their tribute, leaving the gold dust to the traders.

As the remotest place on the gold road to which the gold could reliably be traced, Mali became famous in the Mediterranean world in the fourteenth century. Its ruler, known as the Mansa, attained legendary proportions as a result of diffusion of knowledge of the Mansa Mūsa, who reigned from about 1312 to 1337 and undertook, in 1324, a spectacular pilgrimage to Mecca, which spread his renown far and wide. He was one of three Mansas to make the hajj: this alone indicates the substance and stability of the Mali state, as the pilgrimage took over a year. But Mūsa's trip was undertaken in particularly lavish style and with conspicuous effect. It was remembered for centuries in Egypt, where the Mansa stayed for three months and distributed gold with so lavish a hand that he caused an inflation: by various accounts, the value of gold in Egypt fell by between 10 and 25 per cent. He gave 50 000 dinars to the sultan and thousands of ingots of raw gold to the shrines which received him and the officials who entertained him. Though he travelled with 80 or 100 camels, each weighed down with 300 pounds of gold, he was obliged to finance himself by borrowing on his homeward journey. Reputedly, on his return to Mali, he repaid his loans at the rate of 700 dinars for every 300 he had borrowed.

It was the ritual magnificence of the court of Mali, almost as much as its wealth, that impressed beholders. Detailed accounts of its ceremonial are preserved in the works of Ibn-amir Hajīb and Ibn-Battūta, who claimed that the Mansa commanded more devotion from his subjects than any prince in the world. Negro politics did not always attract respect from Arab or Latin authors: this makes the goggle-eyed awe of the sources in this case all the more impressive. Everything about the Mansa exuded majesty: his stately gait; his hundreds of attendants, bearing gilded staves; his indirect method of address through an intermediary; the acts of humiliation – prostration and 'dusting' of the head – to which his interlocutors submitted; the reverberant hum of strummed bowstrings and murmured approval with which his words were greeted at audience; the capricious taboos which enjoined death for those who entered his presence in sandals or sneezed in his hearing. This exotic theatre of power had a suitably dignified stage setting. The Mansa's audience chamber was a domed pavilion in which an Andalusian poet sang; his bushland capital had a brick-built mosque.

The image of the Mansa's splendour reached Europe. In Majorcan maps from the 1320s, and most lavishly in the Catalan Atlas of 1375, the ruler of Mali is portrayed like a Latin monarch, save only for his black face. Bearded, crowned and throned, with panoply of orb and sceptre, he is perceived and presented as a sophisticate, not a savage: a sovereign equal in standing to any Christian prince. This resplendent impression did not last. By the mid-fifteenth century, when direct contact with the outposts of Mali was briefly opened up by Portuguese penetration of the Gambia, Mali was in decline. Familiarity bred contempt and the heirs of the Mansa came to be seen as stage niggers – crude racial steroetypes dangling simian sexual organs. But briefly, in the fourteenth century, Mali projected an enthralling image for European gold hunters. It was the gold that particularly appealed to the Mediterranean 'public'. 'So abundant is the gold which is found in his country,' said the Catalan Atlas of Mali's ruler, 'that this lord is the richest and noblest king in all the land.'

The Maghribi emporia were the termini of the gold trade, or suppliers of essential items of truck for the Saharan caravans. New attempts, mounted from within Latin Christendom in the middle and late fourteenth century, to make conquests in Barbary may have been inspired in part by a desire to wrest more of the trade. Many explanations have been advanced, for instance, of Luis de la Cerda's plan of 1344–45 to carve out for himself a principality comprising the Canary Islands and the Mediterranean offshore island of Jālita (Galita, Goleta). His enterprise, like many African conquests, projected or perfected, of the late middle ages, wears favours plucked from chivalric romance: Luis was a dispossessed scion of the Spanish royal house who was seeking a kingdom while making a living as a soldier of fortune; he was invested by Pope Clement VI with the title of 'Prince of Fortune' in allusion to the supposed classical name – 'Fortunate Islands' – of the Canaries. His project might signify an attempt to mount a two-pronged attack on Islam; it might reflect the crusading or Petrine policies of the pope. But its most curious feature – the geographical spread of the constituent parts of Luis's intended realm – is best explained with reference to the gold trade. Jālita, like the Jarbāh of Ruggiero di Loria, occupied a strategic position off the 'gold coast' of the Maghrib. It was a staging post between Tunis and Barcelona. The Canary Islands – wrongly, as it turned out – were thought to lie close to the sources of the gold trade, close to the fabled 'River of Gold' which adventurers continued to seek down the west African coast into the fifteenth century. The desire to secure a base at either end – so to speak – of the Saharan gold road remained influential; as we shall see, it may have influenced participants in Louis of Bourbon's Barbary crusade of 1390 and was perhaps an early guiding principle of the Infante Dom Henrique. The pursuit of the gold trade has led us, as it led late medieval explorers, to the edge of the Atlantic. Although Atlantic navigation by Mediterranean mariners had begun earlier and for other reasons, the lure of gold was the decisive stimulus to the new discoveries of the fourteenth and fifteenth centuries. It is time to accompany the gold seekers into the Atlantic.

# PART II

# ... To The Atlantic

# 6. Mapping the Eastern Atlantic

## The Early Phases of Atlantic Navigation

Anyone who has ever seen a late medieval atlas or sea chart will be able to appreciate the sentiments of a Sicilian songster (captured in a mass setting of the mid-fifteenth century), who turned to maps in search of images of beauty.[1] The finest surviving specimen, the 'Catalan Atlas' of the Bibliothèque Nationale, Paris, generally attributed to Cresques Abraham of Majorca, is as rich and intricate as a spilled jewel casket, resplendent with images of exotic beings and untold wealth.[2] Maps of even greater magnificence, larger and more densely illuminated, are recorded but lost.[3] These were royal gifts, intended for ostentation as well as use, but the most modest and practical portolan chart would be drawn with grace and adorned with illustrations or, at least, with fine calligraphy and a delicate web of rhumb lines. It was a period in which maps could inspire more than music. It was almost certainly a map – perhaps even the Catalan Atlas itself – that in 1402 induced the Poitevin adventure, Gadifer de la Salle, to embark on a quest for the mythical 'River of Gold', which led him to his ruin. In the late fourteenth century, the anonymous author of the *Libro del conoscimiento de todos los reynos* constructed from the legends of maps a fantastic journey of the imagination which reached beyond the limits of the known, even the accessible world.[4]

In the present century, historians have been understandably reluctant to succumb to the siren-like allure of these maps, which, while preserving our main evidence of the extent of Atlantic exploration in the fourteenth century, mingle it almost indistinguishably with speculations, fabrications and later additions. Cartographical evidence, therefore, must be read with caution. The maps give us a true picture of men's mental image of the world – that is not in question. But without corroboration from other documents, it would be rash to accept them as proof of a growth in real knowledge of the world, and of the Atlantic in particular. The appearance of new land on maps does not necessarily signify new discoveries. We should remember the warning of the Infante Dom Pedro of Portugal, uttered in 1443, that in maps of his day

151

unknown regions 'were not drawn except according to the pleasure of the men who made them'.[5]

Fortunately, enough corroborative evidence has gradually been compiled, mainly by research in Spanish archives in recent years, to justify a favourable reappraisal of the maps and to build up a convincing picture of prolific activity by Mediterranean navigators in the fourteenth-century Atlantic. Two overlapping phases can now be discerned: first, the inruption of Mediterranean vessels into Atlantic waters in the late thirteenth and early fourteenth centuries; second, from the early fourteenth to the early fifteenth centuries, the creation of a zone of navigation in previously unexplored waters, bounded by the Azores in the north, the Canaries in the south and the Iberian and African coasts in the east, and linked by the Atlantic wind system. French-speaking historians have coined the phrase 'Atlantic Mediterranean' to denote this area: the term is justified, not only because the area was a 'middle sea' surrounded by mainlands and archipelagoes which constituted, for a while, the practical limits of navigation, but also because it was the creation of Mediterranean mariners and came to represent in part, as it was gradually colonised and exploited, an extension or transplantation of traditional Mediterranean civilisation in the new oceanic environment.

In the first of these phases, some seafarers turned northwards when they reached the Atlantic, like the Zaccaria family of Genoa, who tried to corner the northern alum market, or the Frescobaldi of Florence, who got their talons on a sizable share of English wool. They made something of an economic breakthrough, but added nothing to geographical knowledge or to the reach of exploration. Others, however, turned south into waters unsailed – so far as we know – for centuries, off the west coast of Africa. Record of only one such voyage has survived, that of the brothers Vivaldi, who from Genoa in 1291 departed 'for the regions of India by way of the Ocean', thus apparently anticipating the task Columbus was to set himself almost exactly 200 years later. The Vivaldi presumably envisaged a circumnavigation of Africa rather than a transnavigation of the Atlantic, but the galleys they deployed were hardly suited to either purpose, too low and shallow for rough Atlantic waters, too dependent on inshore sailing for the inhospitable African coast. The Vivaldi were never heard of again, but it is likely that there were other journeys in the same direction, some of them in galleys, albeit with less ambitious aims. It was probably in the course of such expeditions that the Canary Islands were discovered. According to Petrarch, writing in the 1340s, Genoese armed ships had sailed to the Canaries 'within the memory of my parents [*patrum*]'. In 1337, he had professed himself almost as well informed about the Fortunate Isles as about Italy or France.[6]

The second phase, in which the archipelagoes of the eastern Atlantic were explored and mapped, began in the 1330s. In 1339, some of the Canary Islands, albeit somewhat misplaced to the north, with three islands in relative positions suggestive of the Madeira archipelago, appeared for the first time on a surviving map.[7] Thereafter, within the span of a couple of generations, there were so many voyages, accumulating so much knowledge, that an almost complete picture of the islands of the east-central Atlantic became available in Latin Christendom. The transformation of that picture by the time of maps reliably dated in the 1380s, in which, as we shall see, the Canaries are shown almost complete, with the Savage Islands, the Madeira archipelago and most of what I take to be the Azores, was a remarkable achievement: hazardous to the vessels, new to the technology and unparalleled in the experience of sailors of the time. To understand why and how knowledge of the Atlantic was so thoroughly transformed in such a short time, it is necessary to reconstruct the stages of the change in some detail. Because the winds of the Atlantic Mediterranean naturally constitute a system of ducts, which tend to take ships south-west from the pillars of Hercules and at most seasons force a wide northward sweep out to sea upon returning sail traffic, the exploration of the Canaries was necessarily the first stage.

## The Exploration of the Canaries

Like patches of twilight in the Sea of Darkness, the Canary Islands in the middle ages lay, never utterly unknown, but long unvisited, except by susceptible imaginations. By the time of their rediscovery at the end of the thirteenth century or early in the fourteenth, knowledge of them transmitted from antiquity was encrusted with fables of St Brendan and St Ursula, Merlin and the earthly paradise.

Indeed, the exact perceptions of the archipelago which early explorers took with them on their first forays are hard to identify among the myths. Of the supposed references to the Canaries in ancient literature, only those of Pliny are convincing. Pliny's circumstantial details – concerning, for instance, the number of islands and their climatic heterogeneity – seem to correspond to the geographical realities of the Canaries. His 'Nivaria' evokes Tenerife, with its snow-capped peak, and his 'Pluvialia' may well refer to one of the relatively rainy westerly isles. His description, repeated by Solinus and Isidore (those great mediators of classical learning in late antiquity) was identified with the Canaries in the era of rediscovery: his collective name, 'The Fortunate Islands', was appropriated by map makers. The rest of his nomenclature was borrowed in humanist circles. The terms 'Canary Isles' or 'Isles of Canary', current from the 1340s, also seem indebted to Pliny's name, 'Canaria', for one island.[8]

Although the aetiological enthusiasm of some historians causes them to 'detect' real places and events in the undergrowth of any myth or legend, no other demonstrable references to the Canaries were inherited from ancient writers. Mentions of remote islands by Plutarch and Horace are too vague to inspire reliance and might refer to any or all of the great mass of islands known or thought, in antiquity and the middle ages, to lie in the western ocean. The same applies to the western isles, Hesperides and Elysian Fields, which have sometimes been taken as allusions to the Canaries or even the Azores, but which might equally be wholly fabulous, without any basis in actual islands. Yet all this material helped, in the period of rediscovery, to shroud Pliny's relatively precise information in mystery, which was deepened by confusion with other island myths of late antique (Brendan and Ursula) or (in the case of the Merlin legend) even preChristian origin.[9] It is hard to say whether the enchantment spun into this tissue of fable increased or diminished the lure of the Atlantic for late medieval explorers. If Arab navigators were deterred by the Sea of Darkness, the mariners of Latin Christendom seem to have evinced a more adventurous spirit. While Arab geography recorded no advances in this field, in western Europe the corrupt traditions gradually changed, in the fourteenth century, in the light of observation and experience.[10]

The chronology of the late medieval exploration of the Canaries cannot be reconstructed with any certainty. The first authenticated visit, at an unknown date probably prior to 1339, was attributed in most sources to the Genoese Lanzarotto (or Lancelotto or Lanzarote) Malocello, who found the island which still bears a version of his name. The dating and authenticity of many of the earliest documents are so much debated that the exact circumstances and motives of Malocello's voyage – whether under Genoese or perhaps Portuguese auspices, whether of reconnaissance, conquest or trade – are matters for speculation. But his chivalric name, vagabond career (in Ceuta, Portugal and, perhaps, France as well as his native city) and attainment of fame are features of the tradition of explorers and early conquistadores as it was to come to be established over the next century or so.

It was perhaps diffusion of knowledge of Malocello's achievement by Genoese and Mallorcan map makers that excited efforts to trade, evangelise, enslave and conquer in the islands, with great intensity in the 1340s and a modest regularity thereafter. Whoever commissioned Malocello's voyage, it is certain that the first expedition of which a detailed account survives (copied, apparently, by Boccaccio and dated 1341) was in part, at least, a Portuguese enterprise.[11] The point is worth emphasising, as it contributes towards a growing picture of Lusitanian maritime activity in the fourteenth century.[12] This expedition, moreover, demonstrates cooperation between Portugal and Italian – specifically, in this case, Genoese and Florentine – experts, which characterises the early history of Portuguese overseas expansion and establishes a prima facie case for continuity between the 'medieval' colonial experience of certain western Mediterranean peoples in their home waters and the 'modern' history of empire building in the Atlantic. Moreover, although it sailed from a Portuguese port under Italian command, the '1341' expedition included, at a lower level, Castilian personnel and mariners 'from other parts of Spain'. Thus, almost at the very outset of the story, a modest Castilian presence can be detected which eventually would grow to preponderance. And it was via Italian merchants in Seville that the surviving account was transmitted to Florence and to Boccaccio's hand. Seville, therefore, appears already in its future role, the role we foreglimpsed in Chapter 2, as the data bank – the overseer and information exchange – of Atlantic navigation.

Because of changes in toponymy, the route of the voyage cannot be retraced accurately. But it is not hard to recognise the Canaries in the account. Depending on how one reads the text, the expedition can be shown to have visited at least thirteen islands (and perhaps as many as eighteen): if all the islets and great rocks are counted, the Canary archipelago can be said to contain thirteen islands (Lanzarote, Fuerteventura, Gran Canaria, Tenerife, La Palma, Gomera, Hierro, Graciosa, Lobos, Alegranza, Santa Clara, Roque del Este, Roque del Oeste). The possible references to more islands may be explained as the product of duplication or ambiguity. Six of the isles visited were inhabited: this fits the real situation in the Canaries closely enough, for, at the time, there were seven inhabited islands, and visitors may not have had an opportunity to observe signs of life on all of them. The description of Tenerife – with its numinous combination of high mountains and low clouds, snow and fierce defenders – is unmistakable. While less obviously unequivocal, the descriptions of the other islands fit the real topography of the Canaries. To the author of this account, the Canaries were 'insulas nuncupatas Repertas' – 'isles called Newfound – or perhaps the punctuation should be made to read, 'insulas nuncupatas "repertas" '. The excitement of new discovery rapidly communicated itself to merchants, like the Florentines of Seville who reported it home; map makers, like Angelino Dulcert who (if a later interpolation is not responsible) recorded the discovery of Lanzarote on his map of 1339; and humanists, like Boccaccio, who, as we shall see, had a particular interest in the anthropological implications of the news. Over the next few years, would-be missionaries and would-be conquerors formed an equally receptive public.

It was in Majorca that the news from the Canaries had the greatest impact. This is not surprising, although the Majorcans' role as early leaders in the late medieval 'space-race' in the Atlantic is too often forgotten or ignored. Majorca was itself something of a 'colonial society' and 'frontier zone': reconquered from the Moors only a century previously, it was briefly (1276–1343) the centre of an island kingdom which lived by trade and, therefore, from the sea. It was a centre, too, for the technical developments in shipping and cartography which helped to make Atlantic navigation practicable on a large scale. Majorca's map makers, the most renowned in Europe, were assiduous gatherers of geographical information, aided by the large Jewish community, from whom many of them were drawn. Exploration of the Canaries was, in a sense, a natural extension of existing Majorcan interests in Africa and the Atlantic: Majorcan shipping carried Catalan trade to northern Europe in the late thirteenth and early fourteenth centuries; and the dispensations Majorcans enjoyed to trade with infidels peculiarly fitted them to take part in navigation along the African coast. The island, moreover, had long been a Genoese staging post for westward navigation: indeed, the Vivaldi themselves had called there. Finally, it was the home of a school of missionaries, chiefly Franciscans, inspired by Ramon Llull's (1232–1316) methods of evangelisation – peaceful persuasion, enhanced by charity and apostolic example, expressed in native tongues. Llullian missionaries were to be among the most frequent early travellers to the Canaries.

At least four voyages from Majorca to the Canaries were licensed in April, 1342.[13] Francesc Desvalers, Pere Margre and Bartolomeu Giges – we know almost nothing of them save their names, though Desvalers has been linked with a certain En Valers, said to be lately returned from Tartary in a document of 1379 – were authorised to make two expeditions in the cogs *Santa Creu*, *Santa Magdalena* and *Sant Joan* to islands 'vocatas perdudes vel de Canaria', also referred to as 'newly found'. This nomenclature seems to establish a link in contemporary minds between these islands, the 'insulae repertae' of the '1341' account, the Plinian 'Canaria' and the islands of the Brendan myth, one of which was traditionally called 'Perdita'. That at least one of the Majorcan licences bore fruit in an actual voyage is shown by the chance survival of a mariner's claim for wages. Other licences were issued in the same month for voyages by Bernat Desvalls and Guillem Safont, 'simile mandatum', and to Guillem Pere, citizen of Majorca, 'to equip and make a voyage to the isles newly found in the parts of the west', again expressly in a cog. A detailed account of what may be a fifth expedition of about this time survives in a corrupt version in a printed book of the next century, which describes a fortuitous landfall in the islands by pirates (probably, though not expressly, Majorcan) pursuing a galley or fleet of the King of Aragon: though dated 1370, the account can be shown from internal evidence more plausibly to relate to the early 1340s. These pirates seem to have regarded themselves as the first discoverers of the islands: this raises the possibility of a casual Majorcan discovery independently of the voyages of Malocello and of the Portuguese, but may be explained alternatively as the result of a corruption in our text.[14]

A gap in the Majorcan archives conceals the next few years'

activity, though it seems unlikely that the hectic pace of the early 1340s can have been long sustained. The wage claim of Guillem Joffre indicates the commercial failure of the voyage on which he shipped and the death of one of its leaders, Pere Margre. This may have been a disincentive to other potential explorers, but continued activity during the sparsely documented years is indicated by the record in the Catalan atlas of the voyage down the coast of Africa to the 'River of Gold' (perhaps the Wad Draa, alchemically transmuted, or even the Senegal) of Jaume Ferrer in 1346.[15] It was formerly thought that Atlantic exploration suffered a 'check' in the mid-fourteenth century because of the effects of the Black Death and the technical insufficiency of ships and nautical aids.[16] Certainly, when archival records become available again from 1351, there is little evidence to support this. It may be, however, that some of the commercial impetus of the earliest voyage was lost, as most of the expeditions of the next generation appear, from surviving records, to have been the work of missionaries.

The voyage of Joan Doria and Jaume Segarra of 1351 is exceptionally well documented. In May, they obtained a Bull from Clement VI for a mission to the Canaries: they were to be accompanied by twelve Catalan-speaking natives of the islands (evidence here of the influence of Llullian methods of evangelisation) who had been captured by previous expeditions. The following month they obtained a royal licence to sail from Majorca. The completion of their journey is strongly suggested by the fact that in November of the same year, Clement VI founded the diocese of 'Fortuna' or of the Fortunate Islands, which was established at Telde in Gran Canaria and lasted until 1393.[17] Records survive of five further missionary expeditions between 1352 and 1386, and it is not unreasonable to suppose that there were others of which no notice has come down to us. It may be that the apparent shift of emphasis in the Majorcan voyages from commerce and conquest to conversion and pastoral care is connected with the reabsorption of Majorca into the Crown of Aragon in 1343.[18] Thereafter, of course, Majorca had no specific interest in making sovereign conquests. On the other hand, it is apparent that the Crown of Aragon inherited, at least for a time, Majorcan pretensions in the region, for a precious document of 1366 preserves royal instructions to the sea captain, Joan Mora, to patrol the archipelago and exclude interlopers from other states. This shows that shipping from outside the Crown of Aragon was active in these latitudes at the time, though, unfortunately, the exact provenance is not given.[19]

## The Mapping of the Archipelagoes

Previous attempts to identify the islands of the eastern Atlantic on early portolan charts and to reconstruct the process of their mapping have foundered on the unreliable chronology of the maps. In the attempt which follows, I avoid arguments which rely on assigning dates to undated maps or on assuming a date equivalent or roughly equivalent, where an almanac is included, to the date of the start of the almanac. The Medici Atlas of the Laurentian Library, for instance, opens with an almanac beginning in 1351;[20] but the Atlas has every appearance of being a collection of folios by more than one hand, drawn at different times. The fifth folio, which shows the Atlantic, most closely resembles the versions of Guillem Soler, one of which is dated 1385, and other maps of similar date or in the same tradition. The Catalan Atlas is conventionally attributed to 1375, because that year is used as the starting point for the composition of the Golden Number, but 1376 and 1377 are also mentioned in its accompanying texts; it conforms closely to the description of such an atlas in the French royal library catalogue, dated 1380 but possibly interpolated or revised later; and its date should also be considered in the light of the record of the imminent despatch of a mappamundi by Cresques Abraham to the king of France by the Infante of Aragon in November, 1381.[21] In view of the fact that Guillem Soler's map of 1385 is almost identical in its representation of the Atlantic, save that it is slightly more complete, the Catalan Atlas can be assigned with some confidence to the late 1370s or early 1380s. For most undated maps, however, it is impossible to suggest anything like so narrow a range of possibilities.

Two Venetian maps, the 'Pinelli-Walckenaer' of the British Library and the dependent 'Combitis' Atlas of the Biblioteca Marciana, are traditionally dated 1384 and c. 1400 respectively, the former because of the starting point of its almanac.[22] But both have features which suggest a much later origin: the perfunctory treatment of a group of islands in the eastern Atlantic, evidently derived from early attempts to represent the Azores, is a feature of maps of the second half of the fifteenth century and is not found on any known late fourteenth or early fifteenth-century example. The Mediterranean toponymy of both maps includes features not found before the fifteenth century.[23] Unless and until reliable dates can be assigned, it is best to leave these maps out of account when trying to establish the chronology of the mapping of the Atlantic.

Even from our limited store of reliable sources, it is possible to discern a gradual increase in the precision with which the genuine archipelagoes of the Atlantic were depicted, during the fairly intense activity by navigators in the fourteenth century. In maps, the discoveries seem to take shape. Whereas, in the early fourteenth century, the Hereford Mappamundi characteristically showed only a speculative mass of Atlantic islands, as though torn from the ragged western hem of Africa, by the time of the Dulcert Map of 1339, at least three islands of the Canarian archipelago were clearly distinguished. These two maps served different purposes: the first was devotional, designed to adorn an altar as an image of the perfection of God's creation (though the visitor to Hereford Cathedral today will find it dismissed to an aisle), while the second was practical, intended as an aid to navigation; but the differences between them also reflect the achievements of Lanzarotto Malocello. Dulcert has 'insula capraria' and 'Canaria' – both names associated with the Canaries – in what are probably speculative positions, about the latitude of northern Morocco, with the legend, 'Insulle s[an]c[t]i brandani sive puellarum', nicely blending the myths of Brendan and Ursula. What could be 'Pluvialia' (one of Pliny's names for the Canaries) lies close by. But off what is perhaps the Wad Draa the map shows 'Insula de lanzarotus marocelus', 'Vegimarin' (indubitably the present Isla de Lobos) and 'la forte ventura'. All are recognisably marked and the first is emblazoned with a Genoese cross, in honour, presumably, of Malocello's provenance. The somewhat later but evidently dependent British Library map, Add. MS. 25691, shows [Ca]praria just below the latitude of the easternmost extension of Africa, with a large 'Insula de columbis' (possibly alluding to the Brendan myth), then just to the south-east 'Canaria', below which comes the legend, 'Insulle de sanbrandini'. But to the south-east again, in roughly the correct position, come the identifiable Lanzarote, Fuerteventura and Lobos.[24]

The next relevant map of reliable date is the Pizigani portolan chart of 1367 in Parma.[25] Here place names associated with the Canaries begin to coalesce into a recognisably single archipelago. Gomera and Hierro seem to be depicted for the first time: certainly, there are eight distinct islands shown. The Catalan Atlas allows no room for doubt concerning the identities of the islands depicted in the positions of the Canaries. Of the eleven largest islands, only La Palma is omitted. 'Graciosa, laregranza, rocho, Insula de lanzaroto maloxelo, Insula de li vegi marin, forteventura, Insula de Canaria, Insula del infernio, Insula de gomera, Insula de lo fero' appear as we read, in order, from east to west. The corresponding modern names are Graciosa, Alegranza, Roque, Lanzarote, Lobos, Fuerteventura, Gran Canaria, Tenerife, Gomera, Hierro. Mount Teide, the great peak of Tenerife, is graphically depicted. The *Libro del conoscimiento*, compiled from the legends of maps at about this time, names eleven islands of the Canaries and includes the name 'tenerefiz', as well as 'Infierno', for the first time.[26] The roughly contemporary work of Guillem Soler improves on the Catalan Atlas and excels some later maps in placing the archipelago in its true position relative to the trend of the African coast. The depiction of the Canaries is also remarkably complete: Santa [Montaña] Clara is added, so that eleven of the twelve largest isles are shown. Hierro has been thought to have been omitted but is in fact clearly visible in the Florentine version of the map.[27] By the time of the work of Pasqualini and Viladestes early in the new century, Hierro was reduced to its proper size, though its shape remained odd.[28]

In view of the ample evidence of frequent sailings to the islands in the period concerned, there is no reason to question the substantial reliability of the evidence of these maps. It is worth stressing that, even were corroborative documents not available, the evolution of the cartographic image of the Canaries, from the speculations of the Hereford Mappamundi to the information recorded in late fourteenth-century portolan charts, would raise a strong presumption in favour of a thorough exploration in the corresponding period. This applies equally to Madeira, which, with the rest of its archipelago and the Savage Islands, appears on dated maps of the second half of the fourteenth century with persistence, consistency and verisimilitude which defy disbelief.

Yet, although the fourteenth-century discovery of the Canaries and the Madeira group is now widely accepted, the case of the Azores has been treated by historians with far more circumspection.

While scholars of a previous generation were inclined to accept the evidence of the maps, the textbooks in current use, especially in the English-speaking world, tend to dismiss or ignore it.[29] Partly, it seems, this is out of respect for the tradition that the Azores, together with Madeira (to which many of the same arguments apply) were discovered by followers of the Infante Dom Henrique of Portugal: Henrique was the first to colonise and systematically to exploit these islands, but that does not preclude earlier discovery. In part, too, scruples concerning the evidence of fourteenth-century knowledge of the Azores have derived from the widespread conviction that navigators of the time were incapable – from timidity or technical insufficiency – of sailing so far out to sea: the Azores are over 700 miles from the nearest land. But this is seriously to underestimate the mariners' proficiency and daring.

Works which clearly recorded the progress of the discovery of the Canaries also displayed knowledge of the Azores: the Guillem Soler maps, the Catalan Atlas, the Pasqualini and Viladestes maps share features in common in their depiction of the Azores which are also to be found in other maps contemporary with them or derived from them, such as the fifth folio of the Medici Atlas and the Catalan portolan charts of Paris and Naples. The islands, though displaced to the east and excessively 'strung out', occupy relative positions which are strongly suggestive of the central and southern parts of the Azorean archipelago. All show the Azores on more or less the same meridian as the westerly isles of the Canaries and on a rhumb north by north-west from a centre near Lanzarote and Fuerteventura, through the Madeira group: although one would actually have to steer a course to the north-west to reach the Azores from the Canaries, magnetic variation, variable winds, unfamiliar currents and cartographical error (assuming that all these maps belong to a single tradition) might account for the difference. The 'stretching' of the archipelago over a far greater area of ocean than in reality, and the exaggerated sizes of individual islands, are typical features of the period and characterise, for instance, the early cartography of the Canaries. All the maps, except the Catalan Atlas, show eight islands, which share a more or less common sequence of names: the Medici Atlas omits or conflates certain names: a central cluster of three islands, for instance, is called 'Insule de ventura sive de columbis', while most of the maps show 'Ventura' and 'columbis' or 'li columbi' as the names of two islands of the group. The

Catalan Atlas omits the two southerly islands – otherwise called 'Capraria' and 'Lovo' altogether, perhaps by inadvertence. The *Libro del Conoscimiento* lists eight islands, with recognisably the same names, in Castilian or Aragonese form, as are shown on the maps. For the identification of the islands depicted, or rather for the solution of the problem of whether they can be identified, the way they are clustered in definable groups is the most important of these common features. To understand the significance of this, it is important to consider how the Azores appear as one approaches them from the south-east under sail. Santa Maria is encountered first, lying well to the south of the main archipelago with little Formigas offshore to the north-west. São Miguel appears as a relatively large island, 'broadside on' to the north. To the north-west again, the central group of the archipelago is formed by two small clusters: Pico, Faial and São Jorge make up the more southerly cluster, Graciosa and Terceira lie slightly to the north-east in relation to it. Beyond the central group again, to the north-west, lie Flores and Corvo.

How does the reality of the Azores, thus described, correspond to the clusterings on the early maps? Two islands stand out, albeit at a greatly exaggerated distance, to the north and east of the central cluster, as do Terceira and Graciosa in reality. The central cluster is formed of three islands, which may be intended for Pico, Faial and São Jorge. The remaining islands are arranged on an approximate north-west to south-west axis. One of them occupies, relative to the central cluster, the position of São Miguel; the others, well to the south, suggest the relative locations and dimensions of Santa Maria and Formigas. Flores and Corvo, which in reality are well to the west of the rest of the archipelago, do not appear in any source before the mid-fifteenth century.[30]

It is, of course, one thing to say that the islands depicted on the maps genuinely resemble the Azores and another to claim that these resemblances derive from real knowledge; one thing to aver that sailors of the time were capable of finding the islands, another to demonstrate that they actually did so. The strongest reasons for doubting the maps lie in the difficulty of verifying their data. Though some bear reliable dates, they are vulnerable to emendation by later hands; their treatment of the Azores, in particular, is open to charges of vagueness, and many islands are alarmingly displaced from their true positions. Moreover, the toponymy of the fourteenth-century cartographers is classical and mythological and they include, elsewhere, many obviously conjectural islands. None of these caveats, however, definitely invalidates the maps. Nothing, indeed, in the cartographers' depiction of the Azores is demonstrably inauthentic. That the Azores appear only as the result of interpolation is possible, but improbable: the Catalan Atlas and the Soler maps, which constitute the essential evidence, betray no hint of the intervention of later hands, and fourteenth-century map makers are unlikely to have wasted parchment in order to give interpolaters space to work in: it gradually became normal to allow increased space to the Atlantic – and that in itself is a strong indication of the vibrancy of late medieval interest in exploration of the ocean – but, among surviving maps, it is only with the Nautical Chart of 1424, in the James Ford Bell Collection, Minnesota, that space seems to be included speculatively, to be filled in later. The surviving maps represent only a small sample of those which must have been available in widely dispersed centres: interpolation would have had to be widespread and systematic to yield such consistent results. Imprecision in the location of islands is only to be expected: if they were completely accurate, it would be a sure sign that they were forgeries, as no means of fixing one's position at sea with exactitude was available in the period. Navigators could take rough readings of latitude and, in our maps, latitudes are always roughly right or, at least, within the margin of error to be expected from cartographers who relied on readings obtained without instruments by direct observation of celestial bodies with the naked eye.[31] Longitudinal accuracy was unknown until the sixteenth century. As far as the classical and mythical toponymy of the maps is concerned, this is again just what one would expect of the period. The modern nomenclature was not fixed until well into the fifteenth century: a fourteenth-century map which appeared to anticipate it would be highly suspect. Learned cartographers who received mariners' reports of newly discovered islands naturally assigned them names which, if not purely descriptive (as, in some cases, they were) would be drawn from existing traditions. As for the inclusion of speculative islands, it was not only in the fourteenth century that such speculations were recorded as if they were facts. Notional islands continued to appear on nineteenth-century Admiralty charts. Genuine discoveries tend to breed speculation in their turn and Atlantic conditions are conducive to false sightings.[32] Inclusion of conjectural islands might as well be read as evidence of the sailors' knowledge of the Atlantic as of their ignorance. Finally, S. E. Morison's influential objection – that the islands appear on our maps on a north-south axis – is simply false. As we have seen, if Flores and Corvo are discounted, the remaining isles are clustered and arranged in the same way, allowing for the exaggeration of size and distance, in the maps as in reality. There are maps which show eastern Atlantic islands, bearing names traditionally associated with the Azores, strung out from north to south, but those are all fifteenth-century works, or, like the Pinelli-Walckenaer and the Combitis, wrongly attributed to the fourteenth. Their sketchy onion strings of eastern Atlantic islands may ultimately have derived from early attempts to depict the Azores, but, in the course of the fifteenth century, evidently became traditional and schematic.[33]

One vital objection to the cartographic evidence remains: why, if the Azores were indeed explored in the fourteenth century, are there no documents of the time, apart from the maps, which explicitly refer to them? Clearly, spurious traditions of later invention, which would throng the north Atlantic in the late middle ages with imaginary precursors of Columbus, must be discounted. But it is hardly surprising that uninhabited islands should be ignored by our written sources: they were understandably of little interest to slavers, conquistadores and missionaries, who, for instance, were responsible for the Canarian voyages documented above. It may be worth pointing out that the Majorcan sailing licences which speak of 'islands to the west' do not specifically exclude the Azores, but it is only common sense to take them as referring to the Canaries.

It is, however, possible to claim the discovery of the Azores as a by-product of the Canary run and to assign a corroborative value, for the alleged voyages to the Azores, to the evidence of navigation to the Canaries; in other words, the documents which refer to the Canaries may be treated by implication as evidence of knowledge of the Azores. Two circumstances may be cited in favour of this proposition. First, there is the sheer scale of navigation to and from the Canaries in the fourteenth century; secondly the influence of the Atlantic wind system. Since the discovery of a formidable body of documents on the activities of the missionary see of Telde and of the document on Joan de Mora's expedition of 1366, the Canary voyage can no longer be seen as an occasional or sporadic indulgence of the period. Once that is admitted, a context in which to understand the discovery of the Azores begins to emerge. It will be remembered that most of the early sailing licences for the Canaries refer to cogs, which were generally unsuitable for tacking against the wind. Though the name 'cog' was relatively new, it does not seem to have denoted a different type of ship from a traditional Mediterranean *navis* (Catalan *nau*). There is no reason to suppose that it was other than square-sailed. Rigged to catch a following wind, such vessels could only return from the Canaries by either of two expedients: they could limit homeward navigation to the most favoured season of the winter, when south-westerlies are frequent enough to grant a safe passage. Indeed, from what we know of the timing of some early voyages, that was understandably the most favoured method and route. But given the frequency of sailings, the duration of the period over which they took place, and the unreliable nature of the winds, it is unreasonable to suppose that the alternative route, making use of the pattern of prevailing winds, was not also employed. This meant striking north in search of the westerlies that would take one home. Such a course would touch or skirt Madeira and it would be generally expedient, if not always necessary, to reach the latitude of the Azores before turning east. The same return route is well attested for some of the Guinea voyages of the fifteenth century. Against the background of current knowledge of frequent sailings to the Canaries, the roughly contemporary discovery of the Azores seems natural, even inevitable. The process can be compared with the Portuguese discovery of Brazil in 1500 in the course of a wide sweep out into the south Atlantic in search of the westerlies that would carry the fleet around the Cape of Good Hope. This, on a larger scale and in reverse was a reflection of the journey the Majorcan cogs might have made on their return from the Canaries in the north Atlantic in the fourteenth century, like an image in a shaving mirror.

## The 'Unknown Pilots'

If it is accepted that the Atlantic Mediterranean was a fourteenth-century discovery, the problem of how it was done must be faced.

Such feats of ocean-going seamanship are often supposed to have been beyond the reach of the ships and men of the time, but if one were to discount the evidence of these voyages on these grounds, it would also be necessary to reject the achievements of Columbus, whose methods of navigation were no more advanced. The true test of a technology is not how sophisticated but how practical it is. Medieval mariners possessed, already in the fourteenth century, techniques different, of course, from their successors' but in no way inadequate to their purposes. Their exploration of the Atlantic was the fruit of the modest miracles of high medieval technology: the cog, the compass, the portolan chart and primitive celestial navigation, not with instruments but with the naked eye. The surviving cartographical evidence is consistent with the observations of dead-reckoning navigators, supplementing their calculations with estimates of latitude of this sort. Their achievement had been effected by Italian – chiefly Genoese – and Majorcan savoir-faire, the art of the 'conners of the sea' (*sabedores do mar*) so highly esteemed by the Portuguese crown.

Looked at collectively, with the early conquistadores and colonisers who form the subject of other chapters, they seem to have displayed motives and sources of inspiration similar to those commonly said to have animated western Europe's great 'age of expansion' in the sixteenth century. They often came from places with a recent crusading history, like Majorca, or had personal crusading experience, like Gadifer de la Salle and Joan Mora. They were sometimes penurious noblemen or even royal cadets, escaping from a society of restricted opportunity at home. They were seeking 'routes of gold' like Jaume Ferrer or 'routes of spices', like the Vivaldi, or slaves, like the Las Casas family of Seville. They were striving to embody chivalric fable, to win fiefs or create kingdoms, like the would-be conqueror of the Canaries, Luis de la Cerda, who was called 'Prince of Fortune', or la Salle's partner, Jean de Béthencourt, who had himself proclaimed 'King of the Canaries' in the streets of Seville. Or else they were missionaries or evangelistically inclined laymen, like Doria and Segarra. They came from a world steeped in chivalric romance and the idealisation of adventure and bore storybook names like Gadifer and Lancelot. They aspired to fame, and most have been forgotten. By contributing to the mapping of the Atlantic Mediterranean, they opened the area to some of the most radical and influential experiments in the creation of colonial government and society ever essayed from within Latin Christendom. It is time to look at those experiments more closely, and at the crucible in which they took place.

# 7. The Atlantic Crucible

The African Atlantic in the fourteenth century was an extension of the western Mediterranean world. Initiatives in the exploration of the area came from the most active maritime powers of the western Mediterranean – Genoa, the Crown of Aragon and, increasingly, Portugal. The progress of colonisation of Maghribi ports was along traditional, mercantile lines, tentatively modified by the Aragonese protectorate in the eastern Maghrib. In the fifteenth century, however, radical new departures occurred, which can, without exaggeration, be said to have introduced into the history of medieval colonisation features original to the Atlantic.

This is not to say that continuity of colonial experience from the Mediterranean to the Atlantic was broken; rather, that the tradition was dynamic and adaptable to new environmental conditions. The environments of the new colonial theatres of the fifteenth century – the Canary Islands, the Madeira archipelago, the Azores and the Cape Verde Islands – were unlike those of the Mediterranean. Climatically, they were compatible with earlier experience; the early cycles of exploitation, for cereals and sugar, reflected both the experience of western Mediterranean producers and the needs of western Mediterranean markets. Demographically, however, and in terms of available labour, the Atlantic archipelagoes presented novel features. Except for the Canaries, they were uninhabited; and the first isles of the Canaries to be colonised – Lanzarote, Fuerteventura and Hierro – were seriously underpopulated. The settlement of these islands therefore necessarily established a pattern of colonisation by settler communities who introduced a system of exploitation unprecedented in the previous history of the region.

This can fairly be contrasted with the medieval, Mediterranean background, where colonial models took other forms: urban and 'aristocratic' colonisation; 'Latin quarters' and *funduks*; the castles and enclaves of crusading or mercenary ruling groups, like the Catalan Company or the nobility of the Latin Empire; or merchant-conquistadores like the Giustiniani of Chios or the Venetian masters of Crete; élites, in short, who took over or modified an existing pattern of exploitation, organising the market or subjugating an existing labour force. In the early and mid-fifteenth century, the colonisation of the Canaries, Madeira or the Azores was closer in character to the settlement of the Iberian peninsula in the course of the conquests from the Moors – what Sánchez-Albornoz called 'a gigantic and uninterrupted process of colonisation'.[1] More particularly, as we have seen, Atlantic colonisation was prefigured in those parts of the Iberian peninsula which border on the Atlantic, or in valleys which drain into that ocean, while in eastern Spain, where the existing Moorish labour force was concentrated, colonisation was less intense at low social levels and conformed more closely to a 'Mediterranean' pattern. The Atlantic model established in the archipelagoes settled in the early fifteenth century was, in the respects we have identified, also typical of some parts of the New World. In the latter part of the fifteenth century, the exploitation of another new archipelago, the Cape Verde Islands, and of the islands of the west African gulf, by slave-fuelled 'plantation' methods, foreshadowed another feature of some of the colonial societies of the New World.

Awareness of distinctive features of Atlantic colonisation clarifies another major problem of the period: why – allowing for the importance of Italian, especially Genoese, and, to some extent, Majorcan capital and expertise – the colonisation of the 'Atlantic Mediterranean' was mainly the work of peoples with little Mediterranean colonial experience – the Portuguese and Castilians. Groups among both these peoples edged, in the course of the fourteenth century, gradually or fitfully towards the goal of exploration and colonisation of the Atlantic, influenced perhaps by the strength of the 'Reconquest' tradition, which habituated them to colonial exploits and provided a conceptual framework in which African and Atlantic conquests could be justified and understood. Of comparable importance was the increasing interpenetration of the Portuguese and Castilian economies with the western Mediterranean commercial world, and, in particular, the growing presence and influence of Genoese merchant-settlers in the Iberian peninsula. The first tentative Portuguese and Castilian steps in the western Maghrib and the African Atlantic in the fourteenth century are intelligible only against these backgrounds.

## Fourteenth-century Beginnings

In 1345, the King of Portugal claimed to have 'turned the eyes of our mind' to the subjugation of the Canary Islands and to have sent an expedition to that effect.[2] This may have been the same expedition as was recorded in a manuscript of Boccaccio's and ascribed, perhaps unreliably, to 1341; yet the internal evidence of the surviving account, which mentions impedimenta of war aboard the ships, suggests no more than an armed reconnaissance, at the private initiative, perhaps, of slavers and merchants.[3] In any event, it is remarkable that Portuguese interest in the islands should have been expressed at such an early date. Projects of conquest of the Canaries were being mooted elsewhere in western Mediterranean Europe at about that time. The Portuguese monarch had an interest in representing his plans as plans of conquest in order to establish a prior claim to the islands. But in the case of one of the Majorcan voyages of 1342, the intention to conquer part of the archipelago seems plainly written into the royal licence, issued on 16 April to Francesc Desvalers and his companions, to go to certain recently discovered islands 'commonly called the Isles of Fortune'. The licensees promised that if they should seize any island or part of an island, they would recognise the King of Majorca as suzerain, for whom they would hold their conquest in fee and to whom they would pay homage. Criminal jurisdiction and the right of appeal would be reserved to the crown.[4] The appearance at an early date of a 'feudal' model for the government of Atlantic conquests established a theme which remained characteristic in the Canaries at least until well into the fifteenth century and, to some extent, in other parts of the Atlantic for much longer. In other respects, the effects of the Desvalers expedition were short-lived. It was back in Majorca by October, 1342 (thus it was only one sailing-season long), with at least one of its leaders dead and no tangible gains to show for it.

The next attempted conquest of which we have specific information was that of Luis de la Cerda in 1344–45, under the aegis of Clement VI. The inclusion of the Mediterranean island of Jalitā in the putative principate conferred on the Castilian adventurer might indicate, as we have suggested, an attempt on the Saharan gold trade. From the pope's point of view, it may have signified a two-pronged crusade into north Africa and an opportunity to extend the patrimony of St Peter. Indulgences equivalent to those of a crusade were announced for prospective participants; again, a feudal model of tenure was adopted: the Principate 'of Fortunia' was to be held of the pope. The choice of de la Cerda, exiled victim of the dynastic insecurity of Castile, owes something, no doubt, to his own initiative, something to his royal blood ('de stirpe ac domibus processit regalibus,' as the pope pointed out) and something, perhaps, to his Iberian provenance. It helped to bring the idea of the conquest of the Canaries within the orbit of Castile (Luis's native kingdom), as well, perhaps, as that of France (his place of exile). Replying in March, 1345, to Pope Clement's request for aid with the project, Alfonso XI of Castile asserted a Castilian claim to the conquest. Indeed, by broadcasting letters and Bulls on the subject all over the western Mediterranean, Clement VI must have assisted the diffusion of knowledge of the Canaries generally. But despite the excited auguries which attended the project – Petrarch recorded a thunderstorm which enlivened proceedings at Luis's investiture and chroniclers all over Latin Christendom reported the event – the actual outcome was disappointing. De la Cerda never saw the Atlantic portion of his seigneury. One expedition at most, despatched from the Kingdom of Aragon, is traditionally thought to have sailed to the islands on his behalf, but there is no contemporary evidence of it. At his death 'Louis of Spain' bequeathed an empty title to the Canaries to his heir. His intervention in the history of the conquest had been, at best, a spur to others; at worst, because of its failure, a disincentive.[5]

For a generation after this episode there were – as far as we know – no more attempts to wrest the islands from their inhabitants by force. The conquest was abandoned to spiritual conquerors – Majorcan missionaries, for the most part, who concentrated their efforts on Gran Canaria. Slavers and perhaps fishermen might be presumed to have frequented the islands but no notice has survived of a renewed attempt at conquest until 1370, when the first partial or temporary success seems to have been achieved, though the disappearance of the original documents, which constituted the evidence, has cast doubt on the whole episode. According to presumed copies of much debated authenticity, on 29 June 1370, the King of Portugal granted two islands, which he called Nossa Señora a Franqua and Gumeyra to Lansarote da Framqua, who is described as 'admiral' and 'our vassal', and said to have found and conquered the islands in question for the Portuguese king ('trobou e nos gaañou'). An interpretation consistent with the other known facts of the islands' history is that this 'conquest' saw the erection of the tower on Lanzarote, attributed by later conquistadores to Lanzarote Malocello, who may have been the same 'Lansarote da Framqua' to whom the grant of 1370 was addressed. The cognomen 'da Framqua' could refer to the island seigneury, part of which the admiral may have wished to dedicate to Our Lady under that avocation for reasons of personal devotion or even possibly as a result of having been in French service, though there is no firm evidence to link Malocello, or any other 'Lancelot' who may be in question here, with France. By this interpretation, the island of 'Nosa Señora' would be Lanzarote, as a marginal note to the lost document is said to have suggested. As the toponymy of the Canaries was not yet definitively established it is not necessary to suppose that 'Gumeyra' was the island we now call 'Gomera', but the balance of probabilities seems to incline that way, as the cartography of the time had assigned more or less accurate positions, with more or less standard names, to all the other major islands of the archipelago. Other copies of documents relating to this seigneurie, of 1376 and 1385, of the same provenance as that of 1370, purport to show that Lansarote da Framqua continued to hold or attempt to hold at least part of his island possessions and died in their defence on Lanzarote in or shortly before 1385. This recalls the tradition that Lanzarotto Malocello spent about twenty years on his homonymous island.[6]

By the time of his death, he had been disputing possession with Castilian interlopers, as well as native Canarians, for at least ten years, in what the 1376 document called 'ficada guerra que ouve com os ditos gaanchos e castellanos (the enduring war he wages against the said Canarians and Castilians)'. It was natural that Castilian interest in the islands should have grown. The expedition ascribed to 1341 included Castilian mariners and it was through Seville that news of it was communicated to Italy. In 1344, a prince of Castilian antecedents had been enfeoffed with the islands by the pope. Reacting to that event the following year, the Castilian king had staked a claim of his own to the conquest of the archipelago on the spurious grounds that the islands, with much of the African mainland, had belonged to his remote Visigothic predecessors and that 'the kingdoms of Africa are of our conquest'.[7] Frequently in the third quarter of the century, Majorcan and Catalan missionaries must have sailed through Castilian waters to reach the islands. And the Portuguese occupation may well have made the Canaries a theatre of war between Portugal and Castile in the 1370s, when, according to tradition, expeditions were sent to the islands from Seville. Such expeditions, if indeed they took place, may have been nothing more than slaving ventures sponsored by Sevillan merchants. By the 1390s, however, a consortium had begun to coalesce in Seville of parties concerned to prosecute rights in the archipelago. In 1390, Gonzalo Pérez de Martel sought royal permission for an attempted conquest. According to a tradition recorded in the sixteenth century, Enrique III in that year made a grant of the conquest to a Sevillan gentleman, Fernán Peraza. The interest of the Peraza family was joined in 1393 with that of the Guzmán, Counts of Niebla, in an expedition (representative, no doubt, of others in about the same period) which wrought much destruction and captured many slaves. According to the account in the *Crónica de Enrique III*, Sevillan and Basque mariners shipped on this voyage, which seized a native chief and his consort on Lanzarote and reported to the king 'how those islands were easy to conquer, if such were his grace, and at small cost'.[8] This was the sort of glib prediction which lured many conquistadores to a terrible fate in the course of Castilian overseas expansion.

From that time onwards, there was no activity in the Canaries without some Castilian, and indeed Sevillan, dimension. It was perhaps not surprising, however, that the first conquest to establish a lasting European presence in the islands came neither from Castile nor any of the other parties to express an interest in the years immediately following the rediscovery, but from France. Until Henry V's invasion disturbed the development of the area, Dieppe was among the most suitable ports in Europe for long-range navigations, and the fishers and merchants of northern France were among the most travelled of men. The Dieppois, in particular, may already have been familiar with the latitudes of the Canaries.[9] In 1390, the Duke of Bourbon prepared an expedition to Barbary, understood by its chivalrous French participants as a new crusade in the spirit of St Louis, but probably intended for other purposes by its Genoese proponents. Al-Mahdīya, the target of the attack, had developed a reputation as a nest of corsairs whom

Genoa wished to eradicate. Additionally, the Genoese may have wished to counterbalance the predominance of the Catalans in the Hafsid kingdom by a show of strength of their own. The expedition is generally thought barren of consequences. Muslim chroniclers virtually ignored it. There were no more French attempts to renew the policy of St Louis in the Maghrib until the nineteenth century. But there were evidently Frenchmen who emerged from the experience with a taste for Maghribi gold.

## Béthencourt, La Salle and the Peraza

Among the men who contracted to serve with Bourbon at Al-Mahdīya were two who were to play crucial roles in the making of the Atlantic Mediterranean: Jean de Béthencourt, Lord of Grainville in Normandy, and Gadifer de la Salle, of the cadet line of a noble Poitevin house, who had served in the household of Philip the Bold and then as royal chamberlain and seneschal of Bigorre. Luis de la Cerda had already combined ambitions in Barbary and the Canaries, and it may be that the ducal expedition to Barbary turned the thoughts of Béthencourt and La Salle towards the same zone. Part of the inspiration, perhaps, and certainly some of the funds, for their venture came from Robert, called Robin, de Braquemont, chamberlain of the Duke of Orleans, who knew Spain well as a result of his participation in diplomatic missions. He was Béthencourt's cousin, through the conquistador's mother, Marie de Braquemont. Another thread of kinship linked him to the Canary Islands through his marriage to Inés, sister of Diego Hurtado de Mendoza, Admiral of Castile, two of whose daughters by his Peraza mistress married members of the Las Casas family, which in turn was allied by marriage to the houses of both the Guzmán and Peraza. These families were among the protagonists of the 1393 Sevillan expedition to the islands, and maintained their interest in the conquest. Braquemont's marriage to Inés de Mendoza took place in 1393 in Castile, where he had an opportunity to hear about Sevillan efforts in the archipelago. Without a loan from Braquemont, Béthencourt might never have attempted the conquest. On the way to the islands, either he or La Salle made a visit to Seville for an unknown purpose. Later, they recruited help there. The first bishop of the see founded in their conquests in 1405 was a member of the Las Casas clan. And it was from Juan de Las Casas, nephew by marriage of Robin de Braquemont, that a ship was despatched to the islands during the presence of the French expedition. Taken together, these facts enable us to see Béthencourt's venture in its Castilian, and specifically Sevillan, as well as its French context.[10]

It may have been the attraction commonly said to exist between opposites that caused Béthencourt and La Salle to link their fates in an attempt to conquer the Canary Islands. Gadifer, with no patrimony of his own, was essentially an adventurer, who had fought once already on the frontiers of Christendom as a crusader in Prussia. Reckless and improvident, of a straightforward and trusting nature, he never took any precautions to protect his interests and never acquired any wealth. He was steeped in conventional lay piety and the chivalric romance that resounds in his very name – a preincarnation of Don Quixote with the insular ambitions of a Sancho Panza. Béthencourt was the more practical partner. For him, the conquest was as much, perhaps, a financial gamble as a chivalric escapade. It is possible that he was heavily in debt, owing fines for infractions of sanctuary and violations of justice incurred in about 1399, and facing lawsuits in connection with his properties and with an act of piracy in which he had been involved with an English ship, after the official cessation of hostilities between France and England. Indeed, in the circumstances, his departure for the Canaries has something of the appearance of a flight. He shuffled his finance together like a card-shark, mixing private loans, small assets desperately realised and dubiously hawked crusading indulgences, without regard for the rights of his wife and heirs. This spirit of 'cut and run' was typical of many later conquistadores and Atlantic frontiersmen. Yet Béthencourt never lost sight of his escape route home. He trimmed efficiently when the English conquered Normandy, manoeuvred his comrade-in-arms out of any share in the spoils of the Canaries, protected the inheritance he left behind at Grainville from allcomers – Englishmen, creditors, cousins – and pursued the entire adventure in the Canaries as if more for gain than glory.[11]

Though most aspects of their expedition are shrouded in obscurity, the balance of probabilities is that, had the original intention been fulfilled, Béthencourt and La Salle would have conquered and colonised the Canaries as a French fief. *Le Canarien*, the chronicle of their deeds, has in part the character of an apologia for the fact that their efforts ultimately redounded more to Castile's benefit than that of France. French ambassadors at Leulingen informed the English of their voyage – which shows that it was executed with the French king's knowledge. And according to Enrique III of Castile it was by command of the king of France that they first set out for the islands.[12]

The original French character of the conquest was soon eroded by the pressing and practical problems of securing material help and a home base close at hand. Castilian aid and jealousy, French preoccupation and indifference, settled the future course of the islands' allegiance. The adventurers' reliance on Castilian help was inescapable. Not only was the financial basis of the expedition unstable; delays en route and dissensions between the leaders and among their complement almost wrecked the enterprise before arrival in the islands: of 280 initial recruits, only 63 completed the voyage. The party left La Rochelle on 1 May 1402. Eight days were wasted on disputes among the crew. At Cadiz, they fell under suspicion of piracy. Gadifer de La Salle was arrested in Puerto de Santa María and released only after examination by the royal council and negotiations of an unspecified nature in Seville. When, after the conquerors had established themselves on Lanzarote, in little condition to fight, Béthencourt returned to Castile to recruit help; Enrique III declared that the conquest so far had been realised in his own 'commendation and defence'. He authorised supplies for Béthencourt and forbade his subjects to prejudice the Norman's interest. By November, 1403, Béthencourt, who made a protracted stay in Spain, much to the chagrin of the isolated and beleaguered Gadifer, appears in Castilian documents as 'Lord of the Isles of Canary, my vassal'. His partisans' chronicle admits he did homage in Castile for the seven habitable islands; and a further act of homage by him, performed before Enrique's successor in Valladolid in June, 1412, was recorded in Castile.[13]

Béthencourt's justification for his submission evoked the grounds on which Portugal had claimed the right to conquer the islands in the previous century: 'the said islands stand closer to us than to any other prince', the Portuguese king had told Clement VI. This was strictly inaccurate, but so were Béthencourt's alleged words to Enrique III: 'You are king and lord of all the lands round about and the nearest Christian king.'[14] In general, Castilian jurisprudence did not accept such arguments from propinquity: Alonso de Cartagena, one of the most prominent Castilian jurists of the day, denied their applicability to Portugal's differences with Castile over title to the Canaries.[15] But for Béthencourt the significance of Castile's relative proximity was probably practical rather than legal. As *Le Canarien* explained, in a late rescension produced by the Béthencourt family:

> If the said Lord Béthencourt had found any comfort in the kingdom of France, there must be no doubt that then or soon after he would have come to an understanding, especially concerning the said Canary Islands. . . . And what is more, by the counsel of his prince and sovereign lord, the King of France, his intention was and still is to carry the enterprise further; but, without help, he could not even maintain his position.[16]

Gadifer de La Salle quarrelled with Béthencourt and withdrew from the adventure after the latter had completed his capitulation to Castile, less perhaps out of resentment at the Castilian connection than because Béthencourt had done homage in his own name only, thereby excluding Gadifer from any title to the conquered lands and any share in the fruits of the enterprise. It has been thought that it was the act of homage to a foreign king that outraged Gadifer: this would not be inconsistent with his character. But the version of *Le Canarien* favourable to Gadifer blames Béthencourt not only for submitting to Enrique III but also because 'he called himself lord of the said isles'. According to the version favourable to Béthencourt, the ground of his colleague's complaint was that he wished 'to have part and portion of the said isles of Canary'. Into Gadifer's mouth it put the words, 'There is one thing with which I am not content. For you have already paid homage to the King of Castile for the Canary Islands and you call yourself lord of all of them.' There is therefore an area of overlap, a kernel – as it were – of compatibility between the two versions which suggests that Gadifer's objection may have been less one of principle than of timing: isolated in the Canaries, he had missed the chance to do homage to Enrique, jointly with Béthencourt. It is also worth noticing that the pro-Béthencourt version of the chronicle is far more eloquent about the expedition's implicit disavowal of French allegiance than the pro-Gadifer version. The dispute between the two conquerors began in factional strife among their respective followers on the voyage out; but it grew acerbic when Béthencourt failed to keep his comrade supplied with provisions from Castile.[17] Béthencourt's adoption of Castilian suzerainty was pregnant with consequences for the future. Henceforth, Castile was to occupy a privileged position in Atlantic expansion. In the long run, the Canaries proved to be the most significant of the Atlantic archipelagoes, in strategic terms, because the wind system linked them to the New World. Béthencourt's 'switch' from French to Castilian allegiance suggests problems comparable with those of the Constantinopolitan and Tunisian crusades of the thirteenth century: was it the product of collusion or an ad hoc expedient? Whether or not Béthencourt had contemplated the Castilian 'option' in advance, it was the only resource open to him by the time of his arrival in the islands. The expedition was seriously underfinanced: Béthencourt had made ends meet by selling property in Paris and borrowing heavily from Robin de Braquemont. After desertions en route it was seriously undermanned. Supplies and men – as well as royal patronage and pay – could be recruited in Castile.

The manpower problem may have been decisive; its consequence seems to have been that Béthencourt founded a distinctly Spanish colony in his island seigneury. The complement of the original expedition was mainly Norman and Gascon (genuinely Gascon, it seems, not trans-Pyrenean Basque, because the names mentioned are French) with some Angevins and Poitevins. Women were included, as we know because of a chroniclers' allegation that some Spaniards tried to rape them.[18] But those who originally embarked contributed little to the process of colonisation. Béthencourt did make subsequent recruitment efforts in Normandy: the last island he annexed, Hierro, was settled by 160 Normans supplied by Béthencourt's nephew and administrator, Mathieu. He also had agents hawking indulgences around the lands of Benedict XIII's allegiance between 1411 and 1414: this effort may have yielded more recruits from a wider area. But already in Béthencourt's day, Castile – and particularly Seville – seems to have been the most productive source.[19]

This pull of Seville's undertow was confirmed by the terms of an agreement of 15 November 1418, in which Mathieu Béthencourt renounced most of his (and, exceeding his brief, his uncle's) rights

in the island to the Count of Niebla. Both Mathieu and Jean are
described as 'citizens of Seville'; the count's worthiness for the role
is said to rest on his nobility, power and royal blood; his intention
to complete the conquest of the islands and fulfil Jean's wish to
convert the inhabitants; his record of service to the Béthencourts –
an allusion here, no doubt, to the help of the Guzmán-Peraza-Las
Casas affiliates in the conquest; and his willingness to perform
further service in the future. Whether Niebla introduced more
colonists is unknown. But members of the Las Casas and Peraza
families who acquired rights, both from Niebla and directly from
the king, in the islands in the next decade, were active in promoting
settlement and attempting to extend the conquest. By the time of
the first surviving records from the islands in the mid-fifteenth
century, the language was Castilian and the institutions thoroughly,
unmistakably Castilian. The only vestige of the 'Norman' conquest
was in Castilianised versions of a few French personal names.[20]

Béthencourt did, however, have a formidable impact on the
society and economy of his island conquests. It is unlikely that he
conceived the conquest primarily as a colonial venture. Not only *Le
Canarien*, but also the documents of papal provenance (like the bulls
of indulgence and the material relating to the foundation of the
diocese of Rubicon) as well as the agreement with the Count of
Niebla, all stress a religious motive: 'to convert the natives', as
King Enrique simply put it.[21] *Le Canarien*, a work of clerical
authorship, expresses the same motive with the ring of truth:
Béthencourt and La Salle 'have undertaken this voyage for the
honour of God and the increase of our holy faith.'[22] It must be said,
however, that these claims, albeit not necessarily insincere, had
great value for the conquistadores as a justification of an otherwise
dubious undertaking. The rights of pagans to undisturbed
sovereignty was a much debated issue. But the right of Christians
to conquer them, save under serious provocation, was not generally
recognised. In stressing the pertinacity of their unbelief; in implying
that, because of the diversity of their customs, they lay outside the
protection of natural law; and in proclaiming the evangelistic
motive of the conquerors, the authors of *Le Canarien* were manifestly
seeking to justify an arguably unjust war. The natives 'are
miscreants and do not acknowledge their creator and live in part
like beasts', they declared in a typical passage.[23] The reference to
beastly habits would have been readily intelligible to a contemporary

reader as a sort of 'code' for behaviour – especially sexual behaviour – which infringed natural law: the followers of 'beastly' instinct belonged in a lower category of creation than observers of law. Whatever credit is assigned to their pious claims, there is no reason to doubt the force of the other motive which *Le Canarien* imputes to Béthencourt and La Salle: to find the 'River of Gold'. The adventurers' knowledge of the region to which they sailed was derived from the *Libro del conoscimiento de todos los reynos*, a source which *Le Canarien* cites and which embellishes the myth of the River of Gold with much circumstantial detail – some fanciful, some derivative – of the ease with which the abundance of gold could be extracted.[24] Like the denizens of the Maghribi *funduks* and the later Portuguese navigators of the west African coast, Béthencourt and La Salle were part of the late medieval gold rush. Unlike their Sevillan backers, they do not seem to have been greatly interested in slaves.

Though they had at first a large expedition under their command, and included women among their complement, colonisation was not a primary objective for Béthencourt and La Salle; and it was only from 1405, when hopes of an easy conquest or a quick killing on the gold-run had faded, that colonisation began in earnest, with Béthencourt's intensive touting in Normandy and the western Mediterranean. Even then, he favoured such craftsmen as carpenters and masons for his colony – potential creators of a fortified base like that attributed to Malocello. Like the Portuguese in the next generation, he turned to colonisation for profit as a sideline from the gold quest, without losing sight of the long-term objective. The expediency of the origins of the programme of colonisation is vividly illustrated by a proposal ascribed to Gadifer de La Salle in *Le Canarien*. As a means of escape from the logistic problems of the conquest, he is said to have exhorted his companions to 'kill all the [native] men, take their womenfolk . . . and live like them'. . . . 'Going native' – foreshadowed here – remained an option throughout the subsequent history of European colonisation in areas inhabited by 'primitives'.

The type of colony Béthencourt founded did not, however, conform to this desperate blueprint. The natives do seem virtually all to have died off or disappeared into slavery abroad, the women along with the men. In their place, the labour needs of the new society were met by a settler-peasantry, and women were brought in from outside: there were, for instance, 23 'young wives' among the first settlers of Hierro. There were no large proprietors on the islands of Béthencourt's conquest, though an élite of big landowners would be introduced, from the 1480s, into the other isles of the archipelago. Béthencourt distributed the lands of Lanzarote, Fuerteventura and Hierro among his peasants and artisans in 'un véritable *repartimiento*' – that is, a division of immovable spoils similar to that which characterised the reconquest of much of the Iberian peninsula. At least, a late and partisan version of the chronicle called *Le Canarien* credits him with such a division: 'And to each he gave part and portion of lands, manors and encampments (*logis*) as seemed good and as suited his rank.' The chronicle passes from facts to judgements when it adds, 'And he did so much that therewith was none discontented.'[25] The settlers brought with them the crops, livestock and ways of life of home; far from 'going native', they imitated metropolitan society.

This was what Braudel has called colonisation 'avec des gros bagages'. The first Atlantic colony belonged to the mainstream of later colonial history, to the sundowner's world of nostalgia. By the end of the fifteenth century, the most remote colony in Christendom, in San Sebastián de la Gomera, the most westerly deep-water harbour of the known world, from where Columbus's first voyage of discovery would depart, had built a parish church of cathedralesque proportions, staring out over the Atlantic through Gothic eyes. Its original portal can still be visited, embedded in the fabric of later reformations, evoking the metropolitan pretensions of a primitive frontier. In the easterly islands, and especially in Béthencourt's two main colonies of Lanzarote and Fuerteventura (which never benefited directly from the sugar boom that enriched the western islands in the last years of the fifteenth century) such pretensions were sustained amid gruelling poverty. Despite the romantic illusions with which they were associated in chivalric tales, islands in the late middle ages generally supported only poor and precarious lives unless they produced rare commodities, like Chios, or mineral wealth, like Sardinia, or specialised crops, like Sicily and Cyprus. The colonies of Béthencourt's foundation had no such advantages. In the earliest surviving self-characterisation, the people of Lanzarote called themselves 'poor, miserable and needy folk', victims of scant harvests, rare rain and economic overreliance on goats.[26] They begged the king of Castile to give them the services of a notary in their suit against their lords because they could not muster enough literacy between them to understand the documents in their case. The reality of life in the 'Fortunate Islands', beneath the civilised airs and chivalric graces affected by early colonisers, was nasty, brutish and short.

The economy was geared to slaving, raiding the African coast and victualling ships. The products Béthencourt brought in with his settlers were pigs, cattle and wheat: the goods they yielded were durable provender – lard, bacon, cheese, ships' biscuit. But Béthencourt's sketchy new agronomy did not entirely succeed in domesticating the economy of his islands. The traditional goats outperformed the new animals. Potential exports listed in *Le Canarien* show the balance between new and traditional products: 'several sorts of merchandise, like leather, fats, orchil, which is worth much money and serves as a dye, dates, dragon's blood and several other things.'[27] Orchil and dragon's blood were naturally occurring commodities, the first a moss-like substance gathered from rocks, the latter a resin, also used in dyeing but equally exploited medicinally: 'it is good for medicines', said a sixteenth-century source, 'and for putting flesh on one's gums'.[28] Pastoralism and gathering were features of the traditional economy of the islands which survived long into the colonial era, even when there were few natives left to pursue them.

Béthencourt's conquest was only a partial success: his declared objectives had been the large, fertile and populous islands of Gran Canaria and Tenerife; he got only the relatively unproductive and depopulated islands of Lanzarote, Fuerteventura and Hierro. Even these modest achievements were registered against native populations diminished and enfeebled by years of depredations by slavers and would-be conquistadores. On Lanzarote, Béthencourt and La Salle established themselves by subterfuge: they posed as defenders of the natives, whom they promised to take 'as friends rather than subjects', guarding them 'from all who would want to do them harm'; this could only have been understood as a reference to the same Sevillan slavers who were increasingly to become Béthencourt's suppliers and close associates. The goodwill thus procured from the natives gave the conquistadores a chance to erect a fort, at Rubicón in the south-east of the island: from there they could dominate Lanzarote and launch assaults on other islands. The example of Malocello's castle was before their eyes; but the classic pattern of Norman conquest was being followed in this last Norman conquest of all.[29] The castle was the first in a series they erected in Lanzarote and Fuerteventura. Neither guile nor intimidation could win them any of the more formidable islands. Their dominance was confined to those where the incursions of slavers had depleted and debilitated the defence. The populous islands – Tenerife, Gran Canaria, La Palma, Gomera – successfully defied them.

Between the end of Béthencourt's conquest and the last quarter of the fifteenth century, Gomera was the only island of the Canaries to fall to Christian arms. The Las Casas-Peraza family disputed the right of conquest, and the possession of the other islands, with numerous contenders – Mathieu Béthencourt, Enrique de Guzmán and the Portuguese – and it was not until the late 1440s that the then head of that house, Fernán Peraza, felt secure enough in the possession of Lanzarote, Fuerteventura and Hierro to give undivided attention to the extension of the conquest. His efforts, successful only in Gomera, were remembered by witnesses at a judicial enquiry some 30 years later and are celebrated in popular verses, still sung in the islands to this day. His attacks on Gomera and La Palma were said to have cost him 10 000 ducats and the life of his son, Guillén, who died on La Palma:

Weep, ladies, weep, if God give you grace,
For Guillén Peraza, who left in that place,
The flower, now withered, that bloomed in his face.
. . .
Guillén Peraza, Guillén Peraza,
Where is your shield and where is your lance?
All is undone by fatal Mischance.

The language of the traditional verses is richly chivalric: the invocation of ladies, the allusion to God, the images of shield and lance, the brooding presence of Mischance or Ill-fortune – *la malandanza* – combine to make La Palma seem an island of romance. In reality, the wars of the Peraza were squalid affairs, waged against neolithic savages who were scarcely fit opponents for a knight. In Gomera, the Perazas' methods of exploitation stand equally outside chivalry and outside the history of the development of Atlantic colonisation. They reverted to a Mediterranean model, reminiscent of the Jarbāh of Ruggiero di Loria. For on Gomera the native population was relatively numerous, and remained so until the 1480s. The traditional economy, yielding cheeses and hides, was not disturbed. Nor was there any colonisation at a low social level. The Peraza shut themselves up in their crude and comfortless keep of stone, which stands to this day, and sustained with their 'vassals' a relationship of mutual fear.[30]

## The Islands of the Infantes

The chivalry-steeped world of Gadifer de La Salle and Guillén Peraza remained the world of the conquistador. The Duke of Bourbon, erstwhile chief of La Salle and Béthencourt, was an epitype of chivalric virtue and one of the heroes of the Infantes of Portugal: a link, therefore, between French and Castilian conquests in the Canaries and Portuguese expansion in the other archipelagoes of the eastern Atlantic. The links go deeper still. The traditional historiography of Portuguese exploration 'has been plagued by the cape-by-cape depiction of the building of empire and the founding of innumerable havens by indomitable adventurers'.[31] It concentrates on the African coast and on the figure of the Infante Dom Henrique. This tradition perhaps obscures the real objectives of Portuguese Atlantic enterprise. To make sense of the story, it is necessary to reduce Henrique to human scale and see his priorities and those of his associates in a more credible order. The Canaries – such is the overwhelming probability – came first for Henrique, in terms both of time and importance; the colonisation of the other Atlantic archipelagoes was an important offshoot. Coastal exploration of the African mainland was, in a sense, a sideshow.

Like many princes of the Renaissance, the Portuguese infantes were prepared to invest heavily in 'fame', because they lived in an age fond of sententious historiography and of appeals to what would nowadays be called 'the judgement of history'. Posthumous repute was a criterion of the good husbandship of political authority and their chroniclers did the Portuguese dynasty proud. No prince drew more praise than Dom Henrique. He is familiar to English-speaking readers as 'Prince Henry the Navigator' but the name, in its modern sense, is misleading for a patron of navigators who

himself made no more than two short sea crossings; the soubriquet
has been current only since the nineteenth century and was coined,
at the earliest reckoning, in the seventeenth.

Henrique's was a world of shabby swagger. His *pourboires* to men
of letters, though money well spent, were squeezed out of meagre
resources. His early fortune seems to have been founded on piracy,
his growing competence on a soap monopoly. One could make out
an amusing case for representing his interest in exploration and
colonisation as an early form of grocer's colonialism, a foreshadowed
'imperialism' of a rising 'capitalist bourgeoisie'; his castle at Sagres,
commonly misrepresented as a sort of salon of savants, may have
been closer in spirit to a prefiguration of the Castle Drogo of Julius
Drewe or perhaps – because of the soap – the Thornton Manor of
William Lever. There is something in comparisons of this sort.
Henrique was, in his own way, driven by the pretensions proper to
a *nouvel-arrivé*. His was a copybook case of a royal cadet with ideas
above his station. Born a prince, he wished to be a king. Sprung
from an impecunious and parvenu dynasty, he wanted the sort of
wealth that control of the gold trade promised. To make up for the
lack of 'ancient riches' that were thought, thanks to Aristotle, to
constitute the essence of nobility, he saturated himself in the
prevailing aristocratic ethos of the day, the 'code' of chivalry.

For at the opposite pole from the image of Henrique the grocer,
is the equally false, but at least contemporary, image of Henrique
the *beau idéal* of romance; an Arthurian figure, surrounded by
Merlinesque cosmographers and adventurous knights and squires,
riding the waves on missions of knightly and Christian virtue,
doing battle with swart paynims, discovering exotic islands, braving
supernatural terrors in seas of darkness and fighting for the faith.
Henrique certainly shared this self-perception. Little survives of
any writing of his own, but the two probably authentic memoranda
attributed to his pen, recommending expeditions against Moors in
Tangier and Málaga respectively, are replete with chivalric images.
Their concern is not with the practicalities of warfare but with the
glamour of great deeds – 'grandes fectos'. Battle with the infidel is
commended as 'more honourable' than war against Christians.[32]
Similarly, Henrique's correspondence with the popes – not, of
course, direct from his hand or brain but reflecting ideas current in
his milieu – while addressing the specific priorities of its intended
audience and stressing the evangelistic possibilities of Henry's

proposed conquests, is always heavily coloured by chivalric influences. The infante's pagan, primitive opponents are either elevated to the status of 'Saracens' – fit targets for the sword stroke of a crusader – or derogated to the ranks of the wild men of the woods, the 'homines silvestri', who, commonly in the art of the time, figured as the symbolic adversaries of knights.[33]

Still, scope remains to subject this chivalric model of Henrique's behaviour to critical scrutiny. In particular, there is a danger of taking the crusading propaganda too seriously. Apart from endowments made late in his career for the study of theology at Lisbon and Coimbra, Henrique never put any resources into spreading the faith. The kingdom whose extension he favoured was, to all appearances, one of this world. His knightly order, the Order of Christ, was religious rather in avocation than vocation. Though his attempted or intended conquests on the African coast were justified in evangelistic terms, and popes often charged him with the labour of converting the inhabitants, there is no evidence that he ever made more than token responses to that charge. Remarkably, the only friars who specifically obtained bulls for missionary activities on the 'Guinea' coast – that is, sub-Moroccan Africa – in or soon after Henrique's lifetime were not even Portuguese subjects but Franciscans of the province of Castile, to whom the Portuguese were 'pirates, Christian in mame'.[34]

As well as a champion – at least, a verbal champion – of knightly ideals, Henrique was a victim of material exigencies. The latter must be assigned an important role in stimulating the interest of Henrique and other Portuguese princes in the exploitation of the Atlantic. The problem of Henrique's 'motives' has been obscured by the dominance in the historical tradition of work executed under his patronage by one chronicler, Gomes Eannes de Zurara (died c. 1474), and particularly of one chronicle, which Zurara devoted to the exploration of the Guinea coast. By making his patron his hero, Zurara implicitly belittled the part of Henrique's brother, Dom Pedro, who, having exerted an important influence on navigators and colonists, was to die as a reviled rebel; his memory was coloured by the circumstances of his demise and his full role can no longer be reconstructed from the surviving evidence. By concentrating on the exploration of the African coast, Zurara created an abiding impression that Henrique's main area of interest lay in extending knowledge in that direction, while other documents seem to point elsewhere. And in a famous analysis of Henrique's 'six' motives, Zurara stressed two sources of motivation – detached curiosity and crusading fervour – which have been accepted as influential by almost all historians but which are unsubstantiated by any other evidence about Henrique. Praise, from humanists and cosmographers, for the scientific possibilities opened up by voyages he patronised, may have made Henrique aware of the usefulness of academic affectations; but it was Pedro who was the literate, erudite and well-travelled infante, patron of scholars. The sort of reading matter Henrique favoured might have inspired a taste for 'mirabilia' – sensational tales of the fabulous and exotic; he may have hoped to find some of them fulfilled in previously unknown lands. But the scientific adulation he attracted in his day was no more than the equivalent of an honorary degree conferred in our times by sycophantic dons on a thuggish 'statesman' or successful business 'pirate'.

The one point in his analysis of Henrique's motives where Zurara seems to have spoken with his master's authentic voice appears, ironically, to have been almost universally dismissed by historians. 'The reason from which all others flowed,' according to Zurara, was Henrique's faith in his own horoscope. This accords with what we know of Henrique's profound interest in astrology: he composed a book on *The Secret of the Secrets of Astrology*, dealing briefly, as a surviving abstract reveals, with the virtues of the planets, extensively with their influence on the sublunar world and duly with the art of astrological prediction. While Zurara's other priorities – science and the crusade – were drawn from traditions tangential to the trajectory of Henrique's life, it is likely that the horoscope was of central importance to the prince. Zurara omits the vital information: he tells us neither how the horoscope was cast nor what it portended, but a good deal of evidence is available to suggest that Henrique was driven by a sense of 'destiny', a 'talent' or 'gift', a 'vocatio qua vocatus est', as King Duarte's ambassadors called it. According to the ambassadors' submissions to Pope Eugenius IV, Henrique preferred 'by far to let the talent handed down to him shine forth before the Lord than bury it in the ground.' The use of scriptural term, 'talent', evokes Henrique's personal chivalric motto and the 'Talent de Bien Faire' which he felt called on to deploy. What did he think this talent was? The ambassadors' memorandum offers further clarifications: 'by amplifying the Christian name' – this phrase can be dismissed as an attempt to endear the infante to the pope – 'he might more expressly fulfil the image and likeness of King João, from whom to him, as by hereditary right, that gift was bequeathed.'[35] The sense of filial duty played an increasing part in Henrique's life. His father died in 1433, and all but the youngest of his grown-up brothers between 1438 and 1449. The death of one brother, the Infante Fernando, in captivity at Fez in 1448 was a heavy charge on his conscience, for he had opposed the possible surrender of Ceuta in ransom. His adoption of an homonymous nephew may have been a response to feelings of guilt over Fernando's death: as well as an heir, Henrique was adopting a quasi-paternal role. In 1449, he became the senior surviving prince of his house when his elder brother, Pedro, fell in rebellion against the crown.

A king's heir is a potential king, and Henrique's sense of his filial duty implied a quest for regality. Like John of Gaunt, he must be a threat to the crown or seek a crown of his own elsewhere. A memorandum of April, 1432, addressed to the king from the Count of Arraiolos, who knew Henrique intimately and himself played a prominent role in Portugal's Moroccan 'crusade', made the point vividly. Referring to the infante's desire to conquer Granada or Morocco, the count observed that Henrique might 'have the kingdom of Granada, or a great part of Castile, and have the affairs of this kingdom [Portugal] in the palm of his hand, and the Canary Islands, which you desire'.[36] The same point is suggested by the quasi-regal household of unruly 'squires' and 'cavaliers' whom Henrique maintained at great cost and no little trouble: a surprising proportion of the surviving documents concerning Henrique are pardons addressed to members of his household for violent crimes, especially murder and rape. This entourage was not only evidence of Henrique's pretensions: it also committed him to seeking to fulfil them in order to generate patronage with which to reward his followers.

An illuminating source, generally dismissed by historians because it occurs only in a late and corrupt version, is the account of Diogo Góes, a squire of Henrique's household, who took part in person, under the prince's auspices, in the African 'run'. Diogo's account of his master's motives is entirely credible: Henrique needed gold with which to reward his followers; the 'sea of sand' which lay athwart the gold road was unnavigable to Christians; only the 'ship of the desert' could cross it. So he sought a way round it in ships of the other sort.[37] Land crossings of the Sahara were attempted in the fifteenth century. In 1413, Anselme d'Isalguier was reported to have returned to Toulouse from Gao with a harem of negresses and three black eunuchs, though how he got so far into the interior of Africa no one knows. In 1447, the Genoese Antonio Malfante got as far as Touat, before turning back with garnered rumours of the gold trade. In 1470, the Florentine Benedetto Dei claimed to have been to Timbouctou and observed there a lively trade in European textiles. And from the 1450s to the 1480s, Portuguese merchants made frequent efforts to cut across country from Arguim, via Waddān, heading for the same destination: at least, they seem sometimes to have succeeded in diverting gold caravans to meet them; by the time of the end of their endeavour, communications with gold-yielding areas had been opened by sea.[38] The intractable nature of the land-route, indeed, demanded a seaborne approach.

By implication, Diogo Góes linked the search for gold with an attempt to re-enact the traditional strategy – anticipated, as we have seen, without success in the previous century – of combining the seizure of a Maghribi port, as a terminus for the gold trade, with the attempted conquest of the Canary Islands. Diogo dates Portuguese sallies against the islands from 1415 – the year of the capture of Ceuta – and while there is no evidence of sustained interest in the Canaries on Henrique's part before the 1430s, Castilian anxiety about Portuguese interlopers in the Canaries is documented from 1416. A large Portuguese expedition, allegedly of 2500 men and 120 horse, apparently inspired by Dom Henrique but paid for by the crown, was launched to defeat in Gran Canaria in 1424. And, if Luis de la Cerda could contemplate a principality which included the Canaries and Jālita, there was nothing inherently impossible about ambitions which may have comprehended the Canaries and Ceuta. The attack on Ceuta is traditionally seen as an extension of the 'Reconquest', or increasingly as part of a widespread Portuguese 'wheat empire' of the fifteenth century (see p.198). It belongs at least as much to the history of attempted European interventions in the Saharan gold trade.

Without having to rely on Diogo Góes' evidence, it is possible to see that the Canary Islands were Henrique's main objective from the 1430s onwards and that the gold trade was his main motive. Zurara concealed the importance of the Canary Islands – perhaps deliberately, because the failure of Henrique's efforts to acquire them would have made an unheroic tale, or perhaps because, as he tells us, the events were covered in another chronicle, now lost. But Henrique's correspondence with the popes reveals the archipelago as the focus of his attention. In 1432, the year of Arraiolos's warning of Henrique's interest in the Canaries, his claims to the right of conquest led the pope to commission opinions from noted jurists on the question of the rights of the pagan inhabitants of the unconquered islands and of the legitimacy of war against them. Documentary evidence abounds of expeditions under Henrique's auspices to Gran Canaria and Gomera in 1434, and it is evident from friars' protests that Henrique's career as a slaver, to be continued in the next decade on the African coast, began then in the Canaries. Henrique suspended his activities in response to papal prohibitions in 1436 but continued efforts to obtain a foothold in the islands by peaceful means – even supplicating for a share in the conquest at the Castilian court. Because the Canaries were evidently understood to be excluded from the series of general 'crusading' bulls issued for Africa to the Portuguese from September, 1436 onwards, he did not cease to beset the pope with requests to renew his conquest rights. There were further Portuguese attacks on the islands in 1440 and 1442, and almost continual efforts to reach a peaceful understanding with the natives of Gomera in the 1440s. In 1446, Henrique sought to ban Portuguese vessels from going to the Canaries without his permission. In 1447 he obtained a dubious title to some of the islands from Mathieu de Béthencourt, who no longer had any legal interest to dispose of. Fortified with this specious claim, Henrique made repeated efforts to seize Lanzarote from its settlers and Gran Canaria from its natives between 1448 and 1454, in no case encountering lasting success. In the mid-1450s, Portuguese anxiety about the Canary Islands subsided, perhaps because the penetration of the Senegambia region offered the chance of an alternative forward base for the search for gold. In 1455, the Counts of Atouguia and Vila Real, who were closely involved in Henrique's service and had both served in Ceuta, obtained a right of conquest of the unsubdued islands – arguably invalid, since it clashed with the concessions of the Peraza family – from King Enrique IV of Castile. On or after Henrique's death, this was made over to the prince's protégé and nephew, the infante Fernando, and further Portuguese expeditions of conquest, of debated date, were launched, probably in the 1460s and certainly in the 1470s. The Treaty of Alcaçovas-Toledo of 1479 explicitly allotted the Canaries to Castile. But even this was not definitive, and Portuguese claims were again advanced in connection with marriage negotiations between the Portuguese and Castilian dynasties in 1482.[39]

This long-sustained effort in the Canaries cannot have been inspired by caprice. Dom Henrique himself always claimed – as did those who wrote or spoke on his behalf – that he was actuated by religious motives alone: 'more indeed for the sake of the salvation of the pagan inhabitants', claimed his brother, 'than for private gain, which was non-existent'. But this claim was disingenuous. For Henrique, as for Béthencourt and La Salle, whose example was before his eyes, the Canary Islands signified a way of outflanking the traditional trans-Saharan gold road, an offshore staging post near the fabled 'River of Gold' – the name is used by Zurara and other sources close to Henrique; he may also have seen them, as I have argued, as part of a sort of bifocal dominion, part Canarian and part Maghribi, which would span the presumed route.

The much vaunted Portuguese 'breakthrough' in African exploration with which Henrique's popular reputation is virtually synonymous – the rounding of Cape Bojador in 1434 – was a product of the effort to seize the Canaries. Coastal toponymy was highly confused and cartography, in those latitudes, imperfectly reliable. It must be doubted whether the Portuguese navigators were consistent in assigning particular names to particular capes. But 'Cape Bojador' probably normally signified nothing more remote than Cape Juby. It had been passed before – probably many times. The Portuguese regarded the Canaries as 'beyond Cape Bojador'. Only in a relatively callow school of navigation, like that of Dom Henrique, can it have seemed significant. If, when Henrique died in 1460, the cape was recalled at all, its memory can hardly have consoled him for his major failures: the Canaries had eluded him; no crown adorned his head; and of the gold of Africa only a few threads had come within his grasp.

## The Rounding of Africa's Bulge

The great litany of exploratory voyages celebrated by Zurara begins in earnest only in 1441. By that date it was doubtless apparent that little or no gold was to be had in the latitudes of the Canaries, which thenceforth became important chiefly as advanced bases, 'for the greater perfection', as Zurara himself wrote, of Henrique's deeds. It was necessary to continue the search further south, and to exploit the chief resource of the region: slaves. Significant amounts of gold, obtained by truck, did start to reach Portugal from west Africa in the mid-1440s, but the big advances, both in the extent of exploration and in the discovery of gold, came in the generation after Henrique's death, as Portuguese explorers worked their way around Africa's bulge.

Towards the end of the prince's life, a navigator of some genius was employed: the Genoese Antoniotto Usodimare, who sailed up the Senegal and Gambia rivers, making contact with outposts of the empire of Mali, in the mid-1450s. On at least one voyage he was accompanied by a Venetian with a remarkable flair for reportage. Alvise da Cà da Mosto was a Vespucci-like figure, disposed to make exaggerated claims, but his acquaintance with the homeland of the Wolof Blacks seems undeniable and his account is full of authentic observations. It might be tempting to see the success of these 'mercenaries', in contrast to the slow progress of Henrique's household knights, as an example of the importance, in the making of the Portuguese empire, of foreign professionalism and enterprise. But da Mosto, as his own account makes clear, was personally interested in exploration and inquisitive about the geography and ethnography of Africa – 'very curious to see the world', as Diogo Góes said – whereas the infante's followers had other priorities, whether crusading, slaving, creating offshore fiefs in island principalities or hunting for gold.

The most dynamic source of enterpreneurism to appear among the Portuguese in west Africa came from within Portugal itself: the 'privatisation' of the right of exploration to Fernão Gomes, a merchant of Lisbon, who commissioned voyages which added 2000 miles of coastline to the area navigated by Portuguese ships. Fernão's monopoly lasted from 1469 to 1475: it seems an astonishing rate of increase over the tortuous gropings of the lifetime of the so-called 'Navigator'. But conditions were now more propitious. The Portuguese had broken through the most adverse of the coastal sailing conditions of the African bulge and had established colonies in Madeira and the Azores which eased the route home. The profitability of the west African navigations had been established by trade in gold, slaves, ivory and malaguetta 'pepper'. The crown retrieved Fernão Gomes's monopoly in 1475, perhaps in order to confront Castilian interlopers. The navigation of west Africa became the responsibility of the senior prince of the royal house, the Infante Dom João. Henceforth, Portugal had an heir and, from his accession in 1481, a king committed to the further exploration and exploitation of Africa. Dom João seems to have conceived the African Atlantic as a sort of 'Portuguese main', fortified by more coastal trading establishments of the sort which had been founded by Dom Henrique at Arguim, because of the hostility of the natives and its suitability as a trading station, in the 1440s. Since then there had been numerous informal and unfortified trading posts set up in the Senegambia region, often by freelance expatriates 'going native' in various degrees. But Dom João had a militant and organising mentality, forged in his war against Castilian interlopers on the Guinea coast between 1475 and 1481.

The most important point on the underside of the bulge, both strategically and economically, was around the mouth of the Volta, and west to the rivers Benya and Pra, where there were local sources of gold, while more gold could be traded from upriver. Here the most impressive establishment – the fort of São Jorge da Mina – was erected at Dom João's orders in 1482 by a party of 100 masons, carpenters and workmen. The inauguration of a new policy of permanent footholds, disciplined trading and royal initiatives was apparent to the native chief who professed a preference for the 'ragged and ill dressed men' who had traded there before. The other prongs of the new policy were the centralisation of the African trade at Lisbon, in the Casa da Mina beneath the royal palace, where all sailings had to be registered and all cargoes warehoused; and the cultivation of friendly relations with powerful coastal chieftains, like the Wolof chiefs of Senegambia, the Obas of Benin and ultimately the 'Kings' of the Congo. At the same time, Dom João tried to give the entire African enterprise enhanced prestige at home. He took the title of 'Lord of Guinea'. He emphasised the Portuguese claim doubtless with a wary eye on Castilian envy – and the duty of evangelisation which was thought to legitimise it. He presided over an extraordinary 'turnover' in baptisms and rebaptisms of rapidly apostasising Black chiefs. In one extraordinary political pantomime in 1488, he entertained an exiled Wolof potentate to a full regal reception, for which the visitor was specially decked out with European clothes and silver plate.[40] None of this implied permanent colonisation of Africa. The longest terms of service were those of the chaplains of the forts. Only the renegades who went native in the woods overcame the problems of acclimatisation and survival which inhibited the development of colonial societies in the fullest sense. Colonisation was an offshore activity, limited to the archipelagoes of the African Atlantic.

## The Portuguese Colonies

Dom Henrique was a failure in his two dearest projects – the quest for the gold source and the desire to acquire the Canary Islands. But he does deserve credit as a patron of the colonisation of Madeira and the Azores; with other members of his family – especially Dom Pedro – he can be counted, after Jean de Béthencourt, among the first creators of Atlantic colonial societies, and so among the makers of the Atlantic civilisation. Again, the tradition derived from Portuguese writers of the fifteenth and sixteenth centuries, exaggerates in some respects. Members of Henrique's household did not discover Madeira or the Azores, as we have seen; nor did the colonisation begin – to judge strictly by the evidence – anything like as early as has sometimes been supposed. In 1433, the king's claim that Henrique was colonising Madeira 'on our behalf' was premature; the following year, Henrique's boast that he had built churches on the island and settled it 'with people of both sexes' shows that he had a colonial strategy by that date; but it was more a pre-emptive stake than a factual account: Henrique seems to have known little about the island, which, he claimed, he was 'liberating from the Saracen yoke'. In 1436, Madeira was thought to be a suitable wasteland retreat for Valencian hermits.[41] But from the summer of 1439, detailed evidence of the beginnings of real colonisation contrasts tellingly with the vagueness of these early, implausible asseverations.

Portugal's Tangier crusade had failed; news from the Canaries was dispiriting. There was both an opportunity and a need to find new outlets for the infantes' energy and new resources for their patronage. Seed, sheep and perhaps settlers were shipped to Madeira and at least one of the Azores in June and July, 1439.

During the next decade, colonisation was 'farmed out' to enterprising intermediate 'lords', whose grants of lordships, as dependents of the infantes, were made contingent on their inducing settlers to populate the islands. Their recruitment was supplemented by using the islands as places of exile for criminals. The first of the 'barons' of Madeira was a knight of Henrique's household who became known as 'Tristão da Ilha'. He lived the romance implied by his Arthurian name, exacting oaths of vassalage from the cutthroats who came to his island. With a fellow member of Henrique's entourage, João Gonsalves Zarco, who was granted the portion of the island not previously enfeoffed to Tristão in 1450, he was regarded by Henrique as 'the first to have colonised the island on my behalf'.[42]

The uneasy relationship of this pair of paladins is tantalisingly documented in a handful of survivals. Some charters of João Gonsalves to his sub-feoffees, reassigning underexploited land; some adjudications, by Henrique or the king, of Tristão's stormy relations with his vassals: these reveal the painful process of inducing settlement. Royal redefinitions of the extent of the barons' respective moieties suggest the dangerous disputes which imperilled the peace. Tristão and João Gonsalves had turbulent followings of desperadoes and cutthroats. Although most of the colonists were probably peasants – 'those of lesser quality', as a letter of King João's says, who lived 'from their labour and cutting and planing wood and from their raising of livestock'[43] – those we know about individually were almost all déclassé *fidalgos*, most of them exiles from Henrique's household for ignominy or crime, serving terms of two or three years. As a result, mid-fifteenth-century Madeira was ruled by a form of gunslinger's law. No incident better captures the tenor of life than a curious abuse of the chivalric conventions in 1452. Diogo de Barrados, a knight of Henrique's service, had been exiled to Madeira, where he served Tristão da Ilha in his household like a knightly retainer, performing 'honour and vassalage'. Ever since Arthur and Lancelot, lords had tended to encounter sexual trouble with their ladies and their household knights. In the present case, Diogo abused his status to seduce Tristão's daughter. The scene (laconically recounted in a royal pardon), in which Tristão chopped off the offender's pudenda and flung him into a dungeon, takes us into a strange world of mingled savagery and civility, not unlike that of the Peraza in Gomera at about the same time: a society of courtly aspirations and crude, desperate reality.[44] The reputation of the Azores at this time was thoroughly unappealing, even to the most desperate of men. In 1453, a sentence of life exile in São Miguel was transferred to Ceuta 'because the said islands [sic] were not such that men could sustain life'. The following year, an exile complained that he could achieve nothing profitable or serviceable in the Azores.[45]

Yet the Portuguese Atlantic islands survived these deprived and dangerous years and rapidly established a stable, economically successful basis of life. Lasting settlement could only be procured by the coercion of exiles. On the Canarian model, which the Portuguese were probably following, it could only be guaranteed by the conferment of extensive privileges: jurisdictional for the 'lords' who promoted colonisation, fiscal for the ordinary settlers. King Alfonso's charter to Dom Pedro for his Azorean island of São Miguel freed the settlers from dues on exports to Portugal 'so that the island may become well populated'. All Henrique's islands enjoyed similar privileges. The grant of João Gonsalves' fief illustrates the conditions which were probably typical of concessions at the top of island society. The grantee and his heirs forever were to have the captaincy of Madeira, outside the limits of Tristão da Ilha's seigneury, with sole rights of jurisdiction, except in cases punished by death or mutilation, in which Henrique reserved the right of appeal. In some islands – Santa Maria and São Miguel of the Azores, for instance – rights of jurisdiction were more limited, all sentences requiring confirmation from Portugal. The 'captain' could grant lands to occupants who promised to stay for at least five years. He had monopolies of flour mills – a traditional seigneurial privilege – bread ovens and the sale of salt and the right to an impost on any sources of water for irrigation and on any mining operations 'extracting veins of iron or other metals'.[46] The last clause was part of a standard formula.

The sort of economy envisaged for Portuguese islands in the grants of the 1440s seems to have been based on the contemporary experience of the Canaries. Sheep, cattle and wheat were specifically mentioned. Imports of Canarian slaves might have turned Madeira into an ersatz Canary Isle, though a settler-peasantry from Portugal rapidly came to form the bulk of the population and the Canarians took specialised roles as herdsmen and, later, sugar-mill staff. To some extent, the Azores fulfilled early expectations; they developed slowly, growing in importance as the Portuguese commitment to the exploitation of mainland Africa gew, favoured by the winds as staging posts for the return trip from the African bulge. They remained wheat producers: Portugal's 'empire du blé'. Madeira, however, was catapulted into early prosperity by the force of a new product which revolutionised the agronomy in the second half of the fifteenth century: with some of the more westerly of the Canary Islands, it became almost a rival spicerie, supplying sugar, the only Atlantic product that could compete as a high-value condiment with the spices of the east. Sugar replaced honey as the western world's sweetener in the fifteenth century. It may have been one of those cases where demand follows supply, for in the last quarter of the fifteenth century, when Atlantic sugar production 'took off' with the development of new sugar-lands in the Canaries, sugar confections were still luxuries, featuring prominently, for instance, in the household accounts of Isabella the Catholic as Christmas gifts for the royal children. But, as with tea and coffee in the eighteenth century or chocolate in the nineteenth, popular taste quickly responded to the increased supply. By the time Piero de' Cosimo painted *The Discovery of Honey*, apiculture was, in a sense, a thing of the past, a primitivist image, which could be used to typify a remote age.

Madeira's rise to prosperity was spectacular. João Gonsalves liked to claim the credit for this himself. A letter of Paul II of 1469 summarises his boasts: 'by your efforts and ingenuity the island was peopled with Christians . . . by your diligence it grew in yield of fruits, especially of sugar, wheat and other things and increased in our days to such an extent that it supplies the greatest possible comforts to inhabitants of Portugal and of the other kingdoms of Spain'. A few years later, when João Gonsalves asked the pope to confer indulgences on a place of pilgrimage which he had endowed on the island, he emphasised the 'labours and dangers' amid which he had populated Madeira. By 1478, Madeira was expected to contribute 1 200 000 *reais* for the needs of the realm out of a total subsidy of 70 000 000. The deputies of the Cortes of 1481–82 praised the wealth of Madeira, claiming that in the single year 1480 'twenty forecastle ships and forty or fifty others loaded cargoes chiefly of sugar, without counting other goods and other ships which went to the said islands . . . for the nobility and richness of the merchandise of great value which they have and harvest in the said islands'. This prosperity – though doubtless exaggerated by the envious peninsular deputies – was lavish enough; and not, of course, despite João Gonsalves's boast, the creation of a single hand. Dom Henrique must be given his due. In fact, his achievements as a colonist in Madeira and the Azores are more conspicuous than the halting progress of his efforts as a patron of explorers, so amply vaunted in the literature. Madeira, as Paul II acknowledged 'was by the said infante first reduced to habitable use'. And though Henrique's brothers and nephew were also important in the development of the Azores, seven of the islands benefited from personal interventions by Henrique to introduce European products or stimulate settlement.[47]

Perhaps most importantly of all, Henrique was involved in the earliest stages of the Atlantic sugar industry. In aptly named Madeira, wood and wood-products were the local 'equivalent' of Canarian dyestuffs – naturally occurring goods, that is, that did not have to be raised from European seeds or stock. The island continued to export wood and pitch in the early sixteenth century, and the legend of rapid deforestation by fire is doubtless much exaggerated. It is true, however, that sugar 'took over' the island's economy within a short span – perhaps as little as a decade – just after the turn of mid-century. For Alvise da Mosto, who visited in 1454–55, Madeira was already 'a land of many canes'. Dom Henrique was a partner in the building of the first recorded sugar-mill in 1452. But the sugar industry was capital-intensive. To plant the canes, build the mills, pay the specialised staff and stoke the furnaces, which were necessary to turn raw canes into refined sugar, demanded capital investment on a scale unprecedented in Portugal, save among the Genoese sugar-producers who had begun production in the Algarve in the first years of the fifteenth century. The active ingredient in the takeoff of the Madeiran economy was the wealth and savoir-faire of Genoese financiers.[48]

Between the aristocratic hoodlums at the top of society and the settler-peasantry at the bottom all three archipelagoes had foreign industrial or commercial élites – Italian, predominantly Genoese, in the Madeira group and in the Canaries, Flemish in the Azores. In Madeira, most foreign investors were absentee-capitalist; in the Canaries and Azores large alien resident communities developed.

The Iberian islands formed a sort of 'enterprise zone' of new exploitation, a *taste-vin* cupped to the lips of the merchants of the two most commercially developed regions in Europe: Italy and the Burgundian dominions. Among the early subinfeudations made by Dom Henrique on his islands were those of Porto Santo (1446) to Bartolomeo Perestrello and of Terceira (1450) to Jacques de Bruges. When Jos van Utrecht was made captain-general of Faial in the 1460s, the appointment was justified on the grounds of the 'good peace and concord' which, as a fellow countryman, he enjoyed with the inhabitants. Bruges, where many of them came from, was the most important northern port of Iberian – indeed, generally for Mediterranean – trade in the fifteenth century, 'where all the nations of the world meet', as Pero Tafur said. Portuguese merchants were granted privileges there by the Dukes of Burgundy from 1411. Such privileges were reciprocated. Merchants from the rich, densely populated southern Netherlands were sure of a market for the grain of the Azores, the sugar of Madeira. By the end of the fifteenth century, a third of Madeira's sugar went to the Low Countries. It is not surprising to find that Netherlanders had an appreciable share of the covert colonialism practised by foreign capital in the nascent Iberian empires.[49]

Until the development of the Cape Verde Islands, from the 1460s, and of islands of the Gulf of Guinea somewhat later, all these Atlantic colonies relied on European immigrant labour, the greater part by far of Iberian provenance, with the Portuguese playing a major role, as small farmers and technicians, even in the Castilian Canary Islands. In the sugar industry, which demanded the intervention of large-scale growers and mill-owners, virtually the only slave labour was employed in the mills, while the land was worked by sharecroppers of European origin. In the Cape Verde Islands, however, in the 1460s, a new model was introduced: the slave-based plantation economy, unprecedented in European experience since the ancient *latifundia*. Cape Verde offered an inhospitable environment in which European immigrants were hard to come by and ill adapted to survive. The Infante Dom Fernando, Henrique's heir, tried to begin to settle them in 1462 but soon found that 'because they are so far from [Portugal] people do not want to go to live there without great privileges and exemptions'. The islands possessed no indigenous population, but were close to sources of black slaves in west Africa. By the 1480s the demand for slaves on the island of Santiago was already so great as to be disturbing for the titular monopolists of the slave trade; in response to complaints of interloping, the settlers of Cape Verde could only reply that the slaves were essential to them for the very maintenance of life. The plantation economy of this remote frontier was a world apart from that of the metropolis, where slaves formed an essentially domestic labour force or in the more northerly island-colonies, where they played specialist roles.

How tenuous life was in the distant plantations is revealed by a series of surviving petitions of 1499 from São Tomé in the Gulf of Guinea, only fractionally north of the equator. The island had been settled at the second attempt in the 1490s, with the intention of creating sugar plantations and exploiting the opportunities of trade on the mainland for slaves, copper, ivory and malaguetta pepper. In April, 1499, the founding captain-general, Álvaro de Caminha, lay dying; his will is a blurred panorama of the economy and society of the island. He bequeathed the copper utensils, slaves and sugar futures which constituted his wealth, while he worried about the island's social problems: the need for marriages among the settlers, the defence of the community's essential privileges at court, the suppression of runaway slaves. In June, following his death, a group of settlers of six years' standing, writing to the king, could profess themselves so content with the effects of his rule 'that none of us regrets his exile from those kingdoms of yours'. Yet this was bravado. Although Caminha's self-appointed successor, his nephew Pedro Álvares, could boast of intending to build a city 'which after it is finished will be one of the most magnificent works one could find', he was obliged to acknowledge the true, desperate state of the colony. The permanent colonists numbered only 50, nearly all of them exiled criminals. So acute was the shortage of food and the prevalence of sickness that no greater number could be accommodated. The so-called captain begged for a ship to send back to Lisbon the most recent arrivals – a group of the converted children of Jews banished from Portugal in the expulsion of 1497. Some of them had already been shipped to Príncipe 'in order to be able to eat'. The land, Pedro Álvares claimed, was evil; and though slaves, pepper and ivory abounded cheaply on the coast, there was no truck on the island with which to buy them.[50] Meanwhile, off Cape Verde itself, Santiago had been the only island to attract permanent colonists: it was still '*the* Island of Cape Verde' in 1500.

A projected colony on Boa Vista never took root: only the livestock remained, running wild, to be hunted by shooting parties from Santiago. Most islands were deserted save for lepers seeking the reputedly prophylactic turtles' blood, or Castilian orchil-gatherers, or merchants collecting the shells esteemed as truck on the African coast. Apart from sugar, contraband was the only source of fortune: in the 'rivers of Guinea' and among the Mandingo, weapons were eagerly traded for slaves.[51] Yet the sugar industry proved rewarding enough, and the plantation model of exploitation sufficiently lucrative, to ensure the survival and gradual growth of the colonies of Cape Verde and São Tomé and to inspire the foundation of a new one, along similar lines, on Príncipe in 1500.

The architect of the settlement of the Cape Verde Islands – and therefore, in a sense, of this new economic model of colonial exploitation which was to become so influential in the New World, was a Genoese, Antonio da Noli, who began and ended his career in Portuguese service but remained a genuine 'free lance', willing and able to transfer allegiance to Castile, if necessary, in order to preserve his fief.[52] On such a remote frontier, he must have been monarch of all he surveyed; his example may have been a deterrent to the Castilian and Portuguese crowns. No more Atlantic territories were formally enfeoffed to foreigners in the next generation (though development continued to rely on foreign capital). The next successful candidate, Noli's fellow Genoese, Columbus, found it hard to get a commission and impossible to enforce its terms.

The years between da Noli's tergiversation (1475) and Columbus's enterprise (1492) were of crucial importance for the Atlantic fortunes of Castile. Those years must be considered, and the context from which Columbus emerged must be described, before the threads of Castile's and Portugal's expansion can be drawn together and the problem of their Atlantic mastery addressed.

# 8. From the Canaries to the New World

## The Context of Columbus

Most books about Columbus have been biographies, which, even at their best, can seem to abstract their protagonist from his proper context. The historical tradition has concentrated on Columbus's credentials as the European 'discoverer' of America, accentuating his heroic individualism or that of rival claimants. Interest in his idiosyncratic geographical theories has fortified his singular image. He is popularly regarded as the great examplar of timeless prowess, registering achievements in the face of contemporary derision. Washington Irving, who popularised this myth in prose, and Cole Porter, who did so in doggerel, have a lot to answer for. In reality, of course, new notes are rarely struck by one-man bands. It is true that Columbus's cosmography was admitted by only a small number of experts, but experts rarely rule, and it was on political and financial backing, not informed assent, that the launching of Columbus's enterprise depended. The background against which such backing for further Atlantic exploration became possible in Castile took shape between the 1470s and 1490s. Many events contributed: Columbus's own suit at court; the prominence and sympathy of many of his fellow-Genoese; the growth of confidence of a purposeful political leadership in and around the persons of the Catholic Monarchs; the effects of Luso-Castilian rivalry and, in some respects, of the war of Granada. The context which bound all these elements together was the progress of the conquest of the Canary Islands.

Castilian interlopers in the African trade had attracted Portuguese complaints in the previous three decades, but the war of 1474–79, in which Afonso V challenged Ferdinand and Isabella for the crown of Castile, acted as a catalyst for Castilian activity. The monarchs were open-handed with licences for voyages of piracy or carriage of contraband; the Genoese of Seville and Cadiz were keen to invest in these enterprises, and Andalusian mariners, including many who were to ship with Columbus or who made transatlantic journeys after him, were schooled in Atlantic navigation. The main action of the war took place on land in northern Castile but was accompanied by a 'small war' at sea in the latitudes of the Canaries. Castilian privateers were licensed by their monarchs to break into Portugal's monopoly of Guinea trade by force; Antonio da Noli deserted to Castile; Portuguese ships made numerous attacks on Castilian settlers in Lanzarote. The importance of the unconquered islands of the archipelago – precisely the largest and richest, Gran Canaria, La Palma and Tenerife – and the fragility of the Castilian hold on Gomera (see p.184) were thrown into prominence. When Ferdinand and Isabella sent a force to resume the conquest in 1478, a Portuguese expedition in seven caravels was already on its way. The intervention of the Catholic Monarchs thus has the character of a pre-emptive strike against the Portuguese.

Other, longer-maturing reasons also influenced the royal decision. First, the monarchs had other rivals than the Portuguese: the Peraza lordship of the islands had effectively descended, by marriage with Inés Peraza, to Diego de Herrera, a minor nobleman of Seville, who fancied himself as a conquistador. His claim, however, to have made vassals of nine 'kings' or native chiefs of Tenerife and two of Gran Canaria[1] was, to say the least, exaggerated. He had raided those islands in the hope of extracting tribute by terror, and had attempted, in the manner of previous conquistadores, to dominate them by erecting intimidating stone turrets. But such large, populous and indomitable islands could not be conquered by the private enterprise of a provincial hidalgo; effective conquest and systematic exploitation demanded concentrated resources and heavy investment, such as could be organised with greater readiness at court. And even had Herrera been capable of completing the conquest, it would have been unwise to permit him to do so. He was not above intrigue with the Portuguese; he might have become a turncoat, like Antonio da Noli in the Cape Verde Islands. And he was typical of the sort of truculent paladin whose power in a peripheral region was an affront to the crown. Almost since the inception of the Canarian seigneurie, lords and kings had been in dispute over the limits of royal authority in the islands. Profiting from a local rebellion against seigneurial authority in 1475–76 – one of a series of such rebellions – the monarchs determined to enforce their suzerainty and, in particular, the most important element in it, the right to be an ultimate court of appeal, throughout the colonies of the archipelago. In November of that year, they initiated an enquiry into the juridical basis of the lordships of the Canaries; embodied in an agreement between seigneur and suzerain in October, 1477, were its findings, that Herrera's rights were unimpeachable, saving the superior lordship of the crown, but that 'for certain just and reasonable causes' which were never specified, the right of conquest should revert to the crown.[2]

Beyond the political motives for royal intervention in the Canaries were economic ones. As always in the history of Latin involvement in the African Atlantic, gold was the spur. According to a highly privileged observer, King Ferdinand's interest in the Canaries was aroused by a desire to open communications with 'the mines of Ethiopia' (that is, Africa).[3] The conclusion of the Portuguese war effectively denied him access to the lucrative new gold sources developed on the underside of the African bulge, around the mouth of the Volta, in the 1480s: this must have helped to stimulate the search for alternative sources and may help to explain, for instance, the emphasis on gold in the journals of Columbus. Meanwhile, however, the conquest of the Canaries was worth completing for the islands' own sake, especially for their dyestuffs and for the potential sugar lands of the unconquered islands. Both these commodities had rapidly growing markets in Europe.

It proved almost as hard to advance the conquest under royal auspices as under those of Herrera. It took six years of unremitting campaigns to reduce Gran Canaria to submission; the conquests of La Palma and Tenerife were not considered complete until 1492 and 1496 respectively. The ferocity of native resistance was responsible in part; but finance and manpower proved almost equally hard to command. Though royal intervention had begun as an attempt to take the conquest out of private hands and bring it into the 'public' domain, as the conquest wore on private sources of money and means of recruiting tended increasingly to displace royal ones. Instead of wages, the conquistadores were promised a plot of conquered land. Instead of the yield from the sale of indulgences or the direct use of the crown's share of booty to meet the costs of the war, booty yet uncollected was pledged as rewards to conquerors who could raise the necessary finance elsewhere. By the end of the process, the conquests of La Palma and Tenerife were being financed by ad hoc companies, in which financiers and conquistadores agreed to share the proceeds.[4]

At the nerve-centre of the monarchs' war effort, scraping contingents together, assembling groups of financial backers, was Alonso de Quintanilla, a treasury official who was one of the most influential architects of policy in the reign of Ferdinand and Isabella. He seems to have been given responsibility for the organisation of the conquest from 1480, when dwindling returns from the sale of indulgences caused a crisis of finance. He devised a wide range of expedients, including the mortgaging of royal booty and recourse to Italian, chiefly Genoese, capitalists. In doing so he adumbrated the circle that would later contribute to the financing of Columbus. Quintanilla himself was instrumental in arranging the backing for the 'Enterprise of the Indies', as for that of the Canaries. In both cases, he was supported by key figures, the Genoese merchants of Seville, Francesco Pinelli and Francesco da Rivarolo. Pinelli had been involved in Canarian finance for as long as Quintanilla, as he administered the receipts of the sale of indulgences on the monarchs' behalf from March, 1480; Quintanilla's first personal subvention was made in April. Pinelli went on to acquire the first sugar mill on Gran Canaria and make loans to the conquerors of La Palma and Tenerife. For his part as a backer of Columbus, the monarchs made him one of the first administrators of the Indies trade when it was organised as a royal monopoly in 1497. Francesco da Rivarolo may have done even better out of the whole affair. There is no evidence that he contributed personally to the conquest of Gran Canaria, but his son-in-law was one of the biggest investors, and the Rivarolo family was a close-knit business partnership carefully managed by the patriarchal Francesco. He took part in the financing of the conquests of La Palma and Tenerife in his own right and became the richest merchant in the archipelago, with interests essentially, but not exclusively, concentrated in sugar and dyestuffs. He was a mainstay of Columbus, whose fourth voyage he financed and who later dwelt in his house. Some non-Genoese of Seville from the fringes of Columbus's world also took a hand in paying for the conquest of the Canaries: the Duke of Medina Sidonia, whom Columbus saw as a possible patron; Gianotto Beraldi, Florentine (according to most sources), who had a share of the New World trade in its early years. But the balance was strongly Genoese. The same is broadly true of the financial circle that sustained Columbus or advanced money for his voyages. There seems to have been sufficient overlap for the conquest of the Canaries and the discovery of America to be seen, to some extent, as the work of the same group of men. The Genoese of Seville played, for Castile in the Atlantic, a role similar to that of the Florentines of Lisbon in the impulsion of Portugal into the Indian Ocean a few years later.[5]

The Canaries were a vital part of the context of Columbus in a further sense: they provided him with his starting point. The port of San Sebastián de la Gomera, from which he set sail, was uniquely suited to his purpose: no deep-water harbour was further west, none closer to the path of the north-east trade winds that would carry him across the Atlantic. It is probably no exaggeration to say that, but for the accidents which made the Canaries Castilian, the New World could not have become predominantly Spanish. Attempts to explore the Atlantic from the Portuguese islands of the Azores, like that of Ferdinand van Olmen in 1487, were doomed to be turned back by the prevailing winds. Gomera only became a safe starting point in 1489, when the last native rebellion was crushed by a force of conquistadores from the lately conquered Gran Canaria. The event left the island in the hands of the exmistress of the king and widow of Gomera's administrator, Doña Beatriz de Bobadilla, who had probably met Columbus in Cordova in 1486.[6]

## The Last Canarian Conquests

The conquests of Gran Canaria, La Palma and Tenerife and of the last native insurgents of Gomera, which form the immediate backdrop to the creation of a Castilian empire in the New World, belong to the traditions of Iberian expansion within the peninsula, in the Mediterranean and in Africa – conceived, or at least represented, in the same way, as 'crusades' or extensions of the 'Reconquest', justified to a remarkable extent in the same terms, 'written up' by chroniclers in the same chivalric language. But before these elements of continuity can be explained, the course of the conquests must be summarised.

Two observations made by one of the most insightful of contemporary chroniclers are helpful for an understanding of the conquests. Although the natives were neolithic 'savages', literally armed with sticks and stones, their stratagems and the defensible terrain brought them frequent victories over technically superior adversaries. And the conquest made 'continuous' demands on the scant resources which Ferdinand's and Isabella's heavily committed monarchy could spare for the task. A remark of the chronicler, the royal secretary, Hernán de Pulgar, about Gran Canaria could be extended to the natives of the other islands as well: they might have proved insuperable, but for the internal rivalries which the conquistadores exploited.[7] As in Naples, Granada, Mexico and Peru, Castilian conquerors were the beneficiaries of indigenous civil wars.

Undermanned and irregularly provisioned, for the first three years of the conquest of Gran Canaria, the Castilians contented themselves with making 'entradas' or raids by land on native villages. Working for wages, and therefore with little incentive to acquire territory, the recruits from urban militia forces did not touch the mountain fastnesses on which the Canarians used to fall back for defence. Rather, they concentrated on places in the low plains and hills, where food, not fighting could be found – the plains where the natives grew their cereals, the hillsides up and down which they shunted their goats. It was a strategy of mere survival, not of victory. Between raids, the invaders remained in their stockade at Las Palmas, where inactivity bred insurrection. The arrival of Pedro de Vera as military governor in 1480 inaugurated more purposeful strategies: he planned amphibious operations to the otherwise barely accessible west coast and the erection of another stockade – a 'second front' – at Gaete. But his first major victory was the result of a miscalculation by the defenders, who descended to the plain of Tamaraseite near Las Palmas, to offer 'conventional' battle with disastrous results: if the chronicler Diego de Valera can be believed, de Vera slew the most formidable native chief in a suspiciously knightly or Homeric encounter, with his own hand.[8] Towards the end of 1480 or early 1481 the natives' seedtime brought a lull in hostilities, probably formalised by a mass baptism, to which the natives would have submitted cheerfully enough, without understanding much of its significance. Certainly a group of chiefs or notables whom the Spaniards had captured and in some sense converted, arrived at the court of Ferdinand and Isabella in May, 1481. The Catholic monarchs wished to impress these new subjects with their clemency as well as their power and, urged on by ecclesiastical advisers, desired to speed the conversion of other Canarians by a timely display of Christian charity. They bestowed a letter of privilege, declaring they had taken the people of Gran Canaria 'beneath our protection and royal defence, like the Christians they are' and guaranteeing their right to move and trade among Castilian dominions on an equal footing with Castilian-born subjects, as well as promising freedom from enslavement.[9] For the time being these stipulations held good and the recipients of this charter must have been well satisfied with their own achievements as well as dazzled by those of the monarchs. From that time on, the movement of 'loyalism' among the natives grew, so that in the coming campaigns Pedro de Vera was able to play off rival factions as a means to final victory. In particular, the capture and conversion of one of the most important chiefs, known to tradition as Tenesor Semidan but better identified by his baptismal name of Don Fernando Guanarteme, in February, 1482, immeasurably strengthened de Vera's hand, as Don Fernando was able to induce many of his compatriots, especially around his power base in the north of the island, to submit.

Yet victory still proved elusive and, frustrated by the inaccessibility of the insurgents of the south who held out in the central mountains, beyond perilous goat walks and precipitous defiles, Pedro de Vera turned to a policy of terror and of scorched earth. Innocent natives were burnt to death in reprisal for the loss of Spanish soldiers. Supplies and livestock were seized to deny them to the enemy. Gradually, coerced by these tactics, or persuaded by the eloquence of Don Fernando, the natives surrendered. Some abandoned hope and ended their struggle by self-immolation, flinging themselves from terrible heights, chillingly described by Spanish chronicles. A remnant continued resistance with justified confidence, for even in the winter of 1483, stalked in a remote defile by a corps of Basque freelances, they were able to win a remarkable victory by their usual practice of precipitating an avalanche against the enemy column. De Vera implicitly acknowledged that force could not prevail against them on their chosen terrain: he withdrew to Las Palmas and invited his adversaries to make honourable terms. Apart from rebels who continued to roam the mountain tops for a few years, without inflicting any serious damage, the entire island was held to have submitted by the summer of 1483.[10]

The condition of Gomera in the 1480s sets its experience apart from that of the other islands. Unique among islands still occupied by natives in having resident Castilian lords, it was also unique among 'conquered' islands, because the indigenous population remained undisturbed (except for the exaction of tribute by the Peraza family) and undisplaced by European colonists. Its very singularity was its undoing. The Genoese financiers of the conquest of the Canaries are unlikely to have tolerated the abandonment of potential sugar lands indefinitely to native herders and gatherers; while the recurring tension between the Peraza and their reluctant 'vassals' made the status quo unstable and gave the crown a pretext for intervention. Gomera's traditional links with the Portuguese, who, as we have seen, strove for an understanding with the natives at intervals from the 1430s, may also have aroused Castilian apprehension. The natives rebelled in 1478, taking the opportunity of the Luso-Castilian war to 'procure favours from Portugal', as was alleged by the Peraza and believed by Ferdinand and Isabella. A further rebellion in 1484 can be inferred from the monarchs' warning that they should obey their lords and pay their tribute. By 1488, they were again in revolt. In 1488 and 1489, royal forces from Gran Canaria made two brutal incursions, between which Hernán Peraza, who ruled the island on his family's behalf, was put to death by the natives. In revenge, the rebels were executed or enslaved in droves, with dubious legality, as 'rebels against their natural lord', and the island permanently garrisoned from Gran Canaria. The treatment of the natives touched tender consciences in Castile; the monarchs established an inquiry by a committee of jurists and theologians into the proprieties of the case; the release of the enslaved Gomerans was recommended and many of them eventually returned to the archipelago to help colonise other conquests.[11] Their native land, however, was now ripe for transformation by European settlers. In the next decade, it became another colonial sugar island.

The conquests of Tenerife and La Palma were relatively rapid but by no means easy. In neither case was success effected by prowess – despite the chivalric postures struck by the Spaniards in the sources – but in the one case by stratagem and in the other by luck. Alonso de Lugo's invasion of La Palma in 1492 was preceded by the missionary activities of a remarkable woman: the native neophyte, Francisca de Gazmira. That an episcopal licence should have been conferred on a lay, native, female missionary suggests remarkable charismatic powers which she seems to have used to good effect among her people.[12] It was perhaps thanks to this preparation that Lugo encountered little opposition and some help when he landed on the western seaboard. Reinforced by Christian tribes of the west, he marched around the coast in a clockwise direction, defeating piecemeal tribes who made no effort to unite in resistance. The interior was the scene of a fiercer defence, for there volcanic activity and erosion have combined to create a vast natural fortress, La Caldera, which was occupied by a single tribe under a leader whom tradition calls Tanausú. If our sole but tardy source can be believed, Tanausú might have resisted indefinitely had Lugo not tricked him into attending a sham parley, at which he was overcome and his followers decimated.[13] Here, for once, the chronicle tradition seems to depart from an heroic version of events. The surviving text dates from the 1590s, when such bold revisionists as the Dominican, Fray Alonso de Espinosa, were challenging the received image of the conquest of the Canaries, praising the natural virtues of the natives and defending their rights. No doubt this version is as warped as that of the contemporary chronicles, which reflect a perception saturated in chivalric literature. But cruelty and ruthless daring are thoroughly characteristic of everything that is known for certain about Alonso de Lugo.

Partly, perhaps, because of his early reputation for rapacity, Lugo's operations thereafter were bedevilled by shortage of finance and legal entanglements with his Genoese (and, in one case, Majorcan) backers. He narrowly averted disaster in both the campaigns to which the conquest of Tenerife committed him. From the first, which occupied the summer of 1494, he barely escaped the near destruction of his force with his life after being lured into a trap at Acentejo near the mouth of the Orotava valley. He was probably making for the land of Taoro – the richest of nine territorial and tribal chieftaincies into which the island seems to have been divided.

He returned with larger forces, probably late in 1495, disabused of his first facile expectation that the conquest would take ten months. Now, however, it was the turn of the chief of Taoro to succumb to overconfidence. That overweening native prince had driven four tribes into alliance with Lugo; the remainder formed a hostile confederacy, which attacked Lugo's camp near La Laguna in the flat terrain that suited the Spaniards' cavalry and gave the islanders little protection from crossbow fire. Even after the inevitable victory, Lugo remained in winter quarters. When he gingerly sallied forth, early in 1496, he found the natives depleted and debilitated by an unidentified epidemic – the first of a series of mysterious diseases, presumably brought by the Europeans, which caused a demographic disaster in Tenerife, comparable, on the islands' smaller scale, to those which later devastated the New World. Lugo resumed his march on Taoro. This time, when he reached Acentejo, he was prepared and avenged the former massacre in a definitive victory. The last chief of Taoro sent his despair the way of his hope and committed ritual suicide, just as some of the defenders of Gran Canaria had done. Surprisingly, no chronicler mentions the event, but the spot where the chief ended his life became a celebrated landmark and is referred to in many early land grants to colonists. After this, the tribes who remained in arms quickly made their submissions and by June, 1496, Alonso de Lugo was able to parade their leaders before his monarchs, under the eyes of the Venetian ambassador, at Almazán.[14]

## Granada, the Canaries and America

The completion of the conquest of the Canary Islands is very close in time to the first conquests in the New World and the last in the Iberian peninsula. Indeed, the overlap is striking, as the conquests of the greater Canaries, from 1478 to 1496, encompassed the years of the Granada War and of Columbus's first two voyages. The crucial question is whether there was any conceptual continuity, because, if people thought of all three conquests in the same way, then there may have been a basis for continuity in other respects – institutional, economic, social.

The juridical passion of Castilian monarchs and their advisers, the obsessive desire to justify in theory – even more, perhaps, than to vindicate in practice – all their doings and especially all their wars, means that their conceptions were often made explicit. The evidence is overwhelming that the conquest of the Canaries was conceived and justified, not only by the monarchs and their advisers, but also at quite humble social and intellectual levels, as an extension of the 'Reconquest', not much different in kind from the subjugation of Granada. The myth of the Reconquest became deeply imbedded in late medieval Spain. It fed on the period's 'Gothic revival' – a pervasive interest in the history of Visigothic Spain and, particularly, in the monarchs' claim to be heirs of the Gothic kings. In the first Castilian reference to the islands, from a letter of the mid-fourteenth century, King Alfonso XI informed the pope – mistakenly but without apparent insincerity – that his predecessors had fought 'the kings of Africa' for those lands and that 'the acquisition of the Kingdom of Africa is well known to pertain to our royal right and no other'. The same or like arguments were not forgotten in the next century, as is apparent from the submissions of one of the most accomplished Castilian jurists of the day, Alonso de Cartagena, who alleged that the Canaries were part of the realms of the Visigothic kings, or at least fell within their rights of conquest: rights which descended with their regality through the line of monarchs of Castile. The same train of thought was current still in the reign of Ferdinand and Isabella: witnesses into the enquiry into the status of the Canarian seigneury in 1476–77 believed that the islands had belonged to Don Rodrigo, the last Gothic king. Arguments reminiscent of Alonso de Cartagena's were recapitulated by Cardinal Carvajal on an embassy to Rome in 1494.[15]

Though its adversaries happened to be infidels, the concept of the 'Reconquest' was secular in part, because in just war theory, as derived from St Augustine, recovery of usurped lands was a valid pretext, whoever the foe. Despite some fantastic attempts – like Oviedo's speculation that the New World might have been part of the realm of King Tubal – the conquest of America could not be convincingly represented in these terms, nor justified on a basis derived solely from a civil-law tradition. Remarkably, therefore – into a world where Christ and Muhammad had never been heard of – echoes of the religious language associated with the 'Reconquest' crossed the Atlantic. Although not formally dignified by crusading indulgences, Castile's American wars were justified by evangelical zeal and sanctified by apparitions of St James. In this respect, the Canary Islands really do look like a conceptual 'half-way house' between Spain and America. The conquests, up to and including that of Gran Canaria, were crusades in the technical sense, for which indulgences equivalent to those of the Holy Land pilgrimage were proclaimed by the popes. And not only were Canarian wars thought of as extensions of the 'Reconquest': the inhabitants seem actually to have been muddled with Moors. For a Venetian ambassador, Don Fernando Guanarteme was 'a Saracen king'. The conquistadores and royal chancery, in making terms with Canarians, adopted the formulae developed during the wars against the Moors and deployed at the time in the 'capitulations' or surrender terms of Granadine cities. It was common for Moors to be ritually 'challenged' to submit before conflict (indeed, this may have been a Moorish practice borrowed by the chivalric world), and the same opportunity was given, if the chroniclers are to be believed, to the Canarians before major encounters. The terms granted to the Canarian vanquished of 1481, which we have described, closely echoed those of surrendering Moors.[16]

In practical and juridical terms, however, the Canarians were unlike the Moors, yet remarkably similar to some of the peoples the Castilians were about to encounter on the other side of the ocean. Their apparent primitivism, as we shall see in the next chapter, set them apart; and, where the Moors were contumacious infidels, they were ignorant pagans who had not explicitly rejected the gospel. As the conquest wore on, the terms offered to the islanders seemed to move away from the model suggested by the Moors and to anticipate the conceptual framework of the early conquests of American Indians; the act of submission was represented as a voluntary reception of Christianity and an acknowledgement that, far from possessing internal sovereignty, the natives were by nature or divine will subjects of the Castilian crown. These terms were recorded in the charter of 1480: 'Reduced and converted to our Holy Catholic Faith, they sent to us to render and tender their obedience and fealty and acknowledged us as their king and queen and natural lords.' Chronicles record numerous offers of similar terms.[17] It must be remembered, however, that Spanish attitudes were protean and unsystematic. For roughly the first half-century of Spanish conquest in the New World, Castilians' conceptions of their rights and of the Indians' status were moulded by reliance on the papal donation – something never admitted in the Canaries. And, even in 1492, it was possible for the natives of Tenerife to be conceived by conquistadores as a sovereign community. One of the most curious documents in the history of the Spanish empire records that in the summer of that year, one of the conquerors of Gran Canaria, Lope de Sálazar, went to Tenerife to make a treaty ('a concertar pazes') with one of the tribes; its terms are unknown but it was a unique case of natives treated on equal terms without starting from an inferior juridical position. The crown's representatives on Gran Canaria honoured Lope's treaty with, if anything, supererogatory zeal: in 1493, when the peacemaker seized three native slaves, the governor pretended to agree to their sale but sent his son with a police force to impound the captives and arrest Lope de Sálazar as a 'treaty-breaker'.[18]

What were the implications, for colonial development, of these elements of conceptual continuity? Although the period of formation of colonial society in Granada, the New World and the major islands of the Canaries lies outside the terms of reference of this book, the essential points demand to be made. The three areas presented widely differing environments which imposed contrasting patterns of settlement and different institutions of government. Granada had an established rural economy and international trade, whereas that of the Canaries had to be constructed *ab initio* and that of the New World transformed to meet European tastes and needs. Granada was an enviable land, conquered by the monarchs in person with the sort of mixture of 'feudal' host and urban militia as had been traditional in Spain; it had a large native population, too, and all three elements had at first to be accommodated: Granada became a mixture of big fiefs and peasant properties, about evenly matched.[19] In the New World, the greater Castilian aristocracy neither sought nor got a stake while the huge indigenous labour force precluded settlement at low social levels until demographic disasters supervened. The Canaries had no such labour force; and in the major islands of the archipelago sugar rapidly came to dominate the economy. Thus the predominant pattern was of big merchant proprietors served by sharecroppers of European – and chiefly Portuguese – origin. The only cases which seem to stand outside this pattern are those of the Duke of Medina Sidonia (the one magnate who contributed to the conquest and who in the Canaries was, through his agents, an active merchant rather than a *rentier*) and the Church, which possessed the only fief granted with rights of jurisdiction by the monarchs in the islands conquered in their reign.[20]

This raises the question of how Castilian conquests were governed and how 'feudal' they were – that is, in this context, how far jurisdiction was reserved to the crown and administered by bureaucrats, or how far it was devolved to local wielders of landed wealth. In Granada, Ferdinand and Isabella were generous with jurisdictional fiefs, but in the Canaries and the New World they and their successors made such grants sparingly or – in most of the territories – not at all and fought hard against the seigneurial pretensions of some conquistadores: the privileges of the Peraza were modestly whittled down; Alonso de Lugo was encumbered with a succession of bureaucratic 'lieutenants'; Columbus was never allowed to exercise the jurisdiction rashly granted him on paper; Cortés was compensated with an admittedly substantial fief for the loss of what threatened to become a territorial principality; conquistadores' rights to the labour services or tributes of Indians in the New World were of strictly limited heritability and were, in the royal conception if not always in practice, regarded as incompatible with the exercise of jurisdiction or the concept of vassalage; a royal army crushed the aspirations to effective independence of the conquerors of Peru, and a network of royal tribunals and itinerant judges was gradually spread all over the New World to make royal justice increasingly accessible and immediate. Within Castile, seigneurial jurisdiction made gains at royal expense in the course of the sixteenth century. In their overseas possessions, however, it was as if the monarchs had seized with relief a tabula rasa, which they were determined to prick with their own stylus.[21]

Nevertheless, in three very important respects it is useful to speak of feudal models in Castilian overseas expansion. First, as Charles Verlinden has argued, the starting points – the lordships of Béthencourt and the Peraza, the jurisdictional 'admiralcy' of Columbus – assumed the alienation of jurisdiction from the crown, and were expressed in the language of lordship and vassaldom.[22] In this respect, Castilian expansion was like that of all the other cases we have noticed. Secondly, the *soi-disant* hidalgos who lorded it over small colonists in the islands or called the natives their 'vassals' in the New World, did not see things from the royal perspective: if not of feudalism, the empire was a world of feudal pretension. Finally, it is true that grants of land and labour services were the most important element in royal policy throughout the empire – at least, for most of the first half of the sixteenth century. They were the means by which exploitation was organised and loyalty tenuously secured. The disposal of substantial rewards of the conquests in patronage forms a link between the peninsular conquests, the Canaries and the New World and distinguishes them collectively from the monarchs' inherited patrimony, which was, by universal agreement albeit not in unwavering practice, inalienable.

## The 'Rise' of Portugal and Castile

Traditionally, the problem of Portugal's emergence as a long-range commercial and imperial power has looked more difficult than it is. Misplaced emphasis on the early fifteenth century – to the exclusion of the long fourteenth-century apprenticeship and the belittlement of the late fifteenth-century leap forward – has made the phenomenon seem dramatic, while misrepresentation of the Infante Dom Henrique has made it seem heroic. Seen in proper context, the emergence of Portuguese imperialism appears more intelligible. The same is true of Castile's education for empire in Andalusia and the Canaries. Yet Castile and Portugal still seem imperfectly fitted for their roles, while the exclusion or pre-emption of other, superficially more likely candidates, demands to be explained.

It may be helpful to recall that the Portuguese phenomenon was not unique. Two hundred years later, the Dutch did something very similar, from a comparable starting point. Both peoples were marginal 'poor relations' of Christendom, numerically feeble, concentrated in coastal settlements where they mingled peasant and piscatorial vocations. Both had experienced recent or current civil wars. Both had maritime traditions based on fishing, with commercial and industrial origins linked to the salting and marketing of fish – cod in the Portuguese case, herring in that of the Dutch. Both practised shipping and piracy in neighbouring seas for a long time before taking up their imperial vocations. Both looked out on the Atlantic but had Mediterranean apprenticeships – the Portuguese as corsairs and carriers in the late fourteenth and fifteenth centuries, the Dutch as pirates and grain shippers in the late sixteenth. Both had rich industrial and urban neighbours who brought in capital and expertise: the Florentines and Genoese to Lisbon, the Flemings to Amsterdam. Looked at together, both cases begin to seem less astonishing. What appeared to be poor equipment begins to resemble a syndrome of success.

None of this, however, helps to explain why Portugal – much less

Castile – was not preceded in the Atlantic by the French, the Catalans or the Genoese. France was the richest and most populous kingdom in Christendom. She had Mediterranean and Atlantic seaboards. Her lands had been nurseries of crusaders and of Mediterranean, Levantine and Iberian colonists throughout the high middle ages. The Barbary crusades show that on the eve of European expansion into the Atlantic, this tradition was not dead. There were communities of long-distance Atlantic fishermen in northern France, just as there were in Portugal. What we have seen of the history of Béthencourt's and La Salle's expedition shows how nearly the Atlantic became French; but it shows, too, why Iberian powers had a crucial geographical advantage. By the standards of the time, the eastern Atlantic was still a perilous sea and the Atlantic archipelagoes distant and dangerous places. Béthencourt switched his allegiance to Castile for the sake of a short lifeline and a handy base. Appeals to the internal divisions of France explain nothing: the achievements of the Genoese, Catalans and Dutch and, to a lesser extent, of Portuguese and Castilians were all launched from home bases riven by dissension. Nor would it be convincing to dwell on France's supposed 'continental destiny' – her commitment to a strategy of European hegemony, imposed by her long and vulnerable land frontier: the country of western Europe with the longest land frontier, relative to its size, is Portugal. More significant, perhaps, was France's position outside the main sea routes that linked the Mediterranean and northern economies in the late middle ages. Early commerce from Genoa or Majorca touched at La Rochelle or Nantes, but from the first the Bay of Biscay was uncongenial: even galleys preferred to skirt it; and increasingly they made their runs directly for the English Channel from Baiona or another Galician or, occasionally, Cantabrian port. Even a galley could complete the voyage in a week or, exceptionally, as little as three days. The big Genoese round ships, carracks and cogs, went straight from Seville or Cadiz.[23]

The Catalan failure is more difficult to understand. It has to be set in the context of a long period of climacteric from the late fourteenth to the late fifteenth centuries, in which the Crown of Aragon gradually and fitfully yielded its prominence in the affairs of Latin Christendom, and in which the commercial might of Catalonia shrank in relation to that of other trading peoples. This 'decline of Catalonia' is one of the great unsolved puzzles of late medieval history. Like the superficially similar problem of the 'decline of Spain' in the seventeenth century, it may to some extent be a matter of distorted perceptions rather than of real decadence, and of relative rather than absolute decline. The great age of Catalan achievement in the thirteenth and fourteenth centuries, like that of Castile in the sixteenth, aroused false expectations. Spectacular victories masked the poverty and vulnerability of the domestic base. Resources were overstretched and energy wasted – especially in the Catalan case, as we have seen, on the Sardinian wars. In the fifteenth century, Catalonia was still robust in many ways; some new openings were exploited and Catalan Levantine trade through Rhodes seems to have increased. If Barcelona was in decline, Valencia was growing.[24] But just as in the seventeenth century the strength of France and the spectacular rise of northern European powers broke the Spanish hegemony and reduced Spain to more limited ambitions, so in the fifteenth century Catalonia was eclipsed by redistributions of forces which created new great powers at either end of the Mediterranean – the Turks in the east, Castile in the west. Why, specifically, did the Catalans withdraw from the Atlantic? From the mainland and Majorca, they had led the Atlantic 'space race' in its early phase; their 'imperial' experience was arguably the most relevant of all potentially interested peoples'. Their commercial motivation must have been at least as strong as that of their rivals. It is tempting to see them excluded from the route to Atlantic archipelagoes by Portuguese control of Ceuta; but the Catalan withdrawal seems to predate that event. The last explicit known evidence of Aragonese attempts to maintain mastery of the seas around the Canaries dates from 1366 (see p.158). Abandonment of the Atlantic may have been a sort of rational economy at a time when Mediterranean commitments were vast and growing. The Aragonese protectorate in the Maghrib gave Catalan traders an established 'route of gold'; further Atlantic exploration was a desperate recourse, of which the Portuguese, Castilians and Genoese had greater need. Catalan traders did return to the Atlantic archipelagoes in the sixteenth century, but only in the wake of Castilian war fleets.[25]

The last of the potential rivals of Portugal and Castile was in many ways the most formidable of all. The Iberian empires depended on Genoese capital and expertise. Why then did no

Genoese Atlantic empire in its own right ever take shape? Apart from an emblem of Genoese sovereignty painted over one of the Canary Islands in the Dulcert map, there is no evidence of any Genoese wish to go beyond the vicarious enjoyment of the profits of Atlantic exploitation. Part of the explanation lies in the nature of the Iberian empires themselves, part in the Genoese tradition. The privileged position of Genoese merchants in Portugal and Castile provided convenient bases for Atlantic operations; their control of resources and their profits on loans could be maintained, at most times, without political control. Their covert colonialism throve in a setting where the Castilians and Portuguese provided manpower and might, the Genoese capital and technical prowess. At times, doubts were expressed in Portugal and Castile about the distributions of the benefits of this informal bargain. In the late fifteenth century, attempts were made to expel or exploit the Genoese of the Atlantic islands.[26] In the sixteenth century, the Castilian monarchs attempted to exclude Genoa from the New World and, for a while, to replace the Genoese as the holders of the monarchy's debts.[27] But, even on the longest-term view, Genoa's involvement in Portugal and Castile seems justified; the Genoese strategy of indirect control was a success.

It was not, of course, a consciously evolved strategy. Genoa, even in the heyday of Mediterranean expansion, never created an étatiste empire on the Venetian model. Collective action was impossible in the hurly-burly of Genoese politics. Empire-building was the work of outcast entrepreneurs, aristocratic adventurers, freebooter factions excluded from civic life or autonomous companies of merchant-conquerors like the Maona of Chios. It was rare for Genoa to hold substantial colonies in anything approaching full sovereignty. The network of Genoese merchant-quarters was the most strictly commercial of the medieval Mediterranean 'empires'. The biggest Genoese traders in Portugal, the Lomellini, were creole expatriates who behaved as if unbeholden to Genoa's state interests; they operated along routes of their own, between Lisbon and Bruges, with Castilian, French and even Irish ports which the merchants of Genoa proper neglected. The Lomellini were an extreme case, but they show how the emulous character of Genoa's commercial life made Genoa's 'empire' fissile. The role of the Genoese within the empires of Portugal and Castile was thoroughly consistent with the parts they had played in the empires of Byzantium and of the House of Barcelona.

Apart from Genoese surrogacy, it is the Canary Islands that are the key to everything that is most spectacular in the rise of Castile. Allegretto Allegretti thought America *was* 'another Canary Island'. It may have been on that sort of confusion that Castile based her claim to the New World before the papal donation, for her treaty rights with Portugal assigned her any 'islands of Canary, still to be discovered'.[28] It was barely more than twice as far from Gomera to Santo Domingo as from Cadiz to Gomera in terms of days of sail.

Yet if the islands were physically close to the New World and anticipated some of the features of colonial societies as they would take shape in the remoter Atlantic, we have repeatedly seen how close they were, in the 'tone' set by the colonists, to the metropolitan world, from which they were a means of escape and of which they were a bodged recreation. In the colonies, Canarian and American alike, the institutions and economies of home were necessarily modified. But a tenacious spirit, an enduring self-perception, survived these changes. What was this 'spirit'? One of the most popular new books of the reign of Ferdinand and Isabella was the one described in *Don Quixote* as 'the best in the world' – the *Tirant lo blanc* of Joan Martorell, an extravagant chivalric romance, in which one of the characters is a 'king of the Canary Islands', who launches, with presumably conscious irony on the author's part, an invasion of Europe. The erection of an island-kingdom is a common dénouement in works of the genre: in *Don Quixote*, the tradition is derided through Sancho Panza's aspiration to rule an island. When the Catholic monarchs added the style of 'King and Queen of the Canary Islands' to the list of titles with which they headed their letters, they were exceeding fiction and making a reality of romance.[29] The same spirit had been evinced by the Peraza and the chroniclers of the conquest of the Canaries. If we were to continue the history of Castilian empire-building into the New World, we should see it there too in overwhelmingly the greater part of conquistadores' surviving literary allusions.[30] The world of Castilian naval warfare is the world of Count Pero Niño, whose chronicle, written by his standard-bearer in the second quarter of the fifteenth century, is a treatise of chivalry as well as an account of campaigns: *El vitorial* celebrates a knight never vanquished in joust or war or love, whose greatest battles were fought at sea; and 'to win a battle is the greatest good and the greatest glory of life'. When the author discourses on the mutability of life, his interlocutors are Fortune and Wind, whose 'mother' is the sea 'and therein is my chief office'.[31] The rise of a Castilian overseas empire, no less – as we have seen – than those of Portugal or of the House of Barcelona, owed a great deal to the strength of chivalric values and to the influence of chivalric romance.

# 9. The Mental Horizon

## The 'Discovery of Man'

Not every brave new world has people in it. Most of the islands of the eastern Atlantic were uninhabited until the first European settlers came. Nor are the indigenous people of frontier regions always such as to excite Miranda's wide-eyed wonder. Most of the natives of the Mediterranean lands traversed in the first part of this book were recognisably akin to the colonists, even when they were infidels, schismatics or Sards. They looked neither, perhaps, like Caliban nor Ferdinand, but somewhere in between.

To the new peoples encountered in the course of Atlantic expansion, however, it was possible to respond with neither the same familiarity nor quite the same contempt. Of all the new features of the Atlantic environment, which made colonial experience in the Atlantic different from what had gone before, the presence of 'primitive' natives was the most challenging. In a famous phrase, Michelet characterised the Renaissance as the period of 'the discovery of the world . . . and of man'.[1] He meant the individuality of man and the newly perceived nature of man's superiority to the rest of creation, the concept of 'the measure of all things' and the vague, collective narcissism of 'What a thing is man!' He was coupling geographical discoveries with what were really no more than the speculations (or maunderings) of moral philosophy. But there was a 'discovery of man' in another sense, too. The geographical discoveries brought anthropological revelations in their wake. By widening the terms of reference of discussion of the nature of man, these may have contributed to adjustments in the self-awareness of the philosophically inclined. The origins of scientific ethnography and of the myth of the 'noble savage' – to take two contrasting examples, both rich in implications for the development of traditions on the relationship of man to the created and metaphysical worlds – are commonly traced back to the discovery of the American Indians and the debates they engendered. Like most supposed features of the Renaissance, the 'discovery of man' in this sense can be found much deeper in the middle ages. The terms of the debates about the American Indians were

223

prefigured in literary and popular traditions, and in the encounters with Blacks and, more particularly, with aboriginal Canarians, which occurred in the course of early Atlantic exploration. The study of those encounters is an inescapable part of the subject of this book for three reasons: it makes an excellent case study of the problem of continuity between Mediterranean and Atlantic expansion, because anthropological or proto-anthropological categories or 'notions' were tested by unprecedented experiences; we can therefore ask how well Mediterranean or other earlier medieval traditions coped with Atlantic conditions. Secondly, some of the configurations of colonial society grew, where indigenous populations existed, from the interaction of incoming, settler communities with established native peoples; colonial institutions developed in part for the regulation of relations between the two. No picture, therefore, of the origins or nature of colonial society and government can omit the problems of how colonists formed their mental images of natives, how much was owed to tradition and how much to experience, and whether such perceptions challenged old institutions or suggested new ones. Finally, it may be of interest to ask what, if anything, 'began' with the discovery of the New World and how early, in the evolution of the tradition – if tradition there was – the essential terms, with which western man has formulated and discussed his perceptions of pagan 'primitives', were fixed.

Some of the notions and categories with which men from Latin Christendom approached the new encounters of the late middle ages derived from classical antiquity, some from folklore, some from canon law and some from examples of relatively recent experience of peoples who, if they scarcely resembled Atlantic 'primitives', were at least different from western man's prevailing self-image. According to Gobineau, cited with approval by Lévi-Strauss, the monsters of medieval legend derived not from the fertility of man's imagination but from his inability to conceive of strangers in the same terms as himself. Most speakers of unwritten languages have no word for 'man' other than that with which they refer to members of their own tribe.[2] Most reporters of pagans and primitives in the late middle ages had no difficulty in recognising kinship with them, but only in establishing its degree. Available paradigms were limited. From classical antiquity derived the concepts of 'the barbarian' – which, to a scholastic mind, demanded further definition – and 'the golden age', which was a literary commonplace of little appeal as a means of understanding pagans and primitives, except to humanists. From popular tradition – much of it made respectable by antique origin – came the images of the *similitudines hominis*, the anthropomorphic monsters beloved of Gobineau, and of the wild man of the woods, understood as a manlike and perfectible but subrational, passionate and instinctive creature. The canonistic tradition on pagans and primitives did not yield useful categories until the thirteenth century, though interest in the classification of societies in terms of their religions and laws is shown in earlier texts. Two ready-made but ill adapted systems of classification were to hand: the classical and biblical panorama of mankind; and the hierarchy of creation or 'chain of being', in which gradations could be added to the category of man and space filled between man and the beasts.

Ethnographical writings became increasingly numerous and specific in the twelfth and thirteenth centuries. First came the 'discovery', in the sense of explicit awareness and detailed scrutiny, of what might be called Europe's 'internal' primitives: the peripheral, pastoral, bog or mountain folk, like the Basques, Welsh, Irish, Slavs and pagan Scandinavians, whose cultures inspired mingled awe and contempt.[3] Then the bloody inruptions of the Mongols came as an intellectual as well as a physical shock: 'of this barbarous race,' as one Rhineland annalist said, 'we hear many things which are incredible and altogether inhuman'. Even for a direct observer like William of Rubruck, they seemed to inhabit 'a kind of other world'.[4] The theoretical framework for assimilating such novel experiences was being amplified, or at least systematised, by the thirteenth-century encyclopedists. Albertus Magnus plotted out a scheme of classification, not only of mankind, but of the whole of creation, based on the range of mental faculties supposedly possessed by different races and beings, their physical characteristics and the presumed relationship between physique, physiognomy, mind and behaviour. His pupil, Aquinas, offered criteria for recognising the barbarian.[5] Both were influential because misunderstood. In subsequent accounts of pagans and primitives, a 'checklist' of ingredients of civility – in language, writing, dress, diet, law, institutions and city life – found most peoples wanting:

from the categories discussed by Albertus Magnus derived a sort of capacious anthropological wastebin to which they could be consigned, as 'beast-men', *homunculi* or barbarians.

Even to minds accustomed to such pliant and useful categories, discovery of the Canary Islanders was a sudden and startling phenomenon. The native races have died out and the evidence of their origins conflicts, but they were probably a pre-Berber north African people, similar, perhaps, to the Imraguen of the western Saharan coast. The first travellers from Christendom arrived in the islands with no inkling of the inhabitants, save the wholly fabulous longevity attributed to them by the *Vita Merlini*.[6] It was natural, therefore, that speculation concerning them should run the whole gamut of the possible and impossible without distinction. At one extreme stands the Hereford Mappamundi, which records ideas on the African Atlantic at only an instant's remove from the first medieval exploration of the area. No figures are actually depicted on the representations of the islands in this map, but the relevant latitudes are peopled with prodigies in plenty: naked men, with round hats, braided hair and eyes in the backs of their heads, appear opposite the legend, 'Canary Island full of large dogs'. And one manuscript of the *Libro del conoscimiento* depicts Canary Islands inhabited by sciapods, each reclining beneath the shade of his one enormous foot.[7] At the opposite pole of speculation, the earliest would-be conquerors expected to find city-dwelling islanders. The expedition recorded by Boccaccio took siege equipment for 'cities and castles' and the Majorcan invaders of 1342 hoped to acquire 'villages, towns, fortifications and castles'. Pope Clement VI admitted the paucity of information when he tried to determine whether the Canarians were blasphemers.[8]

Yet it was at about this time that the first notices and indeed specimens of Canarian natives were beginning to circulate within Europe. The first recorded Portuguese expedition brought back four native captives, the Majorcans twelve. From thenceforth, slaving raids made Canarians a not altogether unusual sight in Mediterranean markets.[9] There was thus a sudden and rapid growth of knowledge of a phenomenon which had been quite unsuspected or anticipated only in a fantastic form.

This may be why the Canarians generated far more interest than the Blacks, who were so much more numerous and economically important. Blacks, because they were more obviously different, might have constituted a more radical challenge to common suppositions about the nature of man. But, as individuals, they were a familiar sight and they made little impact, even when their societies were first directly encountered in the 1440s. They could spring surprises: as the author of the *Libro del conoscimiento* said of the Ethiopians, 'Although these people are Blacks, yet they are men of good understanding and good sense and have learning and science.' In 1488, the eloquence of a Wolof chief reminded a Portuguese chronicler of Attic oratory.[10] But the surprises were more often disappointments. We have seen how Mali was envisaged in Europe as a kingdom comparable with those known at home, and how familiarity with that sadly decayed polity only bred contempt (see p.147). In general, in the second half of the fifteenth century, the elaborate courtesies and assumptions of equality which typified the Portuguese kings' dealings with their black 'cousins' were not shared by the navigators and colonists who knew the Black societies at first hand. The Wolof chief royally entertained in Lisbon in 1488 was unceremoniously murdered by his Portuguese guards back home. The first Congolese ruler to be converted to Christianity apostasised in disgust at the behaviour of his Portuguese 'helpers'. His successor, in a long denunciation, ironically accused the Portuguese of unchristian behaviour and claimed that one of the advisers assigned to him declined to live in his palace so as not 'to have to share a home with a Black'. In his homeland, the Black became a creature of contempt; in Portugal, lampooned upon the stage for his funny talk and slapstick gait, a figure of fun.[11]

Not only were the Blacks easily recognised: they were also readily classified, in a category not far removed from that of the apes, as men made degenerate by sin. In part, this was because of the tradition that the sons of Ham were cursed with blackness, as well as being condemned to slavery; in part through the mental associations evoked by a 'diabolical' colour, generally preferred for the depiction of demons and the signifying of sin. Zurara found the first slaves directly shipped from Africa 'so deformed in their faces and bodies as almost to resemble shadows from the nether world'.[12] Simian features did not help: iconographically, apes signified sin, and especially lust, with its connotations of unnatural vice. In a preinversion of the theory of evolution, they were generally thought in medieval ape-lore to be the degenerate descendants of man.[13] Such characterisations were not an irremediable handicap: freed

blacks could hold positions of honour in both Portuguese and
Castilian society in the fifteenth century. But they do help explain –
together with the force of tradition and the familiarity of custom –
why the legitimacy of the slave trade was not seriously impugned
until the second half of the sixteenth century. It took the example
of the American Indians to suggest the emancipation of the Blacks.
Meanwhile, the Black image was frozen. Alvise da Mosto,
writing early in the second half of the fifteenth century, was almost
uniquely sensitive to the merits of Black civilisation, as observed
among the Wolofs of the Senegambia region. In particular, he
accorded their polity considerable respect. Though their cities and
villages were only of grass huts, they were recognisably urban. And
the chiefs were genuine 'lords', for 'such men are not lords by
virtue of any treasure or money but on account of ceremonies and
the following of people they may truly be called lords'. Da Mosto
emphasised the impressive court ritual of the chief he called
Budomel, of whose friendship he spoke with pride. Budomel rode
on horseback, went everywhere with a train of 200 men in
attendance, struck fear into his subjects by his haughty mien and
arbitrary power, and was courted by grovelling suppliants who
dusted their heads continuously while they addressed him. On the
other hand, da Mosto seems to have harboured no doubts about
the Blacks' general inferiority. He derided their scanty attire,
despised their bestial table manners – 'they eat on the ground, like
animals' – dismissed them as cheats and liars to a man and
apostrophised them as incorrigibly lascivious. Budomel, impressed
at the white man's arcane knowledge, begged da Mosto to tell him
how to satisfy more women. Such departures from reason and
decorum implied a collective derogation of Black society. And yet
da Mosto's account is notable for its relative generosity.[14] After his
time, the picture he left was barely improved for nearly a century;
in the meantime, the development of perceptions of the primitive
was almost entirely limited to literature about the Canary Islanders.

Humanists, missionaries and jurists were the writers most
interested in newly discovered peoples and their respective accounts
can be treated as a basis for classifying the material. I shall deal
with them in that order. Secular chroniclers and conquerors
or would-be conquerors who sometimes wrote accounts or
characterisations of their intended victims, usually in supplications
addressed to popes, shared, on the whole, the jurists' perspective:

their interest lay in establishing that their victims were fair game for enslavement or war, bereft of true sovereignty and consigned to inferior juridical categories; these sources will therefore be considered along with those of the lawyers.

It is easy to see why missionaries and jurists were interested in primitives, but what about humanists? Few new constructions of or glosses on classical texts were likely to be yielded by study of Canarians, Blacks or Amerindians. Yet in other connections the humanists found the primitives appealing: the age of gold was embodied, it seemed, in newly discovered worlds of sylvan innocence; and humanist moral philosophy, following common classical precedent, sought examples of good barbarians for the reproof of civilised sophisticates. Neither tradition had ever been forgotten. The golden age myth was mediated by many well-known Latin sources; unlikely didactic models from the barbarian world had been deployed by writers as various as Adam of Bremen, who praised the Prussians' dismissal of gold 'as dung, much to our discredit', and Roger Bacon or Ramon Llull, who both brandished the example of an 'innocent Tatar'; there even seem to be sententious echoes in Marco Polo's Mongols.[15] Finally, humanists sometimes evinced interest in primitive tongues, for the light they might throw on the history of language. The new opportunities presented by the discovery of the Canary Islanders were significant enough to attract the attention of the leading humanists of the day, Petrarch and Boccaccio. The account Boccaccio copied, though apparently the work of a navigator who actually observed the Canarians on one of the first recorded expeditions (see p.155), reflects the humanist's interest, and perhaps mingles observations by the navigator with comments by the humanist.[16]

Like Columbus confronting the Tainos 150 years later, the first thing this observer noticed about the natives was their nakedness. Evidently, Boccaccio took this to signify innocence rather than savagery: gold and silver coins were shown to them, but they took no notice. They were equally innocent of knowledge of weapons. They respected natural law. They seemed not to know the concept of individual property, but divided everything equally. None of this, except the islanders' nakedness, seems to have had much value for the description of primitive Canarian society, but combined elements of the didactic and golden-age traditions, while clearly implying a riposte to those who might seek to characterise the Canarians with conventional criteria of barbarity. The text seems to depart farther from reality by ascribing civilised attainments and points of comparison with Latin peoples to the natives: they are said to speak a 'polite' tongue, like the Italians, sing sweetly and dance 'almost like the French'. Their houses are built 'of cut stone with wondrous contrivance' (whereas they were really cave dwellers). Their 'temple or oratory' was adorned with a suspiciously classical-sounding statue, the image of a man, sculptured in stone, with a javelin in his hand. Finally, as if these assurances were insufficient, no room is left to doubt the human status and rationality of the natives. They are physically 'normal' – 'indeed, they do not exceed our size': this was important, as Albertus Magnus had denied that reason could subsist in a monstrous frame. And they were 'of great understanding'. A few contradictions in the text suggest that its original author may not have seen in the islands the humanist Utopia envisaged by his editor, but there can be no doubt of the message of the version which has come down to us. Boccaccio turned the first account of the Canary Islanders into a setting of the golden age and an admonition for his times, as Peter Martyr was later to do with Columbus's reports of the Arawaks of the Antilles.

Petrarch's version – though his interest, presumably, was closely allied to his friend's – has a different flavour. He gives the islanders no civilised airs and there are no recollections of the Golden Age in his account. On the contrary, the natives are 'little better than beasts' and seem closer to the wild man tradition than to the classical celebration of primitivism: solitary, subrational, instinctive yet still human creatures. This adds to the impact of their moral superiority over civilised man, which is Petrarch's main point.[17] Indeed, in the humanist tradition, this function of the Canarians seems to have counted for more than their suitability as illustrations of the Golden Age, although at the time of Béthencourt's conquest, the illuminator of the Vienna Codex of the *Roman de la Rose* apparently chose the Canary Islands as the setting for his version of that blissful time, with hide-clad aboriginals dwelling in peace amid trees and mountains.[18]

Petrarch's patron, Clement VI, author of one of the most revealing early accounts of the Canary Islanders, was evidently influenced by the humanists he had in his entourage. His main authority for the geography and nomenclature of the islands was

Pliny; and his information on Canarian religion may have been derived from the same sources as Petrarch's and Boccaccio's: like Boccaccio, for instance, he claims that the Canarians worship 'the works of men's hands' and, like Petrarch, the celestial bodies. But the substance of his work does not support those historians who wish to see Clement as a 'humanist pope'. He looks at the Canarians with a canonist's eyes. His interest is in the great juridical question posed by their discovery: the legitimation of attempts to conquer them in terms of the established canons of just and unjust war, or exercise of sovereignty by pagans and, to a lesser extent, of the propriety of forcible conversion. Indeed, his *collatio* on the creation of Luis de la Cerda as 'Prince of Fortune', preached on 15 November 1344, is the first attempt – and one of the most comprehensive – to marshal all the known arguments in favour of legitimate war against pagan primitives.[19]

Clement's views on the subject of just war in general are known from other texts. He relied on the traditional analysis of Augustine: war had to be proclaimed by a legitimate source of authority and waged for the recovery of usurped possessions or for defence; there must be 'justice and truth' in the cause, 'evil and malice' in the enemy. He specifically authorised a prince to make war on rebellious subjects. All this was the unexceptionable common ground of the period. In a letter to Edward III – not of course necessarily of papal authorship in the same sense as the homilies, but in keeping with the drift of his thought – he adds criteria more obviously relevant to the case of infidels: war is meritorious against those who blaspheme, or 'despise the glory of Christianity' or shed the blood of the faithful or aspire to their confusion or extermination.[20] These implied strictures against Islam may have extended, in the pope's mind, to the Canarians, whom he called 'enemies of the Christian faith' and, somewhat flatteringly, represented as a threat to 'neighbouring Christian peoples'.

But for a convincing case against the Canarians, the pope was obliged to range more widely than in his other considerations of the problem of just war. His attempt to use the argument from the recovery of usurped possessions relied on the fantastic speculation that the isle of Capraria, whither Augustine had sent a letter to Abbot Eudosius, was one of the Canaries. He voiced the suspicion that the islanders 'succoured the persecutors of the name of Christ' to support the suggestion that his proposed war was a war of defence. He argued that there was 'no dominion without virtue' and that pagans could possess no more than the 'image' of virtue: from any other lips, such propositions might have been condemned as heretical. He essayed the assertion that 'pagans ought to forfeit sovereignty, by virtue of their paganism', for which, not surprisingly, he asserted no proof: few, if any, other canonists would have admitted such a crude generalisation. Much of his language reflected the papal imperialism of his day: 'the spread of our faith and our obedience' was a recurrent theme; the lordship over the whole world, which was Christ's, was His vicar's too: 'ours and justly ours'. What he said of the islanders' rights was expressed largely in terms of the superior rights of the pope. Indeed, many of the points he adduced involved no reference to the natives at all, like the notorious doctrine that by the Donation of Constantine 'all the islands of the west' were in the pope's gift. He uttered one important scruple ('unum dubium satis magnum'): that heathen ought voluntarily to assent to the faith, not be forced to it by war. But his answer was generally, by implication, that this question was subsumed in that of the pope's rights. Clement seems to have felt that if he showed his sovereign right to dispose of the islands, the rights to make war on the inhabitants and thereby coerce them to embrace the faith would follow implicitly.

Clement's main argument, however, anticipated all the subsequent juridical literature on pagans and primitives. It derived from a debate among thirteenth-century decretalists and rested on the proposition that sins against natural law invalidated a society or deprived a polity of sovereignty. Hostiensis was the great champion of the argument, but even those like Innocent IV, who stressed the irrevocability of pagan rights in general, were prepared to make an exception of sins *contra naturam*. Sexual perversion was the commonest ground cited – curiously, Clement fails to allege this in the case of the Canarians save by way of what he admits is speculation – but blasphemy and idolatry were commonly held to be unnatural, too: this, of course, placed pagans in an invidious position. Clement rested his case on Canarian idolatry; of their alleged blasphemy, be admitted, 'I have no certainty'.

Much of this ground was reworked in two professional opinions on the legitimacy of Portuguese claims to conquest-rights in the Canaries in the 1430s. The authors were Antonio de Rosellis and Antonio Minucci da Pratovecchio, professors respectively of canon and Roman law in the University of Bologna. Both justified the conquest, without referring specifically to the Canaries, on the grounds that pagans who sinned against natural law forfeited its protection. Their grounds for doubting Canarian obedience to natural law differed, however, from Clement VI's, and reflected the enhanced importance of conversion as an alleged pretext for war. They seem to have assumed that the Canarians refused to receive missionaries in their lands, and that such a refusal was unnatural. There were grounds in canonistic tradition for asserting that an inhospitable response to a peaceful mission was in itself a pretext for war: such a war could be represented as defensive in character. The Bolognese jurists, however, were unequivocal in placing the main weight of their discussion firmly in the terrain of natural law. Because their arguments particularly favoured Portugal, they were the subject of a reply by one of the most brilliant Castilian jurists and textual critics of the late middle ages, Alonso de Cartagena. He wasted no time on the Canarians' rights – no people, he said, was more savage or bestial – but confined himself to impugning those of the king of Portugal and exalting those of the king of Castile.[21] It was not over any issue of principle that the Castilian lawyer differed from the Bolognese, only in the identity of his paymaster.

Outside the ranks of professional jurists, arguments from natural law could be found in lay and popular sources in the shadowy and derivative form typical of oeuvres *de vulgarisation.*, In 1352, for instance, granting a missionaries' sailing licence, Pedro IV of Aragon described the Canarians in terms culled, presumably, from earlier licences issued to would-be conquerors, as 'thoroughly rustic and beast-like' and 'living, indeed, according to no law'. When *Le Canarien* called the islanders miscreants 'of divers laws', the authors may have been concerned only to suggest their political or confessional disunity; but as the remark occurs in a context of justification of the conquest it seems more likely that it is intended to imply respect, on the Canarians' part, for no universal law. It was with the same justification in mind that the Infante Dom Henrique denounced the islanders as 'constrained by no bonds of law' in seeking papal countenance for a projected conquest. Afonso V of Portugal called them 'men without law' with a similar purpose in mind. For the Castilian chronicler, Bernáldez, they were 'idolaters without law'.[22] A work written for the edification of the future Queen Isabel the Catholic, in 1468, wields the same argument with a curious extra cutting edge in the form of a doctrine of natural slavery remotely rooted, perhaps, in Aristotle:

It is said that the barbarous people are those who live without law; the Latins, those who have law: for it is the law of nations that men who live and are ruled by law shall be lords of those who have no law, because they are by nature the slaves of the wise who are ruled by law.[23]

The Blacks were victims of a similar argument. In Ramon Llull's early report (1283) the Blacks of the gold land were idolaters who worshipped beasts and observed no law. When direct experience confirmed this report, they were 'living,' according to Zurara, 'like beasts, with no law of reasonable creatures . . . nor knowledge of good, only of surviving in animal sloth'. He was not questioning their humanity – Zurara is explicit on that point – but justifying their servitude and, by implication, their incapacity for legitimate self-government.[24]

No directly observed missionary accounts either of Blacks or Canarians have survived from the late middle ages, but to some extent, in the case of the Canarians, this deficiency can be supplied from two sources: papal or royal documents – which are plentiful especially for the pontificate of Eugenius IV and the reign of Ferdinand and Isabella – reflecting the submissions of missionaries on behalf of the natives; and a section of the *De Nobilitate ac Rusticitate* of Felix Hemmerlin (1389–1457/64), who, though not a missionary, reports missionary views.[25] He was probably aware of the debate between Rosellis, Pratovecchio and Cartagena, as he had been in Bologna and Basle at material times. Though a canon of Zurich, he knew Franciscan Observant circles well. Into his *De Nobilitate* he introduces what purports to be an account of the fortuitous discovery of inhabited islands 'in the regions of the west' by pirates in 1370: either the date is a misreading or Hemmerlin was misinformed about the priority of this 'discovery'. Like the earlier Boccaccio text, this has the appearance of a first-hand account, modified by its editor. What survives of the original text is critical or, rather, contemptuous of the islanders; it is only Hemmerlin's glosses that elevate them to indisputably human status, attribute to them a capacity for practising natural law and soften their barbarities into plausible innocence. The pirates' first impression of the natives, for instance, was that they were wrapped in raw hides, howled like dogs, had flat faces like monkeys, and ate raw food. Other customs observed by the pirates put the natives beyond the pale of natural law. 'Their bestial customs, especially in the use of food' are passed over quickly in favour of a circumstantial account of more disgusting habits – public sexual intercourse, common possession of women, and the adoption for parturition of a posture 'like that of other brute beasts'. Even Hemmerlin feels obliged explicitly to disapprove, citing Ovid on Scythia 'where men live in a beastly and cruel fashion, deeply differing from the way of life of all men'.

Normally, however, when Hemmerlin raises his editorial voice he utters a different view from his pirate-informants and apparently reflects his Franciscan sources. The sharing of women seems to him to have been taking a basically good principle to excess: 'They did not have the possession of things in any individual sense but all things were common, as in the state of innocence. . . . Indeed, they lived according to natural law . . . and according to divine law.' Following the recent introduction of monogamy by missionaries, 'in this and other things they live as men have been accustomed to do since the Fall'. He seems equivocal too on the question of the natives' sovereignty: 'We do not read that these islands or their inhabitants had ever recognised the sovereignty of anyone from the beginning of the world. . . . And they who professed the lordship of no one among them, nor of any other, now recognise the King of Aragon as their prince and lord.' The work of the friars, however, is sympathetically recorded: they had the advantage of the benevolent disposition of the inhabitants of all but one 'wild' island; they took farmers and artisans with them

and so sagaciously did they work, by God's mercy, that in present times [the natives] have been reduced to the mildness of civilised men and an human way of life and the Catholic faith and their young men have been brought by practice to the knowledge of letters.

Knowledge of writing, like the use of clothes and the building of cities, was a commonly accepted criterion of civility. Though he introduced his digression on the Canarians into a discussion of the origins of diversity of speech, Hemmerlin was evidently aware of the implications, for the islanders, of the debates on which he touched. One of the interlocutors in his dialogue says that he is interested in the problem of the natives' paganism 'because he is a soldier'. The emphasis on successful conversion looks to be designed, in common with Franciscan policy in the mid-fifteenth century, as part of a campaign, waged at Basle and in the papal court, to exempt the Canarians from enslavement, while the emphasis on the natives' obedience to natural law seems intended to protect them from Portuguese or Castilian conquest.

The context of Hemmerlin's work should be sought not only in the Rosellis–Pratovecchio–Cartagena debate, although it seems probable that Hemmerlin is replying indirectly to the jurists' arguments, but also more generally in the history of the Franciscan mission to the Canaries. From its beginnings under Majorcan auspices in the fourteenth century, missionary activity in the islands had been strongly influenced by Llullianism, emphasising the apostolic life, peaceful methods and the mastery of native languages as prerequisites of success or guarantees of legitimacy. The probability that these Franciscans were inspired by Llull is suggested as well by the Majorcan provenance of the early missionaries as by the fact that the works of the mystical doctor are known to have been copied in the islands.[26] The tradition was interrupted in the 1390s by piratical raids and consequent violence, in which the Franciscan mission in Gran Canaria was wiped out, and which was followed by Béthencourt's conquest. But the activities of Observant friars had revived by the 1430s, when friars and their Canarian neophytes, educated by their evangelisers in an atmosphere of total commitment to peaceful conversion, began to work in person on the susceptibilities of Eugenius IV.

He was one of the most suggestible of popes – no doubt because the conciliar troubles which characterised his pontificate made him reluctant to refuse a favour to any potential friend – and was as responsive to Portuguese demands for authority to make war in the Canaries as to the Canarians' cries for peace. In 1434 native islanders were suppliants at his court. Eugenius issued a safe-conduct to a Gomeran chief named Petrus Chimboya, commending him for playing an important role in enlightening his tribe. The case of 'Dux Petrus' must have drawn attention to the islanders' progress in Christian instruction and to the plight to which violent slave-raids and attempted conquests consigned them. More important still was the visit to Rome of a Franciscan neophyte, native to the Canaries, Fray Juan Alfonso de Idubaren, who arrived in the company of the vicar of his mission to plead for action against the slavers. Accordingly, on 25 October 1434, Eugenius addressed the bull *Regimini Gregis Dominici* to him, in which enslavement of Christian Canarians was forbidden, even though enslavement of neophytes seems to have been a generally admitted practice at the time. From the terms of the bull – as well as from the fact that the Franciscans were willing to admit Canarians to their order – elements of the Franciscan image of the islanders can be inferred: fully human, fully rational beings, essentially peaceful and endowed with a natural inclination for goodness, 'on the road to conversion', imperilled in body and soul by the activities of lay slavers and conquistadores. Indeed, at about this time Eugenius actually ordered the suspension of attempted conquests in order to ensure a peaceful setting for the missionaries' work.[27]

In some respects, such views influenced the conquest when it was resumed under Ferdinand and Isabella. On slavery, the monarchs' views were even more trenchant than those received from the pope. Their liberation in 1477 of 'certain Canarians who are Christians and others who are on the way to conversion' on the grounds that 'it would be a thing of bad example and give cause for none to wish to be converted' may be compared with the words of *Regimini Gregis Dominici*: 'that those already converted may enjoy due security and others be not deterred from conversion by fear of such captivity'. For Eugenius, however, this had remained a pious injunction: he had not formerly extended protection from enslavement to unconverted natives. Not only did the monarchs exceed him in this; they followed him in encouraging peaceful conversion, provided the missionaries also taught obedience to the crown of Castile along with the more usual Christian obligations. The mission which the monarchs despatched to Tenerife in 1486 involved a brief both to convert the natives and reduce them to royal authority. Francisca de Gazmira's mission to La Palma (see p.210) produced natives who were considered to be Christians, and who welcomed Alonso de Lugo.[28]

At the same time, the monarchs were unwilling to abandon violent means of extending their influence in the archipelago. Although they professed the conversion of the natives as their principal aim, political considerations counted for at least as much. Their opposition to enslavement of the natives may have derived from their unwillingness to see royal vassals turned into personal chattels, and can be explained by reference to their general distaste for all forms of intermediate lordship which alienated subjects from the jurisdiction of the crown. Ferdinand was prepared to make an exception of rebels 'against their natural lord'. The monarchs' insistence on the justice of their wars against the Canarians is made clear by their response to Sixtus IV's Bulls of Indulgence, for the conversion of the islanders, of 1478. The pope dedicated the funds they received expressly for the conversion of natives and the erection of religious houses in the islands. By an insidious abuse of language, however, the monarchs described the bulls as 'for the said conversion and conquest'. This caused so deep a rift between the monarchs and some of their clergy, and especially the Observant Franciscans who were responsible for the Canarian mission, that the nuncio, Francisco Ortiz, and other opponents of the use of violence attempted to sequester the funds.[29]

Meanwhile, the Franciscans' efforts in the islands were encountering uneven success. Little progress had been made in the unconquered major islands since the 1460s. In a reference to Fuerteventura, Lanzarote, Gomera and Hierro, Pius II had declared in 1462 that 'four islands were now added to the Christian religion', a phrase that Sixtus IV could merely echo as late as August, 1476. In Pius's time the Canaries had been seen as a base for the conversion of the African mainland. Fray Alonso de Bolaños, newly appointed to the Minors' Canarian vicariate, received privileges corresponding to this task, but his efforts seem to have been found unsatisfactory, at least in some quarters. At the beginning of 1464 his rights were suspended. In September of the following year Bolaños was replaced and the friars' concessions restricted. It seems probable that Bolaños's failure was due rather to an excess of zeal than the lack of it; and that opposition to him derived from interested lay competitors. In the pursuit of peaceful conversion, he found himself confronting pirates and conquistadores. In 1476, he obtained from Sixtus IV a bull outlawing the activities of slavers.[30] Perhaps, if the inclusion of Guinea in the area designated by his privileges may be so construed, he was seeking to protect the Blacks, as well as the Canarians, from hostile depredations: if so, it would be a remarkable, almost unique instance of Blacks being directly involved in the terms of the medieval debate about the rights of primitives. It may have been the cause of complaints lodged against him at the papal court by that dedicated raider, Diego de Herrera, lord of the lesser Canaries, in 1465. Despite the machinations of their adversaries, the missionaries made solid endeavours, anticipating the Christian soldiery in the unconquered islands, as when they preceded Herrera's invasion of Gran Canaria in 1460. But the dispersal of their efforts to the Guinea coast and the interruption of Bolaños's apostolate caused a setback in their work in the major islands until Sixtus IV, early in the 1470s, decided to renew the attempt to carry the gospel to Gran Canaria, Tenerife and La Palma. In 1472, Bolaños's privileges were restored. By September, 1475, the vicar was styled apostolic nuncio; and within a year the pope could utter the following eulogy, which shows both how active Bolaños was in proselytising in person and how his methods were designed to introduce the natives not only to the religion of Europeans but also to their customs and material culture:

> For those who hitherto have not known God, now wish to take up the Catholic faith . . . especially in the island which is called Tenerife, to which, we understand, Alfonso, travelling in person, stirred by the fervour of God, that he might supervise the conversion of the pagans in that place, by the example of his own vocation, drew very many to the faith of Christ . . . in such a way that, among faithful Christian people, living in the full observance of the faith, and taking up the mechanical arts and other means of life, they might be more amply and easily instructed and informed in the practice of human industry, which the said pagans and new converts altogether lack.

Sixtus still tempered his praise with caution, for he ordered his legate in Spain, Rodrigo Borja (the future Alexander VI) to examine the nuncio's privileges and make what adjustments he saw fit.[31]

The Franciscans' leading role among the Canarians was not to last long. Their expansion both in the peninsula and on the islands brought them into conflict with the secular clergy, conquistadores and jurists at the royal court, all of whom shared a view of the natives very different from the Franciscans' own. As well as various friaries established in the islands by Bolaños and his successors, the Canarian vicariate had a growing number of dependent houses in Andalusia and the Basque country. There are instances of lapses of discipline from early in the 1470s and a number of individuals were placed under the disciplinary authority of the General Ministry of the Order. Finally, at about the time when, in 1480, Bolaños was preferred to a bishopric, allegations were levelled at the vicars that they had harboured runaway clerks in their houses. Moreover, papal restrictions on the number of houses to be occupied by the Observants had apparently been overstepped and complaints received – for what reason is unclear – from the Duke of Medina Sidonia, who, of course, was an investor in the conquest. As a result, Sixtus revoked all the powers issued to Bolaños, appointed a new nuncio and transferred many houses to the General Ministry. Whereas Pius II had ordered that friars should be welcomed in the Canarian mission houses, even without their superiors' permission, in 1477, the vicar of the Canaries was ordered to send such recruits home.[32]

With the loss of Bolaños's presiding genius, the rapid development of the conquest and the intrusion of the secular clergy, the missionary activity of the friars dwindled. In 1487 their Andalusian houses were incorporated into the Custodia of Seville; those belonging to the African mission were greatly reduced. Their missionary fervour was not assuaged: some of them were soon to provide evangelists for the New World. But for the time being, their adversaries – and an alternative view of the nature and status of the pagan Canarians – had triumphed.

Evidently, there was a chasm between the friars' perceptions of the islanders and those of the conquistadores and potential lay colonists. The former exercised influence disproportionate to their numbers, but the latter preponderated in colonial society. Of the experts who remained in armchairs back home, the humanists were closer, in their image of the primitive, to the missionaries, sharing an appreciative view and an accent on the natural virtue of the natives; the jurists, concerned to justify the conquest, provided raw material for the conquistadores, as we have seen, by scrutinising native society in the light of natural law. It seems improbable, however, that laymen of little education, such as most conquerors and colonists were, should have drawn their prevailing images from learned tradition. Stereotypes of the *similitudines hominis* and the familiar figure of the wild man of the woods seem to have contributed more to popular perceptions. Comparisons with animals came readily to lay lips and pens. For the German physician, Hieronymus Münzer, who saw them in 1497, they were 'beasts in human form'; for Zurara, in the previous generation, they seemed 'drawn from bestiality'.[33] The pirates reported by Hemmerlin likened them, as we saw, to dogs and monkeys and accused them of barking or howling speech, disgusting table manners, and eating uncooked food: these features of beastly life had already relegated the Welsh, Irish, Basques, Slavs and Mongols to the nether links of the chain of being. And those broad, flat faces observed by the pirates, which might suggest cromagnoid origins to a modern anthropologist, were rich in simian associations and suggestive of lust and degeneracy to a medieval onlooker. The same trait had been noticed by most writers on the Mongols. Raw food was a similar commonplace, recalling Mandeville's hairy race of islanders who 'eten bothe flessch and fissch alle raugh'. Even nakedness, which might suggest the golden age to a humanist or primitive innocence to a friar, signified beastliness for most spectators. The pseudo-traveller, 'Jordanus Catalanus' saw nakedness as monstrous: he put men without clothes into his catalogue of prodigies.[34] Even at a learned level, clothes were overestimated as a sign of civilisation. Beatriz de Bobadilla denied the Gomerans' Christianity on the grounds that 'they go about naked'. The first observation of Boccaccio's informant was, 'The men and women were naked and were savage in their way of life and customs.'[35] Such reflections led to the image of the wild man, so prominent in late medieval art that it would have come easily to the mind even of an illiterate or semiliterate man. The traditional heraldic wild men on the scutcheon of one conqueror of the Canaries became assimilated to primitive Canarians. The actual phrase 'wild men of the woods' or close translations of it became a standard term for the natives. They were 'homines naturales', 'silvestres fere homines' and even 'indomiti silvestres'.[36] Yet the romantic view of the wild man as a sympathetic, unspoilt creature, was never applied to the Canarians, except, perhaps, by implication, by Petrarch.

Early Atlantic colonial society was thus an inauspicious milieu for the native. In the Canary Islands, survivors after the conquest were few, to be numbered in hundreds, rather than thousands, even where they were most numerous, in Tenerife and Gran

Canaria, and virtually extinguished in Lanzarote and Fuerteventura. Whom the depredations of slavers and the assaults of conquerors spared, the newly introduced sicknesses depleted. Spaniards of the late middle ages were more sensitive to differences of class than race and members of the native aristocracy found ready acceptance and cultural assimilation. Don Fernando Guanarteme was able to marry his daughters to Spanish hidalgos; the sons of the chiefs of Tenerife were treated as notables and accorded the style of 'Don'. But at a lower social level, natives who survived the conquest did so mainly as domestic slaves or rebels in the hills, or in such solitary occupations as herdsmen and gatherers, or in enclaves apart from colonial society, like that granted to members of Don Fernando Guanarteme's tribe, not in their native Tenerife but on Gran Canaria. Even these were few. The conquerors' and the monarchs' policy was to create a new society of settlers. The natives were deported en masse to the peninsula and forbidden to return, even if they were not enslaved. And the favoured few who remained relatively welcome in colonial society seem to have been victims of adverse discrimination in the distribution of land grants: they received little irrigable land; they were frequently forbidden to grow sugar; and many received their land grants outside their native islands.[37]

Where then does the discovery of Atlantic man stand in relation to the history of 'cultural contacts' and 'race relations' before and afterwards? Mediterranean precedent, strictly understood, was of little relevance. The subject populations of the Mediterranean 'empires' might be considered barbaric, like the Sards or even the Moors of Majorca, 'barbaras nationes' by Catalan standards; or of dubious Christianity, like the schismatic Greeks and Armenians; or infidels, like the Jews and Moors. But none belonged to the same category as the Canarians or Blacks. None was so outlandish in appearance, nor so distinctive in behaviour; none went naked or virtually naked – indeed, in some ways this was the great novelty of Atlantic man. None was strictly pagan, for Jews and Moors belonged to distinct and well-defined classes of heathendom. There had been frequent debates about the propriety of enslavement, especially of schismatic but strictly orthodox Christians such as the Greeks: in the Crown of Aragon, for instance, limitations on the enslavement of Greeks began in the second decade of the fourteenth century and although the trade increased, thanks to the Venetians, who ignored numerous papal prohibitions, and the Catalan Company, who stimulated supply, a fierce sermon campaign of the Bishop of Barcelona from 1396 renewed the attack; Greek slavery disappeared in the fifteenth century.[38] But the debate about the Canary Islanders ranged more widely: the degree to which they were Christians was not the only criterion, but rather the degree to which they were fully rational and endowed with natural rights – in particular, of internal sovereignty.

Though these problems had not specifically arisen in the course of Mediterranean colonial experience, there were precedents in the cases of the Mongols and Lithuanians, who had both been the subject of debates – widely separated in time – on whether they made better allies or enemies. John of Piano Carpini, sent to investigate the Mongols in person in 1245, found that their barbarity excluded them. Paulus Vladimiri, a Polish jurist, replying to the strictures of the Teutonic knights, demonstrated the opposite of the Lithuanians at the Council of Constance. By virtue, particularly, of their practice of natural law, they belonged to 'human society': the rights of that part of human society which lay outside the church had been emphasised, at least since the late thirteenth century, by jurists who were anxious to draw attention to the limits of the pope's authority.[39]

In these cases – and that of the Blacks, as the Portuguese seem to have realised by the time they reached the latitudes of the Congo – discussions of whether particular peoples were fit allies or victims in war raised questions about the limits of papal authority as well as about the status of pagan societies. At one level, the crucial question could be formulated as, 'Did the pope have jurisdiction over infidels?' Another way of formulating it was, 'Did pagans belong to the same society – in the widest sense – as the peoples of Latin Christendom?' This was important because both Castile and Portugal relied on the pope to sanctify or legitimate their Atlantic conquests. Those conquests therefore stimulated the development and acceptance of juridical categories which embraced, or were capable of embracing, the whole of mankind. Thus conclusions similar to those of Paulus Vladimiri on the Lithuanians were advanced, for instance, with somewhat different intent, by Rosellis on the Canarians. Indeed, they belonged, in his submission, to the human race despite admitted offences against natural law. We are approaching a world without barbarians, in Aquinas's sense of the world, in which no human beings are excluded from a common juridical and scientific class which includes all men – in which, according to Las Casas' famous tautology, 'All the peoples of mankind are human'.[40] It was a truth not previously taken for granted.

Did the American Indians pose any new problems, or suggest any new conception, that had not already been encountered on the eastern side of the Atlantic? It is hard to detect any significant elements in the debate about them, at least in the first half of the sixteenth century, that had not been anticipated in discussions of the Canary Islanders. The biggest contribution of the peoples of the New World was probably towards the development of a scientific ethnology, which can hardly be discerned, except in the most shadowy form, in the work of medieval ethnographers.[41] But one should recall, before discounting the significance of the discovery of the Amerindians, the enormous difference of scale between the eastern and western Atlantic discoveries. The Blacks were numerous, but, as we have seen, their impact on late medieval perceptions of man was negligible; the Canarians were a few thousand, and dwindling and marginalised, by the completion of the conquest, even in their own islands. For a brief moment when they were first discovered, they captured the attention of some of the most influential intellects of Latin Christendom: those of Boccaccio, Petrarch, Clement VI; thereafter, interest in them was sporadic and never occupied a prominent place. The Indians of the New World seized and held the attention of an incomparably greater number of observers and commentators, in every discipline and in every position of influence; their impact was spread by the printing press and sustained by the length and brilliance of the process of their discovery.

While the debate about the American Indians raged, the Canarians' relevance was almost forgotten. Las Casas showed an interest in them in his *Historia de las Indias*: but that work remained in manuscript and was little known. Towards the end of the sixteenth century, when the islanders were already almost extinct, antiquarian *amateurs* compiled some ethnographic information, perhaps in imitation of the great compilations, which were coming to be known in Europe, of missionaries in the New World. Only one new polemic was generated. The Las Casas, as it were, of the Canary Islands – the Dominican Fray Alonso de Espinosa – emerged as the great defender and apologist of the Canarians in a work on the Virgin-patroness of the islands, designed largely to demonstrate the natural piety of the preconquest natives. Writing in the 1590s, he was still spellbound by the traditional debate on natural law. 'Although without law,' he claimed, 'they did not live altogether outside law, for in some things their actions were according to reason.' Espinosa could not quite escape from the weight of tradition which condemned them in this respect, but he gave them a redeeming feature in the form of access to reason, which was an essential precondition of recognition of natural law. In other literature spawned by reports or memories of the Canarians, their image became altogether abstracted from reality and assimilated to commonplaces of another popular genre of the time: pastoral literature. In a play of Lope de Vega, in the poems of Cairrasco and Viana, the Canarians led, not real lives, but those of a bucolic idyll, in idealised simplicity, enlivened by coy love affairs, rhetorically elaborated.[42] 'Natural man' had yielded to another, even less apposite literary stereotype.

## The Image of the World

The mariner's occupation, according to Columbus, 'inclines all who follow it to wish to learn the secrets of the world'.[43] Late medieval exploration of the Atlantic fed geographical speculation, even as it increased geographical knowledge. The effects can be observed in three fields: cartography, cosmography and attempted practical navigation.

It was not only the scope of maps that changed in the late middle ages but also their very nature. Until the thirteenth century – to judge from surviving examples – European world maps had been devotional objects, intended to evoke God's harmonious design in a schematic form, appropriate, for instance, for an altarpiece; area maps had been attempts to illustrate an itinerary or sailing instructions in diagrammatic form. By the fifteenth century, map makers were showing the same interest in geographical realism as renaissance artists in naturalism. This renaissance in cartography began with the increasing precision of the sea chart or portulan, in the thirteenth and fourteenth centuries; the experts who made them in Venice, Genoa and Majorca realised that their practical utility as navigational aids was enhanced by accuracy and breadth of coverage. As we saw in Chapter 6, the portulan seems in the fourteenth century to have been a common medium for the recording of new discoveries. Increasingly, this became the map's explicit role. The Genoese maker of an unpublished map of 1403 (now in Yale University Library) recorded how he had checked the details of his work against the 'efficacious experience' and information of seamen. A famous map made in London by Andrea Bianco in 1448 is expressly devoted to a record of the latest Atlantic discoveries of the Portuguese navigators.[44] Nor was it only in the context of navigation that accurate maps were valuable: they had their strategic uses, too. Pere Martell seems to have spread or sketched a map of the western Mediterranean before his interlocutors at the Tarragona banquet of 1229 (see p.15), whereas St Louis was uncertain of the distance from Tunis to Jerusalem as late as 1270, in spite of having a sea chart on board. In the next couple of generations, that gap was plugged: the crusading propaganda of Marino Sanudo was illustrated with maps of uncanny accuracy, drawn by Pietro Vesconte.

Portulans and strategic charts were, by their nature, practical instruments and therefore susceptible to change and responsive to new information. The world map was encumbered with more tenacious traditions, derived from the genre's devotional origins. The convention of depicting the world as the *orbis terrarum*, a continuous landmass, surrounded by islands and ringed by a circumvalatory ocean, was adopted by some of the most up-to-date cartographers: for instance by Henricus Martellus, who included the latest 'descriptions of the Portuguese' in a map probably made in Florence in 1489. To the end of the fifteenth century, it was common to show the earthly paradise at the extreme orient, Jerusalem – at least roughly – in the middle. Concessions to realism, however, began in the thirteenth century and accumulated thereafter. The Catalan Atlas of 1375, for instance, is deliberately encyclopedic, a summa of geographical knowledge and speculation. It also has elements of rough spectroscope, conveying an impression of the earth's roundness. The technique for making a globe was discovered in the *De Sphaera* of Nicholas de Oresma (1320/5–82), and though no medieval globe of the world has survived from before Martin Behaim's of 1492, now in the National Museum of Nuremberg, spherical representations were probably more numerous. Behaim's globe recalls another new development: the use of maps to illustrate geographical theories; Behaim's represented those of the Nuremberg circle to which he and Hieronymus Münzer belonged; the most common source of inspiration, however, was Ptolemy. His *Geography*, the text of which was translated into Latin early in the fifteenth century, invited illustration to supply the want of original maps and to render the difficult language intelligible.

Even in world maps – which gave their compilers a welcome chance to speculate about the Orient and the Indian Ocean – the greatest contribution of novelties of the fifteenth century lay in the Atlantic. The extent of concern with the Atlantic, in both world maps and sea charts, is the most remarkable feature: it shows what a stimulus to the imagination Atlantic exploration was, and how consciousness of an exciting and exploitable Atlantic 'space' grew in the century before Columbus's voyages. To the mythical islands commonly assigned imaginary positions in fourteenth-century maps – those of Brendan, St Ursula and Brasil – the Venetian chart of 1424 adds large and alluring isles, including 'Antilia', the latter identified with the island of 'Seven Cities' to which, in a legend not unlike that of St Ursula, Portuguese refugees from the Moors were held to have repaired in the eighth century. These islands became common in subsequent cartographical tradition and inspired voyages in search of them.[45] As late as 1514, Portuguese official sailing directions gave courses to islands 'not yet discovered' and one of the most amusing forgeries of the sixteenth century is a spurious Spanish 'chronicle' of the conquest of St Brendan's Isle. Attempts have been made to relate these mental divagations to possible real finds, usually in connection with theories of pre-Columbian discoveries of America; the only genuine new discovery of the early fifteenth century which might underlie the phenomenon could be the Sargasso Sea. But once one appreciates the genuine excitement aroused in the fifteenth century by the unlimited possibilities of the Atlantic, the fertility of speculation seems adequately explained. Fresh discoveries were a direct stimulus: the Majorcan cartographers who first placed the Azores in their roughly correct position in maps of the 1430s, also introduced new speculative islands into the tradition. Andrea Bianco was interested in the latest verifiable novelties, as his sea chart of 1448 shows, but in his world map he scattered a handful of imaginary islands about the Ocean, and even in the 1448 chart he included some traditional isles, with an assurance that an 'authentic island' lay 1500 miles out in the equatorial Atlantic.

Bianco seems to have felt that ancient certainties about geography had to be discarded. The same point was made implicitly a few years later by the acknowledged master of the Venetian cartographic school, Fra Mauro, who confessed in a note on his world map – the fullest then devised – that his delineation must be imperfect, since the extent of the world was unknown. The cosmographers of the fourteenth and fifteenth centuries remind one of the prisoners-of-war in one of Marcel Ainé's stories, who, unable to see their cell walls in the light of a tallow candle, could imagine themselves free. Late medieval ignorance imparted a similar sense of boundlessness.

The freedom of conjecture can be sensed in the growth of two revolutionary theories about the Atlantic: the theory of the existence of the Antipodes, and the theory of a narrow Atlantic. Neither was admissible in traditional cosmography. The size of the globe had been consistently underestimated since antiquity, though the best available computation, that of Eratosthenes, was accurate to within five per cent; even these common underestimates implied a huge unknown moiety of the world, the *pars inferior*, like the dark side of the moon. As the image of the *orbis terrarum* – the single, continuous landmass comprising all the known world – was firmly etched in the mind of every educated man, the common, received wisdom was that unrelieved ocean occupied the unknown portion. The daring thought that there might be a second landmass in the midst of the ocean 'opposite' the familiar landmass appealed to the Renaissance taste for symmetry and, more generally, to the medieval preference for an ordered and 'concordant' creation; but it breached two dearly held shibboleths – that all men were descended from Adam and that the apostles had preached 'throughout the world'.

Yet the possibility of the existence of the Antipodes was increasingly widely canvassed. Pierre d'Ailly, the reforming cardinal of Touraine, referred to it in his *Imago Mundi*, of the first years of the fifteenth century, one of the most influential cosmographical works of the period, and in two treatises written a few years later under the influence of Ptolemy. In his *Historia Rerum* of the mid-fifteenth century. Aeneas Sylvius Piccolomini (the future Pope Pius II), considered the theory with implicit approval, only to grant it a pious dismissal with a reminder that a Christian 'ought to prefer' the traditional view. Clearly, that sort of disclaimer was not to be taken seriously and by the time of Columbus, the Antipodes were widely debated and, in some circles, especially in Italy and among humanists, their discovery was seriously anticipated. Speculation about the Antipodes may have been stimulated by the reception of Strabo in the west. The first text arrived in Italy in 1423 and some of Strabo's ideas circulated widely from the time of the Council of Florence in 1439 – a great occasion for the exchange of cosmographical news as well as ecclesiological debate; a complete translation of the *Geography* of Strabo by Guarino of Verona was available from 1458 and in print by 1469. Its peculiar importance was that this text placed the supposed unknown continent roughly where Columbus or one of the other Atlantic navigators of the fifteenth century might have been expected to find it: 'It may be that in this same temperate zone there are actually two inhabited worlds or even more, and in particular in the proximity of the parallel through Athens that is drawn across the Atlantic Sea.' This passage was particularly striking in the context of Strabo's general defence of an Homeric world picture and rebuttal of the cosmography of Eratosthenes: in particular, Strabo intended it as a challenge to Eratosthenes' view that 'if the immensity of the Atlantic Sea did not prevent it, we could sail from Iberia to India along the same parallel'.

That Columbus himself considered the Antipodes as a possible destination for his own projected Atlantic exploration is demonstrated by the response of one of the committees which investigated his plans: 'duda San Agustín'. This can only be an allusion to St Augustine's 'doubts' of the existence of the Antipodes. When Columbus returned from his first voyage, despite his energetic avowals that he had been to Asia, most Italian commentators seem to have assumed that his discoveries were Antipodean in character: the ready acceptance of this theory in so many sources shows that it must have been current before Columbus's departure. Its attraction for humanists was, evidently, particularly strong, perhaps because it appeared to draw support from authorities widely esteemed for their place in the classical tradition, such as the *De Nuptiis Philologiae et Mercurii* of Martianus Capella or the commentaries on Cicero of Macrobius, whose world picture seems to have been based largely on Eratosthenes and therefore to have belonged to a quite different school from Strabo. Macrobius – albeit more obliquely than Strabo – also suggested that 'Antipodean' landmasses might exist in the northern as well as the southern hemisphere.[46]

The second great theory that speculatively 'filled' the Atlantic space was of a greatly extended world landmass, allowing relatively less of the globe's surface to the intervening ocean. Ptolemy had mentioned dismissively the calculations of his fellow cosmographer, Marinus of Tyre, who had sought to stretch the limits of Asia eastwards beyond the limits acceptable to Ptolemy. Following this hint, Pierre d'Ailly speculated that the Antipodes might not be a separate continent, but contiguous with the known landmass. D'Ailly passed on a range of authorities collected by Roger Bacon (1214–92), perhaps with some distortion of the authors' original intentions, to suggest that most of the surface of the world is covered by land: a narrow Atlantic was a necessary inference, which many of d'Ailly's readers drew. In attributing to Aristotle the view that 'the sea is small between the western extremity of Spain and the eastern part of India', d'Ailly was being more faithful to Bacon than to Aristotle, whose text on the subject is ambiguous and obscure. But such authority, once appropriated or arrogated for a particular point of view, carried enormous weight. The theory of the narrow Atlantic was cultivated in the circle of the Florentine cosmographer, Paolo Toscanelli, whose views are expressed in a letter of June, 1474, addressed to the Portuguese king, and a subsequent recapitulation addressed to Columbus. Toscanelli estimated the distance from the Canaries to Cathay to be about 5000 nautical miles – not quite navigable by the standards of the time, but the journey might be broken at 'Antilia' and Japan. This picture of the Atlantic soon came to be shared by the Nuremberg cosmographers: it is, with only small modifications, the picture of Behaim's globe; and Münzer became its spokesman when he wrote to the king of Portugal, urging the exploration of a western route to Asia, in 1493.[47] By then, of course, apparently unknown to Münzer, the attempt had already been made.

Columbus's was not the only practical attempt to exploit the alluring uncertainties of the Atlantic. In 1480 and 1487, certainly, and perhaps regularly in the 1490s, expeditions sailed from Bristol in search of new islands: a big increase in the importation of north Atlantic products to Bristol in the 1480s shows the increased trade with Iceland that such journeys produced or reflected, but these were consciously exploratory voyages, intended to 'serch and fynde'.[48] The Bristolians called their objective 'Brasil'. For the Portuguese and Flemings of the Azores, 'Antilia' was a comparable catch-all name for potential new discoveries. At least eight Portuguese commissions for the discovery of new Atlantic islands, survive from the years 1462–87. Some specifically refer to the evidence of sea charts. The most general terms are those of Fernão Teles's grant (1474) of 'the Seven Cities or whatever islands he shall find'.[49] Despite the minimal results, the Bristolian and Azorean voyages continued unabashed. The Atlantic was becoming a compulsion, a vacuum irresistibly abhorred.

Columbus's first discovery – before, that is, the discovery of America – was of a viable route for further Atlantic exploration. An Azorean point of departure was impractical at most seasons because of the prevailing westerlies; the Canaries, where a favourable wind was at his back, were ideal for the purpose. Whether Columbus fixed on the Canaries by luck or judgment is unknown: but the balance of probabilities is in favour of the latter. He knew Atlantic waters well, and was in a position to judge where the wind was most favourable; the information he had from Toscanelli seems to have favoured – even presupposed – departure from the Canaries; and he reserved his most tenacious campaign for patronage for the crown of Castile, which controlled the Canaries.

The ironies of Columbus's success go deeper. Considered from one aspect, his enterprise was merely another Atlantic exploration like those of his Azorean and Bristolian predecessors. His commission from Ferdinand and Isabella was to discover 'islands and mainlands' in the Ocean Sea; according to his first biographer, he hoped at least to find some new island, even if he found nothing else. As we have seen, he also contemplated, at least at one time, the possibility of an Antipodean landfall. But by the time he made his first voyage, he had virtually staked his claims and his reputation on the promise of a short route to Asia. His belief in a narrow Atlantic was similar to, and in part derived from, the theories suggested or espoused by learned cosmographers like d'Ailly and Toscanelli. Columbus, however, based his hopes not only on their excessive estimates of the eastward extent of Asia, but also on further, less plausible inferences of his own, from Marinus of Tyre and Marco Polo, which exceeded even Toscanelli's expectations. Moreover, Columbus absurdly underestimated the size of the globe by mistaking for Roman miles an estimate in Arabic miles, given by d'Ailly, of the measurement of a degree of the earth's circumference. As with most of his errors, he stuck to this grotesque miscalculation, with pig-headed obduracy, throughout his career.

The crowning irony was that, setting off with a conviction of a narrow Atlantic, and demonstrating indeed that the ocean was by no means as vast as the more pessimistic cosmographers of the time supposed, he nevertheless confirmed its potential and enhanced its mystery. His crossing took 32 days, on his first voyage. That represented, in one sense, the reduction of the image of the Atlantic to navigable proportions; in another, the confirmation of the existence of a huge and exploitable space. In maps of the fifteenth century, which had left increasingly large, blank spaces to westward for the adumbration of new lands, such a development had been prefigured. Not for more than two generations after Columbus were the limits of the Atlantic sufficiently well explored for the ocean to be delineated on maps with reasonable accuracy; indeed, in northerly latitudes, those limits were not fully charted until the nineteenth century. Yet Columbus's voyage does mark a moment of definition in the growth of awareness of the Atlantic 'space' and, therefore, in the modification of men's traditional image of the world. The links, such as they were, between the Mediterranean and the Atlantic had been established in the crucible of the eastern Atlantic in the course of the fifteenth century. Now it was possible for those links to be extended to the ocean's farther shore, in Columbus's crowded wake.

# References

1. THE ISLAND CONQUESTS OF THE HOUSE OF BARCELONA

1. Gil Vicente, *Obras completas*, ed. A. J. da Costa Pimpão (Barcelos, 1956), p.55 (*Auto da Sibila Cassandra*).

2. *Llibre dels feits del rey en Jaume*, chs 47, 57; *Llibre del rei en Pere*, ch. 166, F. Soldevila (ed.), *Les quatre grans cròniques* (Barcelona, 1971), pp.28, 33–4, 577.

3. *Llibre dels feits*, chs 48–55; Soldevila, *Quatre grans cròniques*, pp.28–32; P. Bofarull y Moscaró, *Colección de documentos inéditos del Archivo de la Corona de Aragón*, XI (Barcelona, 1856), 4.

4. P. Bonassie, 'Une famille de la campagne barcelonaise et les activités économiques aux alentours de l'an mil', *Annales du midi*, LXXVI (1964), pp.261–97; J. E. Ruiz Doménec, 'El origen del capital comercial en Barcelona', *Miscellanea Barcinonensia*, XII (no. 31, 1972), pp.55–88.

5. J. Salva, 'Instituciones políticas y sociales', *Historia de Mallorca*, ed. J. Mascaró Pasarius, III (Palma, 1970), pp.387–8.

6. *Llibre dels feits*, chs 48, 56–7; Soldevila, op. cit., pp.28, 32–4.

7. E. de K. Aguiló, 'Actes de venta o de moficació de domini otorgado per primers grans porcioners', *Boletín de la Sociedad Arqueológica Luliana*, XV (1914), 53–62; J. Dameto, V. Mut and G. Alemany, *Historia general del reino de Mallorca*, eds M. Moragues Pro and J. M. Bover (3 vols, Palma, 1841), II, 761–3, 826; P. Negre y Pastell, 'Documentos relacionados con Mallorca otorgados por personalidades de tierras gerundenses', *Anales del Instituto de Estudios gerundenses*, XVIII (1967), 165–260.

8. J. M. Quadrado, *Historia de la conquista de Mallorca* (Palma, 1850), pp.432–535, supplemented by J. Busquets Mulet in *Homenaje a Millas Vallicrosa*, I (Barcelona, 1954), pp.243–300.

9. L. Pérez, 'Documentos conservados en los Registros Vaticanos', *Boletín de la Sociedad Arqueológica Luliana*, XXXII (1961–2), 51, 53; E. Lourie, 'Free Moslems in the Balearics under Christian Rule in the XIIIth Century' *Speculum*, XLV (1970), 628–9.

10. Ibid., pp.630–40.

11. Aguiló, loc. cit.; F. Sevillano Colom, 'Mercáderes y navegantes mallorquines', *Historia de Mallorca*, IV (1971), 513; B. Desclot, *Llibre del rei en Pere*, ch. 14. Soldevila, op. cit., p.421.

12. A. Pons, 'Los judíos del reino de Mallorca durante los siglos XIII y XIV,' *Hispania*, XVI (1956), 185, 205ff, 237, 400–1, 338–40, 349; B. Guasp y Gelabert, 'Para servir a la historia de Castellitx', *Boletín de la Sociedad Arqueólogica Luliana*, XXXIII (1970–1), 371–4.

13. C. Verlinden, *L'Esclavage dans l'Europe médiévale*, (2 vols, Bruges, 1955), I, 253; E. Putzulu, 'Schiavi sardi a Maiorca nell seconda metà del secolo xiv', *Studi storici in once di F. Loddo Canepa* (2 vols, Florence, 1959), I, 213–51; G. Llompart, 'Pere Mates', *Boletín de la Sociedad Arqueológica Luliana*, XXXIV (1973), 93; Sevillano Colom, op. cit., pp.458, 467–70.

14. Ibid., pp.450–1; F. Sevillano Colom, 'Artesanía textil de la lana mallorquina', *Boletín de la Sociedad Arqueológica Luliana*, XXXIII (1970–1), 157–78.

15. *Llibre dels feits*, ch. 106; R. Muntaner, *Crònica*, ch. 8, Soldevila, op. cit. 27, pp.56, 673–4.

16. A. Santamaría Arandez, 'Mallorca en el siglo xiv', *Anuario de estudios medievales*, VII (1970), 165–238; B. Font Obrador, 'Mallorca en 1349', *Boletín de la Sociedad Arqueológica Luliana*, XXXIII (1964), 245–60.

17. F. Soldevila, *Vida de Jaime I* (Barcelona, 1958), pp.98–109; A. Santamaría Arandez, 'Alba del Reino de Mallorca', *Historia de Mallorca*, III (1970), 1–84, esp. 28–43; Pérez, op. cit., p.52.

18. I. Macabich, *Eivissa: los seves institucions històriques* (Barcelona, 1964); 'Formentera', *Hispania*, XII (1952), 572–6; Lourie, loc. cit. p.631; Pérez, loc. cit., pp.55–7, 59.

19. V. Salavert y Roca, *Cerdeña y la expansión mediterránea de la Corona de Aragón* (2 vols, Madrid, 1956), I, 126–7.

20. V. D'Alessandro, *Politica e società nella Sicilia aragonese* (Palermo, 1963), esp. pp.255–80.

21. J. Martínez Ferrando, *Tres siglos de disposiciones reales sobre Menorca* (Ciudadela, 1958), pp.3, 10, 28; Verlinden, op. cit., pp.254–8.

22. Dante, *Paradiso*, VIII, 77.

23. V. Salavert, 'Los motivos económicos en la conquista de Cerdeña', *VI Congreso de historia de la corona de Aragón* (Madrid, 1959), pp.433–45, esp. p.436.

24. J. P. Cuvillier, 'Barcelone, Gênes et le blé de Sicile', *Atti del I Congresso Storico Liguria-Catalogna* (Bordighera, 1974), pp.165–70; F. Soldevila, 'Alguns aspects de la política económica de Pere el Gran', *VI Congreso de historia de la Corona de Aragón*, 187–95.

25. A. M. Aragó Cabañas, 'La repoblación de Sásser bajo Alfonso el benigno, 1330–1336', Ibid., pp.539–49.

26. A. Boscolo, 'La feudalitá in Sicilia, in Sardegna e nel Napoletano nel basso medioevo', *Saggi di storia mediterranea tra il xiv e il xvi secolo* (Rome, 1981), pp.121, 126; *Documenti sull'economia e sulla società in Sardegna all'epoca di Alfonso il benigno* (Padua, 1973), p.2; B. R. Motzo, 'Un progetto catalano per la conquesta definitiva della Sardegna', *Studie in onore di Loddo Canepa*, I, 165–80.

27. Verlinden, op. cit., I, 320–34; J. E. Martínez Ferrando, 'El exceso de población sarda en Menorca a fines del siglo XIV', *VI Congreso de historia de la Corona de Aragón*, pp.319–31.

28. P. Scanu, *Vincles entre Tarragona i l'Alguer* (Barcelona, 1979); J. E. Martínez Ferrando, 'Algunas noticias sobre la situación en el cabo de Logudoro con posterioridad a la victoria catalan del Alguer', *Studi storici e giuridici in onore di Antonio Era* (Padua, 1963), pp.225–30.

29. C. Manca, *Aspetti dell'espansione economica catalano-aragonese nel Mediterraneo occidentale: il commercio internazionale del sale* (Milan, 1965), p.27.

30. M. Mitjà, 'Barcelona y el problema sardo en el siglo XIV', *VI Congreso de historia de la Corona de Aragón*, pp.447–59.

31. I. Carini, *Gli archivi e le biblioteche di Spagna in rapporto alla storia d'Italia* (2 vols, Palermo, 1884–97), II, 177–8; Muntaner, op. cit., ch. 6. Soldevila, *Les quatre grans cròniques*, p.672.

## 2. THE FIRST 'ATLANTIC' EMPIRE: ANDALUSIA AND ITS ENVIRONS

1. See D. Lomax, 'Rodrigo Jiménez de Rada como historiador', *Actas del V Congreso internacional de hispanistas* (2 vols, Bordeaux, 1977), II, 587–92.

2. C. Sánchez-Albornoz, 'Un ceremonial inédito de coronación de los reyes de Castilla', *Estudios sobre las instituciones medievales españolas* (Mexico, 1965), pp.739–63; R. Ximénez de Rada, *Opera*, (Madrid, 1793), pp.153–4; G. Post, *Studies in Medieval Legal Thought* (Princeton, 1964), pp.482–93.

3. J. González, *Reinado y diplomas de Fernando III* (2 vols, Cordova, 1980–1), I, 278–87; M. Ballesteros Gaibrois, 'La conquista de Jaén por Fernando III', *Cuadernos de historia de España*, XX (1953), 65–83.

4. *The Muqaddimah*, trans. F. Rosenthal (3 vols, London, 1958), II, 116–17.

5. J. González, 'Las conquistas de Fernando III en Andalucía', *Hispania*, VI (1946), 584–8.

6. *Primera crónica general*, ed. R. Menéndez Pidal (2 vols, Madrid, 1955), col. 1131.

7. L. Torres Balbas, 'Extensión y demografía de las ciudades hispanomusulmanas', *Studia Islamica*, III (1955), 3ɔ–9; *Ciudades hispanomusulmanas*, I (Madrid, n.d.), 94–106.

8. J. T. Monroe, *Hispano-Arabic Poetry* (Berkeley, 1974), p.334.

9. C. Sánchez-Albornoz, *España: un enigma histórico* (2 vols, Buenos Aires, 1956); A. Castro, *La realidad histórica de Espana* (Mexico, 1954). See P. E. Russell, 'The Nessus-Shirt of Spanish History', *Bulletin of Hispanic Studies*, XXXVI, (1959), 219–25 and H. Lapeyre (p.269 below).

10. *Cantiga 328* (Afonso X, o Sábio, *Cantigas de Santa María*, ed. W. Mettmann [4 vols, Coimbra, 1959–72], III, 191–3).

11. J. Muldoon, *Popes, Lawyers and Infidels* (Liverpool, 1979), pp.111–19; Oldradus de Ponte, *Consilia* (Venice, 1571), folios 126–7.

12. González, *Fernando III*, p.395.

13. J. González, *El repartimiento de Sevilla* (2 vols, Madrid, 1949), I, 236, 238, 285–302, II, 13–185.

14. M. González Jiménez, 'Repartimiento de Carmona', *Historia, instituciones, documentos*, VIII (1981), 66–7; M. González Jiménez and A. González Gómez, *El libro del repartimiento de Jeréz* (Cadiz, 1980), pp.xliv–lxxxiii.

15. M. J. Sanz Fuentes, 'Repartimiento de Ecija', *Historia, instituciones, documentos*, IV (1977), 199–316.

16. M. A. Ladero Quesada and M. González Jiménez, 'La población en la frontera de Gibraltar y el repartimiento de Vejer', *Historia, instituciones, documentos*, IV (1977), 199–316.

17. González, *Repartimiento de Sevilla*, I, 20–1, 47–51; M. Muñoz Vázquez, 'Notas sobre el repartimiento de tierras que hizo el rey Don Fernando III en Córdoba y su término', *Boletín de la Real Academia de Córdoba* (1954), 251–70.

18. A. J. Mur, 'Documentos para el estudio de la Orden de Santiago en Portugal en la edad media', *Actas do Congresso Histórico de Portugal Medievo*, II, (Braga, 1964), 412–15, 417–18.

19. A. Collantes de Terán, 'La aljama mudéjar de Sevilla', *Al-andalus*, I (1978), 143–62; K. Wagner, *Regesto de documentos del Archivo de Protocolos de Sevilla referentes a judíos y moros* (Seville, 1978) gives residents of the XVth-century aljama.

20. A. Collantes de Terán, *Sevilla en la baja edad media* (Seville, 1977), pp.87–94, 207; M. Gaibrois de Ballesteros, *Sancho IV de Castila*, III (Madrid, 1928), pp.cccxcvi–vii.

21. H. Sancho de Sopranis, 'La repoblación y repartimiento de Cadiz por Alfonso X', *Hispania*, XV (1955), 483–539.

22. González, *Repartimiento de Sevilla*, p.377; A. de Capmany y de Monpalau, *Memorias históricas sobre la marina, comercio y artes de la antigua ciudad de Barcelona* (2 vols in 3, Barcelona, 1961–3), II, 53–6.

23. *Libro de agricultura*, ed. J. A. Banqueri (Madrid, 1802).

### 3. A MEDITERRANEAN LAND EMPIRE: SHARQ AL-ANDALŪS

1. 'Juicio interior y secreto de la monarquía' in J. M. Jover Zamora, 'Monarquía y nación en la España del XVII', *Cuadernos de historia de España*, XIII (1950), p.146.

2. R. I. Burns, *Muslims, Christians and Jews in the Crusader Kingdom of Valencia* (Cambridge, 1984), pp.268–80.

3. A. de Capmany y Monpalau, *Memorias históricas sobre la marina, comercio y artes de*

*la antigua ciudad de Barcelona* (2 vols in 3, Barcelona, 1961–3), ii, 40; R. I. Burns, *The Crusader Kingdom of Valencia* (2 vols, Cambridge, Mass., 1967), i, 80–1.

4. R. I. Burns, *Islam under the Crusaders* (Princeton, 1973), pp.126–8.

5. *Llibre dels feits del rei en Jaume*, ch. 130, F. Soldevila, ed. *Les quatre grans cròniques* (Barcelona, 1971), p.63.

6. *Llibre dels feits*, chs 127–9, *Les quatre grans cròniques*, pp.62–3.

7. C. de Tourtoulon, *Jacme I;, le conquérant* (2 vols, Montpellier, 1873), ii, 543.

8. *Llibre dels feits*, chs 336, 363, 436–7, *Les quatre grans cròniques*, pp.128, 135, 157.

9. J. M. Font Rius, 'La comarca de Tortosa a raíz de la reconquista cristiana', *Cuadernos de historia de España*, (1953), 104–28.

10. Burns, *Islam under the Crusaders*, pp.126–7.

11. Ibid., pp.266–7.

12. R. Gallofré Guinovart, *Documentos del reinado de Alfonso III de Aragón* (Valencia, 1968), pp.21, 25, 51.

13. P. Bofarull y Mascaró, *Colección de documentos inéditos del Archivo General de la Corona de Aragón*, xi (Barcelona, 1856), 143–65, analysed by C. de la Véronne, 'Recherches sur le chiffre de la population musulmane de Valence en 1238 d'apres le *Repartimieto*', *Bulletin hispanique*, li (1949), 423–6, S. Sobreques Vidal in J. Vicèns Vives, ed., *Historia de España y América*, ii (Barcelona, 1971), 34–6, and Burns, *Islam under the Crusaders*, pp.82–8.

14. Sobrequés, op. cit., p.38; similar phrases are often used by Burns.

15. *Crònica de Ramon Muntaner*, ch. 29, *Les quatre grans cròniques*, pp.691–2.

16. Burns, *Muslims, Christians and Jews*, pp.61, 73; *Medieval Colonialism* (Princeton, 1975), pp.82, 340.

17. Burns, *Islam under the Crusaders*, pp.357–8.

18. Burns, *Medieval Colonialism*, pp.35–40; *Islam under the Crusaders*, pp.90–8; C. E. Dufourcq, *La vie quotidienne dans les ports méditerrannées au moyen âge* (Paris, 1975), pp.50–1.

19. *Llibre dels feits*, ch. 364, *Les quatre grans cròniques*, p.136.

20. Burns, *Medieval Colonialism*, p.11.

21. Burns, *Islam under the Crusaders*, pp.330–3, 337–51, 301–4, 406–8, 413–20.

22. Ibid., pp.273–86; Burns, 'Los mudéjares de Valencia: temas y metodología', *I Simposio internacional del mudejarismo* (Madrid, 1981), 453–97; 'Social Riots on the Christian-Moslem Frontier', *American Historical Review*, lxvi (1961), 378–400, esp. 383–92; Callofré, op. cit., p.97.

23. *Llibre dels feits*, chs 392, 408; *Les quatre grans cròniques*, pp.145, 149–50.

24. J. González, *Reinado y diplomas de Fernando III* (2 vols, Cordova, 1980–1), i, 460; M. Gual Camarena, 'La corona de Aragón en la repoblación murciana', *VII Congreso de historia de la Corona de Aragón*, ii (Barcelona, 1962), pp.304–10.

25. J. Torres Fontes, 'Jaime I y Alfonso X: dos criterios de repoblación', ibid., ii, 329, 333, 338.

26. J. Torres Fontes, *Los mudéjares murcianos en el siglo XIII* (Murcia, 1961), p.9.

27. Ibid., pp.27–8.

28. H. Lapeyre, *La géographie de l'Espagne morisque* (Paris, 1959), pp.156–7, 191–8; P. Chaunu, *L'Espagne de Charles Quint* (2 vols, Paris, 1973), i, pp.81–98.

#### 4. THE GENOESE MEDITERRANEAN

1. *Cosmographia* (Basle, 1554), pp.139, 178 (1572), pp.178, 248.

2. *Lettres*, ed. R. C. Huygens (Leyden, 1960), pp.76–8.

3. G. Petti-Balbi, *Bonifacio au XIVe siècle* (Bastia, 1980), pp.1–8.

4. G. Petti-Balbi, 'Genova e Corsica nel trecento', *Studi storici del Istituto Storico Italiano per il Medioevo*, xcviii (1976), pp.77–122.

5. M. Balard, *La Romanie génoise* (2 vols, Genoa, 1978), i, 105–25, 355–453; P. Argenti, *The Occupation of Chios by the Genoese* (3 vols, Cambridge, 1958), i, 86–105, 371–415.

6. G. Airaldi, *Studi e documenti su Genoa e l'Oltremare* (Genoa, 1974), p.12.

7. Ibid., pp.12–17; Balard, op. cit., pp.253–337; Argenti, op. cit., i, 569–614, 638–48.

8. *Poesie*, ed. L. Cocito (Rome, 1970), p.566.

9. J. Heers, 'Portugais et Génois au XVe siècle: la rivalité Atlantique-Méditerrannée', *Actas do III Colóquio Internacional de Estudos Luso-Brasileiros* (Lisbon, 1960), ii, 141–7.

10. J. Heers, *Gênes au XVe siècle* (Paris, 1961), pp.200–4, 544–9; *Le clan familial au moyen âge* (Paris, 1974), pp.234–6; Balard, op. cit. ii,522–31.

11. *Cristóbal Colón: textos y documentos completos*, ed. C. Varela (Madrid, 1984), p.329.

12. A. Boscolo, 'Gli Insediamenti genovesi nel sud della Spagna all'epoca di Cristofor Colombo', *Saggi di storia mediterranea tra il XIV e XVI secoli* (Rome, 1981), pp.174–7; F. Melis, 'Malaga nel sistema economico del XIV e XV secoli', *Economia e storia*, iii (1956), 19–59, 139–63; J. Heers, 'Le royaume de Grenade et la politique marchande de Gênes en Occident', *Le moyen âge*, lxiii (1957), 87–121.

13. G. Airaldi, *Genova e Spagna nel secolo XV: il 'Liber damnificatorum in regno Granatae'* (Genoa, 1966).

14. G. Jehel, 'Catalogue analytique et chronologique des actes du notaire Petrus Batifolius', *Cahiers de Tunisie*, xxv (1977), 69–135.

15. Heers, *Gênes au XVe siècle*, pp.271–9.

16. H. Sancho de Sopranis, *Los genoveses en Cadiz antes de 1600* (Larache, 1939); 'Los genoveses en la región gaditano-xericense de 1460 a 1800 [sic for 1500]', *Hispania*, viii (1948), 355–402.

17. *Cristóbal Colón: textos y documentos completos*, p.314, *Cancionero de Juan Alfonso de Baena*, ed. J. M. de Azáceta (3 vols, Madrid, 1956), ii, 497–514, iii, 1105.

18. Boscolo, op. cit., p.111; C. Manca, *Aspetti dell'espansione economica catalano-aragonese nel Mediterraneo occidentale: il commercio internazionale del sale* (Milan, 1965), p.27; Petti-Balbi, *Bonifacio*, p.9; A. M. Aragó, 'Fletes de géneros prohibidos desde el puerto de Barcelona a la Liguria (1358–1409)' *Atti del I Congresso Liguria-Catalogna* (Bordighera, 1974), 214–19; M. del Treppo, 'Tra Genova e Catalogna', Ibid., pp.625–6, 654; G. Calamari, 'Materie prime tra Genova e Catalogna nel quattrocento', Ibid., pp.528–49.

19. J. Heers, 'Les italiens et l'Orient méditerranéen à la fin du moyen-âge', *VI Congreso de historia de la Corona de Aragón* (Madrid, 1959) p.166.

20. C. Verlinden, *Les origines de la civilisation atlantique* (Paris, 1966), pp.167–70.

21. Heers, *Gênes au XVe siècle*, pp.35–46.

22. *Le familiari*, ed. V. Rossi (4 vols, Florence, 1933), iii, 123 [Book XIV, 5]; 'Itinerarium Siriacum', *Opera* (Basle, 1554), f.618.

### 5. THE RIM OF AFRICA

1. *Prose*, ed. G. Martelotti et al. (Milan, Naples, 1955), p.1117.

2. F. Balducci Pegolotti, *La pratica della mercatura*, ed. A. Evans (Cambridge, Mass., 1936), p.22.

3. Petrarch, op. cit., pp.702, 1116: Horace, *Odes*, I, xii, 56.

4. *Vie de St Louis*, ch. cxlv.

5. *The Muqaddimah*, Book I, ch. 2; C. Julien, *History of North Africa* (London, 1970), pp.138–209.

6. H. W. Hazard, 'Moslem North Africa, 1049–1394', K. M. Setton, R. L. Wolff and H. W. Hazard (eds), *A History of the Crusades*, II (Madison, 1969), p.472.

7. C. E. Dufourcq, 'Vers la méditerrannée orientale et l'Afrique', *X Congreso de historia de la Corona de Aragón* (1979), pp.19–20.

8. L. Mas Latrie, *Traités de paix et de commerce et documents divers concernant les relations des chrétiens avec les arabes de l'Afrique septentrionale au moyen âge* (3 vols, Paris, 1868–72), I, 285.

9. J. N. Hillgarth, *The Spanish Kingdoms* (2 vols, Oxford, 1976–81), I, 263.

10. A. Rubió i Lluch, *Documents per l'historia de cultura catalana mig-eval*, Barcelona, I (1908), 52–4; M. Menéndez y Pelayo, *Historia de los heterodoxos españoles*, VII (1948), 232ff; J. Carreras Artau, *Relaciones de Arnau de Vilanova con los reyes de la casa de Aragón* (Barcelona, 1955), pp.43–50.

11. P. Martí de Barcelona, 'Regesta de documents arnaldians coneguts', *Estudis Franciscans*, XLVII (1935), e.g. docs 28, 39, 58.

12. E. Cánovas and F. Pinero, *Arnau de Vilanova: escritos condenados por la Inquisición* (Madrid, 1976), pp.21–5; M. Batllori, 'Orientaciones bibliográficas para el estudio de Arnau de Vilanova', *Pensamientos*, X (1954), 311–25; Dufourq, 'Vers la Méditerrannée', pp.19–24.

13. F. Soldevila, ed., *Les quatre grans cròniques* (Barcelona, 1971), pp.466–77, 704–15.

14. Mas Latrie, op. cit., I, 40; II, 108, 367.

15. Ibid., I, 280–325.

16. M. A. Alarcón y Santón and R. García de Linares, *Los documentos árabes diplomáticos del Archivo de la Corona de Aragón* (Madrid, 1940), p.397.

17. Mas Latrie, op. cit., 304–20; Alarcón and García, op. cit., pp.289, 318.

18. Petrarch, *Africa*, VI, 31–4.

19. Illustrated, for example, in J. Lalinde Abadia, *La Corona de Aragón en el mediterráneo medieval* (Zaragoza, 1979), pp.96–7, from the Poblet Codex of the *Llibre dels feits* in Barcelona University Library.

20. A. Huici Miranda and M. D. Cabanes Pecourt, *Docmentos de Jaime I* (Valencia, 1976 – in progress), I, 187; M. Gual Camarena, *Vocabulario del comercio medieval* (Tarragona, 1968), p.67.

21. C. E. Dufourcq, *L'Espagne catalane et le Maghrib aux XIIIe et XIVe siècles* (Paris, 1966), pp.68–9, 102.

22. J. L. Shneidman, *The Rise of the Aragonese-Catalan Empire* (2 vols, New York, 1970), II, 444; A. Pons, *Los judíos del reino de Mallorca durante los siglos XIII y XIV* (Madrid, 1958), pp.203–6, 238; D. Romano, *Los funcionarios judíos de Pedro el Grande de Aragón* (Barcelona, 1970), pp.13–18, 26–30, 34, 39–41.

23. Pons, *Los judíos*, pp.225, 288; Dufourcq, *L'Espagne catalane*, p.142.

24. A. E. Sayous, *Le commerce des européens à Tunis depuis le XIIe siècle jusqu'à la fin du XVIe* (Paris, 1929), p.7; R. Brunschvig, *La Berbérie orientale sous les Hafsides des origines à la fin du XVe siècle* (2 vols, Paris, 1940–7), I, 339, 430–49.

25. Sayous, op. cit., pp.78, 158; Mas Latrie, op. cit., I, 89–90.

26. Brunschvig, op. cit., I, 433; Mas Latrie, op. cit., I, 90.

27. Huici and Cabanes, *Documentos de Jaime I*, IV (1982), 115–18, 306; C. E. Dufourcq, 'Les consulats catalans de Tunis et de Bougie au temps de Jacques le Conquérant', *Anuario de estudios medievales*, III (1966), 469–79.

28. Huici and Cabanes, op. cit., IV (1982), 84–6, 126; G. G. Musso, *Navigazione e commercio genovese con il Levante nei documenti dell'Archivio di Stato di Genova* (Rome, 1975), 101–2; Mas Latrie, op. cit., I, 302.

29. J. M. Madurell Marimón and A. García Sanz, *Comandas comerciales barcelonesas de la baja edad media* (Barcelona, 1973), pp.33–4.

30. F. Melis in R. C. Cecchetti, G. Luschi and S. M. Zunino, *Genova e Spagna nel XIV secolo* (Genoa, 1970), pp. xvi–xvii.

31. Musso, *Navigazione*, pp.102–8.

32. Cecchetti, Luschi and Zunino, op. cit., pp.421–7; J. Heers, 'Les italiens et l'Orient méditerranéen à la fin du moyen âge', *VI Congreso de historia de la Corona de Aragón*, (Madrid, 1959) pp.168–72.

33. J. Vicens Vives, L. Suárez Fernández and C. Carrère, 'La economía de los paises de la Corona de Aragón en la baja edad media,' *VI Congreso de Historia de la Corona de Aragón*, pp.103–35.

34. M. Gual Camarena, *El primer manual hispánico de mercadería* (Barcelona, 1981), pp.4, 14, 21, 57.

35. C. Manca, *Aspetti dell'espansione economica catalano-aragonese nel mediterraneo occidentale: il commercio internazionale del sale* (Milan, 1966), p.249.

36. Gual Camarena, op. cit., p.105.

37. Ibid., pp.39–42, 172–3, 191–202.

38. Mas Latrie, op. cit., II, 195–223; Alarcón and García de Linares, op. cit., p.252.

39. Madurell and García Sanz, op. cit., pp.152–208; J. Botet y Sisó, 'Notas sobre la encunyació de monedes aràbigues pêl rey Don Jaume', *Congrès d'historia de la Corona d'Aragó*, II (1913), 944–63.

40. Dufourcq, *L'Espagne catalane*, p.531.

41. Ibid.; F. Udina Martorell, 'Un aspecto de la evolución de la economía sarda en el siglo XIV: la acuñación de moneda', *VI Congreso de historia de la Corona de Aragón*, pp.647–61; V. Magalhaes Godinho, *Os descubrimentos e a economia mundial* (4 vols, Lisbon, 1981–4), I, 104.

## 6. MAPPING THE EASTERN ATLANTIC

1. R. L. Gerber (ed.), *Johannes Cornago, Complete Works: Recent Researches in the Music of the Middle Ages*, XV (Madison, 1984), pp.viii–ix. This chapter is based on passages from F. Fernández-Armesto, 'Atlantic Exploration before Columbus: the evidence of maps', *Renaissance and Modern Studies* (1986), pp.1–23.

2. The best reproduction is G. Grosjean (ed.), *Mappamundi: the Catalan Atlas of the Year 1375* (Zurich, 1978); where the map is cited hereafter a reference to sheet III of this edition may be assumed.

3. R. A. Skelton, 'A Contract of World Maps at Barcelona, 1399–1400', *Imago Mundi*, XXII (1968), 108–9.

4. P. E. Russell, *El Infante Dom Henrique e as Ilhas Canárias* (Lisbon, 1979), p.19; *Fontes Rerum Canariarum*, XI, 106; M. Jiménez de la Espada (ed.), *Libro del conocimiento de todos los reynos, tierras y señoríos que hay en el mundo* (Madrid, 1877). Professor Russell will argue for a very late fourteenth or very early fifteenth-century date for this text in a forthcoming work.

5. J. Martins da Silva Marques, *Descobrimentos portugueses* (3 vols, Lisbon, 1940–70), I, 435; *Monumenta henricina* (15 vols, Lisbon, 1960–74), VIII, 107.

6. *De Vita Solitaria*, II, VI, 3, ed. A. Altamura (Naples, 1943), p.125; *Le familiari*, ed. V. Rossi (4 vols, Florence, 1933), ι, 106; R. Caddeo, *La navigazioni atlantiche di Alvise da Cà da Mosto, Antoniotto Usodimare e Niccoloso da Recco* (Milan, 1928), p.51.

7. Y. Kamal, *Monumenta Cartographica Africae et Ægypti* (5 vols in 16, Cairo, 1926–51), IV (fasc. 2), no. 1222; K. Kretschmer, *Die Italianische Portolane* (Berlin, 1909), p.118.

8. *Naturalis Historia*, VI, 37; J. Álvarez Delgado, 'Las Islas Afortunadas en Plinio', *Revista de historia* (La Laguna), XI (1945), 26–51.

9. Plutarch, *Vita Sertorii*, VII and IX; Horace, *Epod.*, XVI, 42; A. O. Lovejoy and G. Boas, *Primitivism and Related Ideas in Antiquity* (Baltimore, 1935), pp.280–303; G. Boas, *Essays on Primitivism and Related Ideas in the Middle Ages* (Baltimore, 1948), pp.168–9; E. Faral, *La légende arthurienne* (3 vols, Paris, 1929–34), III, 334; E. Benito Ruano, 'Nuevas singladuras por las Canarias fabulosas', *Homenaje a E. Serra Ràfols* (3 vols, La Laguna, 1970), I, 203–21.

10. *La géographie d'Aboulféda*, ed. J. T. Reinaud (2 vols, Paris, 1848), II, 263–4; *Description de l'Afrique et de l'Espagne par Edrisi*, eds R. Dozy and M. J. de Goeje (Paris, 1866), p.197; R. Mauny, *Les navigations médiévales sur les côtes sahariennes* (Lisbon, 1960), pp.81–8.

11. *Monumenta henricina*, I, 201–6, replaces earlier editions.

12. C. Verlinden, 'Les génois dans la marine portugaise avant 1386', *Actas do Congresso de Portugal Medievo* (3 vols, Braga, 1966), III, 388–407.

13. F. Sevillano Colom, 'Los viajes medievales desde Mallorca a Canarias', *Anuario de estudios atlánticos*, XXIII (1978), 27–57; A. Rumeu de Armas, 'Mallorquines en el Atlántico', *Homenaje a E. Serra Ràfols*, III, 265–76.

14. A. Lütolf, 'Zur Entdeckung und Christianisung der Westafrikanischen Inseln', *Theologische Quartalschrift*, XLVII (1877), 319–32; Rumeu de Armas, *El obispado de Telde* (Madrid, 1960), p.31.

15. *Mapamundi*, ed. Grosjean, sheet III; Mauny, op. cit., pp.96–7.

16. P. Chaunu, *L'Expansion européenne du XIIe au XVe siècle* (Paris, 1969), pp.95–8.

17. Rumeu, 'Mallorquines', pp.264–73.

18. M. Mitjà, 'Abandó des Illes Canaries per Joan d'Aragó', *Anuario de estudios atlánticos*, VIII (1962), 329.

19. Rumeu de Armas, 'La expedición mallorquina de 1366 a las Islas Canarias', Ibid., XXVII (1981), 15–23.

20. Kamal, *Monumenta Cartographica*, IV (fasc. 2), no. 1246; G. H. T. Kimble, 'The Laurentian World Map with Special Reference to its portrayal of Africa', *Imago Mundi*, I (1935), 29–33.

21. Kamal, op. cit., IV (fasc. 3), no. 1307.

22. Ibid., IV (fasc. 3), nos 1316–19, 1333; A. Cortesão, *História da cartografia portuguesa* (2 vols, Coimbra, 1969–70), II, 49–50.

23. Information of Mr Tony Campbell.

24. Kamal, op. cit., IV (fasc. 2), no. 1222.

25. Ibid., IV (fasc. 1), no. 1289.

26. ed. Jiménez de la Espada, p.50.

27. Kamal, op. cit., IV (fasc. 3), nos 1320–2.

28. Ibid., IV (fasc. 3) 1337, 1350.

29. *IXe Colloque International d'Histoire Maritime* (Seville, 1969), pp.276–9; G. Winius and B. W. Diffie, *Foundations of the Portuguese Empire* (Minneapolis, 1977), pp.25, 61; G. V. Scammell, *The World Encompassed* (London, 1981), p.245; S. E. Morison, *The European Discovery of America: the Northern Voyages* (New York, 1971), p.95.

30. Fernández-Armesto, 'Atlantic Exploration', pp.15–17.

31. P. Adam, 'Navigation primitive et navigation astronomique', *VIe Colloque International d'Histoire Maritime* (Paris, 1966), pp.91–110; C. Verlinden, 'La découverte des archipels de la "Méditerrannée Atlantique" (Canaries, Madères, Açores) et la navigation astronomique primitive', *Revista portuguesa de história*, XVI (1978), 129–30.

32. Morison, op. cit., p.82; H. Stommel, *Lost Islands: the Story of Islands that have Vanished from Nautical Charts* (Vancouver, 1984).

33. S. E. Morison, *The Portuguese Voyages to America before 1500* (Harvard, 1940), p.12.

7. THE ATLANTIC CRUCIBLE

1. C. Sánchez-Albornoz, *España: un enigma histórico*, II (Buenos Aires, 1957), 156.
2. *Clément VI: Lettres se rapportant à la France*, eds J. Glenisson, E. Deprez and G. Mollat (Paris, 1958), no. 1314.
3. S. Ciampi (ed.), *Monumenti di un MS di Boccaccio* (Milan, 1830); *Monumenta henricina*, I (1960), 201–6.
4. F. Sevillano Colom, 'Los viajes medievales desde Mallorca a Canarias', *Anuario de estudios atlánticos*, XXIII (1978), 27–57.
5. E. Serra Ráfols and M. G. Martínez, 'Sermón de Clemente VI Papa acerca de la otorgación del Reino de Canarias a Luis de España, 1344', *Revista de historia canaria*, XXIX (1963–4), 100; L. Lopetegui, 'Las Islas Canarias y la Galeta', *Missionalia hispanica*, III (1946), 579; G. Daumet, 'Luis de la Cerda ou d'Espagne', *Bulletin hispanique*, XV (1913), 38–67; Petrarch, *De Vita Solitaria*, II, VI, 3.
6. C. Verlinden, 'Lanzarotto Malocello et la découverte portugaise des Canaries', *Revue belge de philologie et d'histoire*, XXXVI (1958), 1173–1209; see his debate with E. Serra Ràfols in *Actas do Congresso de Portugal Medievo* III (Braga, 1966), 388–407, and *Revista de historia canaria*, XXVII (1961).
7. *Clément VI: Lettres se rapportant à la France*, no 1317.
8. *Crónica de Enrique III*, ch. 20 (*Crónicas de los Reyes de Castilla*, ed. C. Rosell [3 vols, Madrid, 1875–8], II, 274); *Anuario de estudios atlánticos*, VIII (1962), 346–7.
9. M. Mollat, *La commerce maritime normande à la fin du Moyen Âge* (Paris, 1952), pp.13, 245; cf. R. Mauny, *Les navigations médiévales sur les côtes sahariennes* (Lisbon, 1960), pp.116–18.
10. P. Margry, *La conquête et les conquérants des Îles Canaries* (Paris, 1886), pp.84, 109, 113; J. Peraza de Ayala, 'La sucesión del señorío de Canarias a partir de Juan de Béthencourt hasta su limitación a las islas menores', *Historia general de las Islas Canarias de Agustín Millares Torres*, eds A. Millares Cantero and R. Santana Godoy (5 vols, Santa Cruz, 1974–80), II, 138; *Fontes rerum canariarum*, VIII, 37, 82, 137–47, 409–11, 480.
11. A. Cioranescu in *Fontes rerum canariarum*, VIII, 108–220.
12. A. Cioranescu, 'Dos documentos de Juan de Béthencourt', *Homenaje a E. Serra Ràfols*, II, 75–80.
13. G. Chil y Naranjo, *Estudios históricos . . . de las Islas Canarias* (3 vols, Las Palmas, 1876–91 [1899]), II, 411; *Fontes rerum canariarum*, VIII, 414, 440.
14. *Clément VI: Lettres se rapportant à la France*, no. 1314; *Fontes rerum canariarum*, IX, 101 (the words appear only in the late, pro-Béthencourt version of the chronicle).
15. *Monumenta henricina*, VI, 139–99.
16. *Fontes rerum canariarum*, IX, 193.
17. Margry, op. cit., p.253; *Fontes rerum canariarum*, IX, 31, 33; IX, 107, 215.
18. Ibid., XI, 46.
19. *Fontes rerum canariarum*, VIII, 459, 465, 494; IX, 298, 319–23; C. M. de Witte, 'Un faux en indulgences pour la conquète des Canaries', *Homenaje a E. Serra Ràfols* (La Laguna, 1970), III, 445.
20. Cioranescu, 'Dos documentos', p.77; Peraza de Ayala, op. cit. (n. 10), pp.133–46; L. de la Rosa Olivera, *Evolución del regimen administrativo en las Islas Canarias* (Madrid, 1946), 1–40.
21. Cioranescu, 'Dos documentos', p.79.
22. *Fontes rerum canariarum*, XI, 15, 33.
23. Ibid., p.85.
24. Ibid., pp.106–9.
25. *Fontes rerum canariarum*, IX, 321; M. Mollat, 'La place de la conquête normande

des Îles Canaries dans l'histoire coloniale française', *Anuario de estudios atlánticos*, IV (1958), 548.

26. Chil, *Estudios históricos*, II, 623–6.

27. Cioranescu, 'Dos documentos', p.80; *Fontes rerum canariarum*, IX, 135; A. García de Santa María, *El capítulo de Canarias en la 'Crónica de Juan II'*, ed. J. de M. Carriazo (La Laguna, 1946), p.11.

28. A. de Espinosa, *Origen y milagros de Nuestra Señora de la Candelaria*, bk I, ch. 2.

29. *Fontes rerum canariarum*, XI, 25, 66, 119; E. Serra Ràfols, 'Los castillos de Juan de Béthencourt en Lanzarote y Fuerteventura', *Homenaje a Cayetano Mergelina* (Murcia, 1962), pp.793–6; 'Noticias histórico-arqueológicas acerca de Fuerteventura', *El Museo Canario*, XX (1960), pt. II, pp.368–71; J. Álvarez Delgado, 'El Rubicón de Lanzarote', *Anuario de estudios atlánticos*, III (1957), pp.21–2.

30. J. Álvarez Delgado, 'Primera conquista y colonización de la Gomera', *Anuario de estudios atlánticos*, VI (1960), 456–89; M. Menéndez y Pelayo, *Antología de líricos castellanos*, X (Madrid, 1900), 229; J. Pérez Vidal, *Endechas populares* (La Laguna, 1952), p.38.

31. A. J. R. Russell-Wood, *The Black Man in Slavery and Freedom in Colonial Brazil* (London, 1982), p.20; cf. P. E. Russell, *Prince Henry 'the Navigator': The Rise and Fall of a Culture-Hero* (Oxford, 1984).

32. *Monumenta henricina*, XIII, 118–21.

33. C. M. de Witte, 'Les bulles pontificales et l'expansion portugaise', *Revue d'histoire ecclésiastique*, XLVIII (1953), 715.

34. *Monumenta henricina*, V, 91.

35. *Cronica da Guiné*, ed. T. de Sousa Soares (Lisbon, 1978), p.45; G. Beaujouan, 'Fernand Colomb et le traité d'astrologie d'Henri le Navigateur', *Romania*, LXXXII (1961), 96–105; *Monumenta henricina*, V, 256.

36. Ibid., III, 101–3.

37. Ibid., II, 235–7.

38. C. de La Roncière, *La Découverte de l'Afrique au moyen-âge* (3 vols, Cairo, 1924–7), II, 162–3, III, 1–11; J. Heers, *Gênes au XVe siècle* (Paris, 1961), p.480.

39. P. E. Russell, *O Infante Dom Henrique e as Ilhas Canárias* (Lisbon, 1979), pp.38–52; J. M. Cordeiro Sousa, 'La boda de Isabel de Castilla', *Revista de archivos, bibliotecas y museos*, LX (1954), 35.

40. C. R. Boxer, *The Portuguese Seaborne Empire* (London, 1969), p.32; A. Iria, 'Da fundaçao e governo do castela o fortaleza de São Jorge da Mina', *Studia*, I (1958), 24–69; J. Vogt, *Portuguese Rule on the Guinea Coast, 1469–1682* (Athens, Ga., 1979), pp.8–92; below, p.265 n. 10.

41. *Monumenta henricina*, III, 354–5.

42. C. Verlinden, 'Formes féodales et domaniales de la colonisation portugaise dans la zone atlantique aux XIVe et XVe siècles et spécialement sous Henri le Navigateur', *Revista portuguesa de história*, IX (1960), 1–44.

43. *Monumenta henricina*, III, 150.

44. Ibid., IX, 55, 129; XI, 110, 142.

45. Ibid., XI, 249–51, 351–3.

46. Ibid., IX, 235, X, 105, 312; XI, 236; XIII, 93, 113, 278, 336.

47. Ibid., XV, 4, 73, 83, 88, 92.

48. Ibid., X, 28; T. Gasparrini Leporace (ed.), *Le navigazioni atlantiche del veneziano Alvise da Mosto* (Rome, 1966), pp.16–17; V. Rau and J. de Macedo, *O açucar da Ilha de Madeira nos fins do século XV* (Funchal, 1962); V. Magalhães Godinho, *Os descobrimentos e a economia mundial* (4 vols, Lisbon, 1979–83), IV, 73–93.

49. Ibid., IV, 84; *Monumenta henricina*, X, 192–4; C. Verlinden, 'Un précurseur de Colomb: le flamand Ferdinand van Olmen', *Revista portuguesa de história*, X (1962), 453–9; J. Martins da Silva Marques, *Descobrimentos portugueses* (3 vols, Lisbon,

1940–71), III, 76; see also A. H. da Oliveira Marques, 'Notas para a história da feitoria portuguesa na Flandres no século XV', *Studi in onore di A. Fanfani* (6 vols, Milan, 1962), II, 439.

50. Silva Marques, *Descobrimentos*, III, 500–11, 541, 546–8.

51. Ibid., III, 56, 69, 243–4, 615, 654–5.

52. C. Verlinden, 'Antonio da Noli et la colonisation des Îles du Cap Vert', *Miscellanea storica ligure*, III (1963), 129–44.

8. FROM THE CANARIES TO THE NEW WORLD

1. J. Abreu de Galindo, *Historia de la conquista de las Siete Islas Canarias*, book 2, ch. 7, ed. A. Cioranescu (Santa Cruz, 1977), pp.170–4.

2. G. Chil y Naranjo, *Estudios históricos de las Islas Canarias* (3 vols, Las Palmas, 1876–91), II, 632–4: A. Rumeu de Armas, 'La reivindicación por la corona de Castilla del derecho de conquista sobre las Canarias mayores', *Hidalguía*, no. 32 (1959), p.11.

3. J. López de Toro, 'La conquista de Gran Canaria en la Cuarta Década de Alonso de Palencia', *Anuario de estudios atlánticos*, XVI (1970), 332.

4. F. Fernández-Armesto, 'La financiación de la conquista de las Islas Canarias durante el reinado de los Reyes Católicos', *Anuario de estudios atlánticos*, XXVIII, 343–78.

5. Ibid., p.376; R. Pike, *Enterprise and Adventure* (New York, 1966), pp.3, 99.

6. A. Rumeu de Armas, 'Cristóbal Colón y Doña Beatriz de Bobadilla', *El Museo Canario*, XX (1960), pt II, 263–7.

7. F. del Pulgar [H. de Pulgar], *Crónica de los Reyes Católicos*, ed. J. de Mata Carriazo (2 vols, Madrid, 1943), II, 60.

8. D. de Valera, *Crónica de los Reyes Católicos*, ed. J. de Mata Carriazo (Madrid, 1927), p.108.

9. D. J. Wölfel, 'La curia romana y la corona de España en defensa a los aborígenes de Canarias', *Anthropos*, XXV (1930), 1077–9.

10. E. Hardisson y Pizarroso, 'Sobre la rendición de la Gran Canaria', *Revista de historia canaria*, XV (1949).

11. Archivo General de Simancas, Registro del Sellos, 1478/5/26 f. 100; 1484/8/31 f. 13; 1489/3/4 ff. 76, 300; Wölfel, op. cit., p.1060; Chil y Naranjo, op. cit., III, 289, 332.

12. D. J. Wölfel, 'Un episodio desconocido de la conquista de La Palma', *Investigación y Progreso*, V (1931), 101–3.

13. J. de Abreu Galindo, op. cit., pp.280–7.

14. A. Rumeu de Armas, *Alonso de Lugo en la corte de los Reyes Católicos* (Madrid, n.d.), p.51; *La conquista de Tenerife* (Santa Cruz, 1975), pp.289–309.

15. E. Deprez, J. Glenisson and G. Mollat, eds, *Clément VI: Lettres se rapportant à la France* (Paris, 1958), no. 1317; R. Torres Campos, *Caracter de la conquista y colonización de Canarias* (Madrid, 1901), pp.127, 130, 132; J. de Zurita, *Historia del rey Don Hernando*, book 1, ch. 48.

16. M. Sanuto, *I diarii* (58 vols, Venice, 1879–1903), I, cols 628, 656; Wölfel, 'Curia y corona', pp.1077–9.

17. A. Pérez Voituriez, *Los problemas jurídicos internacionales de la conquista de Canarias* (La Laguna, 1959), p.246; A. de Bernáldez, *Memorias del reinado de los Reyes Católicos* (Madrid, 1962), p.340.

18. F. Fernández-Armesto, *The Canary Islands after the Conquest* (Oxford, 1982), p.127.

19. M. A. Ladero Quesada, 'La repoblación de Granada antes de 1500', *Hispania*, XXCIII (1968), 490.

20. Fernández-Armesto, *The Canary Islands*, pp.9–12, 84–5, 202; E. Aznar Vallejo, *La integración de las Islas Canarias en la corona de Castilla* (Seville-La Laguna, 1984), pp.194–5, 249.

21. Fernández-Armesto, *The Canary Islands*, pp.136–40.

22. C. Verlinden, *Les origines de la civilisation atlantique* (Paris, 1966), pp.164–5.

23. Y. Renouard, 'Les voies de communication entre pays de la Méditerrannée et pays de l'Atlantique au moyen âge', *Mélanges d'histoire du moyen âge dédiés à la mémoire de Louis Halphen* (Paris, 1951), pp.587–94; R. Diehaerd, *Les relations commerciales entre Gênes, la Belgique et l'Outremont* (3 vols, Brussels-Rome, 1941), I, 224; F. Braudel, 'La double faillité coloniale de la France', *Annales*, IV (1949), 451–6; M. Mollat, *Le commerce maritime normande à la fin du moyen âge* (Paris, 1952), pp.13, 245.

24. P. Vilar, *La Catalogne dans l'Espagne moderne* (2 vols, Paris, 1962), I, 476–98; C. Carrère, *Barcelone, centre économique à l'époque des difficultés* (Paris, 1967), pp.640–3; A. Luttrell, 'Actividades económicas de los hospitalarios de Rodas en el mediterráneo occidental durante el siglo XIV', *VI Congreso de historia de la Corona de Aragón* (Madrid, 1959), pp.181–3; discussion between Musso and Del Treppo in *Atti del I Congresso Storico Liguria-Catalogna* (Bordighera, 1974), p.33; A. Santamaría Arandez, *Aportación al estudio de la economía de Valencia durante el siglo XV* (Valencia, 1966).

25. Fernández-Armesto, *The Canary Islands*, pp.35–6, 156–8, 175n.

26. Ibid., pp.23–30; D. Giofré, 'Le relazioni fra Genova e Madera nel I decennio del secolo XVI', *Studi colombiani*, III (Genoa, 1952), 443.

27. R. Carande, *Carlos V y sus banqueros* (3 vols, Madrid, 1965–7), III, 123–499.

28. *Raccoltá colombiana* (14 vols, Rome-Genoa, 1892–6), III, part II, 3; M. Giménez Fernández, 'América, "Ysla de Canaria por ganar"', *Anuario de estudios atlánticos*, I (1955), 309–36.

29. J. Martorell and M. J. de Galba, *Tirant lo blanc*, ch. 5, ed. M. de Riquer (Barcelona, 1970), p.124; *Don Quixote*, II, lii; M. S. Martín Postigo, *La Cancillería real de los Reyes Católicos* (Valladolid, 1959), p.23.

30. I. Leonard, *The Books of the Brave* (Cambridge, Mass., 1949), pp.13–35.

31. G. Díez de Games, *El victorial*, ed. J. de Mata Carriazo (Madrid, 1940), pp.40–7, 86–96, 201, 256–61, 300.

### 9. THE MENTAL HORIZON

1. J. Michelet, *Histoire de France* (17 vols, Paris, 1852–67), VII, pp.ii–iii; cf. J. H. Elliott, 'The Discovery of America and the Discovery of Man', *Proceedings of the British Academy*, LVIII (1972), 101–25.

2. C. Lévi-Strauss, *The Elementary Structures of Kinship* (London, 1969) p.46.

3. R. Bartlett, *Gerald of Wales* (Oxford, 1981), pp.157–210.

4. *Monumenta Germaniae Historica: Scriptores*, XXII (1872), 535–6; A. van den Wyngaert (ed.), *Sinica Franciscana*, I (Florence, 1929), 171; G. A. Bezzola, *Die Mongolen in abendländischer Sicht* (Berne, 1974), pp.130–44.

5. J. A. Weischeipl (ed.), *Albertus Magnus and the Sciences* (Toronto, 1980), pp.263–320, 501–35; H. W. Janson, *Apes and Ape Lore in the Middle Ages and Renaissance* (London, 1952), pp.83–93.

6. E. Faral, *La légende arthurienne*, III (Paris, 1929), 334.

7. A. L. Moir, *The World Map in Hereford Cathedral* (Hereford, 1971), p.22; *Libro del conosçimiento de todos los reynos*, ed. M. Jiménez de la Espada (Madrid, 1877), p.50 n.2.

8. *Monumenta henricina*, I, 201; F. Sevillano Colom, 'Los viajes medievales desde Mallorca a Canarias', *Anuario de estudios atlánticos*, XXIII (1978), 33.

9. C. Verlinden, *L'Esclavage dans l'Europe médiévale*, I (Bruges, 1955), 615.

10. *Libro del conoscimiento*, ed. Jiménez de la Espada, p.63; Rui de Pina, *Crónica de El-Rei Dom João II*, ed. A. Martins de Carvalho (Coimbra, 1950), p.92.

11. A. Brásio (ed.), *Monumenta missionária africana* (Lisbon, 1952), p.319; A. C. de C. M. Saunders, *A Social History of Black Slaves and Freedmen in Portugal, 1441–1555* (Cambridge, 1982), pp.168–71.

12. G. Eannes de Zurara, *Crónica de Guiné*, chs 25-6, ed. T. de Sousa Soares (2 vols, Lisbon, 1978), I, 107–12.

13. Janson, op. cit., pp.94–9; cf. M. Hodgen, *Early Anthropology in the Sixteenth and Seventeenth Centuries* (Philadelphia, 1964), pp.264, 378–82.

14. T. Gasparrini Leporace (ed.), *Le navigazioni atlantiche del veneziano Alvise da Mosto* (Rome, 1966), pp.50–4.

15. R. Bacon, *Moralis Philosophia* (Turin, 1963), p.192; R. Sagranyes de Franch, *Raymond Lulle: docteur des missions* (Schönek-Beckenried, 1954), pp.62, 137.

16. *Monumenta henricina*, I, 201–6.

17. Petrarch, *De Vita Solitaria*, VI, 3, ed. A. Altamura (Naples, 1943), pp.125–6.

18. E. Armstrong, *Ronsard and the Age of Gold* (Cambridge, 1968), plate II.

19. E. Serra Ràfols and M. G. Martinez, 'Sermón de Clemente VI Papa acerca de la otorgación del Reino de Canarias a Luis de España, 1344', *Revista de historia canaria*, XXIX (1963–4), 88–111.

20. D. Wood, 'Clement VI and the Hundred Years' War', *Studies in Church History*, XX (1983), 182–4; E. Déprez, J. Glenisson and G. Mollat (eds), *Clément VI: lettres se rapportant à la France* (Paris, 1958), no. 1582.

21. *Monumenta henricina*, V, 287–343; VI, 139–99.

22. A. Rumeu de Armas, 'Mallorquines en el Atlántico', *Homenaje a E. Serra Ràfols* (La Laguna, 1970), III, 272–4; *Fontes Rerum Canariarum*, IX (1960), 12; XI (1965), 15, 65; C. M. de Witte, 'Les Bulles pontificales et l'expansion portugaise', *Revue d'histoire ecclésiastique*, XLVIII (1953), 718; *Monumenta henricina*, XIV, 323; A. de Bernáldez, *Memorias del reinado de los Reyes Católicos*, ed. J. de Mata Carriazo (Madrid, 1962) p.137.

23. M. de Córdoba, *Jardín de nobles doncellas*, ed. H. Goldberg (Chapel Hill, 1974), pp.138–9.

24. Zurara, op. cit., I, 141–7; Saunders, op. cit., p.39; Llull, *Libre de Evast e Blanquerna*, ch. 84, ed. S. Galmés (4 vols, Barcelona, 1935–54), II, 191.

25. A. Lütolf, 'Zur Entdeckung und Christianisung der westafricanischen Inseln', *Theologische Quartalschrift* (1877), pp.322–32.

26. J. Vincke, 'Die Evangelisation der Kanarischen Inseln', *Estudios lulianos*, IV (1960), 307–14; E. M. Pareja Fernández, *El MS luliano Torcaz I* (La Laguna, 1949).

27. *Monumenta henricina*, V, nos. 37, 38, 52; Verlinden, *L'Esclavage*, I, 457; de Witte, op. cit., p.718; *Bullarium Franciscanum*, n.s., III, 945.

28. E. Aznar Vallejo, *Documentos canarios del Registro del Sello* (La Laguna, 1981), p.3; D. J. Wölfel, 'Un episodio desconocido de la conquista de La Palma', *Investigación y progreso*, V (1931), 101–3.

29. A. Rumeu de Armas, *La política indigenista de Isabel la Católica* (Valladolid, 1969), pp.40–4.

30. *Bullarium Franciscanum*, n.s., II, 510, 619–22; III, 436.

31. Ibid., III, 117, 437; J. Fernández Alonso, *Legajos y nunciaturas en España*, I (Madrid, 1963), 77.

32. *Bullarium Franciscanum*, n.s., III, 230, 677–8, 690–1, 931; *Analecta Franciscana*, II, 455.

33. 'Itinerarium hispanicum', ed. L. Pfandl, *Revue hispanique*, XLVIII (1920), 23; *Crónicade Guiné*, chs 79–86, ed. T. de Sousa Soares (2 vols, Lisbon, 1978–81), I, 295–310.

34. F. Fernández-Armesto, 'Medieval Ethnography', *Journal of the Anthropological*

*Society of Oxford*, xɪɪɪ (1982), 272–6, 282–4; H. Yule (ed.), *Mirabilia Descripta: the Wonders of the World by Friar Jordanus* (London, 1863), p.31.

35. A. Rumeu de Armas, 'Cristobal Colón y Doña Beatriz de Bobadilla', *El Museo Canario*, xxɪ (1960), part ɪɪ, 265; *Monumenta henricina*, ɪ, 202.

36. *Fontes Rerum Canariarum*, vɪɪɪ, 120; ɪx, 15; *Monumenta henricina*, v, no. 129; de Witte, op. cit., p.715; B. Bonnet, 'Un manuscrito del siglo XV', *Revista de historia* (La Laguna), vɪɪ (1940–1), 98.

37. F. Fernández-Armesto, *The Canary Islands after the Conquest* (Oxford, 1982), pp.9–12, 38–40, 66, 124–30.

38. Verlinden, *L'Esclavage*, ɪ, 321–3, 460, 464.

39. A. van den Wyngaert, *Sinica Franciscana* (Florence, 1929), ɪ, 310–43; E. Weise, *Die Staatschriften des Deutschen Ordens* (Göttingen, 1970), pp.118–62. M. Wilks, *The Problem of Sovereignty in the Later Middle Ages* (Cambridge, 1964), pp.104–7, 413–16; W. Ullmann, *Principles of Papal Government and Politics in the Middle Ages* (London, 1966), pp.258–9; *Medieval Papalism* (London, 1949), pp.115–36; J. Muldoon, *Popes, Lawyers and Infidels* (Liverpool, 1979), pp.5–16.

40. *Apologética historia sumaria*, ed. E. O'Gorman (2 vols, Mexico, 1967), ɪ, 257–8.

41. Fernández-Armesto, 'Medieval Ethnography', pp.275–6, 284–6.

42. A. de Espinosa, *Del origen y milagros de Nuestra Señora de la Candelaria*, I, ch. 5. ed. A. Cioranescu (Santa Cruz, 1980), p.35; M. R. Alonso, *El poema de Viana* (Madrid, 1952), pp.311–13, 339–42; Lope de Vega, 'Los guanches de Tenerife', *Obras* (15 vols, Madrid, 1890–1913), xɪ, 301ff.

43. P. Revelli, *Cristoforo Colombo e la scuola cartografica genovese* (Genoa, 1937), p.96; C. Varela (ed.), *Cristobal Colón: textos y documentos completos* (Madrid, 1984), p.277.

44. A. de Cortesão, *História de cartografia portuguesa* (2 vols, Coimbra, 1969–71), ɪɪ, 150–2; H. Kraus, Catalogue no. 55 (New York, 1955), pp.62–6; Y. Kamal, *Monumenta Cartographica Africae et Ægypti* (5 vols in 16, Cairo, 1924–51), v, no. 1492.

45. A. de Cortesão, 'The North Atlantic Nautical Chart of 1424', *Imago Mundi*, x (1953), 1–13; J. de Lisboa, *Livro da Marinharia*, ed. B. Rebelo (Lisbon, 1903), pp.121–2.

46. *The Geography of Strabo*, ed. H. L. Jones, ɪ, 243 (I, iv, 6); A. Diller, *The Textual Tradition of Strabo's Geography* (Amsterdam, 1975), pp.97–134; Macrobius, *Commentaria in Somnium Scipionis*, ed. F. Eyssenhardt (Leipzig, 1893), pp.614–6 (II,8); J. K. Wright, *The Geographical Lore of the Time of the Crusades* (New York, 1925), pp.11, 159–61.

47. *Ymago Mundi*, ed. E. Buron (3 vols, Paris, 1930), ɪ, 207–15; Aristotle, *De Caelo*, ed. W. K. Guthrie (London, 1939), p.253; see G. Uzielli, *La vita ed i tempi di Paolo dal Pozzo Toscanelli (Raccoltà colombiana*, v part ɪ) (Rome, 1894).

48. J. A. Williamson, *The Cabot Voyages* (Cambridge, 1962), pp.197–203.

49. S. E. Morison, *The Portuguese Voyages to America* (Cambridge, Mass., 1940), p.32. J. Martins da Silva Marques, *Descobrimentos portugueses* (3 vols, Coimbra, 1940–71), ɪɪɪ, 124, 130, 278, 317, 320–32, 552.

# Further Reading

The purposes of these pages are to recommend further reading and to complement the notes by mentioning important but previously uncited works, and works or translations in English, where available. References given in the notes are duplicated only if of exceptional importance.

## INTRODUCTION

The present book could not have been written – indeed, the problems addressed would probably not have been formulated – without the work of two great historians of the fate of Mediterranean civilisation, H. Pirenne, *Mohammed and Charlemagne* (London, 1939) and Charles Verlinden, *Les origines de la civilisation atlantique* (Paris, 1966), both from Belgium, a country which, perhaps because it contains the world's most northerly community of Romance-speakers, seems peculiarly interested in the subject. I am an heretical disciple of Verlinden's. Other views of the origins of Atlantic civilisation can be found in M. Kraus, *The Atlantic Civilization: Eighteenth-century Origins* (Ithaca, N.Y., 1966) and R. Davis, *The Rise of the Atlantic Economies* (London, 1973). Apart from Verlinden's, books which overlap with the present book include P. Chaunu, *European Overseas Expansion in the Later Middle Ages* (Amsterdam, 1979) and G. V. Scammell, *The World Encompassed* (London, 1981). J. H. Parry, *The Age of Reconnaissance* (London, 1965) and *The Discovery of the Sea* (London, 1975) are introductory and complementary respectively. V. Magalhães Godinho, *Os descubrimentos e a economia mundial* (4 vols, Lisbon, 1979–82) is on a grander scale than other general accounts and substantially corrects his *L'Économie de l'empire portugais* (Paris, 1969). Some of Verlinden's essays have been collected and translated in *The Beginnings of Modern Colonization* (Ithaca, N.Y., 1970). The venerable works of C. R. Beazley, *The Dawn of Modern Geography* (3 vols, Oxford-London, 1897–1906) and C. de la Roncière, *La découverte de la Terre* (Paris, 1934) still make admirable introductions. On the Chinese explorations, see Ma Huan, *Ying-yai sheng-lan: 'The Overall Survey of the Ocean's Shores'*, ed. J. V. G. Mills (Cambridge, 1970) and P. Pelliot, 'Les grands voyages maritimes chinois au début du XVe siècle', *T'oung Pao*, xxx (1933), 237–452.

## CHAPTER 1

The main narrative sources are published in F. Soldevila, *Les quatre grans cròniques* (Barcelona, 1971) and J. M. Quadrado, *Historia de la conquista de Mallorca* (Palma, 1850). There are English versions of *The Chronicle of James I, King of Aragon*, trans. J. Forster (2 vols, London, 1883), *Chronicle of the Reign of King Pedro III of Aragon*, trans. F. L. Critchlow (2 vols, Princeton, 1928–34), *The Chronicle of Muntaner*, trans. Lady Goodenough (2 vols, London, 1920–1) and *The Chronicle of Pere III of Catalonia*, trans. M. Hillgarth (2 vols, Toronto, 1980).

Essential collections of documents are A. Huici Miranda and M. B. Cabanes Pecourt, *Documentos de Jaime I de Aragón* (Valencia, 1976 – in progress), H. Finke, *Acta Aragonensia ... 1291-1327* (3 vols, Berlin, 1908–22) and *Colección de documentos inéditos del Archivo de la Corona de Aragón* (45 vols, Barcelona, 1849–1970), to all but the last volume of which there is an *Índice cronológico* by J. E. Martínez Ferrando (Barcelona, 1958).

On Barcelona, A. Duran i Sanpere, *Barcelona i la seva història* (3 vols, Barcelona,

1972–5) is an evocation, based on the building history of the city, which does service while A. Duran i Sanpere and J. Sobreques i Callicó (eds), *Historia de Barcelona* (Barcelona, 1975 – in progress) is in course of publication. The new edition of A. de Capmany y de Monpalau, *Memorias históricas sobre la marina, comercio y artes de la antigua ciudad de Barcelona* (2 vols in 3, Barcelona, 1961–3) is invaluable on Barcelona and on Catalan maritime and commercial history generally.

On Jaime I, the fundamental work is J. Miret i Sans, *Itinerari de Jaume I 'el conqueridor'* (Barcelona, 1981); F. Soldevila has written various biographical contributions, most notably, *Vida de Jaume I el conqueridor* (Barcelona, 1958) and *Els primers temps de Jaume I* (Barcelona, 1968); F. D. Swift, *The Life and Times of James I the Conqueror* (Oxford, 1894) is the only biography in English. C. de Tourtoulon, *Jacme I le Conquérant* (2 vols, Montpellier, 1863–7) has not been supplanted as a general account. On the *Book of Deeds* see J. Riera i Sans, 'La personalitat eclesiástica del redactor del "Libre dels feyts"', *X Congreso de historia de la corona de Aragón* (2 vols, Zaragoza, 1980–2), ii, 575–87 and R. I. Burns, 'The Spiritual Life of Jaume the Conqueror', Ibid., pp.322–57. The theme of the Xth Congress was Jaime and his times and many contributions are of great interest. The distinctly secular chivalric ethos (which, I argue, inspired Jaime's values and those of many of the conquistadores in this book) is best described by M. Keen, *Chivalry* (New Haven-London, 1984); see also p.274 below. The editor's arguments for Jaume's authorship of *El Llibre de doctrina del Rei Jaume d'Aragó*, ed. J. M. Sola-Solé (Barcelona, 1977) are unconvincing and, even if correct, would not seriously modify my view.

For the conquest of Majorca, the sources are reviewed in A. Alcover, 'Las fuentes históricas de la reconquista de Mallorca', *Boletín de la Real Acedemia de la Historia*, xcv (1929), 449ff. The best general account of both conquest and *repartiment* remains Quadrado, *Historia de la conquista*, supplemented by J. Mascaró Pasarius (ed.), *Historia de Mallorca*, iii, (Palma, 1970) and materials published in J. Dameto, V. Mut and G. Alemany, *Historia general del reino de Mallorca*, eds M. Moragues Pro and J. M. Bover (3 vols, Palma, 1841), ii, 761–866, and by P. Bofarull Mascaró in *Colección de documentos inéditos del Archivo de la Corona de Aragón*, xi (1856), 7–141 and J. Busquets Mulet in *Homenaje a Millas Vallicrosa*, i (Barcelona, 1954), 243–300. The *Liber Maiolichinus* is edited by C. Calisse (Rome, 1904). Additional sources are in J. Vich and J. Muntaner, *Documenta Regni Maioricarum* (Palma, 1945).

For Ibiza see I. Macabich, *Historia de Ibiza* (4 vols, Palma, 1966–7) (there may be further volumes, which I have not seen) and for Menorca, C. Parpal y Marqués, *La conquesta de Menorca* (Barcelona, 1964).

For the sources on Sardinia, see C. Manca, *Fonti e orientamenti per la storia economica della Sardegna aragonese* (Padua, 1967); I. Carini, *Gli archivi e la biblioteche di Spagna in rapporto alla storia d'Italia* (2 vols, Palermo, 1884) and J. Mateu Ibars, 'Fondos archivísticos sardos para el estudio de la gobernación del reino en el siglo xiv' in *Martinez Ferrando archivero* (Barcelona, 1968), pp.323–50. Important collections of documents include J. Trenchs and R. Sainz de la Masa, *Documentos pontificios sobre Cerdeña de la época de Alfonso el benigno* (Barcelona, 1974), F. Casula, *Carte reale e diplomatiche di Alfonso iii, il benigno, re d'Aragona, riguardanti l'Italia* (Padua, 1971) and L. d'Arienzo, *Carte reali diplomatiche di Pietro IV, il cerimonioso, riguardanti l'Italia* (Padua, 1970). J. Carini and G. La Mantia, *Codice diplomatico dei re aragonesi di Silicia* (2 vols, Palermo, 1917–56) may be consulted for Sicily. The works of V. Salavert and A. Boscolo, cited in the notes, and A. Arribas Palau, *La conquista de Cerdeña por Jaime II de Aragón* (Barcelona, 1952) cover conquest and colonisation. I have not seen F. C. Casula, *Profilo storico della Sardegna catalano-aragonese* (Cagliari, 1983) or O. Schena, *Le leggi palatine di Pietro IV d'Aragona* (Cagliari, 1983), or A. Castellacio, *Aspetti di storia italo-catalana* (Cagliari, 1983). Additional sources on the problem of

Arago-Catalan imperialism are in F. Soldevila, *Pere el Gran* (2 vols, Barcelona, 1950–62), J. Martínez Ferrando, *Jaime II de Aragón* (2 vols, Barcelona, 1948) and *Documentos del Archivo de la Corona de Aragón*, XXIX–XXXI (1886). From the scholarly and perceptive treatment by J. N. Hillgarth, *The Spanish Kingdoms, 1250–1516*, I (Oxford, 1976) and *The Problem of a Catalan Mediterranean Empire, 1229–1327* (London, 1975) I dissent with trepidation. See also J. Lalinde Abadia, *La Corona de Aragón en el mediterráneo medieval* (Saragossa, 1979) and F. Giunta, *Aragonesi e Catalani nel mediterraneo* (2 vols, Palermo, 1959).

On Greece, see A. Rubió i Lluch, *Diplomatari de l'orient català* (Barcelona, 1947); K. Setton, *The Catalan Domination of Athens* (Cambridge, Mass., 1948), A. E. Laiou, *Constantinople and the Latins: the Foreign Policy of Andronicus II* (Cambridge, Mass., 1972) and A. Luttrell, 'La Corona de Aragón y la Grecia catalana', *Anuario de estudios medievales*, VI (1979), 219–52.

On the Jews, the vivid evocation of the nature of a Jewish Mediterranean community in S. D. Goitein, *A Mediterranean Society: the Jewish Communities of the Arab World in the Documents of the Cairo Geniza* (Berkeley, etc., 1973 – in progress) especially I (*Economic Foundations*) and III (*The Family*) should be consulted for its enormous comparative value and richness of insights. Jewish mobility is charmingly illustrated in B. Adler, *Jewish Travellers* (London, 1930). See also the works on Jews in Spain generally, included under Chapter 2 below, and the references supplied by the notes.

## CHAPTER 2

An invaluable introduction to the colonisation of conquests from the Moors is A. de la Torre, J. M. Lacarra et al., *La reconquista española y la repoblación del país* (Madrid, 1951). For the broadest background, see J. Vicèns Vives (ed.), *Historia de España y América* (5 vols, Barcelona, 1971), I and II and A. McKay, *Spain in the Middle Ages: From Frontier to Empire* (London, 1977). Further on the 'Reconquest', see E. Lourie, 'A Society Organised for War: Medieval Spain', *Past and Present*, no. 35 (1966), pp.54–76; J. Goñi Gaztambide, *Historia de la bula de cruzada en España* (Vitoria, 1958) and D. W. Lomax, *La orden de Santiago, 1170–1275* (Madrid, 1965).

The position of C. Sánchez-Albornoz is perhaps best represented by his careful monograph, *Despoblación y repoblación del valle del Duero* (Buenos Aires, 1966). The English version of his magnum opus, *España: un enigma histórico* (2 vols, Buenos Aires, 1956) cannot be conscientiously recommended, but a fair summary of the author's views is in C. Sánchez-Albornoz, 'The Frontier and Castilian Liberties', in A. R. Lewis and T. F. McGann (eds), *The New World Looks at its History* (Austin, Texas, 1963), pp.25–46, and, from an impartial and generous observer, in H. Lapeyre, 'Deux interprétations de l'histoire d'Espagne: Américo Castro et Claudio Sánchez-Albornoz', *Annales*, XX (1965), 1015–37.

A. Castro, *La realidad histórico de España* (Mexico, 1954) has, however, found able translators (as well as devoted partisans) among English-speakers: *The Structure of Spanish History* (Princeton, 1954) is widely preferred to the revised version, *The Spaniards* (Berkeley, 1971). For his essays in translation, see *An Idea of History*, eds and trans S. Gilman and E. L. King (Columbus, Ohio, 1977). Further on the controversy, see J. L. Gómez-Martínez, *Américo Castro y el origen de los españoles* (Madrid, 1975).

On the settlement of Andalusia, as well as the works cited in the notes, S. Sobreques Vidal provides a valuable study in *Historia de España y América*, II, 8–20, and C. J. Bishko, 'The Castilian as Plainsman' in *The New World Looks at its History*, pp.47–69, adds an important dimension. See also the same author's 'The peninsular background of Latin American Cattle Ranching', *Hispanic American Historical Review*, XXXII (1952), 491–515.

Invaluable background works on the Jews are Y. Baer, *A History of the Jews in Christian Spain* (2 vols, Philadelphia, 1966); the same author, writing as F. Baer, provides extensive source material in *Die Jüden in Christlichen Spanien: Urkunden und Regesten* (2 vols, Berlin, 1922–36). On the Moors, I. de la Cacigas, *Minorías étnico-religiosas de la edad media española: los mudéjares* (2 vols, Madrid, 1948–9) is the only attempt at a general depiction of the background, but the deficiency may be partly supplied from the papers presented at *I Simposio internacional de mudejarismo* (Madrid, 1981).

CHAPTER 3

R. I. Burns, *Diplomatarium regni Valenciae, regnante Iacobo Primo*, I (Princeton, 1985) appeared too late to be of help with the present book. Wider coverage – but more selective and less reliable – is provided by J. Martínez Ferrando. *Archivo de la Corona de Aragón: catálogo de la documentación relativa al antiguo reino de Valencia* (3 vols, Madrid, 1934) nd R. Gallofré Guinovart, *Documentos del reinado de Alfonso III de Aragón relativos al reino de Valencia* (Valencia, 1968). Full texts of imperfect accuracy for the period of Jaime I's reign can be found in A. Huici Miranda and M. Cabanes Pecourt (above, p.267).

The principal chronicles are as for Chapter 1 above.

I rely heavily in this chapter on the works of R. I. Burns cited in the notes. Additionally, some of his important *dispersa* are collected in *Moors and Crusaders in Medieval Spain* (London, 1978).

For Murcia, the works of J. Torres Fontes are fundamental: *Repartimiento de Murcia* (Madrid, 1960); *Colección de documentos para la historia del reino de Murcia* (5 vols, Murcia, 1963–80); *Repartimiento de la huerta y campo de Murcia en el siglo XIII* (Murcia, 1971) and works cited in the notes. See additionally on 'Catalan' Murcia, J. M. Font Rius, 'El repartimiento de Orihuela', *Homenaje a J. Vicèns Vives* (3 vols, Barcelona, 1965), I, 417–30, and J. M. del Estal, *Conquista y anexión de las tierras de Alicante, Elche, Orihuela y Guardamar al Reino de Valencia* (Alicante, 1982), which I did not see until the present work was completed.

CHAPTER 4

An important general collection of sources is C. Imperiale, *Codice diplomatico della Republica di Genova* (3 vols, Rome, 1936–42) but most of the important sources for the subjects covered in this chapter are in notarial records appended to works cited in the notes or mentioned in appropriate paragraphs below. Valuable introductory works include V. Vitale, *Breviario di storia de Genova* (2 vols, Genoa, 1955); E. Bach, *La cité de Gênes au XIIe siècle* (Copenhagen, 1955), E. H. Byrne, *Genoese Shipping in the XIIth and XIIIth centuries* (Cambridge, Mass., 1930) and the general narrative outline of R. S. Lopez, *Storia delle colonie genovesi nel Mediterraneo* (Bologna, 1938). Throughout the chapter, I have relied heavily on the works of Balard, Argenti and Heers given in notes 5 and 10. G. Garo, *Genova e la supremacia sul Mediterraneo (1257–1311)* (2 vols, *Atti della Società Ligure di Storia Patria*, n.s. XIV–XV, 1974–5) is a translation of a German work of the late nineteenth century, fundamental for the period it covers.

On Bonifacio, beyond the works cited in the notes, see V. Vitale, 'Documenti sul castello di Bonifacio nel secolo XIII', *Atti della Regia Deputazione di Storia Patria per la Liguria*, LXV (1936) and LXVIII (1940) and G. Petti-Balbi, 'Genova e Corsica nel trecento', *Studi storici del Istituto Storico Italiano per il Medioevo*, fasc. XCVIII (1976), 77–122, and J. Cancellieri, 'Formes rurales de la colonisation genois du Corse au XIIIe siècle', *Mélanges de l'école française de Rome*, I (1981), 89–146. The starting point for further reading on Pera and Kaffa is G. I. Brataniu, *Recherches sur le commerce génois dans la Mer Noire au XIII siècle* (Paris, 1929) and the sources collected by M. Balard, *Gênes et l'Outre-Mer* (2 vols, Paris, 1973–80). Additionally, on Kaffa and Pera, G. I. Brataniu, *Actes des notaires génois de Pera et de Caffa de la fin du XIIIe siècle* (Bucharest, 1927) and M. Lombard, 'Kaffa et la fin du route mongole', *Annales*, V (1950), 100–3, a remarkable little book review which places Kaffa in the context of the 'Mongol' trade route. Argenti's sources for Chico are supplemented by A. Rovere, *Documenti della Maona di Chio* (Genoa, 1979).

For the general background of the Kingdom of Granada, see R. Arié, *L'Espagne musulmane au temps des Nasrides* (Paris, 1973) and M. A. Ladero Quesada, *Granada: historia de un país islámico* (Madrid, 1969). For the north African background, see the notes and further reading to Chapter 5.

For the Genoese in Castile, as well as the works of Sancho de Sopranis and Boscolo mentioned in the note, see L. de la Rosa Olivera, 'Francisco de Riberol y la colonia genovesa en Canarias', *Anuario de estudios atlánticos*, XVIII (1972), 61–198, and R. Pike, *Enterprise and Adventure* (Ithaca, N.Y., 1966). The fundamental outlines of the question, however, must be sought in the works of C. Verlinden, 'The Rise of Spanish Trade in the Middle Ages', *Economic History Review*, X (1960), 44–59, and 'Italian Influences in Iberian Colonization', *Hispanic American Historical Review*, XXXIII (1953), 199–211, which are also vital for my section on the transmission of Genoese influence.

The political background to the survival of Genoese-Catalan trade is recounted in meticulous detail in G. Meloni, *Genova e Aragona all'epoca di Pietro il Cerimonioso* (2 vols, Padua, 1971).

## CHAPTER 5

Relatively little can be added, for his chapter, to what is cited in the notes. The works of Dufourcq (note 22), Julien (note 5) and Brunschvig (note 25) are fundamental throughout. For the background of the African crusades, see also A. S. Atiya, *The Crusade in the Later Middle Ages* (London, 1938) and K. M. Setton, R. L. Wolff and H. W. Hazard (eds), *A History of the Crusades: ii: the Later Crusades* (Madison-London, 1969). C. de La Roncière, *La découverte de l'Afrique au moyen âge* (3 vols, Cairo, 1924–7) covers the background from the point of view of cartography, exploration and – to some extent – trade and includes excellent reproductions of much cartographical evidence. On Mali, see E. W. Bovill, *The Golden Trade of the Moors* (London, 1968) and N. Levtzion, *Ancient Ghana and Mali* (London, 1973).

For the Arago-Catalan background, as well as the works given for Chapter 1, F. Soldevila, *Historia de Catalunya* (3 vols, Barcelona, 1934–5) is the best introduction. For the background to the prophecies of Vilanova, see M. Reeves, *The Influence of Prophecy in the Later Middle Ages* (Oxford, 1969). On the Sicilian Vespers M. Amari, *La guerra del vespro siciliano* (3 vols, Milan, 1886) remains the standard work; S. Runciman, *The Sicilian Vespers* (Cambridge, 1958) takes some account of more recent work.

On the world of medieval merchants generally, see Y. Renouard, *Les hommes d'affaires italiens du moyen âge* (Paris, 1968) and A. Sapori, *Le marchand italien au moyen âge* (Paris, 1952), which has a large bibliography.

On the gold trade, apart from works referred to in the notes, a good introduction can be got from a series of articles in *Annales* and its predecessors: M. Bloch, 'Le problème de l'or au moyen âge', *Annales d'histoire économique et sociale*, V (1933), 1–34; F. Braudel, 'Monnaies et civilisations: de l'or du Soudan à l'argent d'Amérique', *Annales*, II (1947), 9–22, and H. R. Miskimin, 'Le problème de l'argent au moyen âge', Ibid., xvii (1962), 1125–30, and from A. M. Watson, 'Back to Gold and Silver', *Economic History Review*, xx (1967), 1–34. E. Ashtor, *Les métaux précieux et la balance des paiements du proche-orient à la basse époque* (Paris, 1971) and Magalhães Godinho, *Os descubrimentos*, i are useful studies. On the provenance of the gold, see R. Mauny, *Tableau géographique de l'ouest africain au moyen âge* (Dakar, 1961). On Luis de la Cerda, see G. Daumet, 'Luis de la Cerda ou de l'Espagne', *Bulletin hispanique*, xv (1913), 38–67. On early Mediterranean shipping in the Atlantic, see R. S. Lopez, 'Majorcans and Genoese on the North Sea Route in the XIIIth century', *Revue belge de philologie et d'histoire*, xxix (1951), 1163–79; R. Doehaerd, *Les relations commerciales entre Gênes, la Belgique et l'Outremont* (3 vols, Brussels, 1941), Y. Renouard (cited ch. 8, note 23); E. B. Fryde, 'Italian Maritime Trade with Medieval England', *Xe Colloque Internationale d'Histoire Maritime* (Brussels, 1974), pp.291–333; A. A. Ruddock, *Italian Merchants and Shipping in Southampton, 1270–1600* (Southampton, 1951). A useful recent summary of the sources for the Vivaldi voyage is G. Moore, 'La spedizione dei fratelli Vivaldi e nuovi documenti d'archivio', *Atti della Società Ligure di Storia Patria*, n.s., xii (1972), 387–400. R. Mauny, *Les navigations médiévals sur les côtes sahariennes* (Lisbon, 1960) gives the background.

The *Libro del conoscimiento* is translated by C. Markham as *The Book of Knowledge of All the Kingdoms, Lands and Lordships that are in the World* (London, 1912).

CHAPTER 6

The most comprehensive work on late medieval cartography, despite its title, is A. Cortesão, *História da cartográfia portuguesa* (2 vols, Coimbra, 1969–71).

Other works valuable for texts and illustrations are L. Bagrow and R. Skelton, *History of Cartography* (London, 1964) and G. R. Crone, *Maps and their Makers* (Folkestone, 1978). A. E. Nordenskiold, *Periplus* (Stockholm, 1897) offers more accessible reproductions of some of the maps referred to in the chapter than the more comprehensive and detailed work of Kamal cited in the notes.

The best introduction to medieval navigation is E. G. R. Taylor, *The Haven-Finding Art* (London, 1956), which should be supplemented by G. Beaujouan, 'Science livresque et art nautique au XVe siècle', *V Colloque International d'histoire maritime*, pp.61–89 and P. Adam, 'Navigation primitive et navigation astronomique', Ibid., pp.91–111 (both with discussion) and C. Verlinden, 'La découverte des archipels de la "Méditerranée Atlantique" (Canaries, Madères, Açores) et la navigation astronomique primitive', *Revista portuguesa de história*, xvi (1978), 105–31.

CHAPTER 7

The most important collection of sources is *Monumenta henricina* (15 vols, Coimbra, 1960–75). The Majorcan sources can only be consulted in the scattered publications referred to in the notes. Canarian materials are collected in the series *Fontes Rerum Canariarum* (La Laguna, 1933 – in progress).

A corrupt version of Béthencourt's chronicle is translated by R. H. Major as *The Canarian* (London, 1872). The standard account is that by A. Cioranescu in *Fontes Rerum Canariarum*, viii.

On Prince Henrique much has been written but little is of any value. Only scattered lectures by P. E. Russell, especially *Prince Henry the Navigator* (London, 1960) and *Prince Henry the Navigator: the Rise and Fall of a Culture-Hero* (Oxford, 1984) can be recommended without reservation, and by A. J. Dias Dinis, *Estudos henriquinos* (Coimbra, 1960) in part. The commentaries and notes to *Monumenta henricina* must, for the present, do service in place of a general account. On Dom Pedro,

J. Gonsalves, *O Infante Dom Pedro* (Lisbon, 1955) and F. M. Rodgers, *The Travels of the Infante Dom Pedro of Portugal* (Cambridge, Mass., 1961) both broach the question of his role in exploration. Nor are there many good general accounts of late medieval Portuguese expansion, though D. Peres, *História dos descobrimentos portugueses* (Oporto, 1943) and E. Prestage, *The Portuguese Pioneers* (London, 1933) supply now rather dated introductions and B. W. Diffie and G. D. Winius, *Foundations of the Portuguese Empire* (St Paul, Minn., 1977) is of some help. C. R. Boxer, *The Portuguese Seaborne Empire* (London, 1969) is justly renowned, but has little on the period before 1500. C. M. de Witte, 'Les Bulles pontificales et l'expansion portugaise au XVe siècle', *Revue de l'histoire ecclésiastique*, XLVIII (1953), 683–718; XLIX (1954), 438–61; L (1956), 413–53, 809–36; LIII (1958), 5–46, 443–71 does much to fill the gap.

The Chronicle of Zurara now comes in an authoritative edition: *Crónica dos feitos notáveis que se passaram na conquista da Guiné*, ed. T. de Sousa Soares (Lisbon, 1978), though the French translation, edited by R. Mauny et al., *Chronique de Guinée* (Dakar, 1960) remains useful for its notes. An English version by C. R. Beazley and E. Prestage is *The Chronicle of the Discovery and Conquest of Guinea* (London, 1876). On the background, see A. J. Dias Dinis, *Vida e obras de Gomes Eannes de Zurara* (Lisbon, 1949).

For Cà da Mosto, the best edition is that of T. Gasparrini Leporace (cited note 48). There is an English edition, *The Voyages of Cadamosto*, by G. R. Crone (London, 1937), which also prints, with other documents, an English version of Diogo Góes.

On the Portuguese island colonies, see V. Magalhães Godinho, *A economia dos descubrimentos henriquinos* (Lisbon, 1962) and V. Rau and J. de Macedo, *O açucar da Ilha de Madeira nos fins do seculo XV* (Funchal, 1962).

For the period after Dom Henrique's death, further sources are collected in J. W. Blake, *Europeans in West Africa* (London, 1942), A. Brásio, *Monumenta misionária africana* (Coimbra, 1952) and J. Martins da Silva Marques, *Descobrimentos portugueses*, III (Lisbon, 1971). The essays by R. Ricard, *Études sur l'histoire des portugais au Maroc* (Coimbra, 1955), are of great value. On João II, J. V. Serrão, *Itinerários de el-rei Dom João II* (Lisbon, 1975 – in progress) promises to be fundamental. An English biography is E. Sanceau, *The Perfect Prince* (London, 1959).

CHAPTER 8

The best work with which to start an exploration of the historical tradition is probably M. Fernández de Navarrete, *Colección de los viajes y descubrimientos que hicieron por mar los españoles* (5 vols, Madrid, 1825–39). On Columbus, the standard work of S. E. Morison, *Admiral of the Ocean Sea* (2 vols, Cambridge, Mass., 1942) is corrected by the same author's *European Discovery of America: the Southern Voyages* (Oxford, 1974). Of more recent revelations and arguments, only those of A. Milhou, *Colón y su mentalidad mesiánica* (Valladolid, 1984) is of fundamental importance. The chief sources are collected in *Raccoàlta di documenti e studi pubblicata dalla Reale Commissione Colombiana* (14 vols, Rome-Genoa, 1892–6) but, for Columbus's own writings, *Cristóbal Colón textos y documentos completos*, ed. C. Varela (Madrid, 1984) is far superior to any other compilation. A selection in translation has been made by S. E. Morison, *Journals and Other Documents of Columbus* (New York, 1963). A great array of snippets from the sources in translation appears in D. B. Quinn (ed.), *New American World*, I (London, 1979).

On the sea war of 1475–9 see Blake, *Europeans in West Africa* (already cited), P. E. Russell, 'Fontes documentais castelhanas para a história da expansão portuguesa na Guiné nos últimos anos de D. Afonso V', *Do tempo e da História*, IV (1971), 5–33, and A. Rumeu de Armas, *Espana en el África atlántica* (2 vols, Madrid, 1955), which is broader in scope and more reliable than F. Pérez Embid, *Los descubrimientos en el Atlántico hasta el Tratado de Tordesillas* (Seville, 1948). Some interesting details are supplied by V. Cortes Alonso, 'Algunos viajes de las gentes de Huelva al Atlántico (1470–88)', *IX Colloque International d'Histoire Maritime* (Seville, 1969), pp.603–11. A. de la Torre and L. Suárez Fernández add some material in *Documentos relacionados con Portugal durante el reinado de los Reyes Católicos* (3 vols, Valladolid, 1958–63), I.

On Columbus's Genoese environment, see additionally C. Verlinden and F. Pérez Embid, *Colón y el descubrimiento de América* (Madrid, 1967), L. de la Rosa (cited above, p.271) and A. Boscolo, 'Gli insediamenti genovesi nel sud della Spagna all'epoca di Cristoforo Colombo', *Saggi di storia mediterranea tra il XIV e il XVI secoli* (Rome, 1981), qualified by J. Heers, 'Le rôle des capitaux internationaux dans les voyages de découvertes aux xve et xvie siècles', *Travaux du V Colloque Iternational d'Histoire Maritime* (Paris, 1968), 273–93. P. Revelli, *Cristoforo Colombo e la scuola cartografica genovese* (Genoa, 1937) is a heavy-handed but usefully compendious treatment.

On the conquest of the Canary Islands, A. Rumeu de Armas, *La conquista de Tenerife* (Santa Cruz, 1975) is now the most useful work. See also E. Aznar Vallejo, *La incorporación de las Islas Canarias en la corona de Castilla* (Seville, 1983) for an institutional perspective. A general account can be got from J. de Viera y Clavijo, *Historia general de las Islas Canarias*, a work of the 1770s, in editions by E. Serra Ràfols and others (3 vols, Santa Cruz, 1950–2) or A. Cioranescu (2 vols, Santa Cruz, 1981). *Historia general de las Islas Canarias de Agustín Millares Carló*, eds A. Millares Cantero and J. R. Santana Godoy (5 vols, Santa Cruz, 1974–80) contains some excellent contributions.

The standard account of the conquest of Granada is now J. de Mata Carriazo's in R. Menéndez Pidal (ed.), *Historia de España*, xvii, part II (Madrid, 1969), 387–914, with M. A. Ladero Quesada, *Castilla y la conquista del reino de Granada* (Valladolid, 1967). On the background of conceptual continuity, see J. Manzano Manzano, 'La adquisición de las Indias', *Anuario de historia del derecho español*, xxi (1952), 17–45.

On the decline of Catalonia, as well as the works of Vilar and Carrère cited in note 23, see R. Menéndez Pidal (ed.), *Historia de España*, xiv (Madrid, 1966), especially the contributions by R. d'Abdal i de Vinyals, pp.ix–xliv and J. Reglá Campistol, pp.439–605. J. N. Hillgarth, *The Spanish Kingdoms*, ii (Oxford, 1978) and J. P. Cuvillier, 'La population catalane du xive siècle', *Mélanges de la Casa de Velázquez*, v (1969), 159–85, are very illuminating.

On the Genoese in Portugal, P. Peragallo, *Cenni intorno alla colonia italiana in Portogallo* (Genoa, 1907) is fundamental, supplemented by C. Verlinden, 'La colonie italienne de Lisbonne et le développement de l'économie métropolitaine et coloniale portugaises sous Henri le Navigateur', *Le moyen âge*, lxiv (1958), 467–97, and marchands et colons italiens au service de la découverte et de la colonisation portufaises sous Henri le Navigateur', *Le moyen âge*, lxiv (1958), pp.467–97, and qualified by the work of J. Heers (ch. IV, notes 9 and 10). I have not seen G. G. Musso, *Genovesi e Portugallo nell'età delle scoperte* (Genoa, 1976).

On Spanish chivalry, see M. de Riquer, *Caballeros andantes españoles* (Madrid, 1967), E. Prestage (ed.), *Chivalry* (London, 1928) and L. A. de Cuenca, *Floresta española de varia caballería* (Madrid, 1976). *Tirant lo blanc* is translated by D. H. Rosenthal (London, 1984) and *El vitorial* by J. Evans (London, 1928). The link between chivalry and seaborne adventure is one of the main themes of A. Navarro González, *El mar en la literatura medieval castellana* (La Laguna, 1962). On a point of comparison, the equally remarkable coincidence of the imperial and chivalric themes in Victorian and Edwardian England is discussed by M. Girouard, *The Return to Camelot* (New Haven, 1981).

## CHAPTER 9

M. Hodgen, *Early Anthropology in the Sixteenth and Seventeenth Centuries* (Philadelphia, 1964), A. Rumeu de Armas, *La política indigenista de Isabel la Católica* (Valladolid, 1969), A. R. Pagden, *The Fall of Natural Man* (Cambridge, 1982) and H. W. Janson, *Apes and Ape Lore in the Middle Ages and Renaissance* (London, 1952) are essential to this chapter.

On the juridical background, see J. Muldoon, *Popes, Lawyers and Infidels* (Liverpool, 1979) and F. H. Russell, *The Just War in the Middle Ages* (Cambridge, 1975). M. J. Wilks, *The Problem of Sovereignty in the Middle Ages* (Cambridge, 1963) and P. E. Russell, 'El descubrimiento de Canarias y el debate medieval acerca de los derechos de los príncipes y pueblos paganos', *Revista de historia canaria*, XXXVI (1978), 9–32, are also important. J. Friede, 'Las Casas and Indigenism in the Sixteenth Century', in J. Friede and B. Keen (eds), *Bartolomé de Las Casas in History* (De Kalb, 1971), pp.127–234, has at least the merit of discussing the problems in the context of the conquest of the Canary Islands.

On wild men, R. Bernheimer, *Wild Men in the Middle Ages* (Cambridge, Mass., 1952) and T. Husband, *The Wild Man: Medieval Myth and Symbolism* (New York, 1980), which is a Metropolitan Museum of Art exhibition catalogue, are of great interest for the iconography. A partial translation of Espinosa's work is provided by C. Markham, *The Guanches of Tenerife* (London, 1907).

On maps, see the works suggested for Chapter 5 above. G. H. T. Kimble, *Geography in the Middle Ages* (London, 1938) remains the most reliable account of the prevailing mental image of the world. The classical sources can be approached through E. H. Bunbury, *A History of Ancient Geography* (2 vols, New York, 1959) and J. O. Thomson, *History of Ancient Geography* (Cambridge, 1948). On Ptolemy, C. Sanz, *La geographia de Ptolomeo* (Madrid, 1959) is a useful summary. A. Cortesão, 'A carta náutica de 1424', *Esparsos* (3 vols, Coimbra, 1974–5), III, pp.ix–211 makes some corrections to the earlier study of the same subject cited in the notes.

On Columbus, the works suggested for Chapter 8 above can be supplemented by G. E. Nunn, *Geographical Conception of Columbus* (New York, 1924); E. Jos, *El plan y la génesis del descubrimiento colombino* and E. O'Gorman, *The Invention of America* (Bloomington, 1961), which should be read in conjunction with M. Battaillon, 'The Idea of the Discovery of America among Spaniards in the Sixteenth Century', translated in J. R. L. Highfield (ed.), *Spain in the Fifteenth Century* (London, 1972), pp.426–63.

For the background to the Bristolian explorations see D. B. Quinn, *North American Discovery* (New York, 1971) and *England and the Discovery of America* (London, 1974) and, in greater breadth, E. M. Carus-Wilson, *Medieval Merchant-Venturers* (London, 1967), especially pp.98–142 and S. E. Morison, *The European Discovery of America: the Northern Voyages* (Oxford, 1971). There is a careful examination of all the evidence in P. McGrath, 'Bristol and America, 1480–1631', in K. R. Andrews, N. P. Canning and P. E. H. Hair, *The Westward Enterprise* (Liverpool, 1978), pp.81–7.

# Index

University of Pennsylvania Press
MIDDLE AGES SERIES
Edward Peters, General Editor

F. R. P. Akehurst, trans. *The* Coutumes de Beauvaisis *of Philippe de Beaumanoir.* 1992

Peter Allen. *The Art of Love: Amatory Fiction from Ovid to the* Romance of the Rose. 1992

David Anderson. *Before the Knight's Tale: Imitation of Classical Epic in Boccaccio's* Teseida. 1988

Benjamin Arnold. *Count and Bishop in Medieval Germany: A Study of Regional Power, 1100–1350.* 1991

Mark C. Bartusis. *The Late Byzantine Army: Arms and Society, 1204–1453.* 1992

J. M. W. Bean. *From Lord to Patron: Lordship in Late Medieval England.* 1990

Uta-Renate Blumenthal. *The Investiture Controversy: Church and Monarchy from the Ninth to the Twelfth Century.* 1988

Daniel Bornstein, trans. *Dino Compagni's* Chronicle *of Florence.* 1986

Betsy Bowden. *Chaucer Aloud: The Varieties of Textual Interpretation.* 1987

James William Brodman. *Ransoming Captives in Crusader Spain: The Order of Merced on the Christian-Islamic Frontier.* 1986

Kevin Brownlee and Sylvia Huot. *Rethinking the* Romance of the Rose: *Text, Image, Reception.* 1992

Otto Brunner (Howard Kaminsky and James Van Horn Melton, eds. and trans.). *Land and Lordship: Structures of Governance in Medieval Austria.* 1992

Robert I. Burns, S.J., ed. *Emperor of Culture: Alfonso X the Learned of Castile and His Thirteenth-Century Renaissance.* 1990

David Burr. *Olivi and Franciscan Poverty: The Origins of the* Usus Pauper *Controversy.* 1989

Thomas Cable. *The English Alliterative Tradition.* 1991

Anthony K. Cassell and Victoria Kirkham, eds. and trans. *Diana's Hunt/ Caccia di Diana: Boccaccio's First Fiction.* 1991

Brigitte Cazelles. *The Lady as Saint: A Collection of French Hagiographic Romances of the Thirteenth Century.* 1991

Anne L. Clark. *Elisabeth of Schönau: A Twelfth-Century Visionary.* 1992

Willene B. Clark and Meradith T. McMunn, eds. *Beasts and Birds of the Middle Ages: The Bestiary and Its Legacy.* 1989

Richard C. Dales. *The Scientific Achievement of the Middle Ages.* 1973

Charles T. Davis. *Dante's Italy and Other Essays.* 1984
Katherine Fischer Drew, trans. *The Burgundian Code.* 1972
Katherine Fischer Drew, trans. *The Laws of the Salian Franks.* 1991
Katherine Fischer Drew, trans. *The Lombard Laws.* 1973
Robert D. Fulk. *A History of Old English Meter.* 1992
Nancy Edwards. *The Archaeology of Early Medieval Ireland.* 1990
Margaret J. Ehrhart. *The Judgment of the Trojan Prince Paris in Medieval Literature.* 1987
Richard K. Emmerson and Ronald B. Herzman. *The Apocalyptic Imagination in Medieval Literature.* 1992
Felipe Fernández-Armesto. *Before Columbus: Exploration and Colonization from the Mediterranean to the Atlantic, 1229–1492.* 1987
Patrick J. Geary. *Aristocracy in Provence: The Rhône Basin at the Dawn of the Carolingian Age.* 1985
Peter Heath. *Allegory and Philosophy in Avicenna (Ibn Sînâ), with a Translation of the Book of the Prophet Muḥammad's Ascent to Heaven.* 1992
J. N. Hillgarth, ed. *Christianity and Paganism, 350–750: The Conversion of Western Europe.* 1986
Richard C. Hoffmann. *Land, Liberties, and Lordship in a Late Medieval Countryside: Agrarian Structures and Change in the Duchy of Wrocław.* 1990
Robert Hollander. *Boccaccio's Last Fiction: Il Corbaccio.* 1988
Edward B. Irving, Jr. *Rereading* Beowulf. 1989
C. Stephen Jaeger. *The Origins of Courtliness: Civilizing Trends and the Formation of Courtly Ideals, 939–1210.* 1985
William Chester Jordan. *The French Monarchy and the Jews: From Philip Augustus to the Last Capetians.* 1989
William Chester Jordan. *From Servitude to Freedom: Manumission in the Sénonais in the Thirteenth Century.* 1986
Ellen E. Kittell. *From Ad Hoc to Routine: A Case Study in Medieval Bureaucracy.* 1991
Alan C. Kors and Edward Peters, eds. *Witchcraft in Europe, 1100–1700: A Documentary History.* 1972
Barbara M. Kreutz. *Before the Normans: Southern Italy in the Ninth and Tenth Centuries.* 1992
E. Ann Matter. *The Voice of My Beloved: The Song of Songs in Western Medieval Christianity.* 1990
María Rosa Menocal. *The Arabic Role in Medieval Literary History.* 1987
A. J. Minnis. *Medieval Theory of Authorship.* 1988
Lawrence Nees. *A Tainted Mantle: Hercules and the Classical Tradition at the Carolingian Court.* 1991
Lynn H. Nelson, trans. *The Chronicle of San Juan de la Peña: A Fourteenth-Century Official History of the Crown of Aragon.* 1991
Charlotte A. Newman. *The Anglo-Norman Nobility in the Reign of Henry I: The Second Generation.* 1988

Joseph F. O'Callaghan. *The Cortes of Castile-León, 1188–1350.* 1989

William D. Paden, ed. *The Voice of the Trobairitz: Perspectives on the Women Troubadours.* 1989

Edward Peters. *The Magician, the Witch, and the Law.* 1982

Edward Peters, ed. *Christian Society and the Crusades, 1198–1229*: Sources in Translation, including The Capture of Damietta by Oliver of Paderborn. 1971

Edward Peters, ed. *The First Crusade:* The Chronicle of Fulcher of Chartres *and Other Source Materials.* 1971

Edward Peters, ed. *Heresy and Authority in Medieval Europe.* 1980

James M. Powell. *Albertanus of Brescia: The Pursuit of Happiness in the Early Thirteenth Century.* 1992

James M. Powell. *Anatomy of a Crusade, 1213–1221.* 1986

Michael Resler, trans. *Erec by Hartmann von Aue.* 1987

Pierre Riché (Jo Ann McNamara, trans.). *Daily Life in the World of Charlemagne.* 1978

Jonathan Riley-Smith. *The First Crusade and the Idea of Crusading.* 1986

Joel T. Rosenthal. *Patriarchy and Families of Privilege in Fifteenth-Century England.* 1991

Steven D. Sargent, ed. and trans. *On the Threshold of Exact Science: Selected Writings of Anneliese Maier on Late Medieval Natural Philosophy.* 1982

Sarah Stanbury. *Seeing the* Gawain-*Poet: Description and the Act of Perception.* 1992

Thomas C. Stillinger. *The Song of Troilus: Lyric Authority in the Medieval Book.* 1992

Susan Mosher Stuard. *A State of Deference: Ragusa/Dubrovnik in the Medieval Centuries.* 1992

Susan Mosher Stuard, ed. *Women in Medieval History and Historiography.* 1987

Susan Mosher Stuard, ed. *Women in Medieval Society.* 1976

Jonathan Sumption. *The Hundred Years War: Trial by Battle.* 1992

Ronald E. Surtz. *The Guitar of God: Gender, Power, and Authority in the Visionary World of Mother Juana de la Cruz (1481–1534).* 1990

Patricia Terry, trans. *Poems of the Elder Edda.* 1990

Frank Tobin. *Meister Eckhart: Thought and Language.* 1986

Ralph V. Turner. *Men Raised from the Dust: Administrative Service and Upward Mobility in Angevin England.* 1988

Harry Turtledove, trans. *The Chronicle of Theophanes: An English Translation of Anni Mundi 6095–6305 (A.D. 602–813).* 1982

Mary F. Wack. *Lovesickness in the Middle Ages: The Viaticum and Its Commentaries.* 1990

Benedicta Ward. *Miracles and the Medieval Mind: Theory, Record, and Event, 1000–1215.* 1982

Suzanne Fonay Wemple. *Women in Frankish Society: Marriage and the Cloister, 500–900.* 1981